Best wishes,
Mike Bascom

Compliments of:

MICHAEL R. BASCOM, P.C.
ESTATE & BUSINESS PLANNING ATTORNEYS
1203 MACY DRIVE
ROSWELL, GA 30076-6350

About the Authors

Robert A. Esperti and Renno L. Peterson are nationally heralded attorneys, educators, and authors. They have written numerous articles and 18 highly acclaimed books on tax, business, and estate planning for professionals and the public. Their most recent books are McGraw-Hill's *Protect Your Estate* and Viking-Penguin's *The Living Trust Workbook, Loving Trust,* and *The Living Trust Revolution.*

They are cochairmen of the Esperti Peterson Institute, the National Network of Estate Planning Attorneys, and the National Association of Estate Planning Advisors.

They frequently consult with, and lecture to, leading financial companies and professional associations throughout America.

Michael R. Bascom, J.D., is an estate planning attorney with the law firm of Whiteside, Coyle, Bascom & Bergman, P.C. His practice is focused on estate and charitable tax planning, business succession, and asset protection. He frequently teaches seminars on tax, business, and estate planning topics for professionals and the public.

Mike is a graduate of the University of Virginia School of Law and is licensed to practice law in Georgia and Florida. He is a member of the Taxation and Fiduciary Law Sections of the Georgia Bar. He has received advanced training on charitable planning from Renaissance, Inc., the premier charitable trust administrator in the United States.

9066

LEGACY

Plan, Protect & Preserve Your Estate

Practical Answers from America's Foremost Estate Planning Attorneys

— A Special Edition —

Robert A. Esperti Renno L. Peterson

Michael R. Bascom

The authors are not engaged in rendering legal, tax, accounting, financial planning, or similar professional services. While legal, tax, accounting, and financial planning issues covered in this book have been checked with sources believed to be reliable, some material may be affected by changes in the laws or in the interpretations of such laws since the manuscript for this book was completed. For that reason the accuracy and completeness of such information and the opinions based thereon are not guaranteed. In addition, state or local tax laws or procedural rules may have a material impact on the general recommendations made by the authors, and the strategies outlined in this book may not be suitable for every individual. If legal, accounting, tax, financial planning, investment, or other expert advice is required, obtain the services of a competent practitioner.

ISBN 0-922943-09-5

Library of Congress Catalog Number 96-077472

Coordinating editor: Eileen Sacco
Legal review: David K. Cahoone, J.D., LL.M.
Project assistant: Christy Allbee
Marketing services: Eric Johnson, Reneé Garcia, Paul DeLauro
Jacket designer: Richard Adelson
Composition, design, & editing services: C+S Gottfried
Printed and bound in the U.S.A. by Johnson Printing

Esperti Peterson Institute Incorporated
410 17th Street, Suite 1260
Denver, CO 80202

Contents

Preface

Legacy has been written by eighty-five highly talented attorneys who are members of the National Network of Estate Planning Attorneys, of which we are the founders and chairmen. To continue the Network's mission of improving upon the way families estate-plan, *Legacy* explains sophisticated planning techniques that will enable people to work with their professional advisors in properly planning for themselves, their loved ones, and their charities.

Legacy is not an annotated reference book intended to cover every estate planning subject, nor is it intended to cover any specific estate planning subject in overwhelming detail. Each of our contributing authors was challenged with a single goal: *to provide the reader with the best possible answers to the questions they are most frequently asked by their clients.*

The Network was founded in 1989 to bring estate planning practitioners nationwide closer together so that its members might collectively expand their expertise and planning horizons to better serve the estate planning needs of their clients. The Network and each of its members are:

- Dedicated to helping families create their own legacies by assisting them to give what they have to whom they want, the way they want, and when they want and to save every tax dollar, attorney fee, and court cost possible.
- Devoted to providing client families with sound legal alterna-

> tives for achieving their goals and to creating quality legal documents in easily understood language that will perpetuate wealth and values through succeeding generations.

Network members aspire to the highest professional standards of ethics and to behavior that lends dignity to their profession. The Network encourages professionals to work together for the benefit of their mutual clientele in order to offer the best and most effective planning possible. It believes that when professionals work together to combine their respective talents and skills—rather than compete with one another—clients and professionals alike are the winners.

The Network inaugurated, in conjunction with the Esperti Peterson Institute, a 3-year advanced program in estate planning for the more highly experienced attorneys who lead the Network's 800-plus membership. A great many of the participants in this advanced program are also contributing authors of *Legacy*.

Each contributing author was required to submit a minimum of twenty-five important and frequently asked client questions along with his or her responses to those questions. As practitioners of the law for over 50 collective years, we were not surprised to receive a great many duplicate questions from our colleagues. The consistency of these questions reinforced our belief that most families have the same concerns, goals, hopes, and aspirations regardless of the obvious differences in their cultures, economics, and geography.

The responses of *Legacy*'s contributors reflected their differing professional views, feelings, and emotions with regard to just about everything you can imagine. As *Legacy*'s editors, we have attempted to blend the professional differences among our colleagues' opinions into an overall perspective that will provide the reader with the best overview and understanding possible.

Because of the labyrinth of complexities between the various aspects of estate and wealth planning and their significant interrelationships with one another, there is a subtle repetitiveness in the text. This is not a necessary evil but an intended benefit for the reader. Rather than referring the reader back and forth among the pages, we have at times included the same information in several places if it is pertinent to more than one topic. In this way, readers can turn to a specific section of the book and learn about a particular topic without having to read the book sequentially from page 1.

We are delighted to be the editors of this work. It contains an abundance of important planning information and techniques for those of you who care about creating your own legacies.

We are proud of our colleagues and contributing authors; they gave a great deal of their time, energy, and knowledge to make this project and book a reality. We especially wish to thank Michael R. Bascom for his contributions to *Legacy,* and we are honored to dedicate this special edition to him.

Robert A. Esperti
Renno L. Peterson
The Esperti Peterson Institute
August 1996

Introduction

Michael R. Bascom

I am honored to have had the opportunity to participate in the production of this book. It is sure to become a useful resource for all persons concerned with controlling their assets in order to provide for themselves and their loved ones. My contribution to this effort is the result of over 6 years' experience helping people like you plan for the future by carefully examining their current asset distribution strategies in terms of their hopes, fears, and expectations.

This book is based upon the questions that estate planning attorneys have been asked by their clients, and I expect that the information it presents will answer many of your questions. As you use this book, you will read questions that you never thought to ask and will uncover planning tips that you had not previously considered. I hope that you will be inspired by these questions and tips to plan for your real hopes, fears, and expectations.

Estate planning is a team effort. My personal thanks go to all of the professionals who have assisted me in this endeavor over the past 6 years. In particular I want to acknowledge my partners, Jim Coyle, Ken Bergman, and Lee Whiteside, and my colleague, Ken Rutan. Acknowledgment should also be made of Janie Pritchard, who has so carefully assisted in the implementation of my clients' plans.

Accountants, financial professionals, and insurance salespersons are indispensable to my estate planning practice. Each professional brings a unique perspective and expertise to the planning process that ultimately benefits the client since it is impossible for one person to know everything about estate planning.

In 1986 I received a B.S. in economics from Brigham Young

University. Three years later I graduated from the University of Virginia School of Law and joined a large law firm in central Florida. For the next 2 years I applied the laws regarding property ownership and tax planning. In 1991 I moved to the northern suburbs of Atlanta, Georgia, and began helping my own clients with their estate planning needs.

I am licensed to practice law in both Georgia and Florida. Maintaining these licenses is a continuous process requiring that I attend several hours of continuing professional education courses annually. I am a member of the National Network of Estate Planning Attorneys, the Real Property, Probate, and Trust Law Section of the Florida Bar, the Taxation and Fiduciary Law Sections of the Georgia Bar, and the Georgia Planned Giving Council. Additionally, I have received advanced training emphasizing the use of charitable remainder trusts from Renaissance, Inc., the premier charitable trust administrator in the United States.

I am married to the love of my life, the former Susan Hansen. She is responsible, in large part, for my success. We are the parents of a young son, Bradley, and an infant daughter, Kathryn. Because having both quality time and quantity time with my family is important to me, my office is located near our home rather than in downtown Atlanta. In my spare time I enjoy doing volunteer work and playing softball.

I believe in educating clients about the advantages and disadvantages of the estate planning tools before they plan. Toward this end, I have taught several free public seminars about proper estate planning. A significant part of the first meeting with new clients is spent educating them about the various estate planning options and the accompanying advantages and disadvantages. Once clients are sufficiently educated, they are ready to do proper planning.

My philosophy in my work and personal life is to find the solution rather than the problem. It is easy to find reasons why you can't do something; the real challenge is to find a way that you can do something. I love my work, and finding the solution is the best part of that work. At Whiteside, Coyle, Bascom & Bergman, P.C., my colleagues and I are dedicated to understanding and solving our clients' needs. Our firm continues to grow because of referrals from you, our clients.

The next best part of my work is getting to know and work with my clients' professional advisors. Even though I know several professional advisors in every area of estate planning, I prefer to work with the clients' advisors, since they are almost always able to help bring out the true goals and objectives of the clients. Clients are more comfortable sharing this information with a trusted professional rather than a complete stranger. Of course, if a client does not have a team of professionals, I can easily assemble one to fit the client's needs.

At Whiteside, Coyle, Bascom & Bergman, P.C., we are able to assist you with planning for yourself and your loved ones without giving up control of your affairs. We will help you devise a plan to prepare for the possibility of your own disability. Additionally we will help you give what you own to whomever you want, the way you want, and whenever you want. We will help you save every tax dollar, professional fee, and court cost that are legally possible to save. We will prepare all the documents which are needed to carry out your plan, such as living wills, durable powers of attorney for health care, revocable living trusts, pour-over wills, irrevocable life insurance trusts, charitable remainder trusts, and family limited partnership agreements. We can assist you in titling and transferring your assets. We can also assist in handling postdeath administration.

A brief word of caution: Proper estate planning revolves around your relationship with a qualified estate planning attorney who sees that your plan is thorough and focuses on your well-being and that of your family. Do not be tricked into thinking that the same estate plan is appropriate for everyone or that the skill and competence of a qualified estate planning attorney can be duplicated by a cheap computer program. The more you read this book, the more you will become educated, and the harder it will be for you to be tricked. At Whiteside, Coyle, Bascom & Bergman, P.C., we believe that clients should be told the truth.

My goal in working with you and your professional advisors is to listen and understand your estate planning goals, see how your current planning matches up to your goals, educate you as to the advantages and disadvantages of your estate planning options, make recommendations regarding the various options, assist you in designing a proper estate plan, prepare the documentation needed to implement your plan, explain and help you properly execute your estate planning documents, and change the title or transfer your assets to conform with your plan.

This book will be of exceptional value to all persons interested in maximizing the benefit of controlling their assets in order to provide for themselves and their loved ones. It is with your best interests in mind that I am grateful for the opportunity to contribute to the production of this book.

Michael R. Bascom, J.D., is an estate planning attorney with the law firm of Whiteside, Coyle, Bascom & Bergman, P.C. His practice is focused on estate and charitable tax planning, business succession, and asset protection. He frequently teaches seminars on tax, business, and estate planning topics for professionals and the public.

Mike is a graduate of the University of Virginia School of Law and is licensed to practice law in Georgia and Florida. He is a member of the Taxation and Fiduciary Law Sections of the Georgia Bar. He has received advanced training on charitable planning from Renaissance, Inc., the premier charitable trust administrator in the United States.

1

Basic Estate Planning Concepts

"Estate planning" is a term that usually conjures up visions of death and dying. It suggests great wealth and expensive, wood-paneled law offices in the heart of big cities. As you will find as you read this chapter, this commonly held view is the opposite of what estate planning should be.

Estate planning is a process that should be primarily lifetime-oriented. It deals with property ownership, retirement planning, finances, disability concerns, tax strategies, and the preservation and protection of assets. These are the areas addressed in this chapter.

Whether you have a modest amount of assets or great wealth, whether you are young and beginning a career or a family or you are more mature and have children and grandchildren, there is something for you in this chapter. A working knowledge of basic estate planning concepts allows everyone to understand the fundamentals of proper planning. Once these concepts are understood, it is much easier to grasp some of the more advanced strategies that are used.

Each and every idea and technique found in this chapter will help you to build the proper foundation for your estate plan. The information presented will help you discern estate planning myths from reality and make better, more informed decisions as you enter into the planning process.

Our contributing authors have managed to take a great deal of complex information and reduce it to terms that you will easily understand. If you are just beginning your planning or if you have done planning but are confused about what you have and why you have it, this chapter will enable you to better recognize the alternatives available to create the underpinning for your plan.

The Fundamentals of Estate Planning

What is an estate?

There is a common misconception that "estates" are exclusive to multimillionaires. Most people do not realize what actually makes up an estate and only have an idea about estates from watching television shows like *Dallas,* where they see the "Southfork Ranch" estate. A residence, no matter how large or small, is part of an estate. An *estate* is, quite frankly, everything a person owns. Your estate can comprise your residence, cash, stocks, bonds, and other investments, as well as businesses that you may own. Your estate also comprises retirement plans, such as IRAs and Keoghs, and life insurance death benefits. It even includes personal property, such as vehicles, collectibles, and other treasured items.

What is an estate plan?

A proper *estate plan* is a means of preserving and controlling the wealth that you have worked for and accumulated during your life so that you may protect yourself and your loved ones either at your incapacity or at your demise. Your hopes, concerns, dreams, values, and aspirations would be reflected in the plan. A good estate plan, in short, must enable you to achieve the definition of estate planning adopted by the National Network of Estate Planning Attorneys:

> I want to control my property while I am alive and well, care for myself and my loved ones if I become disabled, and be able to give what I have to whom I want, the way I want, and when I want, and, if I can, I want to save every last tax dollar, attorney fee, and court cost possible.

Throughout the estate planning process, you and your attorney discuss and identify your most important goals and visions for you and your family. The coordination of all of this information with appropriate estate planning techniques results in your customized estate plan.

Is estate planning just having a will?

For centuries, that is about all it was. Today, the field of estate planning has grown to be one of the most technically demanding and comprehensive areas of the law.

Estate planning is ensuring that your hopes, dreams, and concerns for yourself and for your loved ones will be accomplished if you become incapacitated or die. It is protecting you and those you love by keeping you, your family, and your sensitive business information out of probate court when you become legally incapacitated or die.

Estate planning is designing a trust agreement which contains your loving instructions for your family's continued well-being after your death and also contains provisions to eliminate estate taxes.

It can include planning for redirecting what would have been paid in estate taxes to useful charitable projects, at no net cost to you or even at a net gain—you and your heirs may have more money for yourselves than would be the case if you had left nothing to charity.

If you are a business owner, estate planning is planning for the survival of that business after your death or the efficient disposition of that business in order to use the proceeds to care for and educate your loved ones.

In this day and age, you never know when you might be sued or what the result might be, even if you have done nothing wrong. For individuals who are particularly at risk from such lawsuits, estate planning can include increased protection from creditor attack.

Through devices such as private foundations, estate planning can keep your family members together and involved for generations in community services while giving them entrée into influential circles they would not otherwise have had.

Estate planning can help you unlock the value of highly appreciated assets which have a built-in capital gain liability and devise retirement vehicles which have the benefits of qualified plans without the restrictions.

What are some of the most common misconceptions about estate planning?

Here are the "Great Myths," as we call them:

MYTH 1: "I'm too young to worry about estate planning."

REALITY: If you're young, you especially need to map out an estate plan to help *protect* your loved ones.

MYTH 2: "My estate isn't large enough to need estate planning."

REALITY: If your estate is fairly small, it will likely suffer a greater percentage of shrinkage from final expenses, probate costs, and so on, than will a larger estate.

MYTH 3: "My estate won't be taxed, regardless of its size, because I can use the unlimited marital deduction to transfer all of my assets to my spouse tax-free."

REALITY: Poorly planned usage of the unlimited marital deduction can simply postpone estate tax problems until your spouse's death. Without proper use of estate tax planning, your estate shrinkage at that time could be substantial, with your children and grandchildren feeling the losses.

MYTH 4: "Most people just have a will; that's all I need."

REALITY: Depending upon who's statistics you read, only about 40 to 60 percent of the population has a will, and it's true that a will is a *must* in every estate plan. But understand, a will *guarantees* the probate process. To avoid the probate process, use a funded revocable living trust as the centerpiece of your estate plan with a pour-over will as a supporting document, not the centerpiece.

What are some common traps I should avoid in my estate planning?

Common traps to avoid in effective estate planning are:

1. Not having any will or trust; having a homemade will; or having a will prepared without proper estate planning analysis
2. Titling too much property in joint tenancy
3. Leaving everything to your spouse

4. Failing to name a guardian for your minor children
5. Failing to prepare a business succession plan
6. Failing to plan for adequate estate liquidity
7. Having too little life insurance
8. Not realizing that life insurance is part of your estate for federal estate tax purposes
9. Having life insurance policies owned improperly
10. Not considering a lifetime giving program

What are the traditional methods of estate planning?

There are six techniques that are traditionally used in estate planning:

- Intestacy
- Will-planning probate
- Joint tenancy with right of survivorship
- Beneficiary designations
- Gifts
- Living trust

Everyone, in some manner, is using at least one of these techniques. Let us briefly look at each one, along with its advantages and disadvantages.

Intestacy A majority of Americans die without a will or a trust. This is called *intestacy*. Intestacy is considered a method of estate planning because by leaving no will, a person has given the state the right to decide who will receive his or her property. Assets that pass by intestacy go through a probate process called *administration* which is almost identical to the probate process for a last will and testament.

Will-Planning Probate A *last will and testament* is essentially a legal document that states how a person wants his or her estate distributed at death. Many people plan their estates by creating a last will and testament.

Unfortunately, wills have major disadvantages: (1) A will does *not* control how or when *all* of the will maker's property is distributed. Property owned in joint tenancy with another person, life insurance proceeds, and retirement benefits all pass outside of a will. (2) A will is not effective until the death of its maker, so it is of no help with lifetime planning. (3) Upon the maker's death, the will must be filed with the probate court, where it becomes a public document and is available to anyone who wants to read it.

Death probate is a court and administrative proceeding. It is required to manage and distribute a decedent's estate at death. Once a will enters the probate process, a person's estate is no longer controlled by his or her family. It is in the hands of the court and the probate attorneys. Because a will guarantees that a decedent's estate will go through probate, it is a very poor estate planning document for families who want to maintain control.

Joint Tenancy with Right of Survivorship There are different forms of how people hold title to property, one of which is joint tenancy with right of survivorship. The *right of survivorship* means that the survivor acquires the entire interest in the property upon the death of the other joint tenant.

Because a joint tenant's interest passes by law to the surviving joint tenant at death, its ownership is not controlled by the deceased joint tenant's will. For example, two brothers, Bob and David, own a piece of property as joint tenants. Bob dies and his will says that upon his death all of his estate should go to his wife, Pat, but because the property passes automatically at Bob's death to the surviving joint tenant, David will own the entire property and Pat will get nothing. This is only one of the many unforeseen problems that joint tenancy creates.

Beneficiary Designations Some types of property pass, at the death of their owners, to those listed in their beneficiary designations. Life insurance policies, annuities, individual retirement accounts, qualified retirement accounts, and pension plans are examples of these types of property.

The advantage of having named beneficiaries is that the property avoids probate. The disadvantage is that since the proceeds from beneficiary-designation property pass directly to the named beneficiaries and are not controlled by terms in the will, the proceeds may not pass to whom the owner wants or the way he or she wants. Like joint ownership, beneficiary designations supersede the terms of a will.

Gifts Giving assets away can be a valuable part of an estate plan, but it should not be done without professional advice.

Living Trust Finally, many people have living trusts, but these documents may be "bare-bones" living trusts. Bare-bones trusts often do not achieve basic planning objectives or avoid probate because their makers failed to transfer their property into their trusts. Bare-bones living trusts are usually sterile documents written in legalese and devoid of meaningful instructions for loved ones. They seldom reflect the hopes, concerns, dreams, values, and ambitions of their makers. However, when someone has a properly drafted and funded living trust, he or she can be confident that the many disadvantages of the five preceding traditional forms of estate planning have been eliminated.

The Need for Estate Planning

I do not have a will or a living trust. What happens if I do no estate planning?

All of us have planned our estates, whether we know it or not. If you do not have a will or a living trust, the state where you live has an estate plan for you, and you are not likely to hold it in high regard.

Should you become disabled, the court, not you or your family, will choose and appoint a conservator to inventory, appraise, and manage your assets and report the information to the court. That information usually becomes part of the public record. There will be attorney and conservator fees imposed against your estate to pay for this privilege.

When you die, your estate will be subject to probate. Again, your assets will be valued and listed in the public record. Creditors will be individually notified of their right to make claims. And the administrator of the estate and the administrator's attorney will each be entitled to a fee.

Once all of the creditors, your administrator, and your attorney have been paid, your assets will be distributed to your beneficiaries according to the preferences set forth in your state's statutes (the laws of intestate succession). If a share passes to your children, it will be given to them immediately and without restriction if they are 18 years of age or older. If a child is not of majority (18 to 21 years of age), a guardian and conservator will be appointed to control his or her person and inheritance until the child reaches the age of majority, at which time the child will receive his or her inheritance, or what's left of it, outright.

If a share is established for your spouse, the size of the share will depend on your state's laws and on the way your property is titled. Your spouse may get all of your estate or very little.

Some assets do not go through probate, but this might not be much better. Life insurance proceeds will pass to whomever you named as the beneficiary. If you forgot one of your children, or if your ex-spouse is still listed as your beneficiary, there may be no recourse because a beneficiary designation supersedes the state's law as to who will receive your property.

Compare this "plan" with the way in which you would like your property to be held and administered in the event of your death or disability. You will probably decide that a plan you design and control is called for.

Can't I simply name as beneficiary the person I want to receive my assets or put his or her name on the title with mine and be done with all of this estate planning business?

Maybe, but not likely. It is important to analyze the nature of the assets you expect to leave behind as well as the individuals you wish to see benefit from them. For some assets, such as an account with a broker, you may not be permitted to name a beneficiary. While in some states you may do so, you need to make sure that your state allows such a beneficiary designation.

Additionally, when you retitle assets in your name and that of another person who is not your spouse, you may be making a taxable gift to that person or setting the stage for some very unfavorable income and estate tax consequences.

Further, by adding another person's name to the title of an asset, you may also be relinquishing your ability to control the asset. Once that person's name is on the title, that person has rights to the property. And so do that person's creditors. You could be subjecting your property to the other person's financial mistakes.

Other problems with this approach include the following:

- Minors cannot receive or control property that is held in their names. If you title an asset in the name of a minor or name a minor as a beneficiary, a guardian must be appointed to handle any property left to that minor. Minors generally will not receive any benefit from property left to them prior to reaching their age of majority, which is usually 18 years. There are some circumstances under which they will be permitted to use their property prior to age 18, but only with the court's permission.

- Disabled or incompetent beneficiaries cannot receive property directly. An incompetent beneficiary must have a guardian and conservator appointed. A disabled individual may be receiving substantial governmental assistance, eligibility for which could be needlessly jeopardized by naming him or her a beneficiary or titling assets in his or her name.
- If your spouse is not the parent of your children, even if he or she agrees on what to do with the property on your death, there is always the possibility that unintended beneficiaries will ultimately receive your property.
- Perhaps most importantly, you must consider yourself and your well-being. You may invest substantial time and energy in planning for your loved ones, trying to save them needless expense and red tape, but you have to take these same principles and intentions and turn them inward, toward yourself. You too deserve to have the best possible plan to care for yourself. Don't sell yourself short in this process.

Simply adding another's name to the title of your assets or naming beneficiaries does not ensure that any planning or real benefits will result for you. In fact, doing so may create more problems for you and your loved ones. Before taking these steps, see an expert estate planning attorney so that you can determine what your alternatives and consequences really are.

I am single and have no children. Why do I need estate planning?

A proper estate plan will provide for the distribution of your estate in the way *you* want after your death. Just as importantly, it will also provide for your care in the event that you become disabled.

One planning concept is to use your assets to do some charitable good after death. Such charitable gifts either can be made outright upon the person's death or, in larger estates, can be held in trust in perpetuity for charitable purposes. Private charitable foundations and community foundations can retain assets after a person's death and pay the income to various charities according to that person's wishes over a period of time.

One way a single person can accomplish this is by purchasing life insurance on his or her life which would be payable to his or her trust, the ultimate beneficiary of which is a private charitable foundation or community foundation.

Taxes

FEDERAL ESTATE TAX

What is the federal estate tax?

The *federal estate tax* is a tax levied against the "right to transfer" property at the time of death. In essence, it is an *everything* tax. Any assets owned or controlled by the decedent at the time of death are included in his or her estate for federal estate tax purposes.

Personal effects such as jewelry, books, and furniture are taxed. Automobiles, real estate, stocks, bonds, and bank funds are all taxed. The federal estate tax also applies to all other owned assets including notes and mortgages held by the decedent. Life insurance proceeds from policies owned by the decedent are also taxed, as are IRAs and retirement plan proceeds. In addition, if the decedent had any rights to transfer property left to him or her by someone else, those rights are also taxed.

How do I determine the value of my estate?

To determine the value of your net estate, you add up the current market value of everything you own and then subtract your debts such as the mortgage on your home, the outstanding balance on your credit cards, and any other indebtedness you may have.

How are assets valued for purposes of this tax?

The value of the assets included in the taxable estate is their fair market value at the time of the death of their owner. If there is an estate tax due, the fair market value of the assets 6 months from the date of the owner's death can be used instead as long as this "alternate" valuation decreases the amount of tax that would be due if the date-of-death value was used.

Who determines the value of the assets?

The trustee of a living trust or the personal representative (modern name for "executor") of a will have the tasks of gathering the information that is necessary to value the estate's assets and hiring the appropriate appraisers.

Who values real estate?

A real estate broker or certified appraiser who is a member of the Appraisal Institute (MAI) appraises and values real estate. A copy of the written appraisal should be attached to the federal estate tax return.

Who values oil and gas interests?

Taxing authorities routinely value producing oil and gas interests on the basis of an arbitrary multiple of four times the annual proceeds from the production of oil and seven times the annual proceeds from the production of gas. This arbitrary rule ordinarily favors the taxing authority.

A petroleum geologist should be hired to provide a valuation of an estate's oil and gas interests where the amount of the tax at issue justifies the additional expense of his or her services. Generally, the petroleum geologist's appraisal will be less than the value established by the arbitrary multiples used by the taxing authority.

Who values publicly held securities and bonds?

Because publicly traded stocks and bonds are valued at the average of the high and low selling prices on the valuation date (if there was no trading on the valuation date, the high and low of the preceding and succeeding trade dates are used), they are easily valued by the estate's trustee or personal representative.

Who values non-publicly traded—closely held—business interests?

The valuation of these interests is always in question or dispute, and as a result, the services of business valuation experts are almost always necessary. A number of professionals—attorneys and accountants—specialize in this area. There are a number of commercial businesses that offer valuation services as well.

Who values life insurance?

Life insurance is valued by the amount of the policy proceeds and is usually valued by the insurance agent of the estate or trust and the trustee or personal representative.

Who values household goods?

Household goods, furnishings, and personal effects are appraised by those persons who routinely buy and sell such items. Household and personal effects ordinarily involve a room-by-room itemization; however, these can be grouped together if no single item exceeds $100 in value, which is rarely the case.

When is the federal estate tax due and payable?

Subject to a limited exception, estate taxes must be paid, in cash, usually within 9 months of the person's death.

What is the exception?

If a decedent owned a business that makes up more than 35 percent of his or her total estate, less debts and expenses, the estate's personal representative can make partial payments over a 14-year period for the portion of the estate tax attributable to the first $1 million of closely held business property. The first 4 years of payments are at 4 percent interest only; no principal payments are necessary during this initial period. After 4 years, interest is paid at the regular rate specified by the Internal Revenue Code; the principal must also be paid off over the remaining 10-year period. This exception applies only to the first $1 million of qualifying property.

What are the estate tax rates?

The rates start at 37 percent for estates over $600,000 and rapidly grow to 55 percent for estates over $2,500,000. For estates between $10,000,000 and $21,040,000, the federal law phases out the exemption of $600,000. This results in an effective rate of 60 percent for these larger estates.

Is the federal estate tax a one-time tax?

Estate tax applies to transfers to each generation, for example, from father to son and from son to grandson.

Are there any deductions, exemptions, or credits?

Every estate receives a *unified credit* of $192,800 against the taxes owed on the estate of the decedent. This $192,800 unified credit is the equivalent of exempting $600,000 from a taxable estate. This means a person can pass to anyone a total of $600,000 free of federal estate tax.

There is also an *unlimited marital deduction.* Each married person may pass to the surviving spouse any amount of assets free of federal estate tax. Thus the value of the deceased spouse's gross estate is reduced by the value of property passing to the surviving spouse.

If my spouse receives an unlimited marital deduction, do I need tax planning?

Absolutely. The unlimited marital deduction has become a tax trap for unwary taxpayers. You can take advantage of the marital deduction only while both of you are alive to plan for its use, because it can only be used by the first spouse to die. The marital deduction is not available to the surviving spouse if he or she wishes to leave the estate to children or grandchildren.

Why can't I leave everything to my spouse and not worry about tax?

If you rely upon the unlimited marital deduction without thought, the $600,000 exemption of the first of you to die will be wasted and result in unnecessary taxes of $235,000. This happens because the marital deduction "swallows up" the exemption equivalent. If you take advantage of both the $600,000 exemption and the marital deduction through proper planning, it is not difficult to save an additional $235,000 in federal estate taxes.

Can I leave money or property to charity free of tax?

You can leave any amount of money or property to qualifying charities without having to pay federal estate tax.

If my estate is not over $600,000, do I have a tax problem?

You will not have a federal estate tax problem if your estate is under $600,000. However, most people are unaware of everything that should be counted and thus undervalue their estates. In calculating your estate size, do not forget to include the total value of your life insurance policy proceeds, your retirement plan monies, the fair market value of all of your personal effects, and any inheritances over which you may have some rights or powers.

It is also important that you consider the effects of inflation on your estate size in the future.

Does my estate have to file a federal estate tax return if it is under $600,000?

If you do not use up any unified credit by making taxable gifts during your life, a federal estate tax return needs to be filed only for a gross estate of $600,000 or more.

If my estate is slightly over $600,000, do I need to be concerned with tax planning?

The federal tax tables indicate that the first dollar over $600,000 will be taxed at a marginal rate of 37 percent; as your estate grows, that rate will rapidly increase to 55 percent. Since inflation alone will increase your estate, you should definitely consider estate planning.

Can the federal estate tax be reduced or eliminated?

There are strategies that can be used to reduce or eliminate federal estate taxes. However, many of these strategies will not always work with a will-planning probate estate plan. This is because the people who draft such plans usually do not coordinate all of the estate's assets but, rather, deal only with the property in the name of the will maker. As a result, major assets such as retirement benefits, life insurance, and joint tenancy property are not included in the plan.

You can easily design a living trust to coordinate all of your assets under one or more subtrusts and thereby take the assets into account in maximizing federal estate tax planning.

Is life insurance taxed?

Generally speaking, life insurance proceeds are not subject to federal or state income tax, and they may not be subject to *state* inheritance or estate taxes. However, life insurance policies owned by the decedent or over which the decedent had any "incidents of ownership" are included in his or her estate for federal estate tax purposes. For example, if you had a life insurance policy with a $100,000 death benefit in addition to other estate assets valued at $600,000, your gross estate would be $700,000. Of that amount, $600,000 is the tax-free exemption equivalent, and the remaining $100,000 will be taxable beginning at 37 percent.

What are incidents of ownership?

They are IRS-specified attributes that put policy proceeds into your estate. These attributes include the ownership of the policy, power to change the beneficiary, right to borrow against the policy, and right to surrender or cancel the policy.

If I give my policy away, can I avoid federal estate tax?

If a policy is given away within 3 years of the death of the insured in order to defeat the incidents of ownership, the proceeds will be drawn back into the gross estate and taxed.

Is there any way to avoid estate tax on my life insurance?

Yes. You can have someone such as your spouse, children, grandchildren, or an irrevocable trust own it. In each of these cases the insurance proceeds will not be taxed in your estate. (Irrevocable life insurance trusts are fully explained in Chaper 3.)

GIFT TAX

What is the annual gift tax exclusion, and how does it work?

You can remove assets and the appreciation on them from your estate by making gifts of the assets. The federal gift tax law provides for an annual gift tax exclusion which allows individuals to give away tax-free up to $10,000 per year per person to as many persons as they wish. Married individuals can combine their exclusions and give up to $20,000 per year to as many persons as they wish; strangely enough, this is called *gift splitting*.

For example, if you are married and have three children, you and your spouse can jointly give each child $20,000 tax-free annually. Payments of any amount for school tuition and medical expenses that are made directly to the school or medical provider are tax-free and are in addition to the annual exclusion.

Can I use my annual exclusion to make gifts in trust?

The $10,000 exclusion amount is only for gifts "other than gifts of future interests in property." Gifts to a trust are gifts of a future interest and usually do not qualify; there are exceptions, however.

Is there a way to qualify gifts in trust for my annual exclusion?

To qualify gifts to a trust for the annual exclusion, the trust must contain "demand-right" language or instructions. This means that the beneficiaries of your trust must have the current right to withdraw the money given to the trust. If they do not request withdrawal of the money within a preset period of time, the trustee will then be able to use the money as you specified in the trust and the gift will qualify for the annual exclusion.

What if I give away more than $10,000 to a family member in a given year?

If you give more than $10,000 to one person in any year, you are responsible for filing a U.S. gift tax return by April 15 of the following year.

Let's say that an individual gives $50,000 to one person in one year. The first $10,000 is free of the gift tax. The donor must file a gift tax return by the following April 15 relative to the portion of the gift which is taxable—the remaining $40,000. The donor's lifetime exemption equivalent, $600,000, will be reduced by the amount of the taxable gift, $40,000, leaving $560,000 to be utilized for future gift and estate tax purposes.

Any gifts in excess of your remaining exemption equivalent amount will be subject to immediate gift tax.

Can I take advantage of my exemption equivalent amount of $600,000?

In addition to using your $10,000 annual exclusion, you may also give away $600,000 of your assets to any one or more persons however you please. To the extent that you use your $600,000 exemption equivalent amount during your lifetime, your estate will not have the benefit of it on death.

Between your exemption and that of your spouse, the two of you can give away $1.2 million during your lifetimes.

When is a gift "complete" for federal gift tax?

A gift is complete when the donor gives up complete dominion and control over the property or interest in property that is given to the recipient. The donor must give away the tree and the fruit that is produced by the tree before the gift is "complete" for gift tax purposes.

How do I value gifts for federal gift tax purposes?

For gift tax purposes, you must value a gift at its fair market value as of the date the gift is transferred to the recipient.

Can I make gifts to my spouse and qualify for the unlimited marital deduction?

You have an unlimited marital deduction when making gifts to your spouse. There are no restrictions on how large these transfers can be or how often you can make them as long as your spouse is a U.S. citizen.

Are gift tax rates higher or lower than estate tax rates?

They are exactly the same; they start at 37 percent and quickly increase to 55 percent.

Who pays the gift tax, the donor or the recipient?

The donor is responsible for filing a gift tax return and paying the tax. If the donor does not pay the tax, payment becomes the responsibility of the recipient. If the recipient does not, or cannot, pay the tax, the property will be used to pay the tax.

Can we review the basic giving methods?

There are five basic methods of making gifts without creating a gift tax:

1. You may give unlimited amounts to your spouse during your life or at death because of the unlimited marital deduction.
2. You may give $10,000 to any person in any calendar year. If you are married, you and your spouse, by "gift splitting," may together give $20,000 per year to anyone provided your spouse consents to the gift. A gift tax return (Form 709) must be filed for the spouse to qualify in such a gift.
3. You may give $600,000 to any one person or to several people during your lifetime or at death. (This is in addition to the $10,000 annual exclusion gifts.)
4. You may pay school or college tuition for any person provided you pay the tuition directly to the educational institution. (This is in addition to the $10,000 annual exclusion and the exemption equivalent.)
5. You may pay medical bills of anyone provided you pay the sums due directly to the doctor or hospital. (This is in addition to the $10,000 annual exclusion and the exemption equivalent.)

THE UNIFIED TAX

What is meant by a "unified" estate and gift tax system?

The federal estate and gift tax is a *unified tax* in the sense that it is imposed upon the cumulative transfers made during life and upon death.

For many years the federal gift tax and the federal estate tax were treated separately under different schedules. Beginning with the Tax Reform Act of 1976, the federal government unified the two taxes so that they are now treated exactly the same. It now does not matter whether transfers are made by gift during life or by will or trust at death; they are taxed at the same rates by the same unified federal estate and gift tax schedule.

What does "cumulative taxation" mean?

If the taxpayer makes taxable gifts while alive, the value of those gifts is added to his or her estate at death and thus the federal estate tax that will be paid is in higher brackets.

For example, suppose a mother made taxable gifts of $600,000 and used up her $600,000 exemption equivalent and annual exclusion; then she gave her daughter a home worth $300,000 and paid the gift tax on the amount of that gift. The mother died 20 years later with an estate of $400,000, which she left to her son. Her estate tax will be based on transfers of $1.3 million ($900,000 during life and $400,000 at death). Her estate will pay the federal estate tax at the $1.3 million bracket, reduced by the unified credit and a credit for the gift tax paid.

STEP-UP IN BASIS/CAPITAL GAIN TAX

What is meant by "basis"?

Cost basis is the term used to describe the original cost of an asset. To determine the taxable gain on the sale of the asset, you subtract the asset's cost basis from its sales price. Basis is important because of the income tax on capital gains that is imposed by the federal government and some of the states.

Doesn't the gift of appreciated assets generate capital gain tax at the time of the gift?

No. A capital gain is triggered only when an asset is sold. Thus, there is no capital gain tax when you make a gift of an appreciated asset, but if the recipient later sells the gift, his or her gain will be taxed.

Is there a way to eliminate the capital gain tax on the sale of a gift?

If you give property directly to charity or to one of several types of charitable remainder trusts and the recipient subsequently sells the property, you and the charity or charitable remainder trust can avoid paying the capital gain tax on the increase in value.

Are there income tax disadvantages to giving property away during my lifetime?

In making gifts—whether or not they fall within the amount of the annual exclusion or your exemption equivalent—there are income tax considerations which a donor should consider.

Property you give away carries your, the donor's, basis with it, and if the recipient sells it, his or her basis is your basis. For example, if you acquired a piece of property for $1000 and the property has a fair market value of $9000 at the time of the gift, the recipient assumes your $1000 cost basis. If the recipient sells the property for $9000, there will be an $8000 gain upon which the recipient-seller will have to pay tax.

Conversely, if you retained that property until your death and left it by will or trust, the property would be included in your estate at its fair market value of $9000 and would acquire a new *step-up in basis* of that amount. If your heirs sell it thereafter, its basis will be $9000 and there will be gain only on any amounts over the $9000.

You must give careful consideration to whether or not the step-up is more valuable to the family than shifting assets and their appreciation from one generation to another through a giving program.

If my spouse and I own property in joint tenancy, does it receive a step-up in basis?

Under Internal Revenue Code rules, property owned jointly by spouses receives a 50 percent step-up in basis on the death of a spouse. This is the same rule as is used for tenancy-in-common property.

What if my spouse and I own property together in a community property state?

Community property receives a 100 percent step-up in basis on the death of either spouse. It does not matter which spouse dies first; all of the community property will receive a new basis equal to its fair market value as valued for estate tax purposes.

What if my spouse and I own property jointly in a community property state?

Only 50 percent of the property would receive a step-up in basis, which would be a tax catastrophe. If you live in a community property state, make sure that you and your spouse own property as community property rather than as joint tenancy property.

Some community property states allow spouses to create a document stating that their joint tenancy property is also community property. However, good planning usually dictates that joint tenancy not be used in any event because of its many other planning disadvantages.

How will we know whether our property is jointly owned or community?

Citizens of community property states take title to their property as community unless they specify to the contrary. In order to own property jointly, an affirmative act to title it as such must be made.

If I am terminally ill, can my spouse give her interest in our joint property to me so that she can get a 100 percent step-up on my death?

Some individuals who know about the step-up-in-basis rules try to take advantage of them when they find that family members or friends are about to die. A person will give property to the dying person with the agreement that the dying person, in his or her will or trust, will leave that same property to the person who gave it. The result these people are looking for is a 100 percent step-up in basis.

To prevent such transactions, the Internal Revenue Code contains a provision that denies a stepped-up basis for any property which was transferred to a decedent within 1 year of his or her death and which is returned to the donor after the decedent's death.

Should I give income-producing assets away?

Assets which produce income are good candidates for giving because the income is removed from the tax return of the donor and put on the tax return of the gift recipient. Note that if the gift recipient is a child who is under the age of 14, this planning strategy may be defeated by the *kiddie tax,* which requires that income from the gift be subject to income tax at the child's parent's highest marginal income tax rate.

If the gift recipient is over the age of 14, a gift of income-producing property may be an opportunity to shift income to a taxpayer who is in a lower tax bracket than the gift maker.

STATE INHERITANCE TAX

Does my estate have to pay state death tax?

Many states have an estate or inheritance tax which is payable on the transfer of assets owned by the decedent.

What is the difference between state inheritance and state estate taxes?

Inheritance tax taxes the beneficiaries on the basis of the specific inheritance they receive. *State estate tax* taxes the decedent or his or her estate on the property that was owned by the decedent at death.

Do I get credit on my federal estate tax return for my state death tax?

Depending upon how your estate planning documents are drafted and the state in which you reside, there may be a credit for state death taxes that is taken on your federal estate tax return. If your state death taxes exceed the amount allowed as a state death credit, no additional credit or deduction is allowed.

Do I receive a $600,000 state exemption equivalent?

State inheritance and estate tax laws do not necessarily follow the federal estate tax law. Some states have transfer tax credits, but others have transfer taxes that are calculated on the net estate itself without any credit. For example, in Pennsylvania a tax is payable on the net estate at 6 percent of assets that are left to lineal descendants and 15 percent of the net estate of the assets that are passing to collateral heirs.

Does the federal government share its estate tax with the states?

In effect, the federal government shares some of its estate tax revenues with the state if the state assesses a tax. Therefore, almost every state has a *pickup tax* or a *gap tax*, which provides for the payment of a tax equal to the amount the federal government allows as a credit for state tax when the federal estate tax is paid.

I have been told that my state imposes a "widow's tax." How is it different from an inheritance or estate tax?

A *widow's tax* is an inheritance tax assessed against property passing to your spouse at your death.

Which states collect the federal estate tax credit?

The gap tax states, those that collect just the amount of the federal estate tax credit, are Alabama, Alaska, Arizona, Arkansas, California, Colorado, Florida, Georgia, Hawaii, Idaho, Illinois, Maine, Massachusetts (after December 31, 1996), Minnesota, Missouri, Nevada, New Mexico, North Dakota, Oregon, Rhode Island, South Carolina, Texas, Utah, Vermont, Virginia, Washington, West Virginia, Wisconsin, Wyoming, and the District of Columbia.

Which states charge estate taxes in addition to the federal estate tax credit?

Massachusetts (through 1996), Mississippi, New York, Ohio, Oklahoma, and Puerto Rico apply tax rates higher than the credit allowed under federal estate tax rates.

Which states charge an inheritance tax?

States that charge an inheritance tax calculate the tax against the value of the share that passes to *each* beneficiary. The inheritance tax states are Connecticut, Delaware, Indiana, Iowa, Kansas, Kentucky, Louisiana, Maryland, Montana, Nebraska, New Hampshire, New Jersey, North Carolina, Pennsylvania, South Dakota, and Tennessee.

Will my estate or heirs pay tax in more than one state?

Unlike the federal estate tax, state taxes pertain to the property within the jurisdiction of the state in which the person is domiciled. Generally, all intangible assets (stocks, bonds, securities, and interest in business enterprises) would be subject to tax in the state in which the decedent is domiciled.

If you own real estate in more than one state that has a death tax, that property will more than likely generate a tax in the state in which it is located.

Estate Tax Planning

Specifically, what can my spouse and I do to reduce the estate tax burden on our children?

In general, you and your advisors can create:

- Marital and family trusts in your will or living trust that will shelter up to $1.2 million of your property
- Irrevocable life insurance trusts to shelter your life insurance from tax
- Family limited partnerships that reduce the value of your assets for estate tax purposes
- A current program of making gifts

I have heard that a living trust does not save federal estate taxes. Is this true?

If a living trust or a testamentary trust in a will contains tax-saving language, it will save federal estate tax; if it does not have tax language drafted into its terms, it will not save tax.

Special language can be placed in a married couple's living trust which will shelter up to $1.2 million in assets from any federal estate taxation under current law. It is not the document itself that saves federal estate taxes; it is the special tax language that is put into the document that will save federal estate taxes.

In addition, special trusts creating charitable foundations and testamentary charitable lead and annuity trusts within the living trust document will keep all of the trust assets free of tax on the death of the surviving spouse (we cover this in more detail in a later chapter).

What are the principal techniques of basic federal estate tax planning?

Basic federal estate tax planning involves utilization of the following four tax principles:

- *Spousal giving:* There is no tax on spousal transfers, either during lifetime or at death. This is due to the unlimited marital deduction. (*Note:* There is an exception to this rule for a non–U.S. citizen spouse.)

- *Exemption equivalent giving:* Each taxpayer has $600,000 to give away tax-free during life or on death. It can be given to as many or as few individuals as the taxpayer chooses.
- *Annual exclusion giving:* Each taxpayer can give away $10,000 each year to as many or as few individuals as he or she likes without any limit on the total number of individuals or years. With gift splitting, a married couple can double the annual exclusion to $20,000.
- *Charitable giving:* There is no federal estate or gift tax on property or cash given to qualified charities.

If I give away property today, will the appreciation be tax-free to the recipients?

Yes. This is one of the great attributes of a giving program. In an inflationary economy, assets that you give away pass the appreciation to the recipients free of federal gift or estate tax.

I plan to leave my property to a family member or charity on my death, but should I consider giving it to them now instead?

If you are comfortable that you will not need the property to sustain your standard of living or to meet future emergencies, you should consider this option. It will remove not only the property from your estate but, as we said earlier, the appreciation from your estate as well.

If the federal gift tax and estate tax are the same, why have I read that gift taxes are really less expensive than estate taxes?

Although both taxes are applied at the same rate, they are calculated differently. The gift tax is "tax-exclusive," whereas the estate tax is "tax-inclusive."

Suppose you are in a 50 percent gift and estate tax bracket and want to transfer $1 million to your children. If you give them $1 million, the federal gift tax is $500,000. Therefore, the total cost of giving the money is $1.5 million ($1 million gift + $500,000 tax).

If you want your children to inherit the $1 million, you must actually leave them twice as much since the amount you leave is reduced 50 percent by the federal estate tax. Therefore, the total cost of leaving the money is $2 million ($1 million inheritance + $1 million tax).

Is removing appreciation from my estate a major issue?

Assume that you have an asset worth $100,000 with no basis, appreciating at 10 percent per year; that your life expectancy is 21.6 years; and that you can do one of two things with that asset in a tax environment that taxes lifetime and postmortem gifts equally at 50 percent:

- Give it to your children today: The cost of giving it to them would be $50,000 ($100,000 × 50 percent).
- Leave it to them in your trust or will: The cost to them would be $400,000 because the inflationary value of the asset will be taxed at 50 percent.

How did you arrive at these amounts?

Under the *Rule of 72,* your asset would double in value every 7.2 years at 10 percent; $100,000 would grow to $800,000 ($100,000 × 2 in 7.2 years = $200,000 × 2 in 14.4 years = $400,000 × 2 in 21.6 years = $800,000).

The estate tax on $800,000 is $400,000, which is 800 percent greater than the gift tax of $50,000.

Can estate tax ever be better than gift tax?

Assume the following: You own a building worth $1,010,000 with a cost basis of $10,000; you have 2 years to live; the building is not appreciating; and you want your children to sell it and travel the world.

If you give the building to your children, you will pay $500,000 in gift tax upon making the gift; when your children resell the building, they will pay capital gain tax of $280,000 on their profit ($1,010,000 – $10,000 basis = $1,000,000 × 28% = $280,000).

If you leave it to them in your estate, the estate tax will be $500,000, and the capital gain tax will be zero because the building will receive a step-up in basis upon your death.

Your children will be $280,000 to the good if you leave them the building rather than give it to them during your lifetime.

What gifts are tax-free?

Gifts to charity and gifts for the payment of medical expenses or tuition are unlimited and free of tax.

Grandparents who are financially able to do so should consider paying tuition for their grandchildren. Such payments constitute tax-free transfers to "skip persons," potentially avoiding both gift and estate taxes as well as generation-skipping transfer tax.

Lifetime use of the unified credit and the $1 million generation-skipping transfer tax exemption are also excellent means of reducing overall gift and estate taxes. You can reduce the size of your estate using current values, thereby removing appreciation from the estate that will be subject to tax.

There are a whole host of other, more sophisticated techniques primarily centered around splitting the bundle of ownership rights in an asset, such as separating the income an asset produces from the underlying asset itself, that permit discounting the value of an asset for tax purposes.

What are other techniques that I could use for saving estate tax besides the unified tax credit and marital deduction?

The following techniques are often used as additional tax-saving strategies:

- *Life insurance trust:* Putting life insurance into an irrevocable trust for the benefit of your children or spouse keeps the death benefit out of your estate and thus can result in substantial savings on estate taxes. You must take care to qualify any premium payments that are funded into the trust for the federal annual exclusion of $10,000.
- *Qualified personal residence trust (QPRT):* A qualified personal residence trust allows you to get your home or vacation home out of your taxable estate by transferring it to a trust for a term of years. During that time, you live in your home; at the end of the term, the home belongs to the beneficiaries of the trust and you can continue to live in it if you pay them rent. A QPRT is an excellent planning vehicle for wealthy taxpayers, as it enables them to pass property to children and grandchildren at a highly discounted value.
- *Charitable remainder trust (CRT):* Charitable remainder trusts work best for taxpayers with built-in capital gains who wish to

avoid paying them. Once an asset is transferred to the charitable remainder trust, the trust can sell the asset without having to pay any tax on the capital gain. This planning vehicle allows you to leave assets to a charity of your choosing, obtain an income tax deduction, and retain an income interest of your choosing for your own and your spouse's lifetimes. The drawback to a CRT is that the principal eventually goes to a charity or charities and not to family members.

- *Charitable lead trust (CLT):* This trust works in the opposite way from the charitable remainder trust: The income is paid to charity for a period of years selected by the trust maker, and the principal or remainder then passes to children or grandchildren at a much reduced value for gift tax purposes.
- *Generation-skipping transfer tax (GSTT) trust:* GSTT trusts are for people who wish to leave property to their grandchildren without having to pay 80 percent federal estate tax in order to do so.

ESTATE PLANNING AND THE SIZE OF YOUR ESTATE

At what amount of net worth should I begin to consider estate planning?

If you have assets and loved ones, you are a strong candidate to consider a revocable living trust–centered estate plan. Although a living trust can be utilized to achieve substantial estate tax savings for estates in excess of $600,000, tax planning is generally not the primary motivation of most clients.

Arguably, a young couple with a relatively small estate and minor children has a greater need for a revocable living trust–centered estate plan than a more affluent couple with no children. The need to provide loving and detailed instructions for the care and well-being of a minor child may greatly exceed the need to do estate tax planning.

The estate planning process should address a host of issues including planning for the trust maker's disability, providing detailed instructions for the care and well-being of the trust maker's family, preserving and expanding wealth, and, finally, avoiding probate and reducing professional fees, court costs, and tax dollars.

Attorneys often ask clients, "What is most important in your life?" Without hesitation, most clients consistently answer, "my family." Clearly, for most clients, tax planning is secondary to planning for their loved ones. The decision to embark on a living trust–centered estate plan is therefore generally not related to the size of a person's estate.

Why should I worry about estate planning if I am young and don't have a lot of assets?

Two common excuses for avoiding estate planning are "I don't have enough assets" and "I'm too young to die." These are misconceptions that can be attributed to a lack of understanding of the consequences of failing to plan and a disinclination to recognize that some day we all die. There are many reasons why estate planning is particularly important when assets are limited.

Estate planning for even modest estates is important because of inflation. This is easily demonstrated through the use of the *Rule of 72,* which holds that 72 divided by the inflation rate equals the number of years it will take to double the size of an estate. For example, if the inflation rate is 5 percent, the rule says that the value of an estate will double every 14.4 years *just because of inflation!* If this seems unlikely to you, just consider how much you paid for your home as compared to the original cost of your parents' homes. Inflation is a certainty of life that simply cannot be ignored. The Rule of 72 does not take into account that the value of assets may grow in excess of the inflation rate. The point is that the value of your life insurance and your house, along with any other assets that you may have or acquire, can be significant, especially over time.

The second reason why estate planning is important is because, according to morbidity tables, the chance of your becoming incapacitated or disabled in the next year is significantly greater than your chance of dying. The absence of an estate plan necessitates a formal, legal guardianship and conservatorship proceeding that involves court costs and the expense of an attorney and would unnecessarily tie up your assets. If you are married and your assets are titled in both your name and your spouse's, those assets will be tied up as well.

In a guardianship and conservatorship proceeding, the court seeks to protect the assets of an incapacitated person, so it requires annual accounting reports justifying the use of assets. Depending upon state law, court permission might be required for the sale of major assets. A performance bond might also be required. The cost of guardianship and conservatorship proceedings far exceeds the cost of an estate plan even for young people with small estates.

In the absence of a properly drafted estate plan, state law determines how assets will be distributed at your death. In states where property is generally owned by married couples in the form of tenancy by the entirety or joint tenancy with right of survivorship, the jointly held property will pass automatically to the surviving joint tenant by operation of law. This may inadvertently create federal estate tax problems when your spouse dies which could deprive your children of an inheritance.

In states where real property is held by spouses as tenants in common, the absence of a written estate plan results in the assets of the deceased spouse passing to the children, with the surviving spouse receiving only a partial share.

If the children are minors, they cannot hold property in their own names and a formal guardianship proceeding is necessary for the court to appoint the surviving spouse as the guardian. An expensive performance bond may also be required. Since a parent has the obligation to support the children, courts generally do not permit the parent to use the children's assets for their support unless the parent is destitute. A further complication is that the surviving spouse may be unable to handle the present house payments and desire to sell the home. With the children owning part of the equity of the home and portions of the deceased spouse's other assets, the surviving spouse may not have access to those funds to purchase a new home.

Thus, even though a person is young and has few assets now, the adverse consequences of failing to plan can be enormous.

My wife and I have more than $600,000 but less than $1.2 million in assets. Do we need to do any estate tax planning?

Yes. If you hold title to your assets in joint tenancy or the survivor of the two of you is the beneficiary of any life insurance, the surviving spouse will wind up owning all of these assets.

The $600,000 exemption equivalent of the first one to die will be lost unless you take steps to preserve that exemption. As an example, for a combined estate of $900,000, by doing proper estate planning, you can save about 37 percent of $300,000, or approximately $111,000, for the benefit of the surviving spouse.

I am single (or widowed) and have more than $600,000 in my estate; what are my options?

You have a number of basic options available to you:

- You can give to as many individuals as you want up to $10,000 annually until you reduce the size of your estate to below the exemption equivalent level of $600,000.
- You can establish an irrevocable life insurance trust to carve your life insurance out of your taxable estate.
- You can give your property to charity.
- You can reduce the value of your property in your estate by transferring it to a family limited partnership.
- You can give a private residence to someone through a qualified personal residence trust.

As an unmarried couple, we do not qualify for the marital deduction. Are there any tax breaks available to us?

The same options available to single or widowed individuals are available to each of you. There are no specific options in the law for reducing federal estate tax with respect to unmarried couples.

My spouse and I have a modest estate and are just beginning to accumulate assets. If one of us should die, couldn't the survivor plan at that later time to avoid tax?

The surviving spouse could consider a number of planning techniques. However, with up-front planning you could easily shelter $600,000 from tax on either or both deaths. This technique would not be available after the first death of you or your spouse.

My husband and I lease a safe deposit box in which we keep all sorts of things for our children and grandchildren. We have written a letter in which we say that everything in the box belongs equally to our children. Will this technique allow our children to receive its contents tax-free?

The Internal Revenue Service is likely to take one of two positions: You have made an incomplete gift, and the property will be taxed in the estate of the surviving spouse. Or you owe back gift tax and interest and penalties for not filing a gift tax return.

I have a number of collectibles, including coin and stamp collections, antiques, and paintings. I have specifically listed some of these items for coverage on my homeowner's insurance policy. Would I be wise to give these items to my adult children, within the $10,000 annual gift tax exclusion, under custody agreements by which they would ask me to "safekeep them" in my home until my death?

Whether this arrangement would withstand an attack by the Internal Revenue Service (for gift tax or estate tax purposes) or by creditors (for enforcement of claims against you) depends upon the answer to two questions:

- *Will your estate be filing an estate tax return?* If a federal estate tax return is filed, it is likely that the IRS will try to tax the value of the tangibles on the theory that you really did not relinquish control and that you did not make a complete gift that would remove the tangibles from your taxable estate.
- *Does your estate have obligations that can be satisfied only from the proceeds of a sale of the assets?* If, at your death, you owe money that could be paid only out of the value of the tangibles under this arrangement, your creditors will most likely ask a court to compel your personal representative to retrieve the tangibles, sell them, and apply the proceeds to the satisfaction of your debts.

Both questions might be answered differently if you should actually store the tangibles in a way that prevents you from enjoying them or if they were scheduled on each child's homeowner's policy.

If I have a Swiss bank account, will my estate have to pay a U.S. death tax on the account?

As long as you are an American citizen or resident of the United States, the IRS will require that your death agent include your Swiss bank account on your federal estate tax return. The attorney and other professionals assisting in the preparation of the death tax return cannot lawfully permit your death agent to omit the account.

Why is it important to plan for life insurance proceeds? I thought the proceeds would pass tax-free to the beneficiary.

While life insurance proceeds generally pass *income* tax–free to the beneficiary, in most cases the proceeds are includable in the estate of the insured person for purposes of estate tax if the insured had "incidents of ownership" in the life insurance. Incidents of ownership include, among other rights, the right of the insured to change the beneficiary. Great care must be exercised in planning for life insurance proceeds so that they can be given to a beneficiary free from income and estate taxes.

A large part of my estate is composed of real estate. Are there specific estate tax issues of which I should be aware?

You should immediately consider the liquidity of your real estate portfolio. Federal estate tax is due in cash 9 months from the date of your death. Ask yourself and your advisors these questions:

- Will the property have to be sold to pay that tax? Do you qualify for any extensions? Does your estate have other assets to satisfy the call on your estate's liquidity?
- Can the real property be sold at its real value in a short period of time?
- Will the appraisal of your real estate portfolio be higher than the property will sell for in certain markets?

The questions so far have involved fictional examples of why people need to do estate planning. Are there any examples of real people who could have benefited from proper estate planning?

Let us look at Elvis Aron Presley's estate as an illustration. When the "King of Rock 'n' Roll" died at the age of 42 in August 1977, his gross estate was valued at more than $10 million. His death probate took 12 long years to complete, and his probate file was finally closed in December 1989. A study made in 1991 by Longman Group USA, Inc., shows that Elvis's gross estate shrank by 73 percent after probate, the most dramatic shrinkage among the famous people listed in the study. By the time his settlement costs were paid, about $2.8 million from the original $10 million was left as the net estate. The settlement costs reported in the study include (1) debts, (2) administrative expenses, (3) attorney's fees, (4) executor's fees, (5) state estate tax, and (6) federal estate tax. The settlement costs and shrinkage of other famous people's estates are shown in Table 1-1.

Groucho Marx's case gives us a graphic illustration of a *living probate* saga that a person may have to face because of his or her failure to plan for incapacity. Groucho had a will, but it did not do him any good on his incapacity. The last 3 years of his life became a living probate battle, in full view of TV cameras, as three parties vied for control over his wealth and care: his live-in friend Erin Fleming, the Bank of America, and Groucho's family. Day in and day out, he was wheeled in and out of court. There was no respect for his dignity and feelings during the lengthy and spectacular trial.

Erin Fleming went to the probate court in Santa Monica, California, to have Groucho declared mentally incompetent. Groucho Marx was indeed judicially declared incompetent in 1974. In addition, Erin Fleming was named his guardian and also his joint custodian along with the Bank of America. All of the court proceedings were open to the public and were covered by the nation's media. The personal life of this famous star was fully exposed. Groucho completely lost control over what was essential to his dignity as a person, namely, his privacy, his personal decisions, and his wealth.

Finally, let us look at Karen Ann Quinlan's case. Karen Ann Quinlan was 21 years old when she slipped into a coma at a party on April 15, 1975. She became a prisoner in a helpless body supported only by medical technology. Her parents, Joseph and Julian Quinlan, decided to take her off the respirator, end her pain, and put her back in a natural state so that she could die in "God's time." However, the doctors at St. Clare's Hospital in Denville, New Jersey, refused to comply with their request because Karen was legally an adult and did not have a living will and a durable power of attorney for health care.

Joseph, her father, had to be appointed her guardian through a living probate, which lasted more than a year. The N.J. State Supreme Court ruled unanimously in the Quinlans' favor on March 31, 1976. Karen was removed from her respirator in May 1976. When she did not die as expected, she was moved to a nursing home. Her parents never sought to have her feeding tube removed during the 9 years she lived after she was taken off the respirator. She died on June 11, 1985. During those frustrating 10 years the Quinlans had to face mounting health care costs as Karen continued to be cared for. The loss of control over their own affairs disrupted and strained the lives of the Quinlan family.

TABLE 1-1 Estates of Famous Persons: Settlement Costs and Shrinkage

Name	Gross Estate	Settlement Costs	Net Estate	Shrinkage
Elvis Presley	$ 10,165,434	$ 7,374,635	$ 2,790,799	73%
J. P. Morgan	17,121,482	11,893,691	5,227,791	69
John D. Rockefeller	26,905,182	17,124,988	9,780,194	64
Dixie Crosby	1,332,571	781,953	550,618	59
Alwin C. Ernst, CPA	12,642,431	7,124,112	5,518,319	56
Frederick Vanderbilt	76,838,530	42,846,112	33,992,419	56
Marilyn Monroe	819,176	448,750	370,426	55
Conrad N. Hilton	199,070,700	105,782,217	93,288,483	53
William Frawley	92,446	45,814	46,632	49
William E. Boeing	22,386,158	10,589,748	11,796,410	47
Henry J. Kaiser, Sr.	5,597,772	2,488,364	3,109,408	44
W. C. Fields	884,680	329,793	554,887	37
Hedda Hopper	472,661	165,982	306,679	35
Cecil B. DeMille	4,043,607	1,396,064	2,647,543	35
Erle Stanley Gardner	1,795,092	636,705	1,158,387	35
Al Jolson	4,385,143	1,396,066	3,036,077	31
Gary Cooper	4,984,985	1,530,454	3,454,531	31
Walt Disney	23,004,851	6,811,943	16,192,908	30
Humphrey Bogart	910,146	274,234	635,912	30
Franklin Roosevelt	1,940,999	574,867	1,366,132	30
Clark Gable	2,806,526	1,101,038	1,705,488	30
Harry M. Warner	8,946,618	2,308,444	6,638,174	26
Nelson Eddy	472,715	109,990	362,725	23
Gabby Hayes	111,327	21,963	89,364	20
Stan Laurel	91,562	8,381	83,181	9

Source: Based on *Your Estate Research Service* (Longman Group USA, Inc., 1990) and Barry Kaye, *Save a Fortune on Your Estate Taxes* (Homewood, Ill.: Business One Irwin, 1993) pp. 24–27.

Estate Planning and Ownership of Assets

What are the most common forms or methods of owning property?

The six most common methods of property ownership are:

- Individual (fee-simple) ownership
- Individual ownership with beneficiary designations
- Joint tenancy with right of survivorship (in some states called *tenancy by the entirety* if between spouses)
- Tenancy in common
- Trustee ownership (Trustee of a revocable living trust holds legal title to the trust property, while trust beneficiaries hold beneficial title to the trust property.)
- Community property

What does "title" mean in relation to property ownership?

Title refers to the manner in which people own their assets. Each manner dictates how much control the individual has over the asset. Title to property consists of two, often confused, subparts: legal title and beneficial title.

Legal title, quite simply, reflects who owns the property for the purposes of buying, selling, or otherwise disposing of the asset. Legal title does not, in itself, confer the right to use or enjoy the property. The *beneficial title* owner retains that right. For example, if you were to lease an automobile, the leasing company would retain legal title to the car. That is, you could not sell or otherwise transfer the car because the leasing company remains the legal owner on the formal written title to the automobile. Nevertheless you, as lessee, have exclusive beneficial, or equitable, title in the car. You, and not the leasing company, have the full right to drive, use, and enjoy the car.

Legal title of many assets is evidenced by a written document naming the owners and the form in which they own the asset—joint tenancy, tenancy in common, and so on. Title to real estate is evidenced by a deed naming the legal owners and describing the property. Title to stock is evidenced by a stock certificate stating in whom legal title is vested; and title to bank, brokerage, mutual fund and

IRA accounts, insurance policies, and certificates of deposit is reflected in an agreement the individual signed when he or she established the account or purchased the asset. Quite often you can determine the legal title to an asset simply by inspecting the bank or brokerage statement, the stock certificate, the insurance policy, and so on.

Beneficial title, on the other hand, is not so easily determined. By simply identifying the legal registered owner of property, one cannot be certain as to the identity of those having the right to use or enjoy the property. Fortunately, however, for estate planning purposes, you need only be concerned with what you own and in what form you own it.

Why is title to my assets so important to proper estate planning?

Title is important because the way an asset is owned dictates the disposition of that asset at your death. For example, if you own an asset in joint tenancy with right of survivorship, at your death, the property passes automatically by operation of law to the surviving joint tenant regardless of what your will or living trust may have directed for that asset. A life insurance policy usually includes a beneficiary designation that will also supersede the provisions of your will or living trust.

Your attorney will suggest different planning alternatives depending upon the type of asset and how it is titled.

INDIVIDUAL OWNERSHIP OF PROPERTY

How does individual ownership work, and what are the advantages and disadvantages of owning property this way?

Individual ownership, legally known as *fee-simple ownership,* means you own both legal and beneficial title to the asset. For example, if you own a bank account, stock, or a car in your sole individual name, you have both the right to control and sell the asset (legal title) and the right to spend the money in the bank account, use the proceeds from the stock sale, or drive the car (beneficial title).

Accordingly, the first advantage of fee-simple ownership is that, because you have full and exclusive ownership of the asset (legal and beneficial title), you can control and distribute the asset at your death in your will. A second advantage is that your heirs will receive a step-up in the cost basis of the property to the fair market value of the property as of your date of death. For example, if you sold this property, you would pay the capital gain tax on the difference between the cost basis and the fair market value. Cost basis is essentially the purchase price of the property, plus any improvements, less depreciation. The cost basis for your heirs, however, will be the fair market value of the property as of your date of death. A step-up in basis can result in significant capital gain tax savings to the person who inherits the property.

There are some disadvantages of individual ownership. Solely owned property may be subject to both living and death probates in the event that the owner becomes disabled or dies. This can create unnecessary expenses and delays. The public nature of the probate process may also cause problems for the owner or for the person who ultimately inherits the property.

INDIVIDUAL OWNERSHIP WITH BENEFICIARY DESIGNATIONS

What is beneficiary-designation property?

While you may have title to certain assets in your individual name, the very nature of the asset may dictate to whom it will be transferred at your death. For example, certificates of deposit, individual retirement accounts, and life insurance contracts typically contain *beneficiary-designation clauses,* wherein you specify who will receive the asset or the proceeds at your death. While you retain legal and beneficial title to these assets during your life, and thus can consume the asset or change the beneficiaries, by designating beneficiaries on these assets, you are, in essence, predetermining who will take legal and equitable title to the asset at your death. As such, your will, despite its provisions, will not control the asset.

May I leave all my life insurance benefits to my spouse?

Many assets, such as insurance policies, individual retirement accounts, qualified retirement plans, and some bank accounts, require a beneficiary designation. When you die, these assets will be paid directly to the person you have named as your beneficiary, without having to go through probate. At least that is the way it is supposed to work.

Spouses often need help and guidance when their marriage partners pass away. Grief, confusion, and lethargy all take their toll during the period of bereavement. By leaving property outright to a surviving spouse through a beneficiary designation, you have no opportunity to provide him or her with guidance and assistance in managing the money. Often, an outright distribution makes more, not fewer, problems after the death of a spouse. At the death of one spouse, the survivor is an easy target for children, relatives, or unscrupulous people who want something. Leaving property outright makes it easier for those predators to feast.

If your spouse is disabled when you die, the court will probably take control of the funds. If your spouse dies before you, or you both die at the same time, the assets will have to go through probate so that the court can determine who will receive them.

Many spouses want to control how their property is to be used after they pass away. Leaving property outright to a spouse affords absolutely no control. If, for example, the surviving spouse remarries, there is no assurance that any property he or she received will ever pass to the deceased spouse's children. Or if the surviving spouse has creditor problems, any property left outright to that spouse is fair game for creditors. If control of your property or creditor planning is important to you, leaving property outright to your spouse is a mistake.

Can't I simply designate my estate as beneficiary of my certificates of deposit, individual retirement accounts, and life insurance policies and then have my will control them?

If you name your estate as the beneficiary of these assets, your will can indeed control them. Doing this, however, does have pitfalls and generally should be avoided. By making your estate the beneficiary of these assets, you are subjecting otherwise probate-free assets to the jurisdiction and lengthy process of the probate court.

JOINT TENANCY WITH RIGHT OF SURVIVORSHIP

What is joint tenancy with right of survivorship property?

Most married couples own their property as joint tenants with right of survivorship, often referred to as *joint tenancy.* Frequently you will also see an elderly or infirm person name a child or close friend as a joint tenant on a bank or brokerage account to facilitate the payment of bills and expenses.

The key element in joint tenancy is its survivorship quality. The last to survive of the joint tenants receives the entire property, thus dissolving the joint tenancy and vesting both legal and beneficial title in the survivor individually. As such, joint tenancy ownership of an asset dramatically affects to whom the asset will be distributed at death.

For example, if you own real estate in joint tenancy with another person, at your death the asset will pass automatically to the surviving joint owner by operation of law.

What is tenancy by the entirety?

Tenancy by the entirety is a type of joint tenancy with right of survivorship. It is available only in some states and only between spouses.

Tenancy by the entirety's unique characteristic is that the creditor of one spouse *cannot* take any part of the property to satisfy the spouse's debt. The creditor may only be able to get a lien on the property. In some states, this creditor protection is not permanent. When the property is sold, its value may no longer be protected. However, if the proceeds are paid to an account which is also owned in tenancy by the entirety, the proceeds may escape seizure by the creditor.

Except for this creditor protection and the fact that it is available only in some states and exclusively for spouses, tenancy by the entirety is almost identical to joint tenancy with right of survivorship.

Are there any disadvantages to owning property jointly with right of survivorship?

Owning property in joint tenancy with right of survivorship has several drawbacks. For example, joint tenancy:

- Only postpones probate
- Supersedes your will or trust regarding distribution of the jointly held property
- Can increase death taxes
- Can lead to capital gain tax
- May cause some children to be disinherited
- May create unintended heirs

Other problems arise if you own an asset in joint tenancy with one of your children. Joint tenancy with a child:

- Can lead to gift taxes
- Can restrict your ability to sell or transfer the property
- Will reduce the over-55 income tax exclusion on the sale of a home
- Subjects the property to possible claims against it
- Might prevent other children from sharing in the property after your death

Doesn't joint ownership between spouses avoid probate?

Let us assume that you and your spouse have two children. You own your home in both your names, as joint tenants with right of survivorship. If you die in a car accident, your spouse automatically becomes the sole owner of your home. There is no probate, but what happens on her subsequent death? There will be a probate. Without proper planning, joint ownership does not really avoid probate; it just postpones it.

I own joint tenancy property with my brother. Upon my death, can I leave my interest in this property to my children?

No, you cannot. A will or a trust cannot control joint tenancy property. When one joint tenant dies, the property, by operation of law, passes to the surviving joint tenant. This greatly misunderstood concept of joint tenancy causes no end of problems and heartache for families.

How can joint tenancy result in increased death taxes?

Joint tenancy between spouses can cause increased death taxes in estates valued over $600,000. This happens because the first spouse to die cannot use his or her $600,000 exemption equivalent amount.

Are there some other tax ramifications of owning property in joint tenancy with my husband?

Under the Internal Revenue Code, a person who inherits an asset on the death of another receives a stepped-up tax basis equal to the fair market value of the asset as of the date of death of the person bequeathing the asset. For example, if a person instructs that his or her corporate stock that originally cost $10,000 be transferred to his or her niece at death, and the value of the stock at death is $20,000, the niece's tax basis is equal to $20,000. Should she sell the stock at its then market value, there would be no capital gain.

Spouses who own property jointly, however, lose the advantage of a complete step-up in the tax basis of an asset on the first death of a spouse. If a husband and a wife own stock jointly and the husband dies first, only his half of the asset will receive the step-up in basis on his death. The wife will not receive a step-up in tax basis on her portion of the asset and would, therefore, have to pay a capital gain tax on any sale of the asset.

I have heard that joint tenancy can cause children to be disinherited. How can this happen?

If you and your husband own property as joint tenants and you die, he owns all of the property by law. If your husband happens to remarry and puts the property in joint ownership with his new wife and then dies, she owns the property by law and your children will be disinherited. The house belongs to her, and she can do anything she wants with it.

How can joint tenancy result in "unintended heirs"?

Here is an example: Dad, about 62 years old, was obsessed about losing everything to a nursing home. His father had to spend his entire estate on nursing home care, and Dad was determined not to let this happen to himself. Dad focused on this to the exclusion of all other estate planning considerations.

Dad talked to a local attorney who did not have much estate planning experience. This attorney recommended that Dad transfer ownership of his home by deed to his two daughters as joint tenants with right of survivorship. Dad retained no ownership interest in his home, relying instead on the loving relationship he had always had with his daughters to allow him to continue living there as long as he could.

Both daughters were married and lived in another state. The older daughter, Ann, had one daughter, Dad's only grandchild. Ann and her husband had a well-thought-out, living trust–centered estate plan. The younger daughter, Betty, and her husband were newlyweds and had no planning. Dad liked Ann's husband but despised Betty's husband and his parents.

Then tragedy struck. Ann, Betty, and Betty's husband were all killed in a highway accident one July 4 weekend. Ann's husband and daughter had stayed at home.

You might think that since the sisters died together, Ann's joint tenancy interest in the home would go to her husband and daughter under the terms of her living trust. But there was litigation in which Betty's husband's parents proved that the truck killed Ann first, then Betty about .02 seconds later, and then Betty's husband, who was in the backseat.

The court held that the laws of joint tenancy controlled instead of Ann's trust. When Ann died, her part of the remainder interest in Dad's home passed automatically to Betty. When Betty died, her remainder interest passed by the laws of intestacy to Betty's husband. When he died, Ann's and Betty's entire remainder interest passed by intestacy to his parents, who now own the home and could legally charge Dad rent or even evict him if they chose to do so.

I am single and I would like to avoid probate upon my disability or death. Why shouldn't I just retitle my home in joint tenancy with right of survivorship with one or more of my children. When I die, won't my property pass to my child without probate? Are there any problems with this?

If you die first, your estate will in fact avoid probate. Of course, when your child later dies, the property could be part of your child's probate estate.

If your child predeceases you, the property will automatically return to you (outside of the probate system), leaving you with no provision as to where the property will ultimately go upon your death. You would be right back where you started, and by then it might be too late to do any further planning.

Also, if either you or your child is disabled and cannot handle your own financial affairs, there might be a living probate required —a guardianship or conservatorship—with respect to the entire property.

Further, you might have created a taxable gift when you put your child's name on the deed with you as a joint tenant. Retitling your home in such a manner is considered a gift because, among other things, after the retitling either you or your child can go to court and obtain an order to divide the property into two separate parcels.

So retitling your home in joint tenancy with your child is treated the same as dividing your home into two parcels and giving one parcel to your child. Depending on the value of the property, you might be required to pay a gift tax. (Generally, if the value of a gift exceeds $10,000, you will incur a gift tax. If the jointly held property is a bank account or brokerage account in street name, the gift is not deemed to have been made until the child withdraws the funds.)

Another problem with retitling your home in joint tenancy with your child is that you may lose control over your home, because your child as a joint owner must consent to any sale or transfer of the property. If you do sell it, you will lose a potential income tax exclusion: a person who is over 55 is allowed to exclude from income taxation the first $125,000 of gain from the sale of his or her home. By placing the house in joint tenancy, you would be able to claim only one-half of this exclusion.

Also, if your child has creditors, say, from a business transaction or from an automobile accident, you are in jeopardy of losing your home to the creditors. The child's joint tenancy ownership in the property can be taken. An even bigger problem can occur if the child gets divorced. His or her joint tenancy interest may be considered marital property under state law and, as such, be subject to the whim of the judge in dividing the marital assets.

All of these rules and results are the same whether the joint tenant is your child or anyone else other than your spouse.

Consider the following example: Lucille, a single woman, was 90 years old and had a farm worth $2 million. She wanted the farm to go to her nephew, John, and she wanted the transfer to be accomplished without probate upon her death. Her advisor suggested that she place the farm in joint tenancy with right of survivorship with John. Tragically, John died before Lucille. The entire ownership of the farm is now back in Lucille's hands. No arrangements had been made to transfer the farm by will or by trust to anyone else, such as John's widow, Martha.

Now enter the IRS. When Lucille conveyed the farm into joint tenancy with John, she made a taxable gift and should have paid gift tax. Now, in addition to the gift tax, there are penalties and interest due.

When Lucille dies, unless Lucille does more planning, Martha will not receive the farm because Martha is not Lucille's heir. To add further insult to injury, when Lucille dies, there will be probate and there will be substantial federal estate tax.

Using joint tenancy to avoid probate can be disastrous. There are better options.

Before my father died, he put all his property in joint tenancy with right of survivorship with my oldest brother, with whom my father was living. My father recently died. Soon after, my brother told me that he had "done more for Dad than the rest of us had" and that he was keeping all of Dad's property instead of dividing it equally among the six children. Can my brother legally keep title to the property and not share it with the rest of us?

Yes. That is part of the tragedy of joint ownership and one of its "unintended consequences." Even if your brother decides to share the property with the rest of you, there can be a gift tax if the value of each sibling's share is more than $10,000.

TENANCY-IN-COMMON PROPERTY

What is tenancy in common?

Tenancy in common is ownership of property between two or more people. Each of the owners owns a percentage of the property, called an *undivided interest.* An undivided interest means that each tenant in common owns a part of the property but there is no way to identify which part he or she owns.

All of the owners of tenancy-in-common property have the right to use and possess the property during their lives, no matter what percentage each person owns. Unless some other agreement is reached, tenants in common may give away or sell their interest in the property. Typically, in dealing with their property, tenants in common are very much like sole owners.

They may also leave their interest in the property to anyone they choose at their death.

Does tenancy in common have a right of survivorship feature?

No. Property owned by tenants in common does not automatically pass to the surviving owners. If you and your two siblings own a cabin in the mountains as tenants in common, you would have legal title to an undivided one-third of the cabin. Not only are you free to dispose of your interest in the cabin as you determine during your lifetime; you are also free to pass your interest at your death to your beneficiaries under your will or trust or by intestacy if you have no formal estate plan.

What are some of the advantages of owning property as tenants in common?

Much like a sole owner, a tenant in common is considered to be in control of his or her share of the property. Each tenant has the freedom to give away or sell his or her interest in the property and to leave it to whomever he or she chooses at death.

Tenancy-in-common interests receive a step-up in cost basis for tax purposes. For example, if two people own a parcel of real estate and one dies, the decedent's interest in the property will receive a step-up in basis, but the surviving tenant's interest will not.

What are some disadvantages of owning property as tenants in common?

Property that is held as tenants in common may be subject to both living and death probates if an owner becomes disabled or dies. This can create unnecessary expenses and delays. The public nature of the probate process may also cause problems for the owner or for the person who ultimately inherits the property.

In addition, since a tenancy-in-common interest is freely transferable, an owner might, involuntarily, become a tenant in common with someone other than the original co-owner of the property.

Is tenancy in common better than joint tenancy with right of survivorship?

In many respects, tenancy in common is superior to joint tenancy as a form of property ownership. Not only can you control to whom the property will pass at your death, but you can utilize estate tax planning strategies unavailable with joint tenancy property. The major pitfall with tenancy in common is that, as with individual ownership, the property may be subject to the probate process.

When would you recommend that couples own property as tenants in common?

A married couple often will have one or two assets which are very valuable and which make up the bulk of their combined estate.

They may be uncomfortable assigning sole ownership of the assets to one spouse or the other. In this situation, it may make sense because of estate tax planning considerations to have each of them own an undivided one-half of the property as tenants in common. This solution meets the need to allocate assets to each of them for estate tax purposes and allows them to continue as co-owners of the property.

For unmarried persons, holding their property as tenants in common rather than as joint tenants ensures that the property will pass to an owner's intended heirs rather than to the remaining co-owners.

TRUSTEE OWNERSHIP

What is meant by "trustee ownership"?

The form of property ownership most rapidly expanding in the estate planning field is that of trustee ownership. By establishing a revocable living trust, you can control who will receive your property at your death and avoid the probate process as well.

When you establish a revocable living trust, you will put most of your assets into that trust. A common misunderstanding is that the trust owns the property within it. This is not really true. The *trustee* of the trust holds legal title to the trust property. The trust beneficiaries hold beneficial title to the trust property. Accordingly, the trustee has the power to invest, reinvest, buy, sell, and trade the trust property (as defined in the trust agreement), while the trust beneficiaries have the right, as provided in the trust, to use the trust property and receive the income or principal of the trust.

It is both common and generally advised that the maker of a revocable living trust be the trustee and the beneficiary of his or her trust (married couples can be joint trustees and beneficiaries of a joint trust). Thus the maker alone can control both the managerial and investment decisions as trustee while using or otherwise spending the trust assets without limitation as beneficiary.

Upon the maker's death, all of the trust property will pass to the beneficiaries named by the maker in the trust upon the terms and conditions that the maker chose. These trust assets are not subject to the legal hoops, costs, and delays of the probate process.

As in the case of sole ownership, the trust assets that are included in the estate of the trust maker receive a step-up in basis at death.

COMMUNITY PROPERTY

What states require community property?

Arizona, California, Idaho, Louisiana, Nevada, New Mexico, Texas, Washington, and Wisconsin.

What is community property?

While the community property laws vary in each of the nine community property states, generally, *community property* is defined as all property acquired by either spouse during marriage which is not considered separate property.

Separate property falls primarily into three categories:

1. Any property owned or claimed by a spouse prior to marriage
2. Any property acquired by a spouse during marriage by partition of community property, by gift, by inheritance, or by devise under a will or trust
3. Any property acquired from recoveries for personal injuries to a spouse's body or reputation during marriage, excluding any recoveries for loss of earning capacity during marriage

All earnings from personal efforts and income from community property are community property. In some community property states, income from separate property remains separate property; in other community property states, income from separate property becomes community property unless the spouses have a written agreement that such income is to remain separate property.

Spouses who own community property are deemed to be partners, each owning an undivided one-half interest in the property. In that respect, community property is much like tenancy by the entirety.

If I look at a deed or title to a car, can I tell if the property is community property?

Not always. Community property is ownership created by law. Who owns the actual title is irrelevant. It is how and when the property is acquired that determines if property is community or not.

What is community presumption?

All property of a marriage is presumed to be community property. This presumption can be overcome if the spouse who is asserting that property is separate property does so with clear and convincing evidence of the separate nature of the property. This evidence is usually found by tracing the property to the time it was acquired, that is, to its *inception of title.*

Separate property acquired with separate property or with the proceeds from the sale of separate property will remain separate property as long as adequate records are kept to properly trace its inception of title.

If my spouse and I have community property, what rights do we have in the property?

Community property is similar to property that is owned as tenants in common in common law property states. As with tenancy-in-common property, each spouse owns 50 percent of the property. This interest is called an *undivided interest* because neither spouse knows which 50 percent he or she owns. For example, if a horse is community property, one spouse doesn't own the front part of the horse and the other the rear. Each simply owns 50 percent of the whole horse.

As a general rule, if one spouse wants to give away or sell his or her interest in community property, the other spouse must approve the sale or gift. Some community property states recognize the concept of *special controlled community property,* that is, community property titled in just one spouse's name. Even though both spouses own the special controlled community property equally, the spouse whose name is titled on that particular property has sole management of and control over it. He or she may dispose of or transfer it without the agreement of the other spouse as long as doing so does not fraudulently affect the other spouse's 50 percent ownership.

A spouse can, on death, leave his or her interest in community property to others by will or trust. There can be no community property on the death of a spouse because the marriage has ended. If a child inherits his or her father's interest in community property, that child becomes a tenant in common with his or her mother.

Are there any tax advantages to community property?

Yes, there is one very important income tax advantage that community property has over any other type of property. At the death of one of the spouses, community property receives a 100 percent step-up in basis. This means that if a married couple bought a vacation home for $100,000 and, at the death of one of them, the house was worth $200,000, the surviving spouse could sell the house for $200,000 and there would be no capital gain tax.

Let's contrast this to the situation in a common law property state. If the home was owned in joint tenancy or tenancy in common, at the death of the spouse only one-half of the house would receive a step-up in basis. In this example, if the surviving spouse sold the house for $200,000, there would be a capital gain tax on $50,000. This is because the deceased spouse's half of the house would get a new basis of $100,000, and the surviving spouse's half would retain its cost basis of $50,000 (one-half its original cost).

Since we are married and live in a community property state, the fact that we hold our property as joint tenants does not defeat the presumption of community property for estate planning and income tax purposes, does it?

In some community property states it does. Unless provided otherwise by statute, joint tenancy and community property cannot exist at the same time on the same piece of property. This seemingly inconsistent result is a product of two conflicting types of law. Community property is a concept inherited from French and Spanish law. Joint tenancy is a concept inherited from English law. Like oil and water, they do not mix. Their legal incompatibility creates an anomaly in the law that can be rectified only by statute.

Without a law to the contrary, joint tenancy property that is owned by spouses in a community property state will lose the full step-up in basis allowed for community property. In addition, joint tenancy property passes to the surviving spouse by law; it is not subject to the control of the deceased spouse's will or trust. Community property can be controlled by will or trust and is therefore much better for estate planning purposes.

What are the three ways to change the character of community and separate property?

Commingling If separate property is commingled with community property to the extent that, even through tracing, clear and convincing evidence of its separate nature cannot be shown, the separate property will become community property.

Partitioning The laws of all the community property states allow spouses to enter into an agreement to divide (partition) their community property into separate property and to declare that certain property is separate property. The agreement must be signed and acknowledged before a notary public. It is now possible under the laws of most community property states for spouses and prospective spouses (through a prenuptial or a postnuptial agreement) to agree not only to partition community property or declare the separate character of separate property presently in existence but also to partition or declare that certain property to be acquired in the future will be the separate property of a particular spouse. Thus, it is possible to agree that income from personal efforts, separate property, and property produced from separate property (such as offspring of livestock) is or will be separate property.

Gifts If one spouse makes a gift of either separate or community property to the other spouse, this property, and all income or property produced from it, is presumed to be the separate property of the recipient spouse. Also, gifts made jointly to the spouses from a third party are deemed to be separate property held jointly, not community property.

What is the character of property owned by a spouse who moves from a noncommunity state to a community property state? What is the character of property acquired in a community property state by a person in a noncommunity state?

If a spouse was domiciled in a common law state at the time he or she acquired property, then the property is generally treated as his or her separate property and will remain separate regardless of whether he or she moves it to a community property state, as long as commingling does not occur. Further, if a spouse domiciled in a community property state acquires property outside the state, its character as to that spouse will be governed by the rules of the community property state. Thus, if the property is acquired with community property, it will be community property; if it is acquired with separate property or by gift, inheritance, or bequest, it will be the separate property of the acquiring spouse, as long as adequate records are kept to trace its inception of title and no commingling occurs. If a spouse who is domiciled in a common law property state acquires real estate in a community property state, the real estate will generally be deemed to be that spouse's separate property since it was acquired with separate property.

Can spouses own community property with right of survivorship?

The laws of most community property states allow spouses to own community property with right of survivorship. Spouses can agree between themselves that all or part of the community property which they presently have or will acquire in the future will become the property of the surviving spouse on the death of a spouse.

Such agreements avoid probate at the first death of a spouse. However, it is strongly recommended that spouses not enter into joint community survivorship property agreements for several reasons. First, the same disadvantages that characterize joint tenancy also exist with joint community survivorship ownership. In addition, such an agreement may have to be adjudicated to the satisfaction of creditors or other third parties. That is, a court hearing may be required to obtain a court order stating that a particular agreement satisfies the statutory requirements for such agreements.

Even though the surviving spouse may prevail, either with or without the necessity of a court hearing, he or she would still be subject to all of the severe shortcomings of joint tenancy. Joint community survivorship property can create more problems than it can solve. Stay away from such ownership.

What is the best way to plan for community property?

If spouses are interested in acquiring the survivorship right and avoiding probate, they should seriously consider creating a revocable living trust. The revocable living trust has all the advantages of joint ownership and then some, with none of the disadvantages of joint ownership.

Wills

What is a will?

A *will* is any written document in which the maker states his or her intention to devise or bequeath his or her real or personal property at death. For a will to be legally enforceable, it must conform to the specific legal requirements of the state in which it is created.

The important features of a will are as follows:

- A will must be prepared and executed with the formalities required by the laws of the jurisdiction in which it is created.
- A will takes effect only on its maker's death.
- A will affects only assets which are owned by the maker alone and which do not pass to others by the operation of law or by contract (joint tenancies and beneficiary designations).

What are the advantages, disadvantages, and consequences of planning my estate with a will?

There are many advantages and disadvantages to planning your estate with a will. Whether the advantages outweigh the disadvantages is a function of many personal factors: the size and complexity of your estate, the degree to which you want to ensure that your assets will, in fact, be transferred to the individuals you choose in the manner you choose, the value you place on privacy, and the importance of minimizing taxes, costs, and attorney's fees. Following is a synopsis of the most significant advantages and disadvantages of will-based planning.

Advantages

1. *Wills avoid intestacy.* If a person dies without a valid will (or funded living trust), all of that person's probate assets will be transferred by the laws of intestacy. State intestacy laws vary considerably depending on whether the decedent is survived by a spouse, the number of children surviving the decedent, and so on. Generally speaking, however, all intestacy laws, in varying degrees and percentages, seek to provide for the decedent's spouse, children, parents, and then more remote relatives. If no individual entitled to inherit the decedent's estate is found within the time prescribed by state law, the property will revert *(escheat)* to the state.

Thus, the primary advantage of having a will is that it permits distribution of your probate estate pursuant to your wishes rather than the state's wishes.

2. *Wills permit the nomination of a personal representative and a guard-*

ian for minor children. In addition to identifying who will receive your probate assets, wills allow you to nominate your personal representative (often referred to as your *executor* if a male or *executrix* if a female). If you do not name a personal representative, the probate court will appoint an individual (often a close family member) who may or may not be the individual you would have chosen.

In a similar vein, a will permits you to name a guardian or guardians of your children. For most people, choosing a guardian of their minor children is a carefully reasoned decision and one that is best made by the parents and not the court.

3. *Wills are easily implemented and maintained.* In most instances, creating a will is an uncomplicated event. While certain individuals wish to handwrite their own wills (called *holographic wills*) or use one of the many forms or computer software applications available to the public, most individuals engage the services of an attorney to ensure that their wills conform to the peculiarities of local laws.

Moreover, as attorneys become more technologically advanced, there is decreasing reliance on amendments, or *codicils,* to wills. Rather, once your will is part of the attorney's electronic files, the attorney often simply incorporates your intended changes directly into your will, reprints the document, and has you execute a new, updated will.

4. *Wills can provide maximum tax savings, protect your children's inheritance from their creditors, and/or establish trusts to "ease" children into their inheritance.* In theory, a "complex" will can provide many of the advantages found in a living trust–based estate plan. In fact, from a legal perspective, the actual language found in a complex will can be almost identical to the trust language of a living trust. Separate trust shares can be created for the benefit of a surviving spouse in an attempt to minimize or eliminate federal estate taxes, and separate subtrusts can be established to provide for the needs of children and loved ones.

The one overreaching caveat regarding wills, however, is that although in theory they may provide tremendous advantages, in practice their usefulness and effects often fall far short of the theoretical optimum. As you shall see, while wills can be effective planning tools for smaller estates, the more complex a person's affairs are, the less effective a will is in planning the estate.

Disadvantages

1. *Wills often fail to control a great deal of the maker's property.* The greatest disadvantage of planning your estate with a will, especially if you have a larger, more complex estate, is that your will may fail to actually control the distribution of much of your property. A will controls only the property that is part of your probate estate. Your probate estate includes:

- All property that is titled in your individual name and does not have a beneficiary-designation clause
- All property that is payable to your estate or subject to a power of appointment
- All property that you own as a tenant in common with another

A will cannot control your joint tenancy assets; they pass automatically to the surviving joint tenant. Nor can your will control assets such as certificates of deposit, individual retirement accounts, Keogh plans, and life insurance for which you have named your spouse, children, or other loved ones as beneficiaries.

2. *Wills offer no protection against conservatorship of the maker.* While a will can effectively appoint your personal representative and the guardians of your minor children, it cannot name or appoint an individual to protect you or handle your affairs in the event of your disability. Quite simply, your will is ineffective until the date of your death. Hence, should you become disabled, your financial affairs may well become subject to your state's guardianship or conservatorship proceedings.

3. *Wills do not easily cross state lines.* In order for your will to transfer the property that makes up your probate estate, it must be filed with the court in the state and county of which you were a resident at your death. While a will executed in one state is valid in another state, it will nonetheless be interpreted according to the laws of the state in which you were domiciled at your death. For example, if your will does not contain a specific clause directing that taxes be apportioned among a certain class of beneficiaries, state A may assess tax liability against each beneficiary according to the amount received by the beneficiary and state B might assess all tax liability against the "remainder" of your estate. Thus, unwittingly, by moving from state A to state B, you could shift the entire tax burden of your estate from each of your beneficiaries to just a select few who were named the recipients of the balance, or remainder, of your assets. Wills are not very portable from state to state.

4. *Wills are fully public.* Despite the fact that most people are reticent to discuss their financial affairs in public, give their latest income tax return to a stranger, or discuss their net worth or cash-flow difficulties at a cocktail party, a person who dies leaving a will to transfer his or her assets may well be exposing this very information. Quite simply, a will, all accompanying inventories, tax returns (in many states), statements of assets and liabilities, the identity of your beneficiaries, the amounts they receive, and the manner in which they are to receive your legacy typically may be filed with the probate court and open to public inspection.

No doubt, the late Jackie Kennedy Onassis had some of the finest lawyers prepare her estate planning documents. Nonetheless, because a will was the cornerstone of her estate plan, it took only a simple drive or a phone call to the courthouse to obtain a complete copy of all such information, and it was a top story on the news.

Your privacy cannot be maintained under a will, and the financial condition of your family and business can be open for inspection by anyone.

5. *Wills ensure probate.* Any asset controlled, disposed of, or transferred by a will must go through probate. Many believe that just having a will (or, more often, their *particular* will) avoids probate; but this is impossible. If your will is used to transfer any of your property, it must first be submitted to the probate court and then be administered in accordance with each and every rule inherent to your state's probate code.

Can you give me an example of what you mean when you say that a will does not control all of my property?

Consider Mr. Smith. Mr. Smith, age 57, is married and has two children, ages 17 and 22. He and his wife have a gross estate for federal estate tax purposes of $950,000, $652,000 of which is deemed for tax purposes to be owned by Mr. Smith. Table 1-2 lists Mr. Smith's assets, as well as how he owns them.

For the purposes of this example, we assume that Mr. Smith made an appointment with a respected attorney and received a complex will that contains tax planning trust provisions for his wife and creates trusts for his children which, upon his wife's death, are designed to retain the remaining principal in trust until each child reaches the age of 35.

Mr. Smith signed his will with great peace of mind, confident that his affairs were finally in order. Assuming that Mr. Smith passes away and is survived by his wife and two children, what does his will control?

Unfortunately, Mr. Smith's will only controls the disposition of his automobile and personal property valued at $34,000! His one-half interest in the family residence, his stocks and bonds, checking account, and artworks will all pass automatically to Mrs. Smith because she is the surviving joint owner. The cabin in the mountains will pass not to Mrs. Smith or to the Smiths' children but to Mr. Smith's brother, despite the fact that Mr. Smith did not name his brother as an heir in his will.

Mr. Smith's certificates of deposit, life insurance proceeds, and IRA will pass to Mrs. Smith, not by virtue of his will but by the beneficiary-designation clauses naming Mrs. Smith as primary beneficiary.

In total, not accounting for court costs, attorney fees, or taxes, Mrs. Smith will receive $602,000 in assets from Mr. Smith, yet only $34,000 pursuant to his will. At first blush, the fact that the will did not control $618,000 of Mr. Smith's assets may seem moot because Mrs. Smith did receive the majority of the property her husband intended. Such a cursory conclusion is flawed.

Mr. Smith's will had federal estate tax planning provisions which sought to hold all assets for the benefit of Mrs. Smith during her lifetime, while paying her the income and, if needed for her health, education, maintenance, and support, the principal as well. By creating such a trust, the will was designed to prevent the assets from being included in Mrs. Smith's taxable estate upon her death. Nevertheless, as Mr. Smith's will failed to control most of his property, $568,000 was transferred outright to Mrs. Smith. Since Mrs. Smith already had assets of her own valued at $298,000 for tax purposes, her taxable estate now totals $866,000. This would generate a federal estate tax of more than $100,740. If Mrs. Smith lives for several years after Mr. Smith's death, the appreciation in value of her estate could cause a much higher federal estate tax liability and added probate costs.

Now let us assume the same set of facts except that Mrs. Smith predeceases Mr. Smith. Her one-half interest in the joint tenancy property passes by law to her husband, thus altering Mr. Smith's federally taxable estate as shown in Table 1-3.

TABLE 1-2 Mr. Smith's Assets

Asset	Value	Title
Principal residence	$175,000	½ joint tenancy with right of survivorship with spouse
Stocks/bonds	100,000	½ joint tenancy with right of survivorship with spouse
CDs	30,000	Beneficiary designation: wife, else children
Checking account	11,000	½ joint tenancy with right of survivorship with spouse
Lincoln town car	24,000	Individually titled
Artworks and collectibles	12,000	½ joint tenancy with right of survivorship with spouse
Other personal property	10,000	Individually titled
Life insurance	75,000	Beneficiary designation: wife, else children
IRA	165,000	Beneficiary designation: wife, else children
Cabin in mountains	50,000	½ joint tenancy with right of survivorship with brother
Total	$652,000	

Now what does Mr. Smith's will control? It still fails to control a great deal of his property, and thus his intended estate plan will not be fully implemented. First, the cabin in the mountains will still pass to his brother, not his children. Second, $270,000 of his estate (again without taking into account taxes, court costs, and attorney's fees) will be transferred outright to his two children as a result of their being listed on beneficiary designations. These assets will not be held in trust for the children until they reach age 35, contrary to Mr. Smith's intentions. Moreover, if Mr. Smith dies while his youngest child is still a minor, a guardian will have to be appointed to receive that child's one-half share of the $270,000 passing outside of Mr. Smith's will.

TABLE 1-3 Mr. Smith's Assets after the Death of His Wife

Asset	Value	Title
Principal residence	$350,000	Individually titled*
Stocks and bonds	200,000	Individually titled*
CDs	30,000	Beneficiary designation: wife, else children
Checking account	22,000	Individually titled*
Lincoln town car	24,000	Individually titled
Artworks and collectibles	24,000	Individually titled*
Other personal property	10,000	Individually titled
Life insurance	75,000	Beneficiary designation: wife, else children
IRA	165,000	Beneficiary designation: wife, else children
Cabin in mountains	50,000	½ joint tenancy with right of survivorship with brother
Total	$950,000	

*Value doubled by reason of Mrs. Smith's death.

Accordingly, if your estate planning goals are to minimize federal estate taxes, court costs, and attorney's fees; to protect your legacy from your children's creditors; or to ensure that your children receive their inheritance when they are mature and not simply of "legal age," yet your estate includes assets that are owned in joint tenancy or controlled by beneficiary designations, then a will is probably not the most effective estate planning tool to accomplish your goals.

Won't a will satisfy the definition of estate planning?

The definition of estate planning that is used by the National Network of Estate Planning Attorneys is:

I want to control my property while I am alive and well, care for myself

> and my loved ones if I become disabled, and be able to give what I have to whom I want, the way I want, and when I want, and, if I can, I want to save every last tax dollar, attorney fee, and court cost possible.

Let's take a look at this definition of estate planning and see how a will stacks up.

A will does allow you to control your property while you are alive and able to do so. A will can do nothing to protect you if you are incapacitated; a will is effective only upon your death.

Does a will actually control property at death? It controls only the property that is not titled in joint tenancy or governed by beneficiary designations.

As far as giving your property to whom you want, the way you want, and when you want, the only thing a simple will can do is give property outright, which may not be in the best interest of the beneficiaries. Often it is not. In order to meet these objectives, your will would have to include a testamentary trust and make sure there is no property titled in joint tenancy or passed through beneficiary designations.

As far as avoiding court costs such as probate, a will does not avoid them. A will guarantees probate, so it also guarantees that there will be professional fees such as those for attorneys and appraisers. Only a will with testamentary trust provisions will provide any type of tax planning or tax savings.

As you can see, a will, in almost all respects, falls short of meeting the definition of proper estate planning.

Probate

DEATH PROBATE AND ADMINISTRATION

Who invented the probate process, and why do we have it?

When people ask this question, they usually are of the opinion that lawyers invented probate for their own benefit. Even though lawyers may have had substantial input in the enactment of probate laws, the necessity of having the probate laws is made clear by the two main purposes of probate:

- To remove the name of a deceased person from title to assets and replace it with the name of a living person

- To provide a way for creditors to be paid

In our country's earlier times, a person would homestead a particular piece of land and obtain a document called a "patent," from the president of the United States, which proved that the homesteaded land was his or hers. As the people who held these patents died, a question arose as to how to remove their names from the patents and put the names of living persons on them. State legislatures had to create a system for transferring property from a deceased person to a living person while protecting family members who might have a claim or interest in the property and giving them an opportunity to be heard. The probate process was "invented" to accomplish such transfers in a fair and orderly way.

Probate also addresses the claims of a decedent's creditors. The process gives creditors an opportunity to make and prove their claims so that valid claims can be paid out of the assets of an estate before they pass to the decedent's heirs.

What is probate?

Probate is a legal proceeding in the probate court to effect the transfer of probate assets to the deceased party's heirs. If the deceased party dies without any estate plan, the process is said to be an *intestate probate;* if the deceased party dies with a will, it is said to be a *testate probate.* The term "probate" actually refers to the proving of the validity of the will. Upon the creator's death, a will is not presumed valid; its validity must be proved in court.

In addition to these death probates, there are also living probates, conducted when persons become mentally incapacitated. So a more complete definition of probate is that it is the process in which a court takes control of certain of your assets if you are no longer able to mange them yourself, either because of death or because of mental disabilities.

What is estate administration?

If a will is proved invalid or if a person dies without a will or without a proper will substitute, the technical term for the public, legal process which ensues is *administration,* not probate. However, the legal process of estate administration is equally as time-consuming and costly as probate, if not more so. Under administration, the disposition of the deceased's assets is governed by state law, not by the deceased person's desires, and thus there is greater opportunity for dispute and disagreement among heirs, family, and friends.

For purposes of this book, we'll treat the terms "probate" and "administration" as meaning the same thing. The primary difference between the two is that in probate a will has to be "proved," whereas in administration, there is no will to prove.

What are the basic steps of probate?

Death probate and estate administration proceedings are made up of six basic steps:

1. Admitting the will (if there is one) to probate and gaining a court determination of its validity
2. Notifying the decedent's creditors, heirs, and beneficiaries of the death
3. Inventorying and appraising the decedent's probate assets
4. Paying (or litigating) the claims of creditors
5. Making certain that any tax obligations of the decedent are paid
6. Distributing assets to the heirs and beneficiaries

What goes through probate and what doesn't?

Anything you own in your own name alone or as a tenant in common with others (including community property) is subject to probate and administration. Beneficiary-designation property for which the "estate" is named as the beneficiary also goes through probate.

Property held in joint tenancy with right of survivorship (including tenancy by the entirety) or in a living trust or property distributed by beneficiary designations (as long as the beneficiary is not your estate) does not go through probate. Property held in a life estate, in which you are entitled to the use of the property and all its income only during your life, also does not go through probate.

What are the disadvantages of the probate process?

The disadvantages of death probate proceedings include:

- *Loss of privacy:* When your estate goes through probate, you lose all privacy. Your will, your assets, and your liabilities all become public record just like any other litigation at the courthouse. Con artists have been known to submit false claims against a probate estate and use the probate record to target heirs and beneficiaries for their next swindle.

- *Will contests:* Wills can always be contested and put aside—it happens all the time. When a will is contested, the estate is frozen and the assets cannot be transferred to loved ones. It is easy for any disgruntled heir to file a will contest since the will is already in probate court.
- *Costs:* The court charges the estate a fee relative to the size of the estate. In addition, attorneys, executors, guardians, and any other fiduciaries acting within the realm of probate (or administration) charge their own fees. The total cost of probate can easily range from 3 to 10 percent of the *gross* estate—or more. For example, if a person dies owning a house that has a fair market value of $300,000 and other assets amounting to $100,000, the value of the gross estate is $400,000. A conservative estimate of the probate costs would be 5 percent of that gross amount, or $20,000. If the house was mortgaged for $200,000, the value of the *net estate* is $200,000. Thus, the probate costs would actually amount to 10 percent of the net estate!
- *Multiple probates:* There must be a probate proceeding in every state in which the decedent owned real property.
- *Delays:* Probate can last from several months to several years. This only adds to the frustrations and anxieties of a grieving spouse and family.
- *Lack of portability:* In our highly mobile society, it is often necessary to have your will reviewed by a lawyer in the state of your new residence to be sure your will complies with and takes advantage of local laws. Usually, a move will necessitate a complete revision of your will.

Probate has been defined as "the lawsuit you bring against yourself with your own money to benefit your creditors." This description is quite accurate, but people usually come to appreciate its veracity only after undergoing the probate of a family member or close friend.

Why should I want an estate plan that can avoid probate?

Probate is obsolete. Death probate was meant to solve the problem of getting title of assets out of a decedent's name. The revocable living trust eliminates the need for death probate because title to your assets is in the name of your living trust instead of your name. There are excellent planning strategies which provide control of assets, privacy, and savings. By planning correctly, you can eliminate the disadvantages of the probate process and have more time and money to create a living, loving legacy.

My spouse and I have wills, so there will be no probate. Each of us gives all property to the survivor or, if neither of us is living, to our children equally. What benefit could possibly be achieved by more estate planning?

First, your wills don't avoid probate. In fact, property passing by a will must go through either a full court probate or a small-estate court proceeding, depending on the value of the estate.

Second, your "I love you" wills can expose your children to unnecessary death taxes, depending upon the size of your estate.

Couldn't I, as a surviving spouse, put everything in joint tenancy with my heirs and avoid probate?

This could be done, but there are a number of drawbacks to this approach. First, you would lose control of your assets. If you need to sell or refinance the property, you must get the signatures of all the joint tenants. If one of the joint tenants is involved in a lawsuit or is responsible for large debts, your property is exposed to that joint tenant's creditors and it is possible that you could jeopardize everything through no fault of your own.

Joint tenancy with an heir also may have serious tax consequences. For most property, when a person adds an heir as a joint tenant, a gift occurs. Also, there may be adverse federal estate tax consequences for the heir if he or she dies before you do.

Lastly, if you change your mind and decide that you want your estate distributed to someone other than one of the heirs that you named as your joint tenant, you might have to get the joint tenant to agree to the removal of his or her name from the title or to the addition of other joint tenants.

Why can't I just give my property away while I'm living?

There are several reasons. First, by giving your property away, you give up control of your property. Regardless of your good intentions, and the good intentions of the person you give the property to, you no longer have any guarantee that the property will be used as you wish or that the property will be used to take care of you.

If you give the property away, it becomes subject to the claims of the recipient's creditors, including his or her spouse. Also, if the recipient predeceases you, the property will pass in accordance with that person's estate planning. If no planning is in place, the property will pass to the recipient's spouse or children. If the children are minors, their share cannot be used for any purpose other than the care of the children. If the recipient divorces, his or her spouse will have a valid claim against the property.

Also, if the property you give away is valued at more than $10,000, you must file a federal gift tax return and pay the appropriate taxes

Can my agent under a durable general power of attorney settle my estate without probate?

No. By law *all* powers of attorney automatically terminate at the death of the grantor of the power.

Can a POD account avoid probate?

A *payable-on-death (POD)* account does avoid death probate. But it does nothing to avoid a living probate. That is, if you are legally incapacitated, no one can touch the account without a court order or a specially drafted durable power of attorney.

If I avoid probate, do I avoid estate taxes?

Nice try. No, your taxable estate includes pretty much everything you own at death or had too much control over. So your gross estate will include joint tenancy property (except the half owned by your U.S. citizen spouse, or any portion to which any non–U.S. citizen spouse contributed), your half of community property, the entire value of life estate property, everything in your revocable living trust, and life insurance proceeds from policies you own.

In addition, if you have the power under a trust someone else created to take some assets out of that trust for yourself, the value of those assets would also be included in your gross estate, even if you never exercised that power.

LIVING PROBATE

What is meant by "living probate"?

It is possible that, prior to your death, you may become mentally disabled due to disease, stroke, or accident.

Legally referred to as a *conservatorship* or *guardianship,* a *living probate* is a legal proceeding in the probate court which is designed to protect a mentally disabled person who is unable to manage his or her financial affairs. It is the duty of the probate court to protect the disabled person's assets, creditors, and personal rights and to appoint someone to manage and assume the mentally disabled person's financial affairs.

There are disadvantages to a living probate:

- It creates expenses. Inasmuch as it is a court proceeding, a living probate often requires the services of an attorney who will prepare the necessary court documents and make court appearances. The court may require the filing of inventories and accountings, along with periodic reports, which may necessitate the hiring of an accountant. The conservator or guardian may be required to post a bond in order to qualify for service before the court. He or she may be also required to make periodic reports to the court during the period of disability and will often utilize the services of attorneys and accountants, as well as other professionals, throughout that entire period. All these factors are very expensive to the estate.
- Just like a death probate, a living probate is a public proceeding which may result in a substantial invasion of privacy and loss of personal dignity.

Why can't I avoid a living probate by giving a general durable power of attorney to a trusted family member?

Unfortunately, general powers of attorney are not always honored by banks, title companies, brokerage firms, and other financial institutions. These institutions have been increasingly fearful of the potential liability inherent in honoring such powers of attorney. Some have established their own specific requirements regarding powers of attorney. The requirements vary from one institution to another, but in general the older a power of attorney is, the less likely it is that an institution will accept it.

Also, the power of attorney, by nature, is a general one and usually gives the designated agent full power and control to do anything with the disabled party's assets. Without caring instructions on how the agent is to apply the funds, this general power can sometimes be abused.

Finally, even if you execute a power of attorney, there is no guarantee that you will not be taken before the probate court by a third party who seeks to have you declared incompetent and himself or herself appointed as your financial guardian. In such a case, your power of attorney would become useless. All too frequently, the general power of attorney causes more problems than it corrects.

How do I most effectively avoid a living and a death probate?

Through a revocable living trust, living and death probate proceedings can be totally avoided. You may incorporate instructions into a revocable living trust which specify how your disability trustee should manage your assets if you become disabled. This simple procedure allows you to have the benefit of your assets, consistent with your directions, during the period of disability while avoiding the expense, delay, and lack of privacy imposed by the living probate process.

Similarly, a revocable living trust enables you to leave instructions for your death trustee, indicating how assets should be distributed. Because the assets are titled in the name of the trust, you avoid the expense, delay, and lack of privacy afforded by a death probate.

LIFE INSURANCE AND PROBATE

Can life insurance policies and proceeds become living or death probate assets?

We usually think of life insurance policies as nonprobate assets. This is because a life insurance contract is a third-party beneficiary contract. In other words, upon the death of the insured, the policy proceeds are payable by the life insurance company to the beneficiary. Probate courts usually have no jurisdiction over nonprobate assets such as life insurance, living trust assets, jointly owned assets, and retirement death benefits.

There are a number of ways, however, that your life insurance policies and the proceeds can get caught up in either a living probate or a death probate, or both. Let's explore the ways this can occur.

You fail to name a beneficiary or a contingent beneficiary. If you fail to name a beneficiary on your life insurance policy or if the beneficiary you have named fails to survive you, the insurance company will pay the proceeds to your probate estate. Most policies provide that the insured's probate estate is the final backup, or default, beneficiary when there is no named living beneficiary.

Your named beneficiary survives you, but dies shortly thereafter. Suppose you and your spouse were involved in an auto accident and you died instantly but your spouse died several hours, days, or even minutes later. If your spouse is named as the beneficiary on your life insurance, the insurance company will pay the proceeds of your policy to your spouse's probate estate. Since your spouse did survive you, your contingent beneficiaries are not eligible to receive your insurance proceeds.

Your beneficiary or contingent beneficiary is under a legal incapacity such as minority or incompetence. If your insurance proceeds are payable to a minor or to an incompetent adult (such as a brain-damaged or comatose spouse who survived the disaster that killed you), the insurance company will have to pay the proceeds to a court-appointed guardian of the minor or of the incompetent adult until he or she gains or regains legal capacity.

You become legally incapacitated, and a guardian of your estate is appointed to take control of all your assets including your cash-value and term life insurance. If you lose your mental capacity or become physically incapacitated due to age, illness, or injury, the probate court may have to appoint a guardian to take control of your assets to conserve your estate from the claims of creditors and other possible losses.

If you own cash-value life insurance, your policy will come under the control of the probate court. The life insurance company will not allow your spouse or anyone else to have access to your cash value, even if it is for your benefit, unless or until your spouse or someone else is appointed by the probate court as the conservator of your estate. Furthermore, once appointed, the conservator will have to get the probate court's permission to withdraw the cash value from the policy, plus post a bond for the amount withdrawn.

Both cash-value life insurance and term insurance carry with them very valuable policy rights which can be exercised only by an owner who is competent. If you become incapacitated, you will not be able to exercise any of these rights, such as your right to convert your term insurance to cash-value life insurance. Approximately 98 percent of all term life insurance never pays off because the policy lapses for nonpayment of premium, the term expires, or the policy is converted to cash-value life insurance. If your insurance policy lapsed or if the term of your term insurance policy expired, an insurance company would declare you uninsurable for purposes of acquiring any new life insurance on your life. If you become incapacitated, only a probate court–appointed guardian can exercise your policy rights for you, and you will have no say over how these policy rights will be exercised.

How can life insurance policies be totally protected from both probate systems?

The best way to totally protect your life insurance policy and proceeds from both probate systems is to designate a revocable or irrevocable living trust as both the owner and the beneficiary of your life insurance policy.

If your estate, including your life insurance, is well under $600,000, it is recommended that you create a revocable living trust which provides that during your life and while you are competent, you are the trustee and you are the life beneficiary of the trust. The trust can own not only your life insurance policies but also any or all of your other assets. While you are the trustee, you will have total control over your policies and all your assets. If you die or become incapacitated, a backup, or successor, trustee that you named in your living trust will control and succeed to all the rights and privileges under your life insurance policy. Your spouse or a trusted friend, relative, or bank trust department can be named as a backup or successor trustee.

In the event of your disability, your backup trustee will have the ability to exercise all policy rights and privileges including the ability to convert term insurance to cash-value life insurance. Likewise, your backup trustee will manage the proceeds of your life insurance for the benefit of your remainder beneficiaries, such as your spouse or children, should you die. At your death, all of your assets, including the life insurance proceeds, will be included in your estate for estate tax purposes. However, if your estate, including the life insurance proceeds, is under $600,000, there will be no federal estate tax anyway.

An irrevocable life insurance trust will also avoid both probate systems, but it is generally used when there is a necessity to save on estate taxes. If estate tax savings are your primary objective, then neither you nor your spouse should be the trustee of an irrevocable trust. Generally a bank trust department or an accountant is the trustee of choice.

If you are not quite ready to take the giant step to a funded, active living trust, you can create a passive trust such as a *standby trust* (an unfunded revocable living trust or a revocable life insurance trust) and name it as the owner and beneficiary of your life insurance. In the event of your death or incapacity, the trust will come out of its passive state and become an active trust. However, you should also give your trustee a specially drafted durable power of attorney to transfer your other assets to your standby trust in the event of your legal incapacity. Furthermore, in the event of your death, your will should name your standby trust as the beneficiary to capture your other assets.

Bear in mind, however, that a standby trust or a revocable life insurance trust is usually unfunded. Inactive trusts will not help you totally avoid the probate of any assets that are not owned by the trust. Only the assets actually owned by a trust will avoid both probate systems.

ANCILLARY PROBATE

What is an ancillary probate, and am I subject to it?

Probate proceedings are brought in the state of which a person was a resident at his or her death. While that probate court will have jurisdiction over all of the decedent's personal property, each state can control only the real property (real estate) within its boundaries.

Accordingly, if a decedent's estate is subject to the probate process and the decedent owns real property in another state, an *ancillary probate* proceeding must be opened in each state where the decedent owned real property. Ancillary probate is simply another probate in another state, conducted for the sole purpose of changing the title to real estate the decedent owned in that state.

In most instances, ancillary probate proceedings require that an attorney in that state be retained, and if the executor of the estate is not a resident of that state, he or she may be required to post a bond with the court. Needless to say, ancillary probate involves additional costs and fees, leaving even less for loved ones.

I have homes in two states, and I spend a considerable amount of time in both. I understand that this can cause tax problems. What should I know?

Although you may have more than one residence, you technically have only one "domicile." It is important to determine which state is considered your domicile, because it is the law of that state which will control the operation of your estate plan and the taxation of your estate. Sometimes, by putting certain language in your estate planning documents, you can select the law of another state to control the operation of those documents in order to obtain more favorable results; your advisors would assist you with the details.

The indications of domicile in a state include the following:

- You vote in that town and state.
- You spend more than half of the year in that state.
- You have your major religious and other community and social activities in that state.
- You have a driver's license for that state, and you have a car registered there.
- You file an income tax return in that state.

If it is not clear from the above indicators which of the two states is your domicile, it is important that you make an informed decision and develop facts and circumstances to support your domicile in the state which you choose. Otherwise, *both* states may consider themselves your domicile and impose state death taxes on your estate.

My mother recently died. She owned property in another state. What problems does this create?

Let's assume for the sake of this answer that your mother's property has already gone through full probate administration in her home state. Let's also assume that everything went well and the administration was completed in 9 months. Now you have to be concerned with the piece of property that is in another state.

You will almost certainly have to retain the services of a probate lawyer in that state. He or she will have to get certified copies of the court proceedings from your mother's home state and file them with the probate court or its equivalent in the county where your mother's real estate is located. In addition, the lawyer will have to file a petition for administration and a certified copy of the death certificate and obtain an order from the probate court admitting the will to probate.

The court will appoint a personal representative who will likely be the same personal representative named in your mother's will. The personal representative will file a notice of administration with a local newspaper of general circulation, and nothing can take place until the statutorily prescribed period of time has expired for creditors to file any claims against the estate. The court will require payment of any claims and taxes, as well as fees of the personal representative and attorney.

The balance of the estate will then be distributed to the heirs. The personal representative will file the final papers with the court to show distribution of assets and close the estate. Assuming everything goes well, this process could take 9 months, in addition to the original 9 months that it took to complete formal probate administration in your mother's home state.

Living Wills

What is a living will?

A *living will,* or advanced medical directive, is a legal document which directs your physician to discontinue life-sustaining procedures if you are in a terminal condition or a permanently unconscious state.

It is considered a final expression of your right to refuse medical treatment which should be followed by your physician. Many people execute living wills so that family members or other loved ones are not put in the position of having to decide whether to terminate or continue life-sustaining treatment when there is no hope of recovery.

The living will is now recognized in virtually all states. Most states have very detailed laws setting forth the language that must be included in order for the document to be valid. As each state has different laws, it is a good idea to check with an attorney in your state to get more information on your state's requirements.

Are there any guidelines that must be followed for a living will?

This document has narrow guidelines that must be met before implementation of its terms can be authorized:

- The maker of the document must be terminally ill from a condition from which there is no reasonable prospect of recovery or must be in a persistent vegetative state.
- Moreover, the maker of the document must be unable to communicate his or her wishes about the course of medical treatment.

Who decides whether or not to invoke the terms of my living will?

You should be aware that most major hospitals have created "ethics" panels or independent review boards which consist of physicians, nurses, and other personnel not currently involved in the treatment of the individual in question. These panels or boards review the situation and give the treating physician(s) direction.

You should ask your local hospital (or the hospital where you may be taken if you have a severe or terminal condition) what its policies are in regard to living wills.

How are living wills misinterpreted?

Living wills are sometimes misunderstood as the equivalent of a "do not resuscitate" (DNR) order, which is an agreement between the patient and the physician that the patient will not be resuscitated if sudden unconsciousness occurs. This situation could occur even if there is no terminal illness meeting the narrow conditions described above for invoking the living will.

For example, a woman who had just had a hip transplant was being wheeled to the recovery room when she suffered a cardiac arrest and lapsed into unconsciousness. The hospital personnel made no attempt to resuscitate her "because she has a living will." This was an improper use of that document because a hip transplant is not a terminal illness from which there is no reasonable prospect of recovery.

What is a power of attorney for health care?

Beyond expressing your wishes as to life-sustaining issues, you may also express your wishes with regard to courses of medical treatment. In a *power of attorney for health care,* you name a surrogate or attorney-in-fact to make medical decisions for you if you are unable to do so yourself. For instance, if major surgery or long-term treatment is proposed and you are too ill to make your feelings known, your surrogate would invoke the power of attorney to facilitate your wishes.

What are some of the issues that I may wish to address in my living will and other medical directives?

Some of the issues you may want to address specifically are terminal conditions or illnesses (such as certain types of cancer, stroke, and major heart problems), vegetative states, and the types of treatments you may want to have withheld (such as tube feeding, artificial nutrition, hydration—in all of their various forms). Your personal medical concerns may dictate other issues that should be included. Be sure to address quality-of-life issues and make an express statement of your desire and philosophy regarding your right to die with dignity.

It is impossible to create the perfect document when you cannot know what the specific situation will be at the time help is needed. With comprehensive medical directives, however, you should have some peace of mind that your wishes have been made known and that your desires will be carried out.

2

Revocable Living Trust–Centered Planning

The subject of revocable living trusts is difficult to cover in so few pages. We have written 1105 pages of prose on the virtues of revocable living trust planning, in *The Living Trust Revolution, Loving Trust,* and *The Living Trust Workbook* (all published by Viking-Penguin). Our contributors have covered those virtues remarkably well in this chapter.

There can be little question that *Legacy's* contributing authors practice daily what they preach. They are devoted to avoiding will-planning probate for their client families and to making each living trust they draft represent, as closely as possible, the hopes, concerns, dreams, values, and aspirations of their clients.

This chapter not only explains why living trust planning is better than available alternatives but also takes you through the process of funding revocable living trusts so that avoiding the publicity, time, delay, and expense of the probate system will be ensured. It discusses everything from taxation planning to planning for beneficiaries and addresses the particular concerns associated with planning for special children and circumstances.

The questions and answers in this chapter present a wealth of material in a lively and informative manner. They supply you with more than enough knowledge to immediately take action to create or enhance your estate plan when working with your professional advisors.

Is a Revocable Living Trust Plan for Me?

Aren't trusts just for the wealthy?

Many people equate the word "trust" with concepts like trust funds or charitable trust foundations—entities that they consider part of the world of the very wealthy and, therefore, not applicable to their situation. Most people equate trust-centered planning with estate tax planning. Thus they conclude that if their estates are less than the federal exempt amount of $600,000, they have no need for any type of trust-centered estate plan.

Nothing, however, could be further from the truth. Most people have assets and personal possessions that they would want to be used for the care of themselves and their loved ones if they should become disabled or die. And most people would want those assets to be used exactly as they would have used them: in a way that promotes their aspirations for loved ones and addresses their specific concerns.

A proper estate plan should be centered on a document that will create a lasting legacy of love, support, and guidance for family and loved ones. Leaving a legacy is not restricted to the wealthy; it can be done by all people. And for those who are not financially wealthy—yet abundantly wealthy in love—it is particularly important that their assets be carefully preserved. Through a revocable living trust, everyone can leave such a legacy for their loved ones.

Isn't creating a revocable living trust just a waste of time and money if my estate is less than $600,000?

Absolutely not. Your estate will pass estate tax–free on your death, but there is more to planning than taxes. In fact, many personal benefits in a revocable living trust may be significantly more important than estate tax savings. Let's go back to the beginning and look at our definition of proper estate planning:

> I want to control my property while I am alive and well, care for myself and my loved ones if I become disabled, and be able to give what I have to whom I want, the way I want, and when I want, and, if I can, I want to save every last tax dollar, attorney fee, and court cost possible.

You will notice that a lot of goals precede the concluding phrase, "and, if I can, I want to save every last tax dollar." It is those preceding goals which have priority in proper estate planning.

For many people with estates of less than $600,000, a revocable living trust is an excellent planning vehicle because, among other things, it can address so many different needs. In creating a revocable living trust, you can, for example, do the following:

- You can provide for your disability by appointing someone to administer your assets while you are disabled in accordance with your detailed instructions on how to care for you and your loved ones.
- You can create a *special-needs trust* to take care of anyone in your family who may have a temporary or permanent disability or who may require special care.
- You can create a *common trust* to care for your minor children from a common pool of the estate assets, just as you would if your family were still intact.
- If some of your heirs are poor at handling money, you can arm a successor trustee with spendthrift provisions to restrain your heirs from their unwise spending or to provide protection from the claims of their creditors.
- You can delay distributions to heirs until they are mature enough to spend their inheritance wisely.
- You can avoid the public, slow, and expensive probate process.
- You can direct the disbursement of your estate in a manner tailor-made to the individual needs and capabilities of each of your heirs.
- If you have contentious family members, you can reduce the likelihood of legal conflicts among them, since a revocable living trust is generally more difficult to contest than a will.

These are but a few examples of the things you can accomplish with a revocable living trust. When you remain mindful of the real priorities in estate planning, you will never choose a planning vehicle solely on the basis of the size of your estate.

How old should a person be before having a living trust plan?

If people knew when they were going to die, they.could see their estate planning attorneys a few months prior to that time. Since no one knows when death will occur, an estate must be planned as though death will happen at any time, whether it be tomorrow or 30 years from now. Age, then, is not a determining factor.

Is living trust planning a good idea for a single parent?

Definitely. In fact, it is the best overall solution to the planning problems of the single parent. How does a living trust benefit the single parent? In most respects, it offers the same advantages to a single parent as it does to a married parent. However, because there is no spouse to assist the parent if he or she becomes disabled or to provide for the emotional and financial needs of the child if the parent should die, living trust planning is particularly beneficial for a single parent. Carefully selected guardians and trustees and detailed instructions for your own care and that of your child will ensure that, no matter what life brings, your wishes will be carried out and your child provided for.

My husband is not well: his memory and his mental acuity have degenerated over the last several years. If I die before my husband, how can I allow him the dignity of his independence and still protect him from the problems related to his failing health?

With a funded living trust as the center of an estate plan, a trust maker can select a cotrustee to serve with the spouse as trustees of the trust. This enables the surviving spouse to retain control and independence while having the advice and counsel of the cotrustee.

In the event that the surviving spouse's health further degenerates, the trust can provide for a smooth transition in the management of his or her affairs. For example, a son or daughter could be named to serve as cotrustee with the father. The selection of a family member provides personal consideration as well as the security of joint management for the ailing spouse.

I have substantial assets and am thinking about getting married. Could a living trust be used to keep the assets I own before my marriage segregated from property acquired by me and my new spouse during marriage?

Yes, a living trust is an excellent way to keep separate property assets, or assets acquired prior to a marriage, from being commingled with assets acquired during the marriage. Since the premarital assets are in a living trust, it would be impossible to commingle them with the assets acquired during the marriage unless the commingling was intentional.

To give even more protection, consider coupling a living trust with a premarital property agreement specifying that all of the assets in the living trust, along with their increase in value, interest earned, dividends earned, and future appreciation, are immune from the claims of the other spouse and his or her creditors.

To properly accomplish your desire, you must discuss your state's marital property laws with an attorney who practices in this area of the law.

The Revocable Living Trust

What is a revocable living trust?

A *revocable living trust* is a written document, which an estate planning lawyer can draft for you, wherein you, or you and your spouse, as the *trust maker* of the trust appoint yourself as your own *trustee* (the manager of the trust) and name yourself as the life *beneficiary* (the person who enjoys the use of the properties of the trust). Thus you, or you and your spouse, are the three essential parties to the trust:

1. The trust maker, sometimes called the *grantor, trustor, settlor,* or *creator*
2. The trustee
3. The life beneficiary

Most of your assets will be retitled in the name of the living trust. As trustee of your own trust, you have 100 percent control over your assets: you can sell assets, buy assets, add assets to the trust, and remove assets from the trust. Since the trust is revocable, you can amend, alter, or revoke your trust and your estate plan at any time.

In the document, you usually name one or more individuals to serve as successor, or backup, trustees should you die or become unable to serve as the trustee. A successor trustee can be one of your adult children or a close friend, a relative, or a trust company or bank trust department.

Most often, the trust includes instructions specifying that upon your death or upon the death of the surviving spouse your children or other loved ones will become the *remainder beneficiaries,* the persons who enjoy the remaining property of the trust. Your trust agreement can also include your instructions on how to distribute the remaining property to those beneficiaries. For example, you can designate that your remainder beneficiaries must attain a certain age or level of maturity before receiving the property, and you can instruct the trustee to distribute that property to them outright or in increments.

If your children are both successor trustees and remainder beneficiaries, they will, as trustees and with the assistance of a lawyer, transfer the property to themselves.

If any of your children are too young to receive their distribution, the successor trustee will manage their shares for their health, support, maintenance, and education until they attain the age you designated. At that time, the trustee can distribute their shares.

How does a living trust differ from a testamentary trust?

Living trusts, also known as *inter vivos* (during your life) trusts, are created and in force during your lifetime. You sign the trust agreement and place the assets you choose in the trust while you are alive. The trust survives both your incapacity and your death, distributing the assets of the trust during your incapacity or after your death to your loved ones in the manner you have provided in the trust agreement.

In contrast, a *testamentary trust* is created within a will and thus is not in force during your lifetime. Since a testamentary trust does not exist until the will takes effect at your death, you cannot place any assets in the trust during your life. Hence, your assets must go through the probate process before being placed in the testamentary trust.

What is the difference between a revocable trust and an irrevocable trust?

As its name implies, a *revocable trust* can be revoked, changed, or amended by the maker of the trust at any time. Its maker can update it as his or her desires and the needs of loved ones change. This flexibility makes a revocable living trust an ideal foundation for almost all estate plans. A revocable living trust can be designed to control all of the maker's property, totally avoid the probate of the maker's estate, and maximize federal estate tax savings.

Irrevocable trusts, on the other hand, cannot be altered or amended without the approval of a court. Accordingly, irrevocable living trusts should be used only in certain circumstances after careful consideration and planning. Most often, irrevocable living trusts are used in conjunction with revocable living trusts to hold certain, select assets of the trust maker for the benefit of the trust maker's loved ones. If the trust maker retains no rights in the irrevocable living trust and is not a trustee or a beneficiary of the trust, the assets of the trust can be excluded from the trust maker's gross estate for estate tax purposes. This allows the trust maker to lower and, at times, eliminate federal estate taxes.

Irrevocable living trusts can be described as an advanced estate planning tool. They are most commonly used by individuals whose gross estates for federal estate tax purposes are greater than $600,000 or by couples whose assets are in excess of $1.2 million. Unlike revocable living trusts, irrevocable living trusts are rarely the foundation of one's estate plan but rather a supplement to it.

I'm afraid I'll lose control of my assets if I don't own them anymore. Why do you say I won't lose control?

First, you create a trust agreement with the help of a qualified estate planning attorney, who makes sure the document fulfills your wishes while staying within the bounds of trust law, debtor-creditor law, marital law, bankruptcy law, and tax law. Among the provisions of your trust are your instructions for the trustee in regard to managing and distributing the assets for and to your beneficiaries—you dictate the terms which the new owner of your property (your trustee) *must* obey. There is no higher duty under the law than that owed by a trustee to a beneficiary.

As if that were not enough control, you can be the sole beneficiary of the trust during your lifetime. Your trust will contain instructions on how to take care of you during a legal incapacity, and your instructions must be followed and your property used for your benefit. If you become disabled, you actually have more control over your property than you would have if you owned it outright, since without the trust your assets would be subject to a living probate.

And finally, for the ultimate in control, you can be your own trustee while you are alive and competent. You make all the decisions to buy, sell, give away, acquire, and use the property, just as you always did.

How does a living trust avoid probate?

The probate process is the court-supervised transfer and distribution of your property in the event of your disability or after your death. The complications, time delays, and expense of probate vary from state to state. However, in all states, the use of a revocable living trust eliminates the need for probate because your assets are in the name of your living trust.

If you have a revocable living trust and become disabled, the trustee is available to utilize the assets for your own care and for your loved ones in accordance with your instructions. Upon your death, the trustee will follow your trust instructions for distribution of your assets to your beneficiaries.

Are assets held in a living trust protected from creditors' claims?

Generally speaking, when assets are held in a revocable trust, they are not protected from the legitimate claims of the trust maker's creditors. This is because the maker can revoke the trust and take back the trust property at any time. The law finds that it is inequitable to allow the trust maker to have this control and full use and benefit from the trust property while denying creditors the power to compel revocation in order to satisfy their just claims.

An *irrevocable* trust may provide some creditor protection because the maker is not able to revoke the trust and get the property back. The maker may have a *beneficial interest* in the trust, such as a right to income or to principal, and that interest may be reached by the maker's creditors. However, if the beneficial interest is subject to the discretion of the trustee and the maker is not the sole trustee, creditors can be thwarted. Since the contribution of property to an irrevocable trust is a completed gift, the property generally is outside the reach of the maker as well as his or her creditors.

Are there ways to draft my living trust so that the trust assets are less vulnerable to my beneficiaries' creditors?

While a revocable living trust cannot protect the maker from his or her creditors, it can protect the beneficiaries from the claims of their creditors. When a special clause is inserted into the trust document to protect trust assets from claims of the beneficiaries' creditors, the trust is said to be a *spendthrift trust.*

Spendthrift trusts are not valid in all states. In addition, the mere presence of a spendthrift clause does not always ensure creditor protection. There are, however, several measures that can be taken to make a spendthrift trust less vulnerable if it is attacked by a beneficiary's creditors. For example, trust agreements may specify that the trustee *must* make distributions for the support of the beneficiary or that the trustee *may* make distributions based solely on the trustee's discretion. Courts have generally held that spendthrift trusts which *require* that distributions be made for the support of the beneficiary may be reached by creditors for support-related debts; creditors generally cannot seize assets of a spendthrift trust that allows the trustee to distribute trust assets based *solely* on the trustee's discretion.

If your objective is to protect your beneficiaries from their creditors, it is generally best to give the trustee of the spendthrift trust sole discretion as to whether or not to pay the trust's income or principal to the beneficiary, as opposed to requiring mandatory payments of income or principal to the beneficiary. Additionally, it is not advisable to name the beneficiary of the spendthrift trust as the sole trustee of his or her own trust. Doing so could invoke the *doctrine of merger* of equitable and legal title, thus allowing the beneficiary's creditors to reach the trust's assets.

Creditors could also reach the assets of a spendthrift trust if the conditions necessary for the trust to terminate have already occurred but the trust has not been terminated. For instance, if the terms of the spendthrift trust require that the trust terminate when the trust beneficiary reaches 30 years of age, a creditor of the beneficiary may require that all assets be distributed to the beneficiary when he or she turns 30. The beneficiary cannot elect to wait out the creditor. To solve this problem, you can make the term of the trust be the duration of the beneficiary's life.

Why do you recommend a revocable living trust as a basic strategy for proper estate planning rather than other traditional methods?

A revocable living trust estate plan meets all of the criteria in the definition of estate planning:

- It allows you to control all your affairs and assets during your life and after your death.
- It minimizes taxes, fees, and costs, thereby preserving your wealth.

If you procrastinate and do nothing, the courts will take control of your assets. When you die, your assets will be distributed according to state law; if you become incapacitated, they will be managed by a conservator. The outcome in either case may not be what you want.

With the traditional methods of planning, you can lose control. A will probably will not control all of your assets, and it does not avoid probate when you die. Furthermore, it provides no protection at incapacity.

Joint ownership doesn't avoid probate; it just postpones it. If a joint owner becomes incapacitated, the other joint tenant could end up in the probate court. Joint ownership can also cause the unintentional disinheritance of a tenant's own family.

Beneficiary designations are not always effective either. They create problems if the beneficiaries are minors or are disabled or if they have creditor or marriage problems.

Finally, none of the traditional methods is particularly useful as a basic strategy for wealth preservation.

If trusts are so good, why don't more attorneys embrace them?

Traditionally, law schools taught will planning and probate planning but offered little instruction in living trust–centered estate planning. Even though the public demand for living trusts is growing, the legal profession is typically conservative and slow to embrace change.

Why are revocable living trusts just now becoming more common among the middle class if trusts have been in use in the common law system since the twelfth century?

Changes in the law and society have made revocable living trust planning much more attractive and necessary. Here is a brief history of some of those changes.

In 1954, the federal tax code was amended so that a revocable living trust is completely ignored for income tax purposes. There is no separate income tax form to file as long as the trust maker serves as trustee of the trust. You report all the income on your 1040, just like you do now.

Many states used to follow the doctrine of merger. Under this legal principle, if you created a trust and named yourself as the sole trustee and sole current beneficiary, the courts would hold that no trust exists because all of the parties of the trust are the same and thus merged together. That was inconvenient for some potential trust makers. Most states have repealed the doctrine of merger, and even those states that have not done so will honor such a trust if it was created in a state which has abolished the doctrine. (New York, which as of this writing still has the doctrine, is reportedly close to abolishing it by statute.)

Durable special powers of attorney, which did not exist anywhere before 1975, provide an important safety-net component in the total living trust–centered estate plan. If you become incapacitated, your agent under the durable special power can transfer your assets into your revocable living trust. This allows your trustee, rather than the courts, to manage your assets according to your instructions.

In 1981, the unlimited marital deduction for estate and gift taxes came into law at the federal level and made possible some very important tax planning. It provides you with the ability to leave as much as you want to your spouse and not have it taxed until he or she dies, and your spouse has creditor protection if you leave the property in trust. This law gave many more people the incentive to create trusts which would continue on after their deaths.

The last piece of the legal picture was put in place with the passage in most states of laws that permit the creation of *health care proxies, durable powers of attorney for health care, appointments of health care representative,* or *designations of health care surrogate.* These documents allow you to designate an agent to make health care decisions for you when you cannot do so yourself. When you combine the health care proxy with a durable special power of attorney and a living trust, you eliminate the need for a financial and legal guardian to be appointed by a court should you become legally incapacitated in the future.

At the same time, the nation's circumstances have been changing. Wealth continues to increase, and inflation constantly erodes the lifetime estate tax exemption equivalent (currently $600,000) and the annual gift tax exclusion (currently $10,000). These factors have made estate and gift tax planning more important for more people.

Although probate has been streamlined in some states, on average it does not seem to be getting less expensive, faster, or more pleasant. Indeed, a number of observers and analysts believe it is getting worse. A fully funded revocable living trust avoids most of the costs of death administration and can usually distribute assets in a matter of months, rather than the 1 to 2 years of a typical probate.

Further, more and more people are entrepreneurs and small-business owners. A small business can be completely wiped out by estate taxes on its owner's death. These entrepreneurs are among a new breed of individuals who are finding estate planning to be vital to their goals and dreams.

The last factor that has propelled revocable living trust–centered planning into the forefront is public awareness. Due to the presence of financial publications which didn't exist 20 years ago, more people are aware of investing, retirement planning, and estate planning. They have educated themselves as to both the lifetime and the post-mortem benefits for themselves and their loved ones of proper estate planning, and they are taking action.

How do I know that the government will not legislate the living trust out of existence?

It is really of no advantage to the government to have a person's estate go through guardianship or probate proceedings because these proceedings add an additional burden to the nation's court systems. The revocable living trust is a major advantage to the government because it frees up the courts' time, enabling the courts to handle more pressing matters.

My bank is currently managing my assets under a trust arrangement. Isn't the bank's document a revocable living trust?

The agreement you signed with your bank may be a revocable living trust. A legal document sets forth the conditions which determine the nature of the legal relationship. If the document describes itself as a "trust agreement" and identifies the bank as your "trustee," a legal trust relationship probably exists. Whether it is a revocable trust depends on the specific terms of the document. The phrase "revocable living trust," as used by members of the National Network of Estate Planning Attorneys, signifies a very complete statement of your intentions that includes your best thoughts on providing for yourself and your loved ones. The bank's document probably contains inadequate instructions in the event of your disability and no provisions for distribution other than to return the assets to your probate estate.

Trust documents prepared by banks for general usage are commonly known as *letter trusts*. Under these arrangements, you, as the maker, designate the bank's trust department as your trustee but retain the right to revoke the trust arrangement. You are designated as the recipient of all of the income. Your estate is designated as the beneficiary upon your death. No provision is made for your disability other than the continuation of income payments to you during your lifetime.

The purpose of the letter trust is to create a specific relationship between you and the bank. The bank is not authorized to be a broker or seller of investment securities. However, the relationship created by the letter trust agreement permits the bank, acting as your trustee, to invest on your behalf and to earn a fee for doing so. These trusts are not designed for estate planning; they are designed to expedite and make easier the bank's investment of your assets.

You should consult your attorney about creating a fully developed revocable living trust as an amendment to the letter trust. In this way your bank, continuing as your trustee, will have full instructions, in the event of your disability or death, for managing and distributing your assets.

What is the difference between a living will and a living trust?

A *living trust* is a document that has your instructions about how your property will be handled while you are alive and after your death.

A *living will* directs your physician not to prolong your life by artificial means if you are terminally ill and mentally or physically unable to convey your desires at that time. Your directive becomes effective when your attending physician determines that your condition is terminal and incurable.

Can a married person create a living trust plan without the knowledge of his or her spouse?

Yes. A spouse can place separate personal property—such as bank accounts, money markets, certificates of deposit, stocks or bonds, and beneficiary designations on IRA accounts—in the name of a living trust without the other spouse's consent or signature on any of the transfer documents.

In most instances, a person would not be able to transfer joint title to real estate into his or her living trust unless the other spouse cosigned any deed that was necessary to put title into the trust.

There are two limitations upon the effectiveness of creating the trust plan without the knowledge of your spouse:

1. Making the maximum use of the unified tax credits, which allow a married couple to leave $1.2 million free of federal estate tax, requires cooperation between husband and wife.
2. In most states, one spouse cannot prevent the surviving spouse from claiming the rights of homestead and of a statutory allowance for inheritance purposes, even if assets are placed in a trust.

Can I have more than one revocable trust?

Yes, you can. For instance, if you plan to be away from the office for an extended period of time, a separate revocable trust can be set up so that you can appoint someone as your trustee to handle the regular business routines of paying bills, depositing checks, and the like, while you are away. This type of trust is like a power of attorney but is safer and more restrictive.

You can also divide property among several revocable trusts and appoint a different member of the family as trustee of each trust to see how each one manages the trust property. This will give you an idea of what would happen in the event of your death. In addition, you can have the sole power to amend or revoke each trust, so that you can terminate a trust if you feel that the principal in it is being mishandled.

In some cases, spouses may each have an individual trust for separate property and a joint trust for marriage property.

JOINT REVOCABLE LIVING TRUST

What is a joint revocable living trust?

A *joint revocable living trust* is a single trust created by a married couple that addresses each spouse's wishes as to his or her property. Both spouses are the trust makers, and both are almost always the trustees.

Can spouses create a joint living trust if they own their property in joint tenancy?

Of course. Joint trusts are good estate planning tools for married couples with joint tenancy property. However, allowing property to pass outright to the surviving spouse pursuant to the survivorship feature of joint tenancy may defeat the trust makers' planning, particularly if federal estate tax planning is implemented. With a joint trust, it is important that, during funding, the spouses "sever" the jointly held property into equal ownership between them to prevent the property from passing outright to the surviving spouse upon the first spouse's death.

If my spouse and I choose to have a joint trust, are we able to direct the trustee to hold our separate property within the same trust?

The creation of a joint trust to hold your assets during your lifetime does not preclude either you or your spouse from directing the trustee to hold one or more specific assets for the benefit of either spouse individually.

If individual assets are part of your joint revocable living trust, the trustee must take care to account for the assets and any income derived from them as separate income. This is particularly critical when the trustee is holding separate property for any of the beneficiaries.

Gift tax and asset tax basis issues must be considered when ownership transfers occur. Therefore, the trustee must carefully document any change of ownership from one spouse individually to the spouses jointly.

When establishing the assets in the separate name of either spouse, you must consult local law with regard to the requirements for a full transfer of the ownership rights. This transfer is more complicated in a community property state than it is in a common law state. Your attorney can advise you of the requirements for documenting transactions involving specific individual assets.

If a joint revocable living trust is established with the spouses as cotrustees, may either spouse act independently or is joint action always required?

Generally, either trustee is able to exercise the full powers on behalf of the trust for the benefit of both trust makers. Limitations requiring joint action by the trustees could be written into the revocable living trust, but such limitations make management of the trust cumbersome.

If there is a lack of trust between the spouses, they should consider having a professionally managed trust during their lifetimes or establishing separate trusts. In this way, concerns that a spouse might use the trustee relationship to take advantage of the other spouse are eliminated. A third-party trustee can also play an important role as a financial manager, record keeper, and investment advisor for your trust.

Advantages of Revocable Living Trusts

What are the benefits of a revocable living trust?

Control, cost, convenience, and confidentiality are the four primary reasons that many people turn to trust-centered estate planning.

Control A fully funded revocable living trust allows the trust maker to retain control of his or her estate planning affairs while avoiding probate and its related pitfalls.

Perhaps the most important attribute of a revocable living trust is that it allows the trust maker to retain control of both personal health care and financial affairs even in the event of his or her disability. Studies have shown that people are much more likely to experience a lengthy period of disability during their lifetime than they are to die suddenly without any period of disability. While a will has absolutely no effect until the will maker has died, a revocable living trust is effective as soon as it is executed by the trust maker. That means that the provisions of the trust can go into effect while the trust maker is alive, so he or she can plan for disability and other issues that may arise during life. Matters including who the successor trustees will be, how the trust maker's medical expenses will be paid, and where the maker will live and what standard of living he or she will retain during the disability can be planned and will take effect immediately upon the trust maker's disability without any need for a living probate. The people designated by the trust maker to handle such matters simply follow the directions that are included within the trust and supplemental documents, including durable powers of attorney for health care.

In the absence of proper planning, the trust maker's wishes may remain unknown and decisions affecting the trust maker may be left to chance.

Cost Because property that is held by a revocable living trust avoids probate, the cost of administering the trust estate after the maker's death is much lower than the professional fees for administering that same property in the probate process.

With a revocable trust, there is no need to retain an attorney to steer the estate through probate. The directions to the successor trustees for the administration and distribution of the trust property are in the trust document. Of course, the successor trustees may seek the advice of an estate planning attorney and a knowledgeable accountant as needed, but in most cases the assistance required from professional advisors is minimal.

Further, trust estates avoid such costs as filing fees, newspaper publication costs, and other expenses associated with the required notices, hearings, and other procedures dictated by probate laws.

The fees and costs associated with administering an estate using a revocable living trust are nominal. A trustee's fee is based upon the "going rate" of bank trust departments, and national surveys show that the average total cost of administering a revocable living trust estate is less than 1 percent of the gross value of the estate!

Let's compare the costs of probate administration with those of trust administration for an estate of $200,000. On average, the costs associated with administering the probate estate equal $14,000, of which $6000 (3 percent of the gross estate) is the probate attorney's fee, another $6000 is the executor's fee, and the remaining $2000 (1 percent) covers the filing fee, publication costs, probate bond, appraisals, and other costs—a total of 7 percent of the gross estate. Now let's suppose that the estate plan consists of a revocable living trust. The costs of administering the estate are now about $1000, or ½ percent. Use of the living trust eliminated the probate attorney's fee, probate filing fee, publication costs, and probate bond and significantly reduced the executor's fee.

Similarly, living probate proceedings are avoided with proper trust-centered estate planning in which health care agents are appointed and successor trustees are designated in the trust agreement. Living probate–related costs, including attorney fees, filing fees, costs of publication, and the like, are avoided, resulting in preservation of trust assets for the benefit of the trust maker.

Convenience While the results of administration of a probate estate or a trust estate are the same—taxes are paid and distributions are made to the beneficiaries—the probate process is cumbersome and time-consuming in comparison to the process of administering a trust estate. The trust maker's specific directions within the trust document address the contingencies of disability and death and appoint successor trustees to carry out those directions.

Upon the disability or death of the trust maker, the successor trustees have legal control of the trust assets immediately, without involvement of any court, so the trust maker's lifetime endeavors may be continued without interruption. If the trust maker was engaged in a business enterprise, the ability to continue its operations is generally critical to the health of the business. In addition, the successor trustees carry out the administration of the trust in a timely manner, whether by creating subtrusts for the benefit of the beneficiaries or making immediate distributions.

Confidentiality Trusts are private. While wills and the entire probate process are open to the public, trusts remain confidential. For many, this in itself is a compelling factor in favor of revocable living trusts.

Most of us have been reared to keep our financial matters private. It is unlikely that we would discuss our income or net worth with neighbors at a social gathering. However, if you die with a will controlling your affairs, then all of your sensitive financial matters are at once open to public scrutiny. Your will and the accompanying inventory of your estate, the value of your assets, and your outstanding debts are all filed with the probate court in the county where you resided at death. Anyone, such as an intrusive neighbor or potential suitor for your business, can simply contact the court, forward a small check to cover the expense of photocopying your estate file, and receive copies of all papers filed in your estate.

Since fully funded trusts are not subject to the rules of the probate court, the inventories, notices to beneficiaries, and accountings of all assets and debts of your estate are not filed with the court and hence not open for public scrutiny.

Can you summarize some of the primary advantages of a revocable living trust?

Revocable living trusts:

- Are easy to create and maintain
- Are easily changed
- Create one receptacle for all your property

- Offer privacy
- Take care of you
- Have no adverse lifetime income tax consequences
- Are probate-free
- Offer continuity in your affairs
- Are good in every state
- Distribute property after your death
- Are excellent for planning for death taxes
- Are difficult for disgruntled heirs to attack

Disadvantages of Revocable Living Trusts

All that you've told me about living trust–centered estate planning sounds really attractive. Are there any disadvantages of a revocable living trust?

There can be, but they are few in number, and most of these problems depend upon the state(s) in which you own real property. Even when there are disadvantages, the benefits of a revocable living trust usually *far* outweigh the drawbacks.

Expense One objection to a revocable living trust is that it is more expensive than a will. True enough. Wills have been priced below cost for years by attorneys who build up huge files of wills and then reap the probate fees in years to come. Executors do not have to use the attorney who drafted the will as their attorney, but in fact, most do.

A living trust–centered plan is only *initially* more expensive than a will. The cost of a will and after-death administration through the probate process almost always exceeds, by a large amount, the cost of a funded living trust and its private after-death administration.

Reducing the cost of death administration is only one benefit of avoiding probate, and avoiding probate is only one (small) benefit of a revocable living trust.

Funding Some people find it annoying to have to determine what they own and how they own it and then have to change ownership of their property to a living trust. Yes, this can be annoying, but it has to be done only once. And if people think it is a problem for them while they are alive and well, think of what a problem it will be for their spouses or children if they become disabled or die.

The choice is this: People can either "probate" their own estates themselves or pay the courts and lawyers to do it for them after they are no longer around to answer questions such as, "Where is the deed to the house?"

Most people who have gone through the funding process, one piece of property at a time, report that they feel a great sense of relief and peace of mind, knowing that they finally have their records in order.

Making Gifts As of this writing, one potential living trust trap has to do with the $10,000 annual gift tax exclusion. Every person can give $10,000 a year per recipient. There is no gift tax, and the gift will not be included in the giver's gross estate upon his or her death. However, the IRS insists that an annual exclusion gift made directly from a revocable living trust must be included in the trust maker's estate if the trust maker dies within 3 years of making the gift. The IRS position on this point has been universally criticized, and it is likely that it will soon be changed by the Congress.

Until that time, however, there is a simple way to avoid this problem. A properly drafted revocable living trust and durable power of attorney, along with some simple instructions from a knowledgeable estate planning attorney, will completely avoid this issue.

Tenancy by the Entirety Property If a married couple own property as tenants by the entirety and transfer the property into their revocable living trusts, the property is no longer tenancy-by-the-entirety property. However, for most people, the benefits of tenancy by the entirety are not that substantial.

Tenancy by the entirety is available only in some states and only between spouses. Generally, the creditor of one spouse cannot get at the house to satisfy the debt; the creditor can get only a lien on the house. But this relief is not permanent. When the property is sold, the proceeds of the property may no longer be protected. Also, if a couple's home has a large mortgage, the mortgage is probably the one debt they are really concerned about, but tenancy by the entirety will not protect their home from its own mortgage when both spouses are liable on the mortgage. If the home is close to being paid for, it is likely the couple do not have pressing bankruptcy concerns. Nonetheless, for some couples, under certain circumstances, tenancy-by-the-entirety protection might have enough psychological benefits to warrant keeping the property outside of their living trusts until the first spouse passes away or until circumstances change.

There are at least two court cases, one in Hawaii and one in Missouri, that held that tenancy-by-the-entirety property, when transferred into a revocable living trust, retains its status as tenancy by the entirety for purposes of creditor protection. Make sure that you discuss with your estate planning attorney the status of the law in your state regarding this issue.

Homestead In some states, homeowners may not be entitled to protections afforded by a declaration of homestead if they place their homes in revocable living trusts. Even in these states, however, there are often ways to title a home so that the benefits of placing the home in a living trust and the declaration of homestead can both be obtained. To what extent a declaration of homestead can protect a home, under what circumstances, and for how long are a matter of state law. Generally, like tenancy by the entirety, it is not permanent protection. And, like tenancy by the entirety, it does not protect the home from claims by the mortgage holder.

Miscellaneous Issues Retirement plans and certain professional practices or franchises may require some special handling for living trusts. In some states, real estate transfer taxes may be triggered upon transfer of real property to a trust (this is very rare); the title insurance company may have some particular requirements; or real estate tax breaks available for owner-occupied residences or the elderly or disabled may not be available when real estate is placed in a trust.

If debt-incumbered property is to be held in a living trust, written assurance should be obtained from the lender that the transfer will not trigger a "due-on-sale clause" (by federal statute this cannot happen in regard to a personal-residence mortgage).

This may seem like a long list, but these issues, when they do occur, are minor and rarely outweigh the substantial benefits of a funded revocable living trust. And more and more state legislatures are sweeping away the few remaining and outmoded quirks of state law regarding living trusts.

Your estate planning attorney should guide you through any issues regarding funding your revocable living trust in your state with your particular assets.

Wills versus Trusts: Which Is Better?

Isn't a will just as good as a trust?

That depends on what contingencies are important enough to you that you wish to plan for their occurrence. How sure are you that you will die suddenly without any intervening period of incapacity? Are all of your intended beneficiaries of legal age and sound mind? Are they solvent, free of other disabilities, capable of handling the assets you wish to transfer to them, in sound marriages, likely to use the assets the way you intend that they be used? Are any of your assets of a nature that makes privacy desirable? Do you care about the potential expense and delay involved in the probate process? These points are just the tip of the iceberg.

Here are six good reasons why a living trust is a better planning tool than a will:

1. A revocable living trust is a private document that can include provisions for your own incapacity, avoiding the need for guardianship proceedings and protecting the privacy of your personal holdings and family relationships.
2. Upon death, assets owned by a living trust are not subject to probate; hence if the trust is fully funded, there is no need for court involvement.
3. Beneficiaries who may be under a legal disability or otherwise incapacitated need not have guardianship proceedings instituted on their own behalf to enjoy the benefit of what you choose to leave to them through a revocable living trust.
4. Individuals who may be legally competent but incapable of handling money can be afforded the protections a trustee can provide in private.
5. The possibility that unintended persons could benefit from your estate can be reduced or eliminated.
6. Benefits can be provided to more than one generation of beneficiaries, privately, and to a whole host of their beneficiaries.

Of course, a trust can be created in a will that will provide many of the same protections as the living trust. However, you still sacrifice disability planning for yourself and any modicum of privacy for yourself and your loved ones, not to mention that you would still have the requirement of probate proceedings. So you decide: Which is better?

Why is having a will and durable powers of attorney not just as effective as having a living trust?

A will is a form of death planning, and durable powers of attorney are a form of disability planning. But a living trust is a form of *life* planning.

A will is used to transfer assets upon death. It takes effect only upon the death of its creator. A durable power of attorney is used to manage the property of a disabled person. A durable power of attorney for health care is used to manage the health and medical care of a disabled person. Both powers cease upon the death of their maker. Thus, a will and durable powers of attorney are limited in duration. While the duration of a living trust cannot be forever, the trust is designed so that the desires, hopes, dreams, and aspirations of its creator can be implemented during life and will survive his or her death.

Although a will and durable powers of attorney are integral parts of a comprehensive estate plan, on their own they are limited in scope. Your control under these forms of estate planning is restricted to stating who will receive your assets and who will act as your agent. A living trust allows you to fill in the "hows, whens, and whys." It can contain any instructions as long as they are not against the law or against public policy. Having a living trust puts you in control during life, disability, and death.

If state law provides for expedited probate procedures with minimal cost, why should I consider a living trust?

Even though a state's probate administration process may be expedited, every probate is a court-administered proceeding that takes some amount of time and entails the possibility of delays. Every probate, no matter how inexpensive, has the possibility of unexpected costs and the disadvantages of loss of control and loss of privacy. In addition, the process eases the way for will contests.

A properly drafted living trust contains comprehensive estate administration procedures that enable successor trustees to have immediate access to the trust maker's assets for the benefit of loved ones. There are usually no unexpected costs, control and privacy are maintained, and it is very difficult to contest a funded trust.

The existence of expedited probate procedures is only one criterion in determining the appropriate estate plan.

My relationship with my ex-husband and my children from my first marriage is not good. I want to leave the bulk of my estate to my current husband, but I am worried that my children and ex-husband will contest my wishes. Will a living trust give me more protection from a contest of this type than a will?

Yes, a living trust is more difficult to contest than a will for several reasons. A will can be attacked as soon as it is filed with the probate court. A fully funded living trust, on the other hand, does not go through probate.

A common way that a will is attacked is by claiming that the maker of the will lacked the intellectual capacity to create the will or that the maker of the will was unduly influenced or succumbed to duress in making the will.

If you create a living trust and serve as trustee, it is difficult for anyone to claim that you were incompetent or under undue influence or duress when you created the trust. The fact that you not only created the trust but also administered and managed your affairs according to its terms on a continual basis from the time you created it until the date of your death is proof that you knew what you were doing and were of sound mind.

Creating a Revocable Living Trust

How long does it take to set up a living trust?

It should take approximately 2 to 3 weeks to establish a trust-based estate plan. It may take a bit longer to get all the documents necessary to fully fund that plan, but the plan itself and most of the funding can be done in this short time. In an emergency, of course, a plan can be drawn up even more quickly.

When does my living trust become effective?

Typically, there is a rather informal "signing ceremony." At that time, you sign all of the various documents that go into a well-designed estate plan. All of these documents are immediately effective when signed. There is no required waiting period.

It is important to keep in mind, however, that your living trust can take care of only the things that you put into it. It may take a little while to transfer some of the property you own into your living trust, but as soon as the ownership of an item is transferred, the trust owns it immediately.

Do I have to record my trust at the courthouse?

The answer to this question depends on the law of your state of residence. Jurisdictions vary widely with regard to their recording requirements. Some states require that the trust be recorded, others require merely the recordation of a memorandum of trust, while still others require only the name of a trustee. For example, Idaho requires that all trusts be recorded, and Florida requires that a memorandum of trust be filed when the maker dies.

Some states require that you record a memorandum of trust or an affidavit of trust when you convey real property to your trust. Such an affidavit or memorandum sets forth certain facts about your trust. For example, you would state the name of the trust, who the current and future trustees are, and some of the powers of the trustees with respect to assets owned by the trust. Ordinarily, you would not disclose the beneficiaries of the trust, the portion of the trust property which has been designated for each of the various beneficiaries, or the provisions for distributing the trust property.

How do I keep my trust confidential if my state requires that it be recorded?

In certain jurisdictions where the recording authorities require that the trust document be recorded, an additional document called a *nominee partnership* can be used to keep your trust confidential. It acts as an agent for your trust, thereby keeping your trust confidential as an undisclosed principal.

If the trust papers are not filed in the courthouse or other places of public record, how are they recognized as legal documents?

Your trust is much like a contract and is governed by contract law. Since it is not a will, it is not governed by laws pertaining to wills.

When you sign your name to any contract, whether it is for the purchase of a car, an item of personal property, or similar goods, the document is generally not filed in a public forum. Without question, such contracts, once signed, are legal documents and are generally binding upon the parties who have signed them. Likewise, when you sign your trust, it becomes a binding legal document without the necessity of its being filed or made of record.

If I am trustee of my revocable trust, do I have to have a separate taxpayer identification number and file a separate tax return for the trust?

No. The Internal Revenue Code classifies a revocable living trust as a "grantor trust." Thus the IRS allows you to use your own Social Security number as the trust's identification number as long as you or your spouse is a trustee of your trust. If you are married and have a joint living trust, you can use either spouse's Social Security number or you can use one person's Social Security number for some assets and the other person's for other assets.

The name of your trust will be on a 1099 form showing interest or other income items, and you will report all of your income on your federal income tax return (Form 1040) exactly as you did before you set up your trust. This is because the IRS still considers your revocable trust assets to be your assets.

After your death—or if you have a joint trust, after the death of one spouse—if the living trust continues, it must get a separate taxpayer identification number and file a trust income tax return (Form 1041).

Can my living trust provide me with any income tax advantages?

No, there are no income tax advantages afforded by a grantor trust.

If I set up a living trust, how will it affect my day-to-day affairs?

The key phrase to remember is "It's business as usual." The only noticeable difference you'll see in your day-to-day affairs is that your bank statements, statements from investment companies, and other such records (except credit card accounts) will be in the name of your trust as opposed to your individual name. The wording of a properly designed living trust allows you, as the trustee, to continue doing anything that you want to do.

Can I change my trust provisions later on?

Because your trust is revocable, it is a very flexible estate planning device. You may revoke, change, or amend your trust document at any time you wish during your lifetime without penalty.

How do I know my estate plan is valid if there are subsequent changes in the law or changes in my personal circumstances?

It is important for you to recognize that an estate plan is constantly changing. As circumstances in your life change, it may be necessary to amend your plan to reflect those changes. You should review your estate plan at least annually to determine whether you need to amend it. If an amendment is necessary, you should contact your attorney for an appropriate modification of the plan.

Your estate planning attorney should notify you of any change in the law that impacts your estate plan and should explain how your plan is affected. The combination of review by you and by your estate planning attorney will ensure that the plan is effective regardless of how long it may be in force.

I've heard that everyone should have a will. Doesn't my living trust replace a will?

Yes. A properly drafted and fully funded trust-based estate plan replaces a will.

As a practical matter, a special will called a *pour-over will* should be a part of your revocable living trust plan. While it may not be needed if your trust is fully funded and you do not have minor children, it is an important fail-safe device should you fail to put all your assets into your living trust. A pour-over will "pours" any assets that are not in your trust at death into the living trust so that they can be controlled by the provisions of the trust.

Whatever property is subject to this pour-over will might well have to be probated. Whether it will or not depends on the type of property and its value. The vastly superior alternative to using the pour-over will and probate is to make sure that all of your assets are placed into your living trust. If that is done, the pour-over will simply "sleeps" inside the trust plan and is never awakened for use.

Planning for a Spouse

If I wish to leave assets to my spouse, is there a preferred way to do so?

One of the best ways to leave assets to a spouse is through a revocable living trust. Following are some of the advantages of using revocable living trust planning:

- Probate can be avoided on the deaths of both spouses.
- A living probate can be avoided if the surviving spouse is unable to manage his or her financial affairs after the first spouse dies.
- Federal estate tax may be eliminated on the first spouse's death and either eliminated or substantially reduced on the death of the surviving spouse, depending on the size of the estate.
- A cotrustee can be named to serve with the surviving spouse and provide him or her with asset and financial management assistance.
- By leaving assets in trust, you may provide your spouse with creditor protection if the spouse is sued.
- The assets left in trust can be protected from a later, unsuccessful second marriage of your spouse. Additionally, your surviving spouse may be able to more comfortably refuse to give away assets or to loan money to other family members or friends by stating that the assets were left in trust and cannot be used for those purposes.

How much property can I leave to my spouse without incurring federal estate taxes?

You can leave an unlimited amount to your spouse without paying any federal estate taxes. Every dollar you leave to your spouse qualifies for the marital deduction, which offsets, dollar for dollar, the assets included in your gross estate. Since your gross estate minus your allowable deductions is your taxable estate—the amount on which taxes are paid—the marital deduction can effectively reduce your taxable estate to zero.

Generally the tax law allows use of the marital deduction to cancel the estate taxes on the first spouse's death, but there is a catch: Those assets which qualify for the marital deduction in the first spouse's estate will be taxable in the estate of the surviving spouse, without the benefit of a marital deduction (unless the surviving spouse has remarried).

If your will leaves all of your property to your spouse, your estate will not pay any estate taxes if your spouse survives you; but upon your spouse's death, the entire value of your property plus your spouse's property will be subject to estate taxes.

TAX PLANNING

How can my spouse and I save on federal estate taxes by establishing a living trust?

A married couple can create a joint living trust, or each spouse can create a separate living trust. Regardless of whether one or two trusts are used, each trust provides that two subtrusts will spring to life upon the first spouse's death. These subtrusts are designed to keep the property free from estate tax.

There are a number of ways this can be done. In the most basic, on the first spouse's death, the first $600,000 worth of assets passes to a *family trust* and the balance to a *marital trust.* The family trust is free of estate tax because of the exemption equivalent; the marital trust is free of tax because of the unlimited marital deduction.

On the death of the surviving spouse, the family trust ($600,000 + its appreciation) will pass free of federal estate tax to the beneficiaries. In the marital trust, the surviving spouse's exemption equivalent amount will shelter the first $600,000, and the balance will be taxed, unless the spouse leaves it to charity.

The end result? A tax savings of $235,000 on an estate of $1.2 million.

How is the $235,000 of tax savings generated?

With subtrust planning, both spouses use their exemption equivalent amounts. If they relied solely on the marital deduction, they would waste one of those exemptions—at a cost of $235,000.

If we set up an estate plan that establishes marital and family trusts when my spouse dies, how can I be sure I will be able to have access to what I need? Won't I lose control of the property in the family trust?

You can be beneficiary of both trusts and can be a cotrustee for your own benefit. Your access to assets in the marital trust can be as liberal or restricted as the trust maker's instructions provide. In regard to the family trust, sound estate tax and trust planning will allow you to have rights to income and principal on the basis of your needs, such as health, education, support, and maintenance.

What are the maximum rights my spouse can have in my family trust?

The maximum rights a spouse can be given in a family trust without having the value of the trust included (and thus taxed) in the survivor's estate are:

- All of the income
- The greater of 5 percent or $5000 of the trust's principal each year
- Any or all of the principal in the trustee's discretion for health, education, maintenance, or support of the surviving spouse
- A limited testamentary power to appoint the property, as the surviving spouse chooses, among your children or other descendants

If you were to grant your spouse greater rights than these in the family trust, your spouse would be deemed to control the assets and, at his or her death, the full value of the trust property would be included in his or her estate for tax purposes—the very outcome you sought to avoid by using the family trust.

What are the minimum rights I can give my spouse in my family trust?

If your spouse either consents to give up his or her rights or receives property of yours at your death that suffices to comply with your state's rules, your family trust does not have to provide for your spouse.

Can I protect my family trust from my spouse's remarriage?

The terms of the trust can provide that on your spouse's remarriage he or she is removed as a beneficiary of the family trust and that on a subsequent divorce or on the death of the new spouse your spouse can again be taken care of by its terms. The appropriate language would be something like the following:

1. Distribute the income and principal to my surviving spouse and children, depending on who needs it.
2. If my surviving spouse dies or remarries, stop any distributions to my surviving spouse and distribute the income and principal among my children.
3. If my spouse becomes single again, go back to my instructions in number 1 above.

If the family trust is worth more than $600,000 on the surviving spouse's death, will it be subject to estate tax?

It will be estate tax–free. Once the $600,000 exemption equivalent is placed in a family trust, estate tax is avoided not only on the assets transferred but also on any growth or accumulation of income in the trust. If, through savvy investing, the trustee triples the value of the trust principal, the entire amount will pass free of estate tax to the remainder beneficiaries at the death of the surviving spouse.

Will there be an income tax on the family trust's income?

Yes, the income earned on the assets in the family trust will generate an income tax which must be paid by the trust if the income is retained in the trust. If the income is distributed to the surviving spouse or to the children, they must report and pay income tax on the trust income at their brackets.

Will the assets in the family trust receive a stepped-up basis upon the death of the surviving spouse?

The assets distributed from the family trust do not receive a stepped-up basis at the death of the surviving spouse. These assets already received a step-up in basis when the first spouse died.

Since the assets in the family trust do not receive a stepped-up basis upon the death of the surviving spouse, would we be better off forgoing the use of the family trust altogether?

You would not be better off. The federal estate tax rates range from 37 to 55 percent (60 percent on estates between $10 million and $21,040,000). The federal income tax rates on capital gains are considerably less at 28 percent and apply only to the excess of the money received for the asset over its tax basis. Even considering state income tax on capital gains, you will always be better off passing property by using your $600,000 exemption than you would be if you retained the property in the survivor's estate so as to obtain a step-up in basis at the time of the second death.

What if the value of our assets is greater than $1.2 million? Where do we put the excess?

Many people create a subtrust called a *qualified terminable interest property (QTIP) trust.* The surviving spouse has a lifetime interest in the income, and sometimes the principal, of the QTIP trust property. On his or her death, the QTIP trust assets will be distributed according to the directions set forth by the trust maker. QTIP planning allows you to provide for your spouse, qualify for the unlimited marital deduction, and control the proceeds after the death of your spouse. QTIP trusts are discussed in detail in Chapter 3.

Am I required by the laws of my state to leave a portion of my assets to my spouse?

The inheritance and succession statutes of most states contain a provision designed to prevent a spouse from being disinherited. Such statutory provisions, often called *elective-share statutes,* entitle a surviving spouse to a minimum distribution from the estate of a deceased spouse and can be used to override the terms of a trust or will. If you do not take this into consideration when designing an estate plan, the enforcement by your spouse of his or her elective share can significantly disrupt the settlement of your estate.

How can I limit the statutory rights of my spouse-to-be prior to our marriage?

You can insist on a prenuptial agreement. Make it fair; be sure that full disclosure takes place; and make sure that your spouse-to-be is separately represented by counsel. If correctly drawn, this agreement can override state statutes regarding spousal inheritance rights.

NONCITIZEN SPOUSES

Do I or my spouse qualify for the unlimited marital deduction if my spouse is not a U.S. citizen?

Federal estate tax law requires that a spouse be a U.S. citizen in order to qualify for the unlimited marital deduction. There is a valid reason for this: Congress does not want a surviving noncitizen spouse to leave the United States with property that has never been taxed. The citizen spouse's estate still has the $600,000 exemption. Even though the surviving spouse is not a U.S. citizen, there is no federal estate tax on this first $600,000. The estate of the U.S. citizen decedent will have to pay federal estate taxes on everything over $600,000 unless the surviving noncitizen spouse is the beneficiary of a special trust called a *qualified domestic trust* (QDOT).

What is a QDOT?

A qualified domestic trust allows the deceased spouse's estate to postpone paying federal estate tax. The trust must meet certain requirements:

- At least one trustee must be a U.S. citizen or a U.S. domestic corporation.
- The trust instrument must provide that no distribution (other than a distribution of income) may be made from the trust unless the U.S. trustee has the right to withhold from the distribution the estate tax imposed on the distribution.
- The trust must meet the requirements of the Treasury secretary as set out in the Treasury regulations to ensure the collection of the estate tax on distributions of principal.

In addition, the decedent's personal representative of the will, or the trustee of the decedent's revocable trust if there is no personal representative, must make an election on the decedent's estate tax return to have the trust treated as a qualified domestic trust.

Can my noncitizen spouse receive the trust's income?

Your spouse can receive the income, just as a citizen spouse can, and will pay federal income tax on the income he or she receives.

What happens if my spouse becomes a citizen after the date of my QDOT?

Your noncitizen surviving spouse will avoid complications if he or she can become a citizen before the estate tax return is due.

Is it difficult to qualify a QDOT?

It is not difficult to qualify a trust for QDOT treatment. However, a huge black hole appears in the Internal Revenue Code provision which mandates that the trust meet the requirements of any regulations issued by the IRS.

Under Treasury regulations, if the cash value of the trust exceeds $2 million, the trust instrument must require that a U.S. bank serve as a trustee or the U.S. citizen trustee obtain a bond equal to 65 percent of the fair market value of the trust assets. If the assets are less than $2 million, the trust instrument must provide that no more than 35 percent of the fair market value of the assets (determined annually) can be held in real estate outside the United States.

My husband is a permanent resident of the United States, but not a citizen. Can we shelter our estate from taxation by putting everything in his name?

To a limited extent this could be a successful strategy if you die first and your husband then sells all of the property, moves out of the country, and dies owning no property in the United States. However, if your estate is substantial or if you want to maintain some control over your property during your life, this type of planning will not defer or eliminate taxation, but will accelerate it.

Unlike gifts between U.S. citizen spouses, who are entitled to an unlimited marital deduction, there is no marital deduction for gifts from a citizen spouse to a noncitizen spouse (whether a permanent U.S. resident or not). However, the annual gift tax exclusion is available, and in the case of gifts to noncitizen spouses it is increased from the usual amount of $10,000 per year to $100,000 per year. So you can give $100,000 per year to your noncitizen husband with no gift tax consequences.

But if your noncitizen husband is a resident alien at the time of his death, his entire worldwide estate will be subject to U.S. estate tax. All assets over his $600,000 exemption equivalent will be taxed. In order to avoid estate tax on amounts over $600,000, he would have to renounce his residency status before his death (and probably have to move out of the U.S.). Moreover, even if your noncitizen husband is not a U.S. resident on his death, his assets located in the United States will be subject to federal estate tax. Unfortunately, a nonresident alien's exemption equivalent is not $600,000 but only $60,000.

A married couple must plan carefully for estate tax reduction if one of the spouses is not a U.S. citizen. Without proper planning, they may unwittingly accelerate and increase the amount of gift and estate tax that must be paid.

Planning for Children

MINOR CHILDREN

Why is planning for minors important?

Virtually all parents want to pass their estates to their children. Unfortunately, whether assets are passed to minor children through beneficiary designations, as a result of joint tenancy, or under the terms of a simple will or bare-bones trust, the assets are often passed without adequate instructions concerning the use of the funds.

Minors cannot own and use assets. Before a minor will be able to use inherited assets, the court must appoint a guardian or conservator to manage the assets for and in behalf of the child under the direction of the court. This process can be expensive and time-consuming.

It is much more sensible to pass the assets under the terms of a revocable living trust. The parents may include instructions in the trust regarding the use of assets for the benefit of their minor children, and they may empower a trustee to handle the assets in accordance with those instructions. Parents can specify the amounts and times of distributions and may provide that the children receive their funds at different times or at different ages, depending upon the personality and character of each child.

Revocable living trust planning affords parents the opportunity to provide for individual children according to each child's unique needs and in ways that will best fulfill their desires for each child.

When will my children be old enough to properly manage their inheritances?

The legal age of adulthood and—unless otherwise planned and provided for by the parents—the time at which a child is entitled to receive his or her inheritance is the age of 18. Since it is often difficult to know how well a child will manage money at age 18, it may be wise to stretch out an inheritance over a period of years. In a revocable living trust, you can provide a trustee with specific directions regarding how and when distributions should be made to your children.

For example, one-third of the inheritance could be distributed to a child at age 18, one-third at 21, and the remainder at age 24. In this way, if the child mishandles the first distribution, he or she has two more chances to learn to manage the money or property responsibly.

Should I divide my property into separate shares for my minor children?

During the period of time when children are minors, a *common trust* is often a good planning tool to use. A common trust is simply one cache which holds all of the trust property for the benefit of all minor children.

While property is in a common trust, there are no separate shares for each child. Rather, the trustee is directed to use any or all of the property for the benefit of all of the children on the basis of the individual needs of each child. This is very much as parents use their resources, in whatever quantities, equal or unequal, in raising their children.

There is no requirement that the children receive equal amounts of property while it is in the common trust. Consider a family with three children, ages 17, 11, and 6. If the trustee is directed to use the common trust property for the benefit of the three minor children on the basis of their respective needs, the youngest child may very likely end up receiving a greater portion of the trust property over time than the two older children simply because the youngest is at least 12 years from being independent and able to seek gainful employment. The oldest child may choose to attend college, which is expensive; but the younger two will have additional needs before they even reach college, and inflation is likely to ensure that their college costs will be significantly higher than those of the oldest child.

When should the common trust terminate?

Normally a common trust terminates when the youngest child reaches a certain age or completes college. At that time, whatever amount of trust property remains is divided equally (or otherwise) into separate shares for each child. The children may receive the property in a lump sum or in some other way, depending on the provisions in the trust.

Sometimes parents are concerned about a lump-sum distribution to one or more children even though the children are already adults at the time the estate plan is established. It isn't uncommon in these situations for parents to stagger the distributions at ages 30, 35, and 40, for example, or even older. Some simply plan to distribute income (i.e., interest or dividends) quarterly or annually during the child's life to ensure that the child always has access to money, but in small-enough portions that poor decision making won't wipe out the full inheritance. Parents who have such concerns need to know that they can achieve their goal of providing support to their children without worrying that the children will accidently or purposefully undermine that goal.

What is the best possible way to protect my estate for my children and still provide for my spouse while deferring federal estate tax?

The best approach is to create a qualified terminable interest property (QTIP) trust in your living trust document. After you are deceased, all or part of your assets passes to the QTIP trust. Your spouse is the only beneficiary of the QTIP trust, and the trust continues for your spouse's lifetime. Upon your spouse's death, the remaining trust assets pass to your children according to the terms of your trust. QTIP trusts are discussed in detail in Chapter 3.

My wife and I travel together a lot and have minor children. What can we do to ensure that they will be taken care of if we both die?

If a catastrophe befalls you and your wife, you want your children cared for, to the extent possible, in the manner in which you would have cared for them. You can achieve this by naming guardians in your pour-over will and by establishing a trust to manage your estate for your children.

It is crucial that you give substantial thought to the selection of guardians and successor guardians who share your values and are willing to love your children and assume the role of raising them. It is equally important that you select trustees to manage your estate for their benefit and that you provide instructions for the financial care of that estate.

If you both die, the court will consider the persons you named as guardians of your children. You should nominate one or more backup guardians to serve in the event the individuals you named are not appointed, since the court will proceed through your list of nominees before considering other parties.

Whom should we name as personal guardians of our children?

A trustee is not a personal guardian but a guardian of the financial estate. Therefore, if you have minor children, it is critical that you name a personal guardian to raise them if both of you become unable to provide parenting. (A natural parent will always have preference with the court unless parental rights have been terminated.) Whom to designate as the guardian of your children is your most important decision. In making this decision, you should not only evaluate the parenting skills of the individual but also consider the impact that the guardianship role will have on the individual's family and lifestyle.

Typically, parents designate family members or close friends to serve as guardians of their children. These individuals usually have similar philosophies and values in raising their own children. Sometimes, people designate their own parents as guardians. However, age is an important factor, since a guardian's death or inability to continue as guardian would precipitate another transition.

You should financially assist the guardian in the raising of your children. For example, your trust instructions could allow the trustee to provide the guardian with a monthly stipend and financial assistance for extraordinary purchases such as a larger automobile or home additions for the larger family. The trustee's discretion as to the appropriate amount of support is important.

To be effective as a guardian, the person you are considering must be able and willing to take on the responsibility. You should discuss the matter thoroughly with him or her to make sure both of you are comfortable with the appointment. After you have made your decision, open and frequent discussions are essential to maintain understanding and better prepare the person for his or her role.

It is important to regularly reevaluate your guardian appointment as facts, circumstances, and family situations change. If you feel that you should designate a new guardian, do so—and be sure that your planning documents reflect the most current appointment.

Should the guardians for our minor children be persons other than our trustees?

Parents should seriously consider naming different persons to serve either as guardians or trustees.

For one thing, each role requires different expertise. Guardians should have the human skills and qualities best suited for raising children, while trustees should have the abilities and qualities best suited for managing finances. Even if you know people who combine the "best of both worlds," it would be difficult for them to shoulder the responsibilities of both positions at the same time. Your guardians will be overwhelmed enough with the sudden, added burden of raising orphans and integrating them into their own family without the additional responsibility of investing, making distribution decisions, and filing technically demanding tax forms for the trust.

Another theoretical problem is that guardians will inevitably be incidentally benefited by distributions to or on behalf of your children. For example, to house your children, your guardians may need to use trust funds to add an addition to their house. If your guardians are the kind of people you want—good, honest, kind people—they might agonize over decisions which would benefit them personally but which also seem to be in your children's best interests. A separate trustee will be able to make such distributions without this kind of agony and relieve your guardians from this pain.

In addition, you may want to benefit the guardians, more than incidentally, for the great favor they will do for you in raising your children. Or you may want to make sure that your guardians' children can enjoy the same standard of living as your children so that there is no resentment between your children and their children.

Your guardians could have a terrible time with these built-in conflicts of interest. A separate trustee will be able to follow your instructions in a balanced way, much as you intended when you created your trust.

Why should I appoint the guardian for my minor children in my will and not in my trust?

Using a trust instead of a will to appoint a guardian does not provide any greater control over the appointment.

There is, however, an advantage to using a will to appoint a guardian for minors. Most states require that any document relevant to such an appointment be filed in the courts for judicial review and approval. If you use your trust document to appoint the guardian, you will have to file the trust with the court, thereby destroying the advantage of privacy generally afforded by a trust. Therefore, it is always preferable that the appointment of a guardian for minors be made in the pour-over will, which is, by nature, a public document that must be filed.

Is the court obligated to follow our appointment of guardian in our wills in the event we die while our children are minors?

Generally, the court will defer to your nomination unless the person designated is determined to be unfit (e.g., because of a drug or alcohol problem). The court may also designate someone other than the person nominated in your wills if there has been a significant change in his or her circumstances (e.g., divorce or a move to another state) since the nomination was made. The court may also give some weight to the wishes of your children, especially if they are old enough to participate in the proceedings.

How can we prevent a certain relative from trying to get custody of our children (and their money) in the event of our premature deaths?

You can specify in your pour-over will that the individual be ineligible to serve as guardian.

SPECIAL CHILDREN

What is the most effective means of planning for special children?

It is probably safe to say that no parent would give a child with special needs and problems a large lump sum of cash without supervision, and yet this often happens after parents' deaths.

If parents make provisions for a special child by leaving an insurance policy payable to that child, they are in effect giving a lump sum to the child: the money is available but without protection, instructions, and guidelines for its appropriate use. Leaving lump sums without proper planning exposes these monies to the processes of the probate court and to the court-appointed guardians, conservators, and lawyers. All too often, the sums left for the care of the special child are diluted by falling into the hands of creditors, fast-talking scam artists, or distant relatives who take advantage.

A better solution would be to leave the property in a *special-needs trust* for the child. If the child is never able to adequately manage the money or the property, he or she will have the benefit of a trustee who will supervise the financial affairs of the child according to the parents' written instructions.

The same kind of instruction and safeguard can be achieved with trust planning for children who are not disadvantaged but who are simply unable to manage their financial affairs. In these circumstances, trust planning can also provide for instructions that will adequately govern the assets so as to provide proper financial management.

What is the primary consideration in creating a trust for my special child?

The primary planning consideration in the creation of a special-needs trust is to ensure that the trustee's powers will not cause the child to be ineligible to receive the federal and state benefits to which the child is entitled. Consequently, the trust should be designed to supplement, not supplant, federal and state benefits.

To that end, the special-needs trust must be discretionary, permitting the trustee to give or withhold funds depending on the condition of the disadvantaged child and the benefits available to that child. For instance, if the child would be denied government aid if he or she received income or assets, the trustee would withhold the funds. The discretionary powers of the trustee should specifically grant the trustee the power to accumulate surplus income and should contain clear and absolute spendthrift provisions that prohibit assignment of any principal or income distributions from the trust.

I have a severely handicapped adult daughter who has lived with me all of her life. What questions should I raise in planning for her?

The planning process always begins with an assessment of the current situation as well as an assessment of what is needed and desired in the future. You should ask yourself the following questions:

- Does she need medical assistance?
- What continuing medication or equipment will she need?
- Is she covered by medical insurance?
- Is she receiving government benefits?
- If so, to what extent do the benefits fall short of meeting her current and future needs?
- What in-home care does she require?
- Is her disability stabilized, or will it get worse?
- What are her total anticipated future needs?
- What will providing for those needs cost?
- Whom do I want to provide for her care in my absence?
- What instructions would I like to give them?
- Are there other family members who can be involved in future caregiving or decision making?

Once you have answered these questions, you and your attorney can prepare your trust with specific instructions for her care.

How should our trust for our disadvantaged child be drafted?

The special-needs trust, often referred to as a *supplemental trust,* should address a host of major considerations. A supplemental trust should specify:

- Your intention that the assets of the trust be used to supplement any government benefits the child may be entitled to

- Your provision that all expenditures of both principal and income of the trust are within the sole discretion of the trustee
- Nonmandatory distributions of income and principal
- A spendthrift clause that insulates the trust from the claims of the child's creditors
- Protective language against the claims of public and private agencies
- Individual trustees who know the purpose of the trust and the needs of the child
- A corporate cotrustee that has experience in administering such a trust
- Remainder beneficiaries, such as siblings, who will share the assets of the trust after the death of the child

How do we allocate our estate to protect our disadvantaged son?

Parents of disadvantaged children often have economic needs that exceed the size of their estates. A couple may wish to divide their estate equally among their advantaged children while leaving that same estate in trust for their disadvantaged child.

Life insurance is often the answer. An insurance policy on the breadwinner or a last-to-die policy on both of you can be earmarked for your disadvantaged son's trust. In this way, your estate can be divided among your advantaged children, and the life insurance can create an independent and liquid estate for the specific needs of your son.

ADULT CHILDREN

Do I have to distribute my assets equally to my children?

Parents often struggle with the decision as to whether or not to distribute their assets equally to their children. Despite what some people may believe, children are not all equal and usually they should not be treated as equals. Facts and circumstances surrounding a particular child will determine how you will distribute assets, if any, to that child or his or her beneficiaries. This can be particularly troublesome if there is a family business and some family members are active in the business while others are inactive.

You should distribute your assets to whom you want, when you want, and in the amounts that are appropriate considering all surrounding issues. You might consider what may be *equitable* for your beneficiaries rather than constraining yourself by arbitrary notions of equality: equitable may end up being equal, but equal is not always equitable.

Your decision on how to distribute your children's shares to them upon your death should take into consideration such factors as each child's age, health, ability to make financial decisions, family circumstances, and situation with creditors. Basically, you should look at what each child truly needs or may need and plan in the most loving and realistic way you can for that child.

Should I leave my property to my adult children outright and free of any trust?

Although your natural inclination may be to give your adult children their inheritances outright, that may not be the best or wisest course of action for them. A well-thought-out series of subtrusts in your living trust can provide for the specific needs of your children. Leaving property to your children in trust can often protect them from their own inexperience with money, from their inability to make wise decisions, or from their creditors. Young adults, and more mature adults, who do not have experience with large sums of money are often overwhelmed when they receive an inheritance. They may make some poor choices and come to realize, too late, that their inheritance has gone to poor investments and frivolous spending.

Perhaps an adult child is easily influenced by friends and family and can't say "no" when asked for a handout. Perhaps he or she has a drug or alcohol problem and a large "windfall" will only increase his or her ability to satisfy the dependency. Or perhaps, at the time of your death, one of your children may have the misfortune of being in the middle of a nasty divorce or a lawsuit.

By using trusts, you can plan for all of these situations very specifically if they currently exist, or you can plan in anticipation of the possibility of those problems and provide some protection for your children if it is later needed.

How do most people leave instructions for their adult children?

They leave each child's share in a subtrust within their living trust document.

Won't we be unreasonably dominating our children from the grave if we leave our property in trust for them?

You have hopes, dreams, and aspirations for your children while you are living; why should they change when you are dead?

Distributions from the trust should be based upon each child's individual ability to manage and conserve money and the dynamics of each child's marriage situation. However, many parents do not like to restrict one child's access to assets while giving the other children full access. Frequently, the practical solution they arrive at is to determine the strategy for the least responsible child and then apply it uniformly to all their children.

What options do I have regarding the distribution of assets?

Once you've decided on the terms for dividing the inheritance into each child's own share or trust, you have the following additional options to consider:

- Whether or not the trust income will be periodically distributed, and if so, when
- When the trust principal (trust assets) will be distributed
- The degree of permitted discretionary distributions by the trustee (Keep in mind that estates and trusts have their own income tax rates.)

What income taxes do trusts pay on the income they retain?

Table 2-1 should make trust taxation very clear.

When a trust distributes net income, the trust receives an income tax deduction. This means that the trust or estate does not pay tax on net income it distributes; the tax is paid by the beneficiary recipient.

Should a trustee accumulate income or distribute it?

If the income accumulated by the trust is insignificant, it may be beneficial to let the net income accrue and be distributed along with the principal of the trust. If there is significant net income generated by the trust, it is generally beneficial to pay the net income to the child since the child is most likely in a lower tax bracket and thus will be taxed on the income at a lower rate than the trust would be.

Distribution of net income helps the child learn how to manage

TABLE 2-1 Income Tax Rates for Trusts (tax years beginning in 1996)

If taxable income is:			
Over:	But not over:	The tax is:	Of the amount over:
$ 0	$1600	15.0%	$ 0
1600	3800	$240 + 28.0%	1600
3800	5800	$856 + 31.0%	3800
5800	7900	$1476 + 36.0%	5800
7900	—	$2232 + 39.6%	7900

money and makes the child less dependent on receiving principal distributions. Once you make the decision to pay income to the children, the next decision is how often it should be paid.

How frequently should income distributions be made?

While once-a-year payments might encourage the child to learn to budget, such an approach may be somewhat extreme. Ideally, monthly income is preferable; however, most stock dividends are paid quarterly. It is administratively difficult to receive income, determine the prorated expenses, and process the checks every month. Arguably there might be a breach of fiduciary duty if the trustee was slow in making monthly distributions. It might be more feasible to provide for distributions at least quarterly; this would still provide an opportunity for the child to learn budgeting.

Should we give our trustee the authority to make discretionary distributions of trust principal?

The pressure of periodic distributions of principal is somewhat alleviated if the trustee has the authority to make interim distributions for legitimate reasons.

Frequently, the trustee is given the authority to make distributions for the health, education, maintenance, and support of the child. These are known as the "ascertainable standards" in the Internal Revenue Code. Collectively they provide for a beneficiary's all-encompassing needs. Thus, the trustee, in his or her discretion, could pay for a child's major medical needs. Similarly, the trust could provide the trustee with a standard for discretionary distributions. For example, some parents prefer a conservative standard which requires the existence of a genuine need, while others prefer a more liberal standard which allows financial assistance for such matters as the purchase of a residence, a business, or any other extraordinary opportunity.

Do discretionary distribution plans provide built-in creditor protection?

Yes. Because the distributions are in the trustee's sole discretion, payments do not have to be made when a beneficiary's creditors are making demands or lurking nearby. The trustee can retain the funds in the safety and protection of the trust.

Are there many strategies for multiple distributions?

There are as many strategies as there are inventive parents and grandparents. In general, however, if a child has not reached middle-age maturity or does not have a track record to demonstrate financial responsibility, it might be appropriate to use a minimum two-stage distribution, 5 years apart, with quarterly payments of net income throughout the period of the trust. In this way, the child can learn from mistakes he or she makes from the first distribution and hopefully be more responsible with subsequent distributions of principal.

For the same reason, staggered distributions are also appropriate if the trust assets are significant. Distributions typically begin when the child reaches a certain age (usually at age 30 or 35) or on the death of the surviving parent and continue at specified intervals over a predetermined period of years. For example:

> Distribute 25 percent of our daughter's share to her on the death of the survivor of us, and distribute the balance in three additional distributions at 5-year intervals from that date.

Can we leave our property equally to our children, but structure the terms and conditions of each of their trusts differently?

This is a common and effective planning strategy. You can provide detailed instructions in each child's trust which specifically meet your hopes, concerns, dreams, values, and aspirations for that child and which specifically address your assessment of that child's strengths and weaknesses.

Is there a general approach that most people use in planning for responsible adult children?

Usually the children are named as their own trustees in a cotrusteeship with others whom they can hire and fire at will (this "creditor-proofs" the trust estate). In this way, adult children can receive what they want from their trusts whenever they wish it.

Can we provide for our children's retirement years through trust planning?

Parents can sometimes reasonably predict that their children will frivolously waste the distributions. A strategy you can use in this situation is to provide net income to the children, and give authority to the trustee to make discretionary distributions of principal with the final distribution at age 55 or later. In other words, the assets are used to ensure the children's retirement.

What if my daughter is a spendthrift?

You could also use the above strategy for a child who "spends money like water." Your daughter's siblings and/or another trustee would be authorized to make net income and discretionary distributions, with a final distribution to her at age 55 or to the grandchildren. The trust could include a provision stipulating that your daughter must be a productive member of society rather than merely rely upon the proceeds of the trust. In this situation, it may be preferable to have more than one sibling as trustee to "take the heat off" any one sibling trustee.

How do we plan for our financially incompetent son?

Because such an adult child is likely to squander or lose money immediately, an outright distribution is out of the question. However, most parents love their children regardless of the shortcomings they may have, and most parents want to help their children with their resources rather than simply disinherit them.

A *lifetime trust* can provide that your son will be taken care of from his share of your estate for his lifetime under definite instructions that take into account the difficulties he is having during life.

An *incentive trust* could provide that your child must alter his behavior in order to receive distributions from the trust.

My son has had drug problems. What can I do to keep him clear of his dependency after I am gone?

A living trust is an extremely flexible document in which you can do anything you want as long as it is not illegal or against public policy. The important thing is to anticipate what might happen to your son and to plan for such an eventuality.

If you want to provide for him upon your death, but are concerned about the possibility of drug or alcohol abuse, you need only to leave appropriate instructions in your trust document. For example:

> Under normal circumstances I would like my child to have all of the income and whatever principal is necessary to provide that child with his or her every need, as long as it is reasonable.
>
> However, if my trustee knows or has reason to suspect that my child is dependent upon or has a problem with drugs and/or alcohol, then my trustee, in my trustee's sole and absolute discretion, may withhold both income and principal distributions until my child is evaluated for drug and alcohol abuse.
>
> If it is determined that my child has a drug or alcohol abuse problem, my trustee shall offer my child the opportunity to enter a treatment program to be paid for from the assets of my child's trust.
>
> If my child refuses to seek treatment which, in the reasonable discretion of my trustee is warranted and proper, my trustee may withhold payments of both income and principal from my child's trust until my child proves to the satisfaction of my trustee that my child no longer has a substance abuse problem.

Can I provide for the costs of food, shelter, and medical care without giving the funds directly to my addicted daughter?

In order to ensure that the payments are used for the benefit of your daughter, as opposed to her using the trust disbursements to further her habit, the trustee could make all mortgage or rental payments directly to the mortgage company or landlord. Similar arrangements could be made for medical expenses, food, clothing, and expenditures for other basic necessities.

Is there an alternative to disinheriting my addicted child?

An alternative is to provide distributions to the child as incentives for the child to overcome his or her drug or alcohol dependency. Incentive provisions, including provisions as to the ultimate distribution of the assets if the child fails to meet certain criteria, may be more beneficial to the child than disinheritance. They can provide goals and initiatives that will hopefully energize your child to seek professional help. Experience suggests that this approach often leads to rehabilitation.

We are concerned with our son's work ethic. Can we structure our living trust to encourage him to work harder?

One client provided that his trustee pay his son an amount each year equal to the amount the son earned independently that year. The trust instructions provide that the son must produce a copy of his income tax return each year to disclose his earned income, which is matched by the trustee after independent verification is completed.

I want my children to lead productive, hardworking lives which contribute to our society. How can I build incentives into their inheritance without being overcontrolling or just giving them too much money?

There are a number of approaches you might consider:

- *Opportunity funding:* You may instruct your trustee to create or buy an "opportunity" for your child. The benefits to the child will occur primarily if the child successfully develops the opportunity.
- *Testamentary charitable foundation:* You may want to create a trust or foundation in your living trust that springs to life after your death and directs that, under certain guidelines, your children assist in the philanthropic endeavor of giving away the income of the trust. This strategy not only encourages children to look beyond themselves but also enhances their personal and social status in their communities.

- *Staggered distributions:* You may simply want to stagger distributions to children at certain more mature ages or after certain periods of time. A second- or third-chance formula allows your children to have resources left if they fail to handle their first distributions wisely.
- *Trustee discretion with criteria:* Your trustee can hold a child's share for life with the discretion to make certain distributions. You can set any number of specific criteria for the exercise of that discretion, such as liberal or conservative standards for distributions, and you can suggest or direct under what circumstances the children's trust principal should be distributed.
- *Milestone incentives:* You may condition distributions from your trust on your child's reaching certain milestones which can either be clearly defined or be left to the discretion of your trustee.

The opportunities for creating incentives for your children are almost endless; however, you must also be sensitive to the risks of overcontrolling. With the assistance of an experienced, knowledgeable estate planning team, you can create the structures which encourage the desired outcome without the negative responses.

How can I make sure that only my children receive their inheritance?

In your living trust, you can create at your death a trust share for each child so that a child's spouse, or ex-spouse, or even your child's creditors cannot get to the trust share property.

The trust will contain instructions that all trust shares are created only for their beneficiaries. There will also be *spendthrift* provisions stating that distributions will be used only for the child's health, support, maintenance, and education expenditures and that on the beneficiary's death, the proceeds of his or her trust share will pass directly to grandchildren and others.

How can we protect our children from losing control of their inheritance through the influence of their spouses?

In some cases, parents have a negative perception of their sons- and daughters-in-law. In these instances, parents delay principal distributions to the child in the hope that the child will recognize the error of his or her ways and will not remain married or controlled by the spouse. Although somewhat drastic, you could condition your child's full access to principal upon his or her no longer being married to a specified person. Establishing a convenience trust is a good strategy, but it may have limited application if the son-in-law or daughter-in-law has enough influence or "control" over the child to get him or her to withdraw the assets from the trust and place them in joint accounts. In that situation, a discretionary trust might be more appropriate.

Will my daughter's husband get half or more of her inheritance from a divorce?

In almost every state, an inheritance is considered to be separate property, so unless your daughter takes property from the trust share and commingles it with the marital or community property or gives it to her husband as a gift, the inheritance should remain your daughter's separate property. However, how a divorce court ultimately decides to divide the property of the respective spouses is generally within the court's equitable discretion.

I have eight children, four of whom help me operate my dairy farm. The assets of the dairy farm comprise 90 percent of my $2 million estate. I want the four who operate the farm to receive it. But I also wish that the other four could receive an equal share of my estate. Is there a way to accomplish this?

This is a very common agribusiness situation. Life insurance made payable directly to the noninvolved children or payable to a trust for their benefit can go a long way toward equalizing the children's shares. A trust agreement can be structured so that it pays the proceeds to these children free of federal estate tax.

How can our family's vacation retreat be made available to all of our children without unfairly burdening any one of them with the cost of upkeep and taxes?

Family retreats (cottages, camps, cabins, etc.) are often the most cherished of estate assets; their use by family members can have a positive effect on family dynamics after parents are gone. However, leaving a fractional share of the cottage, along with a share of the upkeep and taxes, to each child may place a burden on some of the sibling owners and may not provide a mechanism for equitably dividing the use of the retreat.

Creating a *family-retreat subtrust* in your living trust can afford a workable alternative to fractionalizing the interest among your children. In the subtrust, you can name all of the children as trustees and create a fund for maintaining the property regardless of its use.

If my son predeceases me and I leave his share to his descendants, do they automatically receive those assets at age 18?

They will receive the assets at the age of majority in their state—18 or 21 years of age—unless you provide otherwise for them with language and protection in your will or trust.

Using Powers of Appointment for Tax Planning

What is a power of appointment?

A *power of appointment* is a legal instrument that authorizes a person to designate who will receive property. This power is given to the person by someone else. For example:

> Ralph gives his son, Dave, the power to designate which of Ralph's grandchildren will receive Ralph's property 10 years after his death.

Ralph is the *giver* of the power, and Dave is the *holder* of the power. Dave has the right to *appoint* which of Ralph's grandchildren will receive Ralph's property.

Powers of appointment are very important and are frequently used by attorneys in planning the estates of their clients.

What is a general power of appointment?

A *general power of appointment* gives the power holder the power to direct property to anyone, including the holder, his or her creditors, his or her estate, or the creditors of his or her estate.

What is a testamentary general power of appointment?

A *testamentary general power of appointment* comes into effect at the death of the holder and is generally exercised in a will or trust. The document giving rise to the power may specify how and where it is to be exercised.

What is a limited power of appointment?

A *limited power of appointment* is any power which is not a general power. In other words, a limited power enables the holder to transfer property to anyone *other than* to the holder, the holder's creditors, the holder's estate, or the creditors of the estate.

A limited power of appointment can be crafted so that the holder may use it only to vary the timing or the proportion of distributions to a class of individuals or to specifically named individuals. For example:

> I give my son the power to distribute this property to or for the benefit of his children, outright or in trust, in equal or unequal shares among those children as he shall exclusively determine.

In this example, the property must pass to the grandchildren, but the son can leave out one or more of his children or distribute the property equally or unequally either outright or in trust. The power does not give the son the right to leave the property to his spouse, a charity, or friends.

What is the tax effect of giving someone a general power?

When a person has a general power of appointment over property, the property will be included in the taxable estate of that person for federal estate tax purposes. Practitioners often use general powers in planning clients' estates when they wish to place, or "trap," specific property in a person's taxable estate.

Should I give my child a general power of appointment?

Parents usually give a general power of appointment over the property they leave to a child upon their deaths to make sure that if the child dies, the property will not be subject to a generation-skipping transfer tax. Frequently, if the child has no estate, the child's $600,000 tax-free exemption equivalent amount will wipe out the tax on the property. Ironically, if the property were to pass straight to the grandchildren without being included in the child's estate, it could be subject to the horrendous 55 percent flat generation-skipping tax on gifts to grandchildren in addition to the federal estate tax in the child's estate.

Can I leave my spouse a limited or general power of appointment in my living trust or will?

Yes, you can. If your spouse survives you, he or she will then have the opportunity of exercising the power, within the discretionary parameters you set in your document, for the benefit of certain beneficiaries.

Planning for Disability

Why do I need to plan for my potential mental incapacity or mental disability?

We are living in a society where medical science is becoming increasingly proficient at sustaining and extending physical life. However, treatments to extend our mental faculties are not expanding in direct proportion to life-extension treatments: more and more people are becoming mentally incapacitated prior to becoming physically incapacitated.

If you fail to plan for disability, the onset of disability will necessitate a living probate proceeding, in which a probate court will appoint a conservator and guardian to manage your finances and physical well-being.

What is a guardianship?

If an individual becomes mentally incapacitated, the probate court appoints a *guardian* of the person to administer his or her affairs. The guardian is usually, but not necessarily, a family member. Who the court selects is the court's business and rests with the discretion of the judge.

What is a conservator?

A *conservator* manages the financial affairs of a judicially declared incompetent. He or she must keep scrupulous records to account for expenses down to the penny and must file an annual report which is subject to the approval of the court. Because this procedure is so exacting, more often than not, an attorney and/or an accountant is necessary to assist in the process.

Most families resent the fees involved and feel that the guardian-conservator process is humiliating.

Why won't my will take care of my disability planning?

A will is not a valid instrument until you die. If you become incapacitated or incompetent, you are still alive, so your will is helpless to provide for your well-being.

Will putting our assets in joint tenancy solve the living probate problem?

Placing assets in joint tenancy is not a satisfactory solution. Upon the disability of one of the joint tenants, the asset is frozen because the sale of the asset requires the signatures of both joint tenants.

Why can't I just give my spouse or child a power of attorney over my affairs?

Giving a power of attorney (called a *durable* general power of attorney because it remains in effect upon your disability) to an agent may provide some relief. However, these powers generally grant the agents considerably more power and authority than they need and thus become dangerous instruments in the hands of the agents. When you rely on such a document, you are relying on your agent to act only for your benefit. If the agent does not act for your benefit, there may be no one to intervene on your behalf.

Most durable powers of attorney include a *ratification clause* which states that the maker will not contest the transfer of any assets to any person who has relied upon the authority granted to the agent. The third party is, therefore, protected against your claims to recover the property. If your agent squanders your assets, your only recourse would be a lawsuit against that person, who is almost always a family member or close friend.

Furthermore, durable general powers of attorney may become "stale" and difficult for agents to use. Most institutions will accept durable powers of attorney only on their own forms and will not usually recognize them if they are over 3 years old.

Can't I just include limitations in the power of attorney?

A general power of attorney provides unlimited discretion on the part of the individual to whom the authority is given. The general power of attorney is not intended to contain limiting instructions. The inclusion of such limitations would only raise questions by third parties which could cause them not to accept the power of attorney as proper authorization.

Aren't a number of states passing new and better laws for using powers of attorney?

Many states have added to their statutes new and nontraditional powers for an agent authorized under a general power of attorney. These statutes typically give power holders the right to make gifts, to provide for donation of the power giver's organs upon his or her death, and to select or designate a successor agent.

The fact that the agent may be authorized to provide more services or to take broader action regarding your property does not eliminate the usual concerns about powers of attorney. Under a general power of attorney, even one with a number of specific powers, the agent is not provided with sufficient instructions regarding your wishes and does not have discretion and flexibility to deal with a wide variety of unforeseen circumstances.

If my mother gives me a general, broad durable power of attorney, can I make lifetime gifts of her assets after she becomes incapacitated?

IRS private letter rulings, federal case law, and the common law of most states indicate that if the giver of the power wants the agent to make gifts, the power of attorney must clearly spell out that authority. Powers of attorney that do not specify this authority are routinely challenged by the IRS, and any such gifts made have been included in the deceased power giver's estate for federal estate tax purposes.

Will the Social Security Administration recognize a power of attorney?

The Social Security Administration does not recognize powers of attorney for the purpose of dealing with Social Security accounts.

The administration recognizes only an individual who is appointed through the representative payee designation process.

Does a power of attorney avoid probate on my death?

A power of attorney cannot avoid probate. Regardless of whether or not you have a power of attorney, if you do not have a fully funded revocable living trust, your assets will pass through probate in order to be retitled in the name of your heirs or testamentary trustees.

Can my living trust provide for my disability?

Current statistics tell us that over one-third of us will be disabled for 6 months or longer at some point in our lives. As a result, comprehensive disability instructions in a revocable living trust are tremendously important.

With proper planning, you can provide for the uninterrupted administration of your affairs without the cost, delay, public exposure, court supervision, and accounting that accompany a conservatorship. This is the lifetime equivalent of avoiding probate on death.

Through a revocable living trust, you can designate a trustee to administer your trust and its assets in the event of your disability. You can retain control over your estate by including detailed disability instructions, and you can even define the conditions under which you will be deemed disabled.

What is the most important matter I should consider in my disability planning?

Of utmost importance is the proper selection of your disability trustee: Who do you want to control your assets and make decisions as to their investment and use? Who will have the authority to write checks, sell assets, invest income, or cash checks in order to pay the ongoing expenses of your care or the upkeep of your residence?

You should select someone who will be loyal to you in handling your assets, is adequately prepared to deal with the investment and tax issues that may arise, and is able to dedicate the time needed to follow through on the responsibility. Both you and the person you designate must also be aware of the responsibility inherent in managing the financial affairs of another person, including the possibility of surcharges and lawsuits for mishandling the account.

How does the disability trustee of my living trust get the authority to act in the event that I am disabled?

As with nearly all aspects of a revocable living trust, the disability trustee gets his or her authority from the trust document. In a properly drafted living trust there will be specific definitions of what constitutes a disability. For instance, the trust may define "disability" in any one of these different ways:

1. If two licensed physicians say that I am unable to care for myself or my financial affairs, that is a definition of my disability.
2. If my doctors and family cannot agree that I cannot take care of myself or my financial affairs, and my loved ones ask a probate court to determine my competency, and the probate court determines I am not competent, that is a definition of disability.
3. If I am missing or have been kidnapped or otherwise held against my will, that is also a definition of my disability.

In the event of a disability as defined by the trust, your disability trustee gives an *affidavit of trust* to third parties or institutions, demonstrating that he or she is authorized to act on your behalf.

A well-drafted document will also include instructions as to how the disability trustee should use the assets of the trust. The usual provision is any one of the following:

1. Provide for me only.
2. Provide for me and my spouse.
3. Provide for me, my spouse, and any children who may be dependent upon me for support.
4. Provide for me and anyone else who may be dependent upon me for support, such as my parents.

Of course, you can set forth your own specific limitations or exceptions.

Can I create enough flexibility so that my trustee can handle unforeseen circumstances?

In your trust, you can include instructions for the trustee in regard to specific instances and provide general guidance in the event of unforeseen circumstances. You may, for instance, provide that some of your assets be used for your benefit and for gifts to loved ones during your lifetime or for improvements to your property.

Why is having a successor trustee under a trust better than having an agent with a durable power of attorney?

In the event of your disability, the power and authority granted to your successor trustee is limited and controlled by your specific instructions in your trust agreement. In contrast, a power of attorney provides the agent with unlimited power.

In addition, trustees are governed by fiduciary law to act in good faith on behalf of the trust beneficiaries and can be held liable if they do not follow your specific instructions. Agents under a power of attorney are not always governed by such fiduciary law and may not be held liable to the same extent for their actions.

In the event of your death, the successor trustee can continue in that capacity to carry out your instructions as set forth in the trust. Any power of attorney, whether durable or not, by law automatically terminates at your death. Therefore, after your death, your agent under a power of attorney no longer has authority to act on your behalf.

If I have a living trust, do I need powers of attorney on my disability?

As part of your disability planning, you will need to include a *special limited power of attorney* with your living trust so that your agent under the power of attorney can transfer to your trust, subsequent to your disability, any assets you forgot to place there. Without this special limited power, assets outside of your trust could not be controlled by it and could not be placed in your trust without a court proceeding.

Will my trustee make my health care decisions?

You should also have a *durable power of attorney for health care,* in which you appoint an individual to make medical decisions for you during any periods when you are not able to communicate your wishes to your physicians. A durable power of attorney for health care allows the power holder, on your behalf, to agree to or refuse surgery or treatment, determine which hospital you should be in, and make other important medical decisions involving your health and welfare.

What about life-sustaining procedures?

Another document that you should have for disability planning is a living will. A *living will* is a directive to your physician which states that you do not want "extraordinary means" employed to keep you alive should you be in a terminal condition. This will not only relieve your family or trustee of the burden of applying to the courts to make this decision but also relieve your family from having to make this decision at all.

This decision also affects your overall estate plan because you cannot estimate the length of time or the cost of employing "extraordinary means" until you succumb to your final illness or injury.

Can I specify that I don't want to go to a nursing home?

Yes, such a provision is not unusual in a living trust. You can request that you be allowed to remain at home and be periodically taken to church or synagogue, parks or museums, even to play bingo or to dine out.

Can I update my disability instructions?

Of course. In fact, it is quite common to do so. For example, you may want to include a preference for certain nursing home care or home health care should you require it.

Who should be the beneficiary of my disability insurance?

If you have disability insurance personally or through work, your trust should be the beneficiary so that the proceeds of the policy will not have to go through a living probate.

I own and operate my own business. How can it function during my disability?

You can name successor trustees in your living trust whom you authorize and direct to run the business in your absence. Dedicated employees are often named in this regard.

How can my wife and I be assured that we, rather than the probate court, will be in charge of each other's affairs?

A fully funded revocable living trust enables you to plan for disability. On the disability of one spouse, the other may serve as the disability trustee. If both of you become disabled, or if one becomes disabled after the other is deceased, your designated successor disability trustee will continue to follow the trust instructions.

My life partner and I are concerned about what will happen should one of us become incapacitated or die. Neither of our families is truly accepting of our relationship. What can we do to protect what we have?

The marriage contract imposes certain rights and obligations on a husband and wife. Such obligations include the duty to support each other and provide necessaries; in some states, there is protection from disinheritance, and so on. In the absence of such a contract, the partners must fashion their own.

These agreements are sometimes called *living-together agreements* or *antenuptials.* They are enforceable as contracts provided that they are supported by "fair and adequate consideration," which, in this context, generally means that there is full disclosure between the partners. Such agreements can cover almost anything the couple considers important, such as ownership of particular items of property used in the household; how jointly acquired assets are to be divided in the event of a breakup; and each partner's obligation, if any, with respect to supporting a disabled or even unemployed partner, and for how long. Each partner should expect to carry disability income insurance and health insurance.

To protect one another in the event of incompetence or death, each of you should consider living trust–based planning, with cross designation of one another in representative capacities. This will enable you to retain control over your joint estate and be involved in the decision-making process. Your living trusts can also handle property distribution on death to avoid probate.

If I become disabled and my family does not approve of the disability trustees listed in my trust, can they fire them and take control of my affairs?

They would not have the power to terminate them. They would have to bring a lawsuit—most probably in your county's probate court—to have the trust set aside, and this is enormously difficult to do.

The court would be restricted to two issues: Were you competent when you signed your trust? (Arguments over whether or not you are disabled would be moot: if you aren't, you control your trust anyway; and if you are, its terms are operational.) Are your successor trustees competent to act in their fiduciary capacity?

If the answers to these questions are yes, the court will have no right to interfere with your planning.

Disinheriting a Family Member

DISINHERITING A SPOUSE

Is it possible to disinherit a spouse?

Federal tax law does not prohibit the disinheriting of a spouse. Disinheritance of a spouse is a state law issue, and all states but one—Georgia—have statutes preventing it.

At common law, a wife was entitled to a "dower" right, which was a percentage of the husband's estate. A husband had a "curtesy" right, which entitled him to a specified percentage of the wife's estate. Some states have abolished dower and curtesy rights, while others have specifically codified the rights. Similarly, some states require that one spouse cannot dispose of real property without the approval of the other spouse. This deters reducing an inheritable estate by giving it away. If a state has a dower-curtesy statute or limitation on real estate dispositions, total disinheritance of a spouse may well be prevented.

What if I try to disinherit my spouse by the terms of my will?

State statutes uniformly protect surviving spouses who are disinherited by will planning.

What if I try to disinherit my spouse by the terms of my living trust?

In a number of states this can be successfully accomplished because the state statutes apply only to disinheritance by will and not by a living trust. Your attorney will be able to tell you what your state statutes and case law provide.

Can I disinherit my spouse if we own property jointly?

You cannot disinherit your spouse in regard to any property titled jointly with him or her. Such joint property will be distributed in accordance with the title to each particular asset. The surviving spouse will receive outright ownership of those joint assets along with responsibility for any liens or encumbrances on them.

Changing jointly titled assets to your sole ownership will require your spouse's consent and signature.

My spouse has failed to support me for many years. We are living together but maintaining separate finances. May I disinherit my spouse in favor of my children or other relatives and friends?

State statutes almost always provide that if the spouses were living together at the time of death, the surviving spouse has specific statutory rights to a share of the deceased spouse's estate. If, however, they were not living together and one abandoned the other, disinheritance might be allowed depending upon state law. You should see an attorney for an explanation of the specific statutes in your state.

Can an individual give up the right to inherit from his or her spouse?

Under the laws of most states, spouses may sign prenuptial or postnuptial agreements waiving their rights to elect against the deceased spouse's estate.

DISINHERITING A CHILD

Can I disinherit a child?

While the states generally do not allow citizens to disinherit their spouses, all states allow parents to disinherit children.

What are potential consequences of disinheriting a child?

If you are faced with the prospect of disinheriting a child, remember that your decision may have a substantial impact on the future relationships among your children. Disinheriting one child may adversely affect that child's relationship with his or her siblings. Therefore, you should carefully and thoroughly evaluate the relationships of all beneficiaries before you elect to disinherit a child.

What is the most common reason children are disinherited?

The most common reason parents disinherit their children is directly related to drug or alcohol dependency. Parents fear that distributing assets to the dependent child will only lead to an increased dependency.

I wish to disinherit my son. What must I do to ensure that he will not get my property after my death?

State laws vary on the disinheritance of a natural heir. In some states such disinheritance can be accomplished by simply failing to name the child in a trust or will. In other states, the will maker or trust maker must acknowledge the existence of a child and then specifically disinherit him or her. In the latter states, a child who is not mentioned is considered to have been "forgotten" and, therefore, is included under the terms of the will or trust by state law.

You should specifically and intentionally name your son in both your will and your revocable living trust and state that it is your intention to disinherit him.

How can I prevent my disinherited children from successfully contesting my planning?

It is wise to anticipate such a challenge and to take measures to prevent it from being successful.

A primary basis for challenging an estate plan is that the decedent did not have the requisite testamentary intent due to his or her incapacity, undue influence, mistake, or duress. The challenger must prove that the lack of testamentary capacity existed as of the time the decedent executed the trust or will. If you are able to create a record establishing your proper capacity at the time you sign your estate planning documents, your trustee or executor will be better equipped to defeat such a challenge.

There are a number of ways to do this:

- Have a psychiatrist, a psychologist, or your attending physician examine you and give a written opinion regarding your sanity. Such a report—if it is contemporaneous to the signing of the estate planning documents—is likely to carry far more weight than anecdotal testimony raised many years in the future.

- Amend your plan on a frequent basis, with each amendment reincorporating the disinheritance language. In this way, a child who later challenges the plan will have to prove your lack of testamentary capacity not only at the time of your signing of the last documents but at the time of your signing of each of the preceding documents as well.
- Have a retired judge question you—for the record—about your understanding of your disinheritance wishes.
- Videotape the signing of your estate planning documents. Although a good presentation on videotape can prove to a later court that you were competent, not everyone leaves the impression of being a Hollywood movie star. You should critically evaluate your "star appeal" before committing to a videotaped signing ceremony.

While these approaches may seem like overkill, they work well and should be employed in particularly difficult family situations.

Ultimate-Remainder Planning

What happens to my assets if my designated beneficiaries do not survive me?

Unless you specify who is to ultimately receive your property upon your death, your state's *descent and distribution statute*—commonly referred to as the "laws of intestacy"—will control who receives your assets. Every state has this statute, which originated in English common law, and all the states' versions are amazingly uniform.

Distribution entails creating and following family trees. The statutes generally provide that in the absence of planning, property shall pass to spouses, children, and lineal heirs thereafter, and in their absence, the assets will pass to parents, aunts and uncles, nieces and nephews, grandnieces and grandnephews, and so on.

What ultimate-remainder strategies do most people employ in their planning?

Most people use any one or a combination of the following strategies:

- I leave my property to my family in accordance with my state's descent and distribution statute.
- My estate shall be divided in two equal shares: one for my family and one for my spouse's family, both of which shall be distributed by the laws of intestacy in my state.
- I name specific relatives or friends to receive my property in specific dollar amounts or percentages, or both.
- I leave my property to designated public charities.
- I create a testamentary charitable foundation in my living trust and leave my property to it.

Trustees

What is a trustee?

A *trustee* is a person or a licensed corporation that owes a special duty of care to the beneficiaries of a trust.

What is a cotrustee?

A *cotrustee* is a person or corporate fiduciary that is currently serving as trustee with one or more other trustees.

What is a successor trustee?

A *successor trustee* is a trustee who takes over for a prior trustee when that trustee is no longer able to perform the duties of a trustee, for whatever reason. Usually the trust maker names the successor trustees in the trust agreement.

It is common to have two or three successor trustees acting at once. Theoretically, there is no limit to the number of successor trustees you can have acting at the same time but, as a practical matter, having too many can be costly and cumbersome.

What does the term "fiduciary" mean?

The word "fiduciary" comes from Roman law and is derived from the same word as are "fidelity" and "faith." A person who is a fiduciary has been put in a position requiring him or her to be faithful and trustworthy. A trustee is the ideal example of a fiduciary. When a trustee controls trust assets, he or she must be faithful to the beneficiaries by performing the trustee's duties in their best interests, and in accordance with fiduciary law, as he or she carries out the terms of the trust agreement.

What do trustees do?

Each state has statutes that detail the powers and duties of a trustee in carrying out the management of the trust estate. It may be necessary for the trustee to seek professional management or investment advice if such expertise is not within the trustee's experience. Some of the general duties of a trustee include:

- Preparing a complete inventory and valuation of the trust assets
- Obtaining a federal tax number from the IRS
- Paying applicable expenses (medical, funeral, etc.) and taxes (federal estate tax, if applicable, and inheritance tax)
- Dividing and allocating assets to the subtrusts created in the trust if required by the terms of the trust
- Distributing assets according to the directions of the trust
- Preparing accountings as may be required

How does the law measure the performance of trustees?

Each state has statutory guidelines governing a trustee's responsibilities, and these guidelines vary from state to state.

Recently, some states have adopted the *prudent investor rule,* a model rule requiring that the trustee use reasonable care, skill, and caution in investing and managing trust assets. The investment decisions and actions of the trustee are judged in terms of the trustee's reasonable business judgment regarding the expected effect on the portfolio of investments as a whole given the facts and circumstances existing at the time of the decision or action. It is important to note that the prudent investor rule is a test of the trustee's conduct and not of the resulting performance of the investments.

Under the prudent investor rule, the trustee has certain duties. The trustee has the duty to review the portfolio assets at the time he or she receives control of the trust assets. The trustee has the duty to diversify the investments of the portfolio unless it is reasonably believed that diversification would not be in the best interests of the beneficiaries. In exercising his or her investment powers and duties, the trustee must pursue an investment strategy that considers both the ability of the investments to produce income and the safety and preservation of capital.

Although the laws that govern the responsibilities and conduct of trustees are precise, they simply boil down to using common sense and good judgment. In many cases, that will mean consulting a professional advisor for guidance. Making your chosen trustees aware of what responsibilities lie ahead is a good first step toward achieving proper administration of your trust property when you are no longer able to do so due to your incapacity or death.

What characteristics should a good trustee have?

A good trustee should:

- Be honesty and trustworthy
- Have the ability to make and handle investments
- Be financially accountable for any mistakes he or she makes
- To the extent possible, be situated in the area where your beneficiaries and your assets are located
- Have good relationships with the beneficiaries
- Be likely to survive you
- Be someone who you feel confident will manage your affairs wisely

What advantages do family-member trustees have?

- They will often serve for little or no fee.
- They are free from corporate technicalities which can slow down decisions and actions.
- They are known, trusted, and loved by trust beneficiaries.

What disadvantages do family-member trustees have?

- They often make decisions on an emotional basis rather than an objective one.
- They may have a lack of expertise.
- They may not have the financial resources to cover mistakes.
- They may die, become incapacitated, become greedy, or even file bankruptcy.

What are the advantages of corporate trustees?

Corporate fiduciaries have several advantages:

- They act objectively and follow trust instructions without emotion.
- Managing trusts is their business; they do it professionally day in and day out.
- They have investment, tax, and estate administration expertise.
- They don't die or become incapacitated, and if they go out of business, their obligations will be assumed by another corporation.
- They are highly regulated by state and federal agencies.
- They have the resources to cover errors and mistakes.

What are the major disadvantages of corporate trustees?

- They charge fees for what they do.
- Because they are supposed to make decisions on an objective and unemotional basis, they are often thought of as being mean-spirited and uncaring.
- They are not always the best choice for an estate that includes mostly real estate and/or a family business.

What kinds of questions should I ask myself when assessing potential trustees?

You should ask yourself a great number of questions when selecting trustees:

- Are they free of monetary problems of their own?
- Have they demonstrated financial managerial ability?
- Do they have any history of substance abuse?
- Do they know the beneficiaries well?
- Are they reliable?
- Do they have the required specialized skills to manage my assets?
- Have they demonstrated problem-solving ability?
- Are they the right ages?
- Are they likely to be available when needed?
- Will they seek and utilize professional assistance when circumstances require it?
- Will they accept the appointment?

Do my trustees put my trust property in their individual names?

Trustees do not have equitable or real title to your property; they merely have legal title in accordance with their responsibility of prudently managing your property for the benefit of your trust's beneficiaries.

Can my trustees appropriate my property for their own use if they are not beneficiaries of my trust?

Trustees are charged with the highest duty and responsibility imposed by law in carrying out their functions. They are absolutely prohibited from using trust assets or income for their personal use, enjoyment, or benefit.

What if they make mistakes and lose my funds?

If they make mistakes which are proved to be costly to the trust or its beneficiaries, they are liable to the beneficiaries for those mistakes. However, whether or not the funds are collectible is another matter.

How can I protect my beneficiaries from the mistakes of a trustee?

Name a corporate fiduciary as a cotrustee. By law, corporate fiduciaries are liable for their mistakes and, as such, can be collected against. They must post all of their assets as their bond for the faithful performance of their duties.

Do trustees receive compensation?

In the absence of specific instructions in a trust document, most state statutes specify trustee compensation that can range from whatever is reasonable to specific statutory schedules that hover around 1 percent of the value of what they manage annually. Your trust document should always provide for compensation of your various trustees.

Do I have to pay a trustee while I am alive and healthy?

There is no reason to pay trustees until you need them. While you are alive and healthy, you can serve as your own trustee.

Should I compensate family members?

While family members often are willing to serve without compensation, the duties of a trustee are significant and ill feelings can arise if the person shouldering this burden is not fairly compensated.

How is a corporate trustee compensated?

Generally, a corporate trustee publishes a fee schedule which it will follow during the time that it renders services. You can get an idea of what a corporate trustee will cost by obtaining a copy of its current fee schedule.

Can I be the trustee of my own living trust?

This is commonly done. However, if you become disabled or die, it will be easier to continue the affairs of your trust if you had a cotrustee serving with you who can continue to carry out your trust instructions in your absence.

Whom should I name as a cotrustee?

If each spouse has his or her own trust, it is common practice to name the other spouse as a cotrustee. If both spouses use the same joint trust agreement, they are its initial trustees.

If my spouse and I are both trustees of a joint living trust, do we both have to sign everything?

Most couples want each spouse to be able to act without the consent of the other. You can include a provision in your trust that allows either spouse to act as trustee in the administration of the trust.

Can my children be cotrustees with me?

Children are commonly named as cotrustees, but seldom named as sole trustees, of their parents' living trust plans.

Whom do I name to serve as trustee if I become disabled?

Your spouse can become the sole trustee or can continue as a cotrustee with others you select to help him or her. Children and close friends or colleagues are often named as cotrustees for disability planning purposes and it is not uncommon for a corporate fiduciary to be named as a cotrustee as well.

Selecting an appropriate team of trustees to manage your specific affairs is generally preferable to naming a single individual or corporate trustee.

If I name more than one trustee, who controls?

This depends solely upon your trust instructions. You can provide for a majority vote, or you can provide otherwise. Your instructions could specify that your spouse must agree or that he or she must carry the vote of at least one other trustee to block a specific action or to institute a certain action.

How do multiple trustees work together?

They can delegate to each other the tasks in which each has significant expertise.

In what circumstances do most people need cotrustees?

Many people want to name as a trustee a loving family member who is not good with money or investments but who is trustworthy and personally close to the trust's beneficiaries. In such instances, naming a trusted accountant or a corporate fiduciary as a cotrustee can shore up the individual's weaknesses while maintaining his or her many strengths.

Why do you feel so strongly that the appointment of cotrustees is so beneficial?

A combination of several individuals or professional trustees is beneficial for a great many reasons that center around qualifications and balance. Also, it is prudent to have trustees watching trustees for the benefit of the trust beneficiaries.

If I leave a will, I know the courts will oversee the distribution of my property. With a living trust, the courts will not be involved. Therefore, how can I be assured that my estate will be distributed the way that I want?

Choosing successor trustees to serve on your death is one of the most important tasks that you, as the trust maker, will be faced with. Successor trustees can be either individuals, such as adult children, other relatives, trusted friends, a CPA, or an attorney, or a corporate trustee, such as a bank or a trust company. A corporate trustee can be a good choice if the estate is large or will remain in trust after the death of the trust maker.

If my living trust becomes an irrevocable trust at my death, does that interfere with the ability of my spouse to buy and sell and manage the assets in my trust?

You would simply name your wife as trustee, giving her the power to manage the trust property and to add property to or remove property from the living trust as conditions at that time warrant.

Can my spouse be the sole trustee after my death?

There has been significant professional debate over this question. While technically a spouse can be a trustee of a family trust, we believe it to be a risky practice from a tax standpoint. Your spouse can be sole trustee of his or her marital and QTIP trusts but generally should not be a sole trustee of the family trust.

Why shouldn't I name my spouse to be the sole successor trustee of my trust?

When a husband or a wife dies, the surviving partner is usually at a loss in many ways. Putting him or her in a position to make all the financial decisions alone, without any help, can be a burden and often results in poor decisions on the part of the vulnerable and bereaved spouse.

It may be wiser to give your spouse some assistance by naming one or more cotrustees. This can relieve some of the burden of decision making, but it does not have to mean a loss of control. You can always give your spouse the right to remove a trustee and replace that trustee with the next person you have chosen.

In addition, having your spouse serve as a cotrustee, rather than the only trustee, offers some creditor protection to the assets you left in trust for your spouse.

Why is a bank a good choice for trustee?

Banks are generally very experienced and extremely capable. A bank's trust department is staffed by trust officers who are trained to be full-time trustees, and they have access to its computer systems for accounting and record keeping. Banks have a good track record on their investment and management of trust assets and are frequently audited by banking authorities to be certain they are adhering to prudent trustee practices.

In the case of liability for fiduciary mismanagement, trust beneficiaries can more easily obtain compensation from a bank because banks are held to a higher performance standard by regulatory agencies and courts. It is much more difficult to prove liability and obtain compensation for improper trust management from individual trustees. Finally, banks do not die or become incompetent.

Why might a bank be a poor choice as trustee?

Although banks are adept at the "nuts and bolts" of being trustees, they are often very poor at making personal, discretionary decisions about the distribution of trust funds. Since the bank is not a member of the family, it feels very uncomfortable making decisions about whether or not beneficiaries should receive trust funds and how much should be distributed. Usually such determinations are made by an impersonal trust committee.

What happens to my trust if a bank is trustee and the bank fails?

When a bank is trustee, it is merely holding your assets in its fiduciary capacity. If the bank fails, those assets are not subject to claims by either depositors or creditors of the bank. Instead, the regulating authority, usually the state bank examiner, the Federal Reserve Bank, or the FDIC, arranges to have another financial institution in the geographic area take over the trustee responsibilities of the failed bank.

Even though the bank fails, your trust doesn't. The new trustee will continue to manage your trust assets in the same manner as did the failed trustee. If your trust was invested in various stocks, bonds, and mutual funds, those same stocks, bonds, and mutual funds will now be managed by the new trustee. Your trust remains completely intact as long as the value of the investments remains intact.

Should I name a bank or trust company as sole trustee over my spouse's trusts?

Most spouses do not want to have their affairs managed by a corporate entity over which they have no control, but many trust makers do want the benefits offered by corporate trustees. You could name your spouse as a cotrustee with the corporate trustee and provide that your spouse can terminate the corporate trustee and then name another fiduciary in its place.

Why would I give my spouse the right to fire a corporate fiduciary?

Experience has taught most practitioners that if a spouse—or any other beneficiary for that matter—is "locked into" a trustee, it is likely that the trustee will not be very responsive to the needs of the beneficiary.

If I allow my spouse to terminate a trustee, can I provide a list from which the replacement must be selected?

You can specify the precise replacement or furnish a list from which the replacement can be selected.

Should I name the guardians of my children as their trustees?

This is frequently done but can often be dangerous. Most professionals recommend that the guardians be named as cotrustees if they are named at all. This will lessen their burden and provide an extra layer of fiduciary protection for minor children who cannot protect themselves.

Should I name the same trustees for all of my children?

This would be wise if the trustees are charged with caring for more than one child or grandchild from the same common trust fund. If you have created separate shares for each child, you can name the same trustees for all the children or different trustees for each child.

Should I name my children to be trustees of each other's trusts?

It is generally not a good idea to put one child in charge of another child's inheritance even if they get along famously. There are certain things you can do in estate planning that bring families together upon death, while other things can pull them apart. This is one of the things that can pull them apart. In most circumstances siblings should not be each other's trustees.

Can I name my adult son as his own trustee?

This is commonly done with adult children, but you should name at least one other person or institution as a cotrustee with the child. By naming a cotrustee, you creditor-proof your son's trust.

How does a cotrustee "creditor-proof" my son's trust?

A properly drawn trust is generally not subject to the claims of creditors unless the sole trustee is also the sole beneficiary. If your son is sole trustee of his own trust and gets into financial or legal difficulties, creditors can obtain and execute judgments against him. If your son resigns as trustee, a creditor would have a difficult task in asserting rights against his trust or its trustee.

Whom should I name as trustee of an adult child's trust?

You should name a trustee team that will take into account the child's needs and your wishes for his or her success and happiness. You might not want to name the same trustees for a spendthrift child as you would for an accomplished professional or executive child whose trust needs protection only from creditors and a potential divorce.

What kinds of trustees can help my spendthrift child?

Corporate fiduciaries and certified public accountants make excellent cotrustees for spendthrift children.

Can I name my financial advisors and planners as cotrustees?

Although commonly done, this has a single significant disadvantage: If advisors make their living selling investments or services, state law may preclude them from selling to a trust under which they serve as trustees.

Is there any way that I can name my financial advisor and allow her to sell to the trust?

You can include instructions stating that you want her to be able to sell or charge for her investment advice but that she cannot participate in any decisions with other cotrustees whenever she has a conflict of interest.

Should a trustee also serve as my personal representative (executor)?

Your executor is responsible for handling the probate administration of your estate, including distribution of all of your probate assets. It is important to have someone who will follow your written instructions as set forth in your estate planning documents. Likewise you will want someone who will give appropriate attention to any of your personal-property items that have a high sentimental value even though they may not have a high economic value.

If you have a living trust–centered estate plan, it is good practice to have a trustee also be your personal representative. A trustee who is a family member or close friend is often a good choice.

Can we appoint our attorney to be a successor trustee of our living trust?

You can name anyone you want to be a successor trustee; however, most attorneys will respectfully decline. Attorneys are not in the business of acting as trustees, and you may be better served by using the attorney's services as an advisor.

What if someone we have named as a successor trustee doesn't want to serve?

You cannot force a person or institution to act as your trustee, so you should name alternatives in case one of your choices refuses or cannot serve.

What kind of problems would there be if one of the trustees I named is involved in a divorce or other legal problems while he or she is serving as a trustee?

A trustee of a trust is not an owner of the assets that are inside the trust. The trustee is a manager or agent. Therefore, a trustee's divorce or other legal proceedings involving his or her personal matters are not related to the trust and should not, in any way, jeopardize the assets that are owned inside of your revocable living trust.

In general, should my beneficiaries be allowed to remove a trustee that I have named in my trust agreement?

It is not a good idea to have a trust that does not provide some method for removing a trustee. Matters change over time, and it is entirely possible that a particular trustee may become inadequate.

If the beneficiaries are not satisfied with a trustee's performance, they should be allowed to fire the old trustee and hire a new one. When this happens, the next person you named as a successor in the trust agreement becomes the new trustee in place of the removed trustee.

In the event that the list of named trustees runs out, it is customary to provide in the trust agreement that a court can be allowed temporary jurisdiction over the trust for the sole purpose of appointing a new trustee. Courts usually appoint corporate trustees under such circumstances. This method prevents the beneficiaries from "trustee shopping" (constantly hiring and firing trustees until they find one that meets their needs or does what they want), since continually going to court would be expensive and unproductive. At the same time, it does enable them to remove a trustee who is unsatisfactory.

If a court is named to appoint a trustee, won't my trust be back in probate?

Your instructions can provide that the court will name a successor trustee *ex parte,* which means it will not gain jurisdiction over your trust.

Who looks over the trustee's shoulder?

As with any trust, the trustee of a revocable living trust has a legal duty to do two things: to follow the rules set down by the trust maker and to act in the best interests of the beneficiaries. In normal circumstances there will not be anyone looking over the trustee's shoulder. And this is what most people want—that the trust operate or distribute after they are gone with no outside interference.

If you have an unusual situation in which a successor trustee does not follow the rules or does not act in the best interests of the beneficiaries, anyone hurt by that trustee's actions can ask the county court with jurisdiction over estates and trusts to review what the trustee has done.

Pour-Over Wills

What is a pour-over will?

A *pour-over will* is used in conjunction with a living trust. Its primary function is to name the guardians of minor children and to transfer, or "pour over," any assets in the decedent's probate estate to his or her trust after death.

If a revocable living trust avoids probate, why do I still need a will?

All proper, trust-centered estate plans include pour-over wills. Having a pour-over will ensures that any property not owned by the trust at the time of your death will pass to the trust.

The pour-over will, however, provides additional fail-safe features. If, for any reason, your trust is invalidated (improper drafting, faulty execution, destruction or disappearance of the trust document without replacement), the pour-over will then determines the disposition of your assets.

In addition, the existence of the pour-over will allows for the appointment of an executor, which is necessary if your estate becomes involved in any litigation. This happens most frequently in the case of the wrongful death of the trust maker. The executor is generally the only fiduciary with the authority to conduct a wrongful-death suit on behalf of the estate.

With a pour-over will that has been drafted as a complementary backup to your living trust document, you can rest assured that, no matter what happens, the terms of your trust will be protected and acted upon in your absence.

If I have a pour-over will, does it have to be probated when I die?

All wills go through probate, but a pour-over will probates only the assets it controls. If you fail to transfer your assets to your living trust, your pour-over will is designed to fund the trust for you. Unfortunately, those assets will go through the probate process. This is not the situation for which pour-over wills are created.

Pour-over wills are designed to gather forgotten or newly acquired assets that a trust maker inadvertently neglected to place in trust, so that the probate on those assets will be minimal and will, hopefully, fall under the small-estates acts of the various states.

Am I required to write a new pour-over will each time a child or grandchild is born or adopted?

You can provide in your trust agreement for a gift to a class of individuals which will remain open until the distribution puts the gift into effect. In this manner children born or adopted into your family after you prepare your will and trust are automatically included in your plan.

Funding the Revocable Living Trust

THE FUNDING PROCESS

What is meant by "funding" a revocable living trust?

A revocable living trust can control only those assets which are titled in the name of the trust. "Funding" refers to the act of transferring the ownership of assets to a revocable living trust. It also refers to changing beneficiary designations on life insurance or deferred compensation benefits, if appropriate, to the name of the trust.

Funding—the process of retitling assets to the name of the trust—is the power behind living trust planning. It obviates the need for a conservatorship and guardianship while you are alive and totally avoids the administrative process of the probate court upon your death. It preserves the privacy of your affairs and places the control, or planning power, behind your document in the hands of those persons or institutions you have named as successor trustees.

Can you give me an example of funding?

Suppose you created the John Doe Living Trust, dated May 26, 1996, and you are the initial sole trustee. The property that is currently titled in your name will be retitled to read:

> John Doe, Sole Trustee, or his successors in trust, under the John Doe Living Trust, dated May 26, 1996, and any amendments thereto.

This retitling of your assets enables your successor trustees to deal with the property, according to your instructions, in the event of your disability or death.

In practice, using the full name, as shown above, may be cumbersome. It may not fit into certain computer software programs used by brokerage houses or public agencies. To abbreviate, you could use the following:

John Doe, Trustee, u/a dtd 5/26/96.

This is sufficient for purposes of holding title in the name of the trust, since it identifies the current trustees and refers to a particular trust document ("u/a" is an abbreviation for the words "under agreement").

If I place my property in trust, haven't I given my property away?

Your property is titled in the name of the trust, but its instructions provide that you are the beneficiary of the trust and have the right to use, possess, and enjoy the trust property. By retitling your assets to your trust's name, you change nothing other than avoiding the judicial system upon your disability or death. *It is imperative that your assets be transferred into the trust in order to avoid probate.*

If all my assets are titled in the name of my living trust, how do they avoid probate upon my death?

Let's look at what happens upon death. An individual might have two types of assets—probate assets and nonprobate assets. *Probate assets* are subject to the jurisdiction of the court system (surrogate, common, or probate court depending upon the state of the decedent's domicile) so that title can be changed from the name of the decedent to the name of his or her heirs.

Nonprobate assets are not controlled by a court. Assets such as life insurance, pension benefits, IRAs, annuities, and similar property "pass by contract": the benefits are paid upon death to the beneficiary designated in the applicable contract. No probate is needed. Real estate or other property held as joint tenants with right of survivorship passes "by operation of law": when one of the joint owners dies, the owner who survives automatically owns the entire property. Probate is not needed to pass title on the first death.

A living trust enables probate property to become nonprobate property. The property in the living trust is held, administered, and distributed according to the terms of the trust agreement and thus avoids the judicial process of retitling.

I've heard that funding a revocable living trust makes estate planning more difficult, expensive, and time-consuming? Is this true?

This view is often promoted by will-planning probate practitioners as a reason to avoid living trust–centered estate planning. Interestingly, funding your trust is one of the major *advantages* of electing to use living trust–centered estate planning.

The argument that funding a living trust makes estate planning more difficult and time-consuming runs counter to both legal and common sense. If it is indeed so difficult to locate and transfer assets during your lifetime, how can the process be more easily accomplished during probate—*without* the very assistance of the person who owned the assets and knew more about them than anyone else? Most people do not have their financial paperwork well organized at the time of their death or disability. This results in a legal "scavenger hunt" on the part of those left behind. The time it takes to locate assets is often a major cause of delay in the average probate estate.

It's only human to procrastinate. Very few people look forward to the paperwork involved in retitling their assets into the names of their trusts. However, many people go through the funding process, sometimes with the assistance of an attorney or financial advisor, and most have accomplished the complete funding of their trusts with little, if any, hassle.

With your participation, problems that loom today can be solved easily. Without your participation, those same problems can cause lengthy delays, costs, and aggravation for your loved ones.

The title to real estate is often illustrative of the difference between funding your trust while you are capable and allowing the judicial system to do so after you are incapacitated or deceased. For example, a person may believe that real estate is owned by a partnership, when in fact the land was never deeded to the partnership but remains in the individual name or joint names of one or more of the partners. This mistake in ownership is quite common, and it will cause massive partnership and tax problems that will not be solved to anyone's satisfaction after a partner's death.

Are you saying there are no additional costs to funding a trust during my lifetime as compared to retitling the assets after death?

In almost every instance, there is a nominal to small cost for transferring assets into most living trust plans. These costs are almost always far less than the costs that would be incurred after your disability or death without living trust planning.

For example, most brokerage houses will handle the retitling of your stock certificates to your living trust at no charge if the shares are transferred into a *street name* account (a single account that holds all of your securities with that particular company) or at a nominal cost if you wish to continue to hold the individual certificates. In addition, most full-service financial institutions or brokerage houses will transfer certificates from street name back to your name at no additional cost.

Some asset transfers will clearly result in fees. The documentation of a real estate transfer, for instance, should always be prepared by an attorney, who will charge for doing so. However, this cost is almost always insignificant.

If I create a revocable living trust, can I keep assets in my own name and have them transferred to my trust at death without going through probate?

In some states certain kinds of assets can be owned in your own name and be transferred to your living trust at death without going through the probate process. For example, Ohio allows you to own bank accounts with a designation, *payable on death (POD),* to a beneficiary. All bank checking, savings, and money market accounts can be owned with the designation payable on death to your living trust. Ohio has also adopted a *transfer-on-death (TOD)* designation for stocks and brokerage accounts. Therefore, in Ohio it would be a good idea for you to own your stock or brokerage accounts with a TOD designation to your living trust so that your trust will be funded with these accounts at death. In Ohio, and in a number of other Uniform Probate Code states, subchapter S corporation stock or stock in a professional corporation can also be owned with a TOD designation without causing you to lose your subchapter S election.

In states that allow POD and TOD designations, it is therefore possible to utilize different funding strategies so that you can maintain ownership of many of your assets outside of your living trust while you are alive and still get them into your trust probate-free after your death.

Other kinds of assets, including life insurance, annuities, and retirement plans, provide for beneficiary designations in all of the states. As long as your living trust is designated as the beneficiary, the proceeds from these assets will be distributed to your trust at death without going through probate.

Can I sign my living trust and leave my assets titled in joint tenancy with my spouse?

How assets are titled is critical to the proper planning and execution of your estate documentation. For example, if you have a perfectly drafted living trust that contains an "A-B," or marital-family, subtrust provision, you and your spouse could lose massive federal estate tax benefits if you continue to hold your assets jointly. This is because the joint ownership property rules of your state will override the federal estate tax planning contained in your trust. When you die, your jointly held property will be automatically transferred to the surviving owner and thus will not be controlled by the tax instructions in your trust.

The pitfalls of holding assets jointly with right of survivorship can best be explained through an example:

> Assume that Bill and Mary own their house, their cars, and their other major assets as joint tenants with right of survivorship. Additionally, they have a well-drafted testamentary trust will or a living trust with A-B trust estate tax provisions. When Bill dies, these jointly held assets automatically pass to Mary. Mary now owns the property outright. Bill's trustee or executor collects the rest of Bill's property, which Bill owned in his name alone. Because a preponderance of Bill's property is in joint tenancy and automatically vests in Mary outside of Bill's will or trust, Bill's estate is unable to take advantage of keeping his $600,000 estate tax exemption equivalent amount out of Mary's estate on her death. When Mary later dies, the entire value of all of the assets which Mary and Bill formerly owned as joint tenants is included in Mary's gross estate for estate tax purposes. Mary can transfer $600,000 worth of this property to her children free from estate taxation, but the rest is taxed.
>
> Had Bill and Mary owned their property individually, rather than jointly with right of survivorship, each of them could have transferred $600,000 worth of property to their children (a total of $1.2 million) without incurring any estate tax liability, and they would have saved $235,000 of unnecessary estate tax.

How do we fund a joint trust with our jointly held property?

Each of your respective assets is contributed to the trust and listed on a schedule to the trust document. Jointly held property contributed to the trust is listed as belonging to each spouse equally, with 50 percent going to each spouse's schedule.

Practitioners vary on how they fund a joint living trust. One school of thought advocates first converting the jointly held property to tenancy in common and then conveying each spouse's tenancy-in-common interest to the joint trust. Another school of thought believes that the conversion to tenancy in common is a wasted step and that the jointly held property can be transferred directly to the trust. This group believes that the conveyance to the trust automatically converts the property to tenancy in common (50-50 ownership between the spouses) and destroys the survivorship feature. Regardless of which funding technique is followed, the use of a joint trust is ideal for spouses who own their property in joint tenancy.

How does a married couple decide which marital assets will be funded into the husband's trust and which marital assets will be funded into the wife's trust?

The objective in funding trusts for married couples is to allocate assets in a way that satisfies their respective ownership needs and desires while minimizing the effect of income and estate taxes on the couple and their children. In addition, liability concerns are often addressed as part of the allocation of assets in the funding process.

What are the determining factors in funding the spouses' respective trusts?

There are four main factors to be considered.

The Psychological Factor Many spouses feel that all of their marital assets are marital property and that both spouses have equal rights and ownership to all of their marital assets. Others feel that some assets are more clearly associated with one spouse than the other. For example, a wife who has inherited property from her parents, such as a family vacation home, may feel stronger emotional and legal ties to that property than her husband does. Or a husband whose hobby is investing in the stock market may have a desire to maintain control over the couple's brokerage accounts. These factors, and others like them, need to be taken into consideration when allocating assets between the spouse's respective trusts.

The Predetermined Ownership Factor Another consideration is whether there are significant qualified retirement plan assets that by their nature have a predetermined ownership. Qualified retirement assets must be owned by the plan participant. Any other arrangement will result in the premature payment of income taxes. Couples with large concentrations of assets in qualified plans should consult their advisors because the rules governing the lifetime and after-death use of qualified plan funds are enormously complicated.

The Capital Gain Factor Yet another concern when allocating assets between the spouses is the age and health of each spouse. Is it likely that one spouse in particular will die before the other? If so, have any of the properties appreciated in value? This determination is made by looking at the cost basis and fair market value for each of the spousal assets. If there is appreciated property, the spouses will want to consider a transfer of the appreciated property to the trust owned by the ill spouse in order to obtain a step-up in basis for the appreciated property.

This technique can yield significant capital gain tax savings for the surviving spouse. However, asset transfers within 1 year of death will not receive a stepped-up tax basis.

The Liability Factor Does one spouse have greater exposure to liability claims as a result of his or her occupation or of the type of property that he or she owns (e.g., rental real estate or a business that deals in hazardous materials)? If so, it is important to make sure that assets necessary for the family's basic needs are not jeopardized. For this reason, it makes sense to have the spouse who is not exposed to the threatened claims own the bulk of the family assets if the marriage is stable and the spouses are comfortable with that arrangement.

In some cases, couples may own some assets which create liability exposure and other assets which do not. In this situation, it is often appropriate to have one spouse own all of the high-liability assets and to have the other spouse own the "clean assets."

Couples who have significant assets and are concerned with liability issues may also want to consider employing more sophisticated asset protection strategies such as family limited partnerships or offshore trusts.

Will placing all of my assets into a trust protect me from my creditors?

You cannot create a living trust for your benefit to avoid your creditors during your lifetime. Upon your death, however, a living trust, in forty-four of the states, completely cuts off the claims of your unsecured creditors. In California, Massachusetts, Michigan, New Jersey, New York, Oregon, and Florida, creditors' claims are not severed after the trust maker's death. In these six states, creditors of the trust maker can prevail upon the trust to the extent of the trust maker's interest in the trust, just as they can against any other estate.

Can my living trust cut off the claims of my beneficiaries' creditors?

If properly drafted, your living trust can protect your beneficiaries from their creditors through state laws called *spendthrift* statutes. Spendthrift provisions in a revocable living trust insulate trust funds from the claims of your beneficiaries' creditors.

Will there be any gift tax consequences as a result of my putting property into my living trust?

A properly written living trust qualifies under the Internal Revenue Code as a grantor trust for income tax purposes, and all of its income is taxed to the individual trust maker as though the property was still in his or her name. Gift taxes are not generated through the funding of a revocable living trust, and gift tax returns do not need to be filed.

Are all assets retitled in the same way to my trust?

Different assets are retitled in different ways, and specific information about each asset is required in order to successfully transfer the asset into your revocable living trust.

For real property, the current legal description and the ownership of the property is important. Most attorneys require a copy of the deed that conveyed the property to you so that they can then accurately reconvey the property to your trust by using the same property description.

For bank accounts and street name investment portfolios, you should provide the account number, name and address of the institution, and name of the individual with whom you work so that these assets can be easily retitled to your trust.

Retitling closely held business interests usually entails a review of applicable buy-sell agreements, partnership agreements, or other documentation which may restrict the transfer of their ownership. The permission of third parties is often necessary before the transfer of these types of assets can be completed.

Retirement plan assets and life insurance do not require a change of ownership but, rather, a change of beneficiary designation. You name your revocable living trust as their beneficiary in the event of your disability or death.

Is there a simple way to determine what methods should be used to place my various assets in my trust?

Most assets have some sort of paperwork which indicates their owner for legal purposes. As a general rule of thumb, the same paperwork which originally conveyed those assets to your name will be used to reconvey them to your trust. Most law firms that regularly prepare living trusts can provide you with letters of instruction that will assist you with the paperwork.

Do I have to show my bank, broker, or anyone else a copy of my trust when funding it?

When transferring assets to your revocable living trust, more often than not the transferring agents need to see certain information from your trust to help them make the transfer. They need to know that the trust exists and that you have actually signed the trust. They need to know the names of the trustees and cotrustees and what powers they have. They also need to know the name of your trust and the date it was executed or last amended.

However, your trust is and should remain a confidential document. In a well-drafted estate plan, an *affidavit of trust* should be available in lieu of your actual trust document. It is a shortened version of the essential elements of the trust and suffices as a substitute document without disclosing the private information contained within the actual trust document.

What if I don't want to involve myself in the funding process?

If you do not wish to actively participate in the funding process, you can delegate the process to others. Through a specially designed limited power of attorney, other individuals can do everything necessary to transfer assets to your trust *without* obtaining any control whatsoever over your assets. Thus, you can offer your heirs the chance to do the funding paperwork for you now rather than after your death. Alternatively, you can pay someone to help with the transfer process. Either way, you can supervise the process; in stark contrast, you will have no control if your assets are transferred by the probate process.

Most law firms which regularly prepare revocable living trusts are happy to make their paralegals available to prepare your trust funding documents. And, in many instances, your own financial advisors can perform a major portion of the necessary work.

It seems like there's still a lot of work to do after we sign our estate planning documents. Is it really worth all that effort?

If you wish to avoid both a potential living probate and probate upon your death, you will want to fund your trust. If you want to be able to take advantage of basic federal estate tax planning that will save $235,000 of tax, you will want to fund your trust.

Trust funding is not complicated or expensive, but it does involve finding documents of title and doing administrative follow-up. When compared to the delays, publicity, and expense of probate and the burden of paying federal estate tax, these minor inconveniences appear trivial and can be easily tolerated.

TRANSFERRING SPECIFIC ASSETS

Should I change the ownership of assets that I wish to give to my children?

In order to make cash gifts that may be part of your estate plan, you should keep a checking account in your individual name rather than retitling it in your name as trustee of your living trust. The reason for doing so is that gifts made from an account in your individual name are immediately and permanently removed from your taxable estate.

The IRS has taken the position that gifts made from a living trust within 3 years of your date of death may be brought back into your estate and become subject to federal estate tax. Knowledgeable practitioners can draft around this problem in a living trust plan; however, it is reasonable for you to make sure that all property to be given away is placed in your individual name prior to being given away.

How do we transfer our bank accounts to the trust?

You take an affidavit of your trust to the bank, give it to your account representative, and request that the account be transferred into the name of your trust.

Do I have to have the name of my trust on my checks, and do I have to change my checking account number?

You do not have to have the name of your trust on your checks, and you do not have to change your checking account number. You do not even need to put the word "Trustee" after your signature. To change the bank account to the trust, you need only change the name on the bank's signature card.

How do we transfer our CDs into our living trust?

You take the affidavit of trust to the institution that issued them, give it to your banking representative, and request that they be transferred into the name of the trust.

Should I change the ownership of my pension, profit-sharing, and Keogh plans and my IRA to my living trust?

The ownership of your pension and profit-sharing plans, Keogh plans, and IRA should *not* be transferred to your living trust without first consulting with your estate planning attorney. The tax-deferred amounts that have been contributed to a qualified retirement plan are considered taxable income when received, whether received by the owner of the plan or a designated death beneficiary. However, if the beneficiary of these plans is the spouse of the deceased employee, the spouse may transfer, or "roll over," the benefits into his or her own IRA and defer income tax until the spouse actually receives the proceeds.

If the living trust has not been drafted properly and you designate it as the primary beneficiary of your deferred compensation plans, the trust may have to pay income tax on the distributed proceeds after your death and your spouse will not have the ability to role them over to a new IRA. However, a well-drafted trust will allow a rollover of the proceeds to an IRA for your spouse.

You may consider naming your spouse as the primary beneficiary of your retirement plan proceeds and your living trust as the secondary or contingent beneficiary. Or you may name the trust as primary beneficiary and give the trustee the authority to disclaim the funds in favor of the surviving spouse if this would produce a more desirable tax result. On your death, your spouse can consult with his or her advisors as to the law at that time in order to determine whether or not he or she should elect to receive the benefits or disclaim them and let them flow into your living trust for his or her benefit.

If the surviving spouse's income tax planning needs are greater than the available federal estate tax planning needs, he or she will generally elect to take the proceeds outside of the trust and continue to defer the payment of the income tax. If, however, the surviving spouse needs to begin drawing on the retirement plan benefits, or if the family trust is underfunded, the spouse can be advised to *disclaim* his or her interest in the retirement plan proceeds so that they will flow into your living trust for estate tax planning purposes.

How do I transfer my publicly held securities if I have the certificates in my possession?

If you hold the individual certificates, you need to contact the transfer agent and get a blank transfer form. You complete the form and have your signature guaranteed, and then you send the form and the certificate to the transfer agent. As we discussed earlier, it may be easier to have the transfer made by a stockbroker by having the stocks placed in a street name account.

Should I transfer my Section 1244 stock to my living trust?

If you own stock in a small-business corporation which is qualified under Section 1244 of the Internal Revenue Code, that stock should not be transferred to your trust.

In general, if the business represented by Section 1244 stock is sold at a loss or liquidated at a loss, a Section 1244 shareholder may deduct the loss from his or her ordinary income up to $50,000 per year ($100,000 for married couples filing a joint return).

If Section 1244 stock is transferred to a living trust, the Section 1244 ordinary-loss treatment will be lost, and the losses incurred will be deemed to be capital losses, which are only deductible against capital gains or up to $3000 per year against ordinary income.

Should I transfer my stock certificates to my living trust if they are subject to a restriction agreement?

Transfers of stock in closely held corporations, regardless of whether they are regular corporations, S corporations, or professional corporations, may be subject to restrictions imposed by agreement or by statute. It is important that you have your attorney evaluate these restrictions to determine if they preclude you from transferring your certificates to your living trust or if advance approval is needed from other persons or entities.

Can my S corporation stock be held in a revocable living trust without breaking the S corporation election?

Since a living trust is a grantor trust under the Internal Revenue Code, it may hold S corporation stock without adversely affecting the S election.

Should I transfer my stock options to my living trust?

Transferring your stock options to your living trust may generate an income tax on the difference between the option price and the value of the stock at the time of transfer. The stock option plan may also prohibit such a transfer. Many practitioners believe that the preferable approach is to wait until you exercise your option and to allow all holding-period requirements to expire before transferring your stock into your living trust.

Does transferring partnership interests present difficulty in the retitling process?

Most partnership agreements require the permission of all of the general partners in order for an individual partner to transfer his or her partnership interest. This requirement is designed to prevent a *stranger* from becoming a party to the partnership, but it inadvertently slows down the innocent attempts of trust makers to convey their partnership interests into their revocable living trusts. The correspondence or telephone calls required to explain the situation both to the other partners and to the partnership's legal counsel take time and cost money.

Can I transfer my house to my living trust without losing any federal tax benefits?

A transfer to a revocable living trust is an income tax–neutral event. The Internal Revenue Service recognizes that, in effect, there has not been a true conveyance of your property since the control of the property and the beneficial right to receive the rights and profits from the property have not been transferred. The property starts in your individual name and is moved to your trust name very much like moving coins from your left pocket to your right pocket; it never leaves your person for tax purposes.

If I transfer my principal residence to my revocable living trust, will this affect the one-time exclusion of capital gains for persons over 55?

No, the one-time exclusion of capital gains is not forfeited if the residence is transferred to a revocable living trust.

However, there is an additional matter which you must consider prior to making the transfer. If, after death, your trustees place your residence into a family trust, your spouse cannot take advantage of the one-time exclusion; but if your residence is placed in the marital trust, your surviving spouse can take advantage of the exclusion. This issue may be of minor concern because of the stepped-up basis the residence will receive subsequent to your death.

Should I be concerned with state tax issues when transferring real estate to my living trust?

You should always consult with your attorney before conveying real estate into the name of your living trust. Tax issues vary from state to state and can sometimes lead to unwanted consequences. For example, in Pennsylvania, a transfer fee is placed on the fair market value of any real property transferred into a trust if any beneficiary, stated or contingent, could be a nonexempt transferee under the Pennsylvania Real Estate Transfer Tax Act. In New York, the eligibility for a senior citizen exemption might be lost when a residence is transferred into a revocable living trust if there is a cotrustee other than the senior citizen trust maker.

Can we lose the benefit of creditor protection if we transfer our real estate to a living trust?

While many other assets such as publicly traded stocks, bonds, bank accounts, and tangible property can be easily transferred to a revocable living trust, real estate has certain peculiarities which require closer scrutiny before transferring the property.

In some states there are protections against claims of creditors when property is held by husband and wife as tenants by the entirety. These protections may be lost if the property is conveyed into a living trust. Many states have homestead exemptions which protect the family home from the claims of creditors. The homestead exemption may be lost in some jurisdictions through trust funding.

It is therefore important that you seek the advice of your attorney before transferring real estate into the name of your trust.

Should I change the ownership of environmentally contaminated real estate to my living trust?

Real property that is contaminated not only pollutes the environment but can "pollute" your trust as well. If contaminated property is in the name of your living trust, your total trust assets are at risk of being used to pay for any resulting environmental liabilities and your trustee is personally at risk under federal law for the costs of cleaning up the property and paying damages claimed by third parties.

It is absolutely essential to consult an attorney with specialized knowledge of both environmental legislation and estate planning before transferring your contaminated property to your living trust.

Should I transfer real estate to my living trust if my mortgage contains a due-on-sale clause?

Many mortgages and deeds of trust that encumber real estate contain *due-on-sale clauses.* These clauses provide that the entire unpaid balance of the underlying debt is due in full if the property is transferred. Federal law precludes such clauses from being enforced when residential real estate is transferred to a revocable living trust.

However, with respect to nonresidential property and residential property containing more than five units, the clause may be enforceable. Therefore, you should not transfer such property to your living trust until you have evaluated the potential consequences of the transfer or obtained a waiver from the lender.

Do I need the approval of my lender before transferring real estate subject to a mortgage?

It is generally advisable to notify mortgage holders of proposed transfers to living trusts and seek their assent to prevent any default under the terms of the mortgage. Generally, mortgage lenders are agreeable to permitting the transfers for estate planning purposes. They may, however, require certain written documentation and a small fee to cover their cost of reviewing the paperwork involved in the transfers.

Do we have to have new deeds drawn whenever we want to put real estate in our trust?

The only way you can transfer your existing real estate into your trust is by signing a deed showing that the property is owned by your trust. Most attorneys charge only a nominal fee for the preparation of such deeds because they routinely do this type of work.

If our attorney prepares a deed to transfer the title to our home into our trust, do we have to record the deed?

As a general rule, you should record any deed which transfers real estate into a revocable trust. Recording the deed is the official record that the trustees of the trust are the owners of the real estate. After the deed has been recorded, there is official notice that the real estate is in the trust, even if the deed is later lost or destroyed.

Can I have my local attorney transfer real estate that I own in other states to my trust?

The mechanics of transferring real estate vary widely among the states. The use of local counsel is necessary to confirm that the form of deed used will be acceptable to the title companies and will meet the various recordation requirements of the particular jurisdiction.

Should I notify my insurance agent when I place real estate into my trust?

Once real estate has been placed into your revocable living trust, you should notify your liability insurance carriers so that they can make the necessary notations in their files.

Should I transfer the titles to my automobiles into my living trust?

Many practitioners believe that cars should be owned outside of your trust in order to protect your trust assets from creditors' claims resulting from the ownership of the vehicles.

Generally it is not absolutely necessary to transfer title of most vehicles into the name of your living trust. Collector vehicles, antique vehicles and vehicles with a high value, or those which you plan to keep for an extended period of time should be placed into your trust.

If I don't put my vehicles in my living trust, will they go through probate?

This depends upon state law. For example, the Michigan vehicle code allows any individual to transfer up to $60,000 worth of motor vehicles to a spouse or children without the necessity of probate. The small-estate statutes of many states accomplish the same result as the Michigan statute. It is therefore important that you ask your attorney what your state's law is prior to making this funding decision.

How do I retitle my horse or livestock in the name of my trust?

In order to transfer ownership of a registered thoroughbred horse you will need to transfer the title on the back of the Jockey Club registration certificate. Many other breeds of horses also have registration certificates as evidence of title, and transfer of ownership to your living trust can be accomplished by making the transfer on the certificates. Livestock in general is transferred into a living trust by changing the ownership of the livestock brand to the name of the trust.

How do I transfer assets that do not have formal titles?

Assets that do not have formal titles, such as furniture, furnishings, silverware, china, collectibles, and so on, are conveyed to trust ownership by a general bill of sale or assignment.

Do I need to precisely describe each article I want to put into my trust?

For personal property such as clothing, jewelry, furniture, and household effects, you simply sign a general assignment or transfer document transferring all of this property to your living trust. There is no need to do a detailed inventory of your personal property.

How do I transfer my art collection to my living trust?

If there are personal collections of substantial value, such as coin, stamp, or art collections, most practitioners tailor specific assignment documentation to convey them into the trust.

How do I transfer promissory notes or installment contracts into my living trust?

Promissory notes and installment contracts are transferred to your living trust through a written assignment prepared by your attorney.

Do I transfer my debts into my trust?

When you put your property into your trust, you do not have to put your debts into it. Your trust has nothing to do with your creditors or what you owe them. You will still be liable for your debts regardless of whether you have established a living trust.

Should life insurance be owned by my revocable trust?

If you own life insurance on your life, you should name your living trust as the primary beneficiary of your policies. In cases where the estate asset values are low, and there is little danger that the assets will be subject to estate taxation now or in the future, it makes sense to make your living trust the beneficiary of your policies.

When the value of an estate is such that it will be taxed (generally, estates over $600,000 for a single person and over $1.2 million for a married couple), ownership of life insurance by the insured's revocable trust will only add to the estate value and increase the estate tax burden. In such cases, it may make sense to employ an irrevocable life insurance trust as the owner of the policies.

If you do not use an irrevocable life insurance trust and your policy has a cash value, your living trust should be the owner and the beneficiary of the policy. If you become disabled, this allows your trustee to "control" the policy so that the cash value can be accessed.

Why should my living trust be the beneficiary of my life insurance policies?

Although life insurance benefits pass directly to the named beneficiary outside of probate, the beneficiary on your policies should be your living trust so that the proceeds can pass to the trust to be distributed in accordance with your instructions. It may also be necessary to have the life insurance proceeds pass into your living trust in order to facilitate your federal estate tax planning.

If I make my living trust the beneficiary of my life insurance policy, will the proceeds be subject to creditor claims in the same way they would be if my estate were the beneficiary?

In virtually every state, the proceeds will not be subject to the claims of your creditors if you name your living trust as the beneficiary of your life insurance. To fully protect the proceeds from the claims of creditors, your living trust should contain a spendthrift clause.

Maintaining Your Revocable Living Trust

If I title all of my assets in the name of my living trust, how can I buy and sell assets and keep track of my income? Must I keep two sets of books?

There is no need for two sets of books. Your living trust is your alter ego. You continue to keep your books and records in precisely the same manner that you did prior to the trust's creation.

Is there a penalty when I take something out of my living trust?

You can put assets into your trust and take assets out of it without incurring a penalty or tax of any kind.

If my assets are titled in the name of my trust, do I need anyone else's permission to access them?

If you are your own trustee, you are not restrained in any way as to how you use, manage, invest, or handle your trust assets. Accordingly, you control the assets that are titled in the name of the trust in the same manner that you controlled them prior to putting them into trust.

How do I get assets out of my living trust?

You retitle the assets in your name through the same procedures that you used to place them into the trust. Real estate is redeeded, investment accounts are retitled, partnership interests are reassigned, and so on.

How do I sell my real estate after I place it in my trust?

As trustee, you are in complete control of the real estate in your trust. If you decide to sell it, you will have a deed prepared from you as trustee to the buyer and you will sign it as trustee.

Will the buyer's attorney want to know about my trust?

Yes. The buyer's attorney will want to know that your trust exists, that it owns the property being sold, and that the trustee has the authority to sell the real estate. Your affidavit of trust provides this information.

Do we have to change our living trust every time we want to add property to, or remove property from, our trust?

It is not necessary, or even advisable, to change your living trust every time you add or remove trust property. You need to change it only if your planning goals or your family situation has changed.

Do I need to see an attorney when I buy or sell trust assets?

You can buy, sell, or do anything else with your trust assets, just as you could when they were in your individual name, without the need to consult anyone. However, you may need the assistance of your attorney when buying or selling real estate, as discussed earlier.

Do I need an attorney every time I want to place a new asset in my trust?

Your attorney will generally get very involved in the initial funding of your trust. As you acquire new assets thereafter, however, you take title to them directly in the name of your trust. For example, if you acquire additional real property, you instruct the seller to prepare a deed which conveys title directly to your trust rather than to you personally.

If I put all of my assets into my trust, can I borrow against those assets to get a loan?

A properly written living trust will always allow you to pledge trust assets as collateral for your borrowings.

Can I avoid creditors or nursing home care costs with my revocable living trust?

As the trust maker, you retain the right to control, amend, and revoke the trust at any time. There is no protection from creditors or nursing home care costs.

What happens if I die, or become incapacitated, and some of my assets have not been transferred to my trust?

A properly prepared living trust–centered estate plan should always include a pour-over will and durable powers of attorney. A pour-over will leaves to your trust upon your death any assets that you neglected to place in it while you were alive. Durable special powers of attorney allow others to place assets into your trust should you be unable to do so because of a medical condition or for any other reason during your lifetime.

Maintaining Your Estate Plan

Where should I keep my estate planning documents?

The answer to this question depends upon how many sets of documents you receive from your attorney and in what form you receive them.

Generally, the trust maker receives two sets: a complete set of original documents in one or more binders (including a duplicate copy of the pour-over will), which can be kept in his or her home or office, and an unbound set of original documents (including the original pour-over will), which can be kept in a safe place such as a safe deposit box, home safe, or office vault.

The best place to keep your documents is someplace where they will be safe and where they can be easily located when they are needed by you, your family, or your authorized agents after you are disabled or deceased. Your attorney should also keep a copy in case your sets are lost or destroyed.

How often do I have to revise my estate plan?

As a general rule, it is a good idea to review your plan once every year or two and to have your estate planning attorney review it with you at least once every 5 years. It is also wise to update your estate plan in the event of a change in the law, in your family situation, or in your financial situation.

You should ask your estate planning attorney whether he or she will advise you of any changes in the law that may have an impact on your overall estate plan. However, trust law is one of the most stable areas of the law and generally does not change as frequently as other legal areas. Additionally, if your estate planning attorney takes careful measures in drafting your estate plan to ensure that it is flexible, minor changes in the tax laws will not require a modification of your estate planning documents.

From time to time, you may want to fine-tune your estate plan. This does not require abandoning your current plan, and it can usually be accomplished at a minimal cost. During your initial interview with your estate planning attorney and other advisors, you should discuss the procedures and estimated expenses that may be incurred in modifying your estate plan.

When should I review my estate plan?

You should review your existing estate plan:

- Upon any change in the federal estate and gift tax laws or state succession laws
- If any of the following events occur to you, your family, executors, trustees, or designated guardians:

  Marriage
  Divorce or separation
  Birth or death
  Disability or illness
  Incompetency
  Move to a new state
  Inheritance
  Change of wishes
  Business or work changes
  Retirement
  Formation, purchase, or sale of a business
  Significant change in net worth

- Whenever you desire to change names or amounts with respect to beneficiaries
- Whenever you wish to make changes in the appointments of your trustees or guardians

If I wish to change my distribution pattern, say, by reducing a gift to my niece, do I have to redo my entire trust?

You simply execute an amendment to your trust revoking the section or clause pertaining to your niece and replacing it with your new wishes.

You should not attempt to change your trust by yourself (e.g., by crossing out the old clause and writing in your new instruction). A written amendment prepared by an attorney is necessary to properly change the provision of any trust document.

It's quite possible that my wife and I may relocate within the next few years. Will we have to replan our entire estate with an attorney in our new home state?

The U.S. Constitution guarantees that full faith and credit must be given in any state to any living trust agreement which was valid in the state in which it was created and executed. Hence, if your trust was valid in the state in which you lived when it was signed, then it will continue to be valid should you relocate to another state. It will generally not need revision to carry out your wishes should you choose to relocate.

However, your new state's laws will be applied in interpreting your pour-over will, so you should have it reviewed by an attorney in that state.

Do my other estate planning documents, such as my powers of attorney, need to be reviewed if I move to a different state?

Having these documents reviewed by an attorney in your new domicile is a sound idea given the differences in state laws.

3

Advanced Estate Planning Strategies

This chapter can save many readers and their families a great deal of money. It presents complicated estate planning strategies in an understandable manner. By answering clearly and concisely the advanced planning questions that their clients repeatedly ask, our contributing authors have made it easy for you to grasp the complexities behind these cutting-edge planning techniques.

The material covered in this chapter is not esoteric. It emphasizes the practicality of advanced planning so that you can take affirmative steps to avoid the ravages of what many people believe is a confiscatory federal estate and gift tax system. This chapter will be of special interest to anyone who:

- Wants to pass property to grandchildren without incurring transfer taxes of up to 80 percent
- Has a high-net-worth estate and does not want to lose up to 55 percent of the property to egregious federal estate taxes before passing the remainder on to children
- Has a significant life insurance portfolio and wants to avoid losing 50 percent or more of the insurance proceeds to federal estate or gift tax
- Has a residence that has appreciated significantly over the

years and would like to leave it to children without having to sell it to pay federal estate tax

- Wishes to make significant gifts to family members without incurring federal gift taxes and to shift the appreciation in his or her estate to children and grandchildren

In this chapter, we discuss many planning strategies that include the use of irrevocable trusts. To help you better understand the questions and answers regarding each type of irrevocable trust, we begin with a discussion of general concepts that pertain to all irrevocable trusts.

Irrevocable Trusts

What is an irrevocable trust?

An *irrevocable trust* is a trust that cannot be changed or amended after it is signed. Irrevocable trusts are used to make gifts to others—the trust beneficiaries—"with strings attached."

When making gifts to children or grandchildren, parents and grandparents can either give funds directly to the beneficiary or place the funds in trust, accompanied by a set of written instructions. These instructions are the strings attached to the gift.

Gifts in trust enable the donor to control the use for which the gift is intended.

Why would anyone want to create an irrevocable trust?

Irrevocable trusts are created to make gifts with strings attached and to protect assets from federal estate and gift tax. They are used to support children, grandchildren, and other family members to whom the trustmaker feels a responsibility.

Why would I want to set up a trust in which I relinquish total control?

You don't really give up total control. You establish the ground rules in the trust document through your instructions, and you appoint the trustees to enforce those instructions.

What do I have to give up in order to get the tax benefits of an irrevocable trust?

To keep the trust's assets out of your taxable estate and keep the trust's income out of your taxable income, you have to give up the power to revoke or amend the trust, and you also have to give up the right to receive the income from the trust or to subsequently designate—outside of the trust's instructions—to whom or in what amounts trust income or principal is to be paid.

In addition, you can't keep the power to vote stock in a "controlled" corporation—a corporation in which you and related persons have 20 percent of the voting power—or the stock will be included in your estate.

What's the difference between an irrevocable trust and a revocable living trust?

The major difference is reflected in the name—you can't keep the power to "revoke" or change the terms of an irrevocable trust. If you could, the trust property would be treated for tax purposes in the same way as your revocable living trust property: it would be included in your taxable estate.

A revocable living trust is like a will in that it can be changed or amended, canceled, or revoked at any time without the requirement of a reason for doing so. An irrevocable trust is nothing more than a complete and absolute gift which is made with strings attached. You can place the contingencies, requests, and prohibitions you wish into your irrevocable trust terms, but you cannot retain the right to change or alter it after you execute it.

What are demand-right trusts?

To understand demand-right trusts, you must first understand the gift tax annual exclusion. The gift tax law allows you to exclude from the gift tax computation the first $10,000 you give in any year to any person, as long as that gift is a gift of a present interest. The tax law defines a *present interest* as the "unrestricted right to the use, possession, or enjoyment of property or the income from property."

For example, if you give one of your children $10,000, whether in cash or by transferring assets into the name of the child, so that you have no further control over the property, you've made a gift of a present interest, which qualifies for the annual exclusion. But suppose you give the cash or assets to a conventional irrevocable trust of which your child is the only beneficiary, which calls for the trustee to hold the trust assets during the child's lifetime and make payments from income or principal as needed for the child. In this case, you have not given a present interest—you have made a gift of a *future interest*—and the transfer to the trust will not qualify for the annual exclusion unless the transfer is accompanied by "demand rights."

A *demand right* in estate planning is normally a right given to beneficiaries of an irrevocable trust to demand up to $10,000 of the contribution made to the trust within a certain period of time (usually 30 to 45 days). This demand right qualifies the gift as a gift of a present interest for purposes of the annual exclusion. The shortest time that the tax court has approved for the demand right is 15 days.

Of course, your purpose in setting up your irrevocable trust will be undermined if your beneficiary—your child or grandchild—actually exercises his or her power to withdraw what you give to the trust. While the demand right must give your beneficiary the legal right to demand a withdrawal, in the usual family situation all that is required is to explain to the beneficiary that your overall estate plan, and the family's best interest, will be served by not exercising the demand right.

Can a demand right be given to a minor beneficiary?

The demand right can be given to a minor beneficiary through his or her guardian. In most states, a minor's parent is the natural guardian of the minor, and legal appointment of a guardian will not be required to make the demand right effective. If you have minor children and make gifts to an irrevocable trust on their behalf, your spouse as their natural guardian has the legal power to exercise or refuse to exercise the demand right on their behalf and qualify the demand right for tax purposes. But you need to make sure that your trust document properly provides for the giving of reasonable written notice to the minor's guardian and that your trustee carefully follows the prescribed procedure.

What's a Crummey Trust?

A *Crummey trust* is an irrevocable trust with demand rights in it. There is nothing crummy or shabby about a demand-right trust. The name "Crummey trust" comes from a tax court case which approved the use of a demand right to make a gift to a trust eligible for the trust maker's gift tax annual exclusion.

What happens if my lifetime beneficiary dies before I do?

If a lifetime beneficiary predeceases the trust maker, the beneficiary's share of contributions made to the trust before the beneficiary's death is held and distributed according to the trust maker's instructions.

Can creditors attack my irrevocable trust?

You may not create a trust and place your assets beyond the reach of your existing creditors to defraud them in the case of an existing obligation or requirement. If, however, you place assets in good faith into a trust in which you are not a beneficiary or potential beneficiary, and you are subsequently sued by a future creditor, such a creditor will generally be prohibited from accessing the trust or the gifts you made to it.

What is a spendthrift clause, and why would it be included in the trust provisions?

Every properly drawn trust document will have such a clause. It protects the beneficiaries from the claims of creditors and from their own attempts at improper actions with regard to the trust's income or principal.

What types of investments can the trust own?

The trust may own all types of assets. You can specify or list which assets it can own, refer to the state statute that lists those assets, or combine both in your trust instructions.

Does the IRS require that a gift tax return be filed when my trust is created?

You will be required to file a gift tax return if you transfer property to your irrevocable trust which results in the use of your exemption equivalent amount or creates a gift tax liability, if you are electing to gift-split with your spouse, or if you wish to allocate any of your generation-skipping transfer tax exemption to the gift.

What happens to my property after I place it in an irrevocable trust?

It is administered according to your instructions and, in their absence, by the discretion of the trustees you have named.

Can assets be removed from an irrevocable trust once they have been placed in it?

Once you have placed the assets in an irrevocable trust, you no longer have any control over them. Since you should not be the trustee of an irrevocable trust that you have established, you can have no authority to remove assets.

What if I place a term life insurance policy in an irrevocable trust?

If you place a term life insurance policy in an irrevocable life insurance trust or if the life insurance policy is placed there when purchased by the trust, you can, in effect, remove the policy by discontinuing the gifts to the trust. The trustee will not be able to pay the life insurance premiums, so the policy will lapse. However, if you use a whole life policy that has an automatic premium loan provision or if you have universal life insurance that has cash value, you may not be able to let it lapse until the cash value has been used up.

Why shouldn't I be a trustee of my irrevocable trust?

In order to keep the trust assets outside of your estate and avoid federal estate and gift tax on those assets, neither you nor your spouse should be a trustee of the trust.

How many trustees will I need for my irrevocable trust?

You may appoint as many trustees as you wish. The number of trustees you choose will be the number that your best judgment indicates you need. You should take into consideration the purposes for which you have created the trust and the assets that are to be managed by the trustees.

How is the fee for my trustees determined?

Most institutional trustees charge a percentage of the value of the assets in the trust as an annual fee for acting as trustee. The fees charged by corporate fiduciaries approximate 1 percent of the assets they manage, but this amount varies widely depending upon geographic location.

If my children cannot get along with the trustees in the future, can they change trustees?

You should consider including a provision in your trust document which authorizes your beneficiaries to terminate the services of a trustee and to appoint a successor or a different trustee when your beneficiaries so desire or according to standards that you set forth for trustee removal and replacement.

When I die, is my irrevocable trust a part of my estate for federal estate tax purposes?

Only the assets you own or have an interest in at your death are a part of your estate for federal estate tax purposes. When you transfer assets to your irrevocable trust, you no longer have title to those assets. Therefore, any assets owned by the trust will not be included in your probate estate.

Estate Freeze Strategies

IRREVOCABLE LIFE INSURANCE TRUSTS

What is an irrevocable life insurance trust?

An *irrevocable life insurance trust (ILIT)* is an irrevocable trust that is created to own and be the beneficiary of life insurance policies on the trust maker's life.

Why would I want my irrevocable trust to own life insurance?

If you own life insurance, it is included in your taxable estate and the proceeds will be taxable for federal estate tax purposes. (This comes as a surprise to most people but has been the case almost since the inception of the federal estate tax.) If it is owned by an ILIT, however, the proceeds will be free of federal estate tax.

What if I don't own my insurance but control it through someone else?

Your life insurance will be included in your taxable estate as long as you possess any *incidents of ownership* for federal estate tax purposes. Incidents of ownership include your rights to borrow on a policy or pledge it as collateral, name or change the beneficiary, and assign the policy to someone else.

If you maintain any right to a life insurance policy, the IRS will take the position that you retained incidents of ownership and will include the proceeds in your taxable estate.

What is the theory behind an ILIT?

Because the trust is irrevocable, you do not have incidents of ownership in it or in the life insurance policies owned by it. Thus the proceeds of those policies will not be taxed upon your death nor will they be taxed upon the death of your spouse if he or she survives you. They completely avoid the federal estate tax.

You are able to control the disposition of the policy proceeds through your trust instructions as to:

- Who the trustees will be while you are alive, upon your disability, and upon your death
- How the proceeds will be distributed to your beneficiaries or left in trust

Can I provide that my spouse be cared for in my ILIT's terms and still avoid estate tax on his or her subsequent death?

You can provide for your spouse precisely as spouses are provided for in the family subtrust of your living trust. There are a number of alternatives that are possible. For example:

- I want my trustee to pay my spouse all of the trust income and whatever he or she needs from the principal in the trustee's discretion.
- I want my trustee to provide for the needs of my spouse.
- I want my trustee to provide for the needs of my spouse and children.
- I want my trustee to provide for the needs of my spouse, children, and grandchildren.

- I want my trustee to provide for the needs of my spouse, children, grandchildren, my parents, and my spouse's parents.

Can my spouse and I sign a joint ILIT as well as separate ones?

Joint ILITs are used when both spouses wish to be insured on a last-to-die basis. Individual ILITs are used when one or the other spouse has life insurance on his or her life.

What are an ILIT's components?

There are three components in an irrevocable life insurance trust, similar to those found in a living trust:

- Trust makers, who control their ILITs through their instructions
- Trustees and their successor trustees, named by the trust makers
- Beneficiaries and contingent beneficiaries, named by the trust makers

Who buys the life insurance on my life or my spouse's and my lives?

The life insurance is purchased by the ILIT's trustees.

Can I or my spouse be a trustee?

A third-party, independent trustee should be named in order to keep the proceeds out of your estate.

Can I terminate the trustees?

You can provide instructions in your trust document as to how trustees are to be hired and fired. You cannot directly retain the hiring and firing rights without possessing incidents of ownership in the trust policies, which would place them right back in your or your spouse's taxable estate.

Who should be trustee of my ILIT while I am alive?

Trust specialists uniformly agree that ILIT trustees should be professionals. Corporate fiduciaries and CPAs make excellent ILIT trustees.

Who should be the trustees of my ILIT if I become disabled?

Your CPA or corporate trustee should be augmented with the same persons that you have named for this purpose in your living trust.

Who should the trustees of my ILIT be after my and my spouse's deaths?

Your initial trustee should be augmented or replaced by the same persons whom you named for this purpose in your living trust.

Do gifts to my ILIT qualify for the annual exclusion for federal gift tax purposes?

Gifts to a trust do not qualify for the annual exclusion. However, they can be made to qualify if your attorney drafts *demand-right* language into your ILIT.

What happens if my beneficiaries do not demand their pro rata share of the gifts to the trust?

The trustees apply for insurance policies and pay the premiums after they are issued.

How do my beneficiaries even know that I am making gifts to an ILIT?

You give them formal notice in a *demand-notice letter* that you have made a gift to the trust and that they have a certain amount of time to demand their shares of the gift. If they do not make such a demand within that time period, their right to demand automatically lapses and the trustee is free to make the premium payments.

What is the maximum amount I can contribute each year to an ILIT which names my three children as the only beneficiaries without having to pay gift tax?

You can contribute up to $30,000 from your annual exclusion

and up to $600,000 from your lifetime unified credit exemption equivalent if it is available. When joined by your spouse, you can double these limits.

Should I use my exemption equivalent for life insurance premiums in excess of my annual exclusion, or should I use it for other purposes?

The answer depends on your other circumstances; however, using your exemption equivalent amount to purchase life insurance is generally a wise decision, since the death proceeds are usually far greater than the premiums. This is especially true if you do not live a long life.

When life insurance premiums are paid from a person's exemption equivalent, professionals refer to the transaction as a *leveraging of the client's credit* because the life insurance proceeds are far greater than the premium amount against which the exemption equivalent amount is applied.

My lawyer told me that even though I can qualify gifts to my ILIT for the annual exclusion, there are other laws that prohibit me from giving more than $5000 a year to it. Is this true?

This is technically a true statement, but a planning falsehood. If your trust creates separate shares for your beneficiaries, rather than lumping them together in a single trust share, you can avail yourself of the full amount of the annual exclusions.

Can I name grandchildren as contingent beneficiaries of my trust in order to multiply my available annual exclusions?

As a result of recent case law, this is permissible.

Who owns the life insurance policies?

An ILIT, through its trustees, is both owner and beneficiary of life insurance policies it owns on the trust maker's life. Since you are not the owner and have been careful not to retain any incidents of ownership in the policies, the proceeds will flow into the trust after your death totally free of federal estate tax and will remain estate tax–free upon the subsequent death of your spouse.

What happens if I don't have a spouse, or my spouse predeceases me?

The proceeds will be paid to your ILIT free of federal estate tax.

Can my ILIT pay my estate taxes directly to the government?

By law, your ILIT cannot pay the estate tax directly, but it can buy assets from or make loans to your living trust so that its trustees will have the necessary liquidity to pay the taxes.

How can I be sure that my trustees will coordinate the insurance proceeds between the respective trusts?

Properly drawn ILITs provide that, following their makers' deaths, their trustees will be the same as the trustees of the makers' living trusts. Having the same people or institutions serving in both fiduciary capacities makes good planning sense and eliminates communication and coordination oversights.

Who is responsible for collecting my life insurance proceeds?

Your ILIT trustees have this responsibility for policies owned by your ILIT.

What can my ILIT trustees do with the proceeds?

By following your exact instructions in the trust, they can invest and distribute them for the benefit of your trust beneficiaries, or, as just discussed, they can make some or all of the proceeds available to cover the taxes and expenses of your estate.

Are ILITs only for rich people?

ILITs are an enormously useful planning tool for anyone who has, or will have, an estate over $600,000 and would like to keep the proceeds of his or her life insurance portfolio free of federal estate tax.

Does an ILIT protect my insurance proceeds from creditors?

Life insurance owned and made payable to a properly drafted

ILIT is free from the trust maker's creditors, the creditors of his or her estate, and the creditors of the trust beneficiaries.

Does my life insurance go through probate if it is made payable to my ILIT?

Life insurance made payable to an ILIT does not go through the probate process.

Are there disadvantages to using an ILIT?

While ILITs are a safe and attractive way of transferring assets and providing liquidity, their main disadvantage is their irrevocability. If circumstances change beyond what you envisioned in your trust instructions, the results could be less than you expected, since you are incapable of changing the terms.

Isn't there any way around this "changing-circumstance" problem?

Many practitioners invoke the equitable doctrine of *trust reformation,* which provides that a court can reform or change an irrevocable document if the change is consistent with the intent of the trust maker at the time the document was created. It is not difficult for judges to invoke this doctrine on the request of an ILIT's counsel when the circumstances are compelling and when no one will be hurt by the reformation.

Is naming a family limited partnership as the owner and beneficiary of life insurance policies a good alternative to using an ILIT?

In some situations, a family limited partnership (FLP) is more advantageous than an ILIT, while in others it is less advantageous. Each planning situation is unique, so you should consult your attorney about which is better for your circumstances.

What advantages does an FLP have over an ILIT when it comes to owning insurance?

The FLP is flexible and, unlike the ILIT, can be amended to meet changing needs and family conditions. The insured can retain control of the policy if he or she also controls the FLP as general partner.

Since the FLP is run by the members of the family, there is no need to seek out and appoint outside trustees. And since the contributions to an FLP qualify as present-interest gifts, the annual exclusion is always available.

Money to pay for the policy premiums can be contributed to the FLP by either the general or the limited partners, or if there are sufficient earnings in the FLP, the partnership can pay for the premiums out of current earnings and avoid any "withdrawal-rights" issues. At the death of the insured, the FLP receives the proceeds from the insurance policy income tax–free and can apply them in the same manner as they would be applied within an ILIT.

Couldn't I solve the estate tax problems with regard to my life insurance by simply having my spouse as owner and beneficiary of my policy?

If your spouse survives you, the policy proceeds will be in his or her estate, so you will not have accomplished your goal of keeping them tax-free. If your spouse predeceases you, either they will be back in your estate or the ownership will pass to others without your control.

Why can't I just have my children own the life insurance on my life?

If you hope to use life insurance to provide the liquidity to pay estate taxes, you are strongly advised to hold the policy in an irrevocable life insurance trust. The irrevocable trust offers flexibility and safety over outright ownership of the policy by children in a number of ways:

- Minor children cannot own a policy.
- Adult children do not always act in a coordinated, timely, and responsible manner when called on to pay premiums to keep the policy in force.
- Even when adult children are responsible, a misfortune such as a lawsuit, bankruptcy, divorce, or death may put the policy at risk.
- Assuming the policy is kept in force by the children until the

death of the insured parent, there is no assurance that all of the children will act in concert to use the proceeds to provide the liquidity needed for paying the taxes on your or your spouse's estate.

- Outright ownership of a policy by the children precludes the use of generation-skipping transfers and thus may unnecessarily subject unexpended proceeds to estate tax in the estates of the children.

Can I place an existing policy on my life in an irrevocable life insurance trust, or do I have to purchase a new policy?

There are two disadvantages to using an existing life insurance policy in your newly established ILIT. First, the Internal Revenue Code specifies that if you die within 3 years of the transfer, the value of the policy will be included in your gross estate for estate tax purposes. Second, there could be a gift tax on the cash value (interpolated terminal reserve value) of the policy when you transfer it into the ILIT.

For these reasons, it is preferable to have your ILIT purchase a new policy if at all possible. This procedure will eliminate the problem of the 3-year rule and will also prevent the possibility of your incurring a gift tax.

Can my spouse and I use one trust for all of our life insurance policies?

You can if neither of you is a beneficiary of the trust. If you want your spouse to benefit from a policy on your life or if you want to benefit from a policy on your spouse's life, the life insurance policies on one or the other of your lives must be owned by your respective individual ILITs.

Can my trustee purchase term insurance for my ILIT?

Your trustee is free to purchase term, whole life, variable life, universal life, or any other form of life insurance for your ILIT. There are reasons for the purchase of each, and your trustee should coordinate the necessary decisions with the trust's insurance advisor and attorney.

Our attorney has advised us to establish a joint irrevocable life insurance trust funded with a "second-to-die" insurance policy. We like the idea but want to know the cost of the insurance before we set up the trust. What can we do?

Keep in mind that the purpose of an ILIT is generally to pay the estate tax that arises on the death of the surviving spouse or to provide replacement funds for the beneficiaries after taxes are paid. A last-to-die policy is a perfectly designed product for these situations.

Second-to-die life insurance is also far less costly than life insurance that is purchased on the life of any one spouse or policies purchased separately on both spouses' lives.

Can I have any contact with the life insurance company and still keep my life insurance estate tax–free?

As the trust maker, you sign the life insurance application only as the potential insured to authorize release of medical records and attest to the accuracy of medical information you give in the application. As the trust maker/insured, you have no incidents of ownership. The ILIT trustee has the incidents of ownership. Accordingly, if you die within 3 years of the date of the insurance policy, the insurance proceeds will be excluded from your estate for estate tax purposes.

Why should I go to the time and expense of establishing an ILIT, only to find out that I am uninsurable?

Most people are justifiably reluctant to go to the time and expense of establishing an ILIT until they know whether they are insurable and at what cost. For this reason, they frequently sign insurance applications before their trusts are drafted and signed. This exposes the insurance proceeds to taxation if the insureds die within 3 years.

To avoid this dilemma, you can have someone else sign the insurance application as the proposed owner. Adult children, close relatives, or a business partner all have a potential insurable interest in the trust maker and could sign the application.

Once the insurance underwriting is completed, and you complete and sign your ILIT, the policy can be transferred to the ILIT trustee without concern for the 3-year rule by the friendly accommodating party.

Can I borrow from the policy to reduce the value of the gift for gift tax purposes?

You cannot directly borrow from a policy that is not owned by you. However, if access to the cash value is important to you, you can have your life insurance advisor and attorney split the policy's cash value from its death value and keep the cash value out of your ILIT through a split-dollar agreement.

What is a split-dollar agreement?

It is an agreement that separates the ownership of a life insurance policy's death benefit from the ownership of the side fund, or cash value. With this agreement, one party can own the cash value and another can own the death benefit.

Must my ILIT file a federal income tax return?

Unlike a revocable living trust, an ILIT is a separate entity for tax purposes. For this reason, the ILIT trustee should file for a federal taxpayer identification number for the ILIT by using IRS Form SS-4.

An ILIT must file federal income tax returns if its gross income exceeds $600 in any year. This should not present a problem to most ILITs because the cash value, or inside buildup in the policy, is not taxable income until it is withdrawn in excess of the policy payments.

On the basis of your experience, do you have any particular cautions concerning ILITs?

Do not write the checks for life insurance premiums to the insurance company; if you do, you may defeat your planning. Write your checks to your ILIT; then let the trustee deposit the money in the trust checking account and write the check on the trust's account to the life insurance company.

Care should be taken to make certain that the bank account owned by the ILIT trustee is exclusively used for the purpose of depositing the gifts from the trust makers and paying the insurance premiums.

Can international trusts be used to hold my life insurance?

The law does not require that ILITs be domestic trusts. As long as a foreign trust meets all of the necessary requirements of a domestic ILIT, the same tax result will occur.

Are international trusts more favorable than domestic ILITs?

International insurance trusts may be more favorable under some circumstances due to certain exceptions under the Internal Revenue Code. Although the policy proceeds are income tax–free, any buildup of assets within the domestic insurance trust after the life insurance policy proceeds are received will be subject to income tax if the trust income is not distributed to the beneficiaries annually.

What are the benefits of using international variable insurance products for estate planning?

There is a growing desire among many affluent individuals to be able to control the investments within their policies rather than have the insurance companies invest their money. Internationally, most insurance companies allow the policyholder substantially greater input in the determination of how the funds are invested. Because of this added flexibility, some investors elect to purchase their life insurance offshore.

How do I find and choose an international insurance company?

Most international insurance companies do not market their services within the United States. This is not only because of the regulatory issues faced by U.S. carriers but because international insurance companies would lose substantial tax benefits if they operated within the United States.

Because foreign insurance companies are adamant about not soliciting U.S. business, it is usually necessary for prospective policyholders to travel internationally to establish their offshore portfolios. Although this may be inconvenient, the benefits of using international insurance products are often substantial.

QUALIFIED PERSONAL RESIDENCE TRUSTS

What is a qualified personal residence trust?

A *qualified personal residence trust (QPRT)* is an irrevocable trust in which the grantor or donor—usually parents—gives a personal residence to family members—usually children—while retaining the right to live in the home for a period of years (the personal-use period, or initial term of the trust).

What is the purpose of a qualified personal residence trust?

By placing your residence in a QPRT, you can reduce its value for federal gift tax purposes and eliminate its value from your estate for federal estate tax purposes while still retaining the right to enjoy and live in the home.

What residences qualify for a QPRT?

A personal residence of the grantor is either:

- The principal residence of the grantor
- Another residence considered to be used for personal purposes (e.g., a vacation home)
- An undivided fractional interest in either of the above

To qualify for a QPRT, the residence must be occupied as a residence by the grantor. Recent letter rulings by the IRS permitted residences with appurtenant structures such as small guest houses or coach houses to also qualify.

Can we transfer our house on our working farm to a QPRT?

You can establish a QPRT for your house but only if you can separate the house from the farm. This will require a survey and title work.

If my house has a mortgage on it, can I transfer my house to a QPRT?

Yes, but if you keep paying the mortgage, the IRS may take the position that you are making a taxable gift to the QPRT every time you make a mortgage payment. It would be preferable to pay off the mortgage before you transfer the property to the QPRT.

Do I have to have an appraisal?

Yes. Otherwise, the IRS may scrutinize the transaction and later successfully dispute the value used. It is important to retain an appraiser who has good credentials.

Does the gift to my children qualify for the annual exclusion?

A gift to a QPRT is a gift of a future interest, so it does not qualify for the annual gift tax exclusion.

Can we use our $600,000 exemption equivalent?

The gift to the QPRT can be applied against your $600,000 exemption equivalent. You will not have to pay any gift tax unless you have exhausted your exemption equivalent in making prior gifts or the value of the gift to the QPRT exceeds your remaining exemption equivalent amount.

Does the initial term of the trust affect the value of my gift?

The longer the initial term of the QPRT, the less the value of the remainder interest passing to the beneficiaries; consequently, the gift amount and the gift tax will be lower.

How is the value of the gift calculated?

The value of the gift for gift tax purposes is determined by referring to the U.S. Treasury Department valuation tables.

Can you give me an example of how a QPRT saves federal estate or gift tax?

A father, age 65, has a home with a fair market value of $500,000. He transfers the home to a QPRT and retains the right to live in the home for 10 years, with the remainder interest going to his children. Assuming an 8 percent applicable federal interest rate, the present gift value of the remainder interest to the children is $170,600. At the end of the trust's initial term, the value of the residence is $1 million.

By means of the QPRT, the father reduced the size of his estate by $1 million, used the home for 10 additional years, and utilized only $170,600 of his exemption equivalent amount by transferring ownership to his children.

Can you provide another example?

Let us assume the following facts:

- A 72-year-old father owns a home worth $500,000 and believes he will live more than 10 years.
- He has an estate in excess of $3.5 million, which places it in the 55 percent federal marginal tax bracket.
- He expects that his residence will increase in value at approximately 4 percent per year and that it will be worth $700,000 at the time of his death, sometime after 10 years.

The value of the gift at the time of the creation of the trust is $139,660 ($500,000 less his 10-year use valued at $360,340 using an applicable federal rate, or AFR, of 7.6 percent). Thus the federal estate tax savings for having used the QPRT amount to $308,187 (55 percent of the difference between $700,000 and $139,660).

The gift of $139,660 does not qualify as a gift of a present interest and must be reported as a taxable gift. If the donor has not used his $600,000 equivalent unified credit exemption, the value of the gift would reduce the exemption and no gift tax would be payable.

Will an outright gift of my residence accomplish almost the same tax consequences?

If you give your home directly to your children, two things will happen immediately:

- You will lose the legal right to continue to live in your home.
- The house will be valued at full fair market value for gift tax purposes rather than at the discounted rate permitted to the QPRT.

What happens if the donor dies before the initial term is completed?

The fair market value of the home is *included* in the donor's estate as if the trust never existed.

To protect against this risk, the grantor may purchase life insurance in an amount equal to the projected taxes on the residence.

What happens if the donor dies after the initial term is completed?

If the donor survives the personal-use period, the full value of the home is *excluded* from the donor's estate.

What is the amount of the discount the donor receives?

The discount available depends upon the actuarial life expectancy of the donor, the prevailing official IRS interest rate—based on 120 percent of the applicable federal midterm rate—and the term of the QPRT.

Who should be the trustee of a QPRT?

During the initial term, the grantor may be the sole trustee of the QPRT, with complete control over the trust and the residence. If desired, the grantor may also designate a cotrustee to serve.

After the initial term, the grantor cannot be a trustee of the QPRT. However, the grantor may designate in the trust agreement a chain of trustees to serve in the event of his or her disability during the initial term and during his or her lifetime after the initial term.

Is appreciation in the value of the residence still subject to federal estate tax?

All appreciation in the value of the residence after the time the QPRT is established is removed from the grantor's estate provided the grantor survives the initial term. Transferring a residence to a QPRT freezes the value of the residence at its value at the time of the transfer.

Who's entitled to the income tax deduction for the property taxes?

Because the QPRT is a "grantor trust" under the Internal Revenue Code during the initial term, the grantor is treated as the owner of the property for federal income tax purposes. If the grantor pays the real estate taxes on the residence, the grantor is entitled to the income tax deduction for such taxes.

Who pays expenses of the house during the trust's initial term?

During the initial term of the trust, the grantor typically pays the normal and customary expenses of repair and running the house.

Can the residence be sold during the initial term of the QPRT?

Yes. You can create the trust so that it will dissolve upon the sale of the trust property and the proceeds will be distributed to you. Or you can specify that your trustee acquire another residence for you, of your choice, with any excess proceeds from the sale of your original property to be placed in a special investment account which will pay income to you until the end of the initial term. At the end of the initial term, both your new residence and the capital in the investment account will become the property of your beneficiary.

The trust may also prohibit the sale of the residence during the initial term without the consent of the grantor.

Is the grantor entitled to the deferral of $125,000 on sale?

If the residence is sold, the grantor is entitled to the deferral of gain on sale if the residence is replaced with a new residence. If the grantor is age 55 or older, he or she is also entitled to the one-time exclusion of $125,000 of gain on the sale of a principal residence.

Can a QPRT residence be rented?

A residence in the trust cannot be rented full-time. The grantor must use the house more than 10 percent of the amount of days rented or a minimum of 2 weeks per year, whichever period is longer.

When do the trust beneficiaries get the use of the residence?

The beneficiaries, usually family members, have the right to possess the home only after the retained personal-use period of the donors has expired.

What if my spouse and I want to live in our residence after the initial term has expired?

If you want to continue to live in the house after the initial term has expired, you will need to pay the remainder beneficiaries—usually the children—a fair market value rent.

Will my heirs lose the step-up in basis on my home if it is in a qualified personal residence trust?

Yes. Your heirs assume your original basis in your home. They will pay tax on the appreciation of your home in excess of your original basis at the capital gain rate when and if they sell the property.

If the property is not in a QPRT and is still includable in your estate, your heirs will pay the estate tax of between 37 and 55 percent on the value of the property at your date of death and the tax will be due 9 months later. They will, however, receive a step-up in basis.

Can you summarize the benefits and drawbacks of a QPRT?

A QPRT provides a number of tax benefits to its maker:

- The donor can transfer the ownership of the personal residence to his or her beneficiary in the future without paying taxes on the appreciation on the personal residence.
- The residence is transferred today at a discounted value from its appraised value for gift tax purposes.
- The donor is allowed to live in the house.
- The value of the house is removed from the donor's taxable estate.

There are two potential disadvantages to using qualified personal residence trusts:

- The grantor must survive the personal-use period, or the value of the home will be included in his or her estate.
- The beneficiaries do not receive a step-up in basis on the gift of the home and thus may pay a higher income tax when the home is sold.

SELF-CANCELING INSTALLMENT NOTES

What is a self-canceling installment note?

A *self-canceling installment note* is a promissory note given by a buyer to a seller that calls for installment payments of principal and interest over a set period of time. It also provides that if the seller dies before all of the payments under the note have been made, the remaining payments will be canceled and the buyer will owe nothing further.

How is a self-canceling installment note different from a regular note?

The unpaid balance owing to the seller at the time of the seller's death is not included in the seller's taxable estate. Thus, if a parent sells her business to her children in exchange for a self-canceling installment note, and dies soon after the sale is completed, the parent's taxable estate will not include either the value of the business or the remaining balance owed by the children at the time of the parent's death.

What is the main disadvantage of a self-canceling installment note?

Such a note must include an extra premium to compensate the seller for the possibility that the seller will die before all payments are received. The installment payments are therefore greater than those under a note having the same terms but without the self-canceling feature.

How is the risk premium determined?

The risk premium may be either an increase in the principal amount of the note over the business's fair market value or an increase in the interest rate to be paid by the buyer on the unpaid principal.

What if no risk premium is included?

If no risk premium is added to the note, the IRS will consider that a gift has been made by the seller to the buyer.

Are self-canceling installment notes frequently used?

Because of the perceived cost of the risk premium, use of self-canceling installment notes has not caught on as a viable tax planning strategy. However, it is a technique that should be considered in a variety of situations.

PRIVATE ANNUITIES

What is a private annuity?

A *private annuity* is an agreement under which an owner transfers an asset to a buyer—the obligor—in exchange for the buyer's promise to make fixed periodic payments to the seller—the annuitant—for the rest of the seller's life.

Why are private annuities used?

By using a private annuity, the annuitant is able to remove the asset in its entirety from his or her estate while retaining a fixed income stream for the rest of his or her life.

How is the amount of the annuity payment determined?

The amount of the annuity payment the buyer must pay to the seller is determined by the fair market value of the asset and the life expectancy of the seller. Specifically, the payment is calculated on the basis of two variables:

- The number of years the annuitant is expected to live, according to the IRS tables
- The interest rate that must be charged, which is equal to 120 percent of the federal midterm rate in effect for the month in which the annuity is being valued

How are a private annuity and a self-canceling installment note alike?

Like a self-canceling installment note, a private annuity removes the asset from the seller's/annuitant's taxable estate while providing a stream of income to the seller. And as with the note, when the seller dies, the buyer's obligation to make payments ends.

How does a private annuity differ from a self-canceling installment note?

Unlike a self-canceling installment note, a private annuity carries no upper limit to the amount a buyer may have to pay to fulfill his or her obligations. That is, if the seller/annuitant lives significantly beyond his or her life expectancy, the buyer will have to continue making installment payments until the seller's death.

There is also no limitation on the ability of a buyer to resell the purchased asset soon after acquiring it from the seller. In intrafamily transactions, the deferral of capital gain otherwise available in installment sales (including self-canceling installment sales) will be lost if the asset is sold by the buyer within 2 years of the date of the transaction. No such acceleration of gain occurs if the buyer in a private annuity transaction resells the acquired asset.

A private annuity must be unsecured, whereas a self-canceling note may be secured by collateral.

If I am diagnosed with a terminal illness, can I enter into a private annuity to avoid federal estate tax?

No. The IRS will disallow any annuity created when the annuitant is or was terminally ill.

How does the IRS define terminally ill?

The IRS says that a person is "terminally ill" if the individual is known to have an incurable illness or other deteriorating physical condition and there is at least a 50 percent probability that the individual will die within 1 year. If the individual actually survives for 18 months or longer after that date, then the individual is presumed not to have been terminally ill unless the contrary is established by clear and convincing evidence.

If you are very ill, you should obtain a letter from your physician stating that, in his or her opinion, death is clearly not imminent and that there is every statistical certainty that you will survive for more than 18 months.

What if I die within a year?

The IRS will ignore its actuarial tables and assess death tax against your estate.

What is the disadvantage of a private annuity?

A private-annuity obligation is extinguished on the death of the annuitant. If, however, the annuitant turns out to have the longevity of Methuselah, the private annuity will backfire and the cost to the family-member buyer will be far more than the savings in federal estate tax.

FAMILY LIMITED PARTNERSHIPS

What is a family limited partnership?

A *family limited partnership (FLP)* is a legal entity formed under your state's limited liability partnership law between you and some of your family members.

Does an FLP work just like a standard limited partnership?

An FLP works like any other limited partnership under your state's statutes. The FLP has two kinds of partners: general partners and limited partners.

The *general partners* have 100 percent control over and responsibility for the management of the partnership and its assets, and they are 100 percent liable for the acts or omissions to act of the partnership and all the other general partners. They decide when assets are bought and sold and the timing and amount of the partnership's income and capital distributions.

The *limited partners* have no control over either the assets or the income of the partnership. They also have no authority over the general partners. They cannot fire the general partners or replace them. Their legal authority and roles are narrowly defined by all states' statutes. Limited partners are not liable for the acts of the general partners and are not liable for claims against the partnership or for partnership debts. They are liable, or at risk, only up to the amount of their partnership investment or interest.

Who are the general partners of an FLP?

The general partners almost always are parents or grandparents or corporations, limited liability companies, or management trusts controlled by those individuals.

Why would anyone want to create a corporation, limited liability company, or management trust to be an FLP general partner?

By law, a limited partnership dissolves upon the death or disability of its general partner. These entities are used to provide continuity within the partnership if such an event occurs. They are also used to create an additional layer of protection from the claims of aggressive judgment creditors.

Using a corporation as a general partner also provides income tax planning options. The corporation may charge fees and receive income for management of and duties performed for the FLP. This shifts some of the income from the limited partnership to the corporate general partner. The corporation can then use the income to pay salaries or set up retirement and other tax-advantaged plans such as welfare benefit trusts, defined-benefit plans, and medical reimbursement plans. As a result, the family is able to shift income from higher to lower income tax brackets and at the same time set up retirement pension plans for family members who are employees of the corporate general partner.

Who are the limited partners?

The limited partners are often children and grandchildren of the general partners, irrevocable trusts created by the senior family members for the benefit of junior family members, or revocable living trusts created by senior family members as part of their own estate planning.

What are the advantages of an FLP?

An FLP effectively allows its creators to:

- Make gifts of limited partnership units at significantly discounted values to children and grandchildren, thereby removing the assets from their taxable estates, while retaining control over those assets as the partnership's general partners.
- Segregate income and equity interests in the underlying asset (whether it be an operating business, income-producing real estate, stock portfolio, or life insurance policy) from the managerial control over those assets.
- Thwart the claims of creditors.

Why is an FLP an effective planning tool for saving federal estate and gift tax?

The interests of the FLP's limited partners are discounted for purposes of current gift and estate taxation.

Why do the limited partners' interests receive discounts for federal gift and estate tax?

Limited partners have few, if any, rights. They do not manage, vote, or control anything; they are passive investors.

A buyer of those interests would be aware of the lack of marketability and control reflected in a minority position and would not pay an amount directly proportionate to the partnership interest. Any thinking buyer would demand a substantial discount through his or her purchase offer regardless of the success of the partnership.

What discounts can we generally expect to receive from an FLP?

FLP discounts for gifts of limited partnership interests usually range from 20 to 60 percent and average between 35 and 40 percent.

Suppose $15 million of securities and real estate is transferred to an FLP in exchange for a 1 percent general partnership interest and a 99 percent limited partnership interest An average discount of 40 percent would generate an immediate $6 million reduction in value. At an estate tax rate of 55 percent, this would produce estate tax savings of $3.3 million.

Who appraises the partnership interests for purposes of the discount?

Before a partnership interest can be appraised and valued, a qualified appraiser must appraise the value of the partnership assets. Once that is completed, a second qualified appraiser generally appraises the value of the limited partnership interest in terms of its lack of marketability and control.

Can the two appraisals be completed by the same individual or company?

The person who appraises the value of the partnership assets will be a specialist in the valuation of those particular assets (e.g., a commercial real estate professional specializing in appraising rural office buildings will be used if such buildings are part of the FLP's holdings or business). On the other hand, a person specializing in business valuation will be used to establish the discounted value of the limited partners' interests.

How do qualified appraisers value the gifts of limited partnership interests?

The Internal Revenue Code says that a gift will be taxed on the basis of its fair market value on the date of its transfer and that "fair market value" is what a knowledgeable buyer and a knowledgeable seller would exchange for the asset.

Does the total amount of the discounts escape taxation?

The amount of the net gift—the gross gift less the discounts—may or may not be gift tax–free. The answer depends upon whether or not the annual exclusions of the grantors are being used and whether or not the grantors have any exemption equivalent left.

How do I know whether FLP discounts work?

For a great many years, the national case law has been overwhelmingly in favor of allowing discounts.

How can an FLP separate income and equity interests in the partnership assets from the managerial control over those assets?

Limited partnership statutes in all fifty states specify that this must be the case. These statutes not only allow parents and grandparents to give away massive amounts of equity but also allow them to continue to manage that equity.

How can an FLP be an effective device for thwarting the claims of creditors?

If you or your children have debts that result in judgments against you or them, the judgment creditors' remedies against your respective interests in the FLP are significantly restricted by law. The only way a judgment creditor can execute against your FLP interests is through a *charging order,* which allows the creditor to receive the distributions in lieu of the partner's receiving them. Because the FLP is controlled by its general partners, the general partners can decide to eliminate income distributions to partners if a charging order has been issued.

Who pays the income tax on partnership income attributable to the debtor partner?

Since the creditor stands in the shoes of the partner as a result of the judgment, the creditor will be charged with all income tax attributable to that partner's interest. This is true even if there are no distributions of income! As a result, the creditor will not receive satisfaction of the judgment but will be charged with phantom income upon which he or she must pay federal income tax.

Put yourself in the place of the judgment creditor: You have a judgment against a partner, but you cannot seize the partner's interest. As you wait for distributions to be made that you can seize, you are required to pay income tax on the share of the partnership income upon which you have a charging order. In effect, you have won a Pyrrhic victory and suffered an additional business loss. You have not recovered assets or income, but you are generating an expense. Would you be willing to settle such a judgment for less than full value?

Can an FLP hold life insurance on the life of the general-partner parents or grandparents?

An FLP offers a meaningful alternative to the irrevocable life insurance trust and may in many instances be superior to it.

If the partnership is the owner of life insurance on the life of a general partner and most of the FLP's ownership interests are in the hands of the children and/or grandchildren, the life insurance proceeds attributable to their limited partnership interests will not be taxed in the estate of the general-partner parents or grandparents.

How can an FLP be superior to an irrevocable life insurance trust?

An ILIT is irrevocable, and the maker or his or her spouse cannot be a trustee. An FLP can be changed at will by the general partner pursuant to the terms of the partnership agreement and the state statutes under which it was created. By law, the FLP must be managed by the general partners—the parents or grandparents—for the benefit of all of the partners.

How do parents (or grandparents) create an FLP and transfer their interests to their children and grandchildren?

Parents, with the help of a qualified attorney, set up a limited partnership with themselves or controlled entities such as trusts, corporations, or limited liability companies as the general partners. Typically, each general partner owns a 1 percent general-partner interest and a 49 percent limited-partner interest. They fund the FLP with such assets as investment real estate (other than their primary residence), stocks, bonds, cash, and other business or investment property.

After the partnership is formed, the parents typically give limited partnership interests to their children and grandchildren, or to irrevocable trusts created for them, by using either their $10,000 annual exclusions or all or part of their $600,000 exemptions. They also hire appraisers to calculate the discounted value of those interests to children and grandchildren.

Can gifts be made in more than one year?

Gifts of limited partnership interests can be made as often and in whatever amounts the grantors wish. They can be made in a single year or over a number of years.

Are the costs of preparing a family limited partnership deductible?

There are some deductions that may be taken:

- Expenses for the collection or production of income or for the management, conservation, or maintenance of property held for the production of income and tax planning under Internal Revenue Code Section 212 are deductible subject to a minimum requirement of 2 percent of adjusted gross income.
- A partnership's organization expenses may be amortized over not less than 60 months.
- In addition, a corporation, which is typically the general partner in the limited partnership arena, may elect to amortize organization costs over 60 months.

Do we pay tax when we fund our FLP?

No gain or loss is generally recognized to the partnership or the partners on the transfer of their property to the partnership in exchange for a partnership interest. Be careful, however, if you transfer property subject to a mortgage. If the mortgage is greater than your tax basis of the asset, the excess will be taxed.

Does my FLP have to have its own federal identification number for income tax purposes?

Although the partnership itself does not pay federal income tax, it does need a federal tax identification number and a partnership return must be filed.

Who pays the income tax on the partnership's gains?

The partnership is a pass-through entity for income tax purposes. All income, deductions, gains, and losses are passed through to the partners, who pay taxes individually in proportion to their percentage interests.

This arrangement can lower the income tax liability of general partners. If parents place income-producing assets into the limited partnership, their tax liability is only their pro rata share of the profits rather than all of the profits. The remaining liability is divided among the limited partners, who are usually in a lower tax bracket. Thus, it is possible not only to reduce the parent's personal income tax liability but also the total taxes paid.

Do my children or grandchildren pay taxes on partnership income that is not distributed to them?

Partners pay income tax on their share of the partnership's income whether or not it is distributed to them. Therefore, in the normal course of managing the partnership business, most general partners make distributions to their limited partners equal to the limited partners' income tax liability.

Once we have placed assets into an FLP, how do we get money out of the partnership?

There are five ways that money can be distributed from an FLP:

1. The general partners are entitled to receive a reasonable fee for managing the FLP. If the general partner is a corporation, the corporation can pay salaries to officers and employees of the corporation.
2. The general partners may authorize pro rata distributions of partnership income or principal to the general and limited partners.
3. The FLP may make loans to any of the limited partners. The loans must be allowed by the FLP agreement.
4. Specific items of income or gain may be specially allocated to one or more specific partners.
5. The FLP can be terminated by consent of the general partner and all of the limited partners, allowing each partner to receive his or her pro rata share of the partnership assets.

Can you provide an FLP example that illustrates what you've been saying?

Consider the following example:

- Parents contribute vacant real estate holdings appraised at $2 million to an FLP in exchange for a 2 percent general partnership interest and a 98 percent limited partnership interest.
- A qualified business appraiser applies a valuation discount of 40 percent on the limited partnership interests for lack of control and lack of marketability.
- The 98 percent limited partnership interests originally valued at $1,960,000 are thus discounted to a value of $1,176,000.
- The parents give their limited partnership interests to the children.
- No gift tax is due because the value of the gifts is less than the parents' combined $1.2 million exemption equivalent.
- The parents are able to maintain control over the real estate portfolio. The amount of the discount—$784,000 in this example—totally escapes federal estate and gift taxes.
- The appreciation attributable to the limited partnership interests in the vacant lots will not be taxed in the parents' estates.
- Interests worth $1,960,000 before discount were transferred to the children. If the interests appreciate at the rate of 7.2 per-

cent per annum, at the end of 10 years the interests will double in value to $3,920,000.

- The parents will have removed $3,920,000 worth of real estate from their estates at a current value that is less than their $1.2 million combined exemption equivalent amount.

Can you give another example of how an FLP works?

Assume the following:

- You are 74 years of age, your spouse is 72, and you have five children. You have a $5 million estate that consists of $500,000 in bonds and publicly traded stocks and a $4.5 million farm.
- You are in a 55 percent marginal estate tax bracket on the death of the surviving spouse and wish to reduce your potential federal estate taxes.
- Your assets are appreciating at 5 percent per annum; and you expect to live for 14.4 more years, during which time your assets will double in value to $10 million.
- On your death at that time (assuming your spouse has predeceased you), the taxes on your $10 million estate—even with a bypass family trust in a living trust–centered estate plan—will be $4,618,000.

Now let us see what will happen if you create an FLP:

- You and your spouse form an FLP that has one general-partner unit and ninety-nine limited-partner units.
- The two of you transfer the farm into the partnership and get all of the partnership units—both the general unit and the limited units—in return.
- There is no income tax generated by your funding of your partnership.
- The two of you no longer own the farm, but you own the partnership which owns the farm.
- You hire an appraiser to value the farm, which she values at $4.5 million.
- You hire a partnership valuation specialist who appraises the

limited-partner interests at a discounted value of 60 percent of their real worth (a 40 percent discount).

- The 99 percent limited-partner interest is now worth $2,673,000.
- You begin a program to give the limited-partner units to your children—99 percent of the partnership—while keeping the 1 percent general-partner unit.
- On Christmas Day of the first year, you and your spouse begin your gift program:

  You give your five children $1.2 million worth of partnership units tax-free because of your combined exemption equivalent amount.

  Since each of the children is happily married, you give each couple $40,000 without tax because of your collective annual exclusions.

  Since you have ten grandchildren, you give an additional $200,000 of partnership interests to them as well.

- You make additional gifts of $400,000 on New Year's Day, a week later.
- You have now moved $2 million out of your estate tax-free.
- Two Christmas seasons later, you make another $400,000 worth of annual exclusion gifts, and give the remaining $273,000 on New Year's Day, a week later. You have now completed your program of giving away $2,673,000.
- As the FLP's general partners, you and your spouse still run the farm. You still control the assets and the income it generates.
- You receive a salary from the partnership for managing the partnership's affairs as general partners.
- Nothing has changed except that you have achieved massive federal estate and gift tax savings.
- On the death of the survivor of you or your spouse, the survivor's estate will consist of only 1 percent of the family farm and the stocks and bonds.
- Only the 1 percent FLP interest and the stocks and bonds will be taxed.

What can we do about protecting our portfolio, which is outside of our FLP?

In the above example, you and your spouse will have a stock and bond portfolio of $1 million that will generate $408,000 in estate tax on the death of the surviving spouse. If the partnership purchases a $410,000 last-to-die life insurance policy on both spouses' lives, the policy will pay 99 percent of its proceeds tax-free to the partnership. You have now covered the remainder of your tax liability.

Are there any disadvantages to using a family limited partnership?

One disadvantage is that the interests given by the parents retain the parents' income tax basis. Unlike assets the parents leave at death, the FLP interests do not receive a stepped-up basis to date-of-death value. When the limited partners—children and grandchildren—sell their interests at a later date, there will be capital gain tax due if the sales price exceeds their parents' and grandparents' basis in the units.

How do I know whether capital gain tax planning is more important than federal estate and gift tax planning?

Calculations can easily be made comparing the effect of the loss in step-up in basis with the effect of getting the assets out of the taxable estates of the parents or grandparents. In such comparisons, the numbers almost always show that the estate tax savings with an FLP far outweigh the potential capital gain tax savings without an FLP.

Can an FLP disqualify my estate from special-use valuation?

In order to qualify for the installment payment of estate taxes, your closely held business or farm must be at least 35 percent of your total estate. Caution must be taken when transferring such interests to your FLP.

A transfer by a parent or grandparent to an FLP could potentially disqualify the estate from special-use valuation. It is therefore important that your attorney or accountant make the appropriate calculations prior to the transfer of special-use property to an FLP.

Does my FLP have to have a business purpose?

Your FLP must have a business purpose other than tax avoidance if it is to survive an attack by the IRS.

What are some of the reasons I can set forth in my partnership agreement to satisfy the business-purpose requirement for my FLP?

Your partnership will need to have a purpose such as:

- Managing and/or developing real estate
- Providing a reasonable and smooth economic arrangement among the members of your family to maintain the partnership assets in the family
- Ensuring family harmony by providing that any dispute will be resolved by arbitration rather than going through the court system
- Preventing assets of the family from being taken through the probate court system on the death of a family member
- Providing for smooth succession and control of your family's assets
- Consolidating family assets which are held in fractional interests
- Creating an orderly and consolidated management system for all assets held by the partnership

Are there any other potential traps of which I should be wary?

There are several other complications of which you should be aware prior to creating an FLP:

- Immediate gain will be recognized if your debt on property contributed to the FLP exceeds your basis.
- You cannot transfer installment notes into an FLP and immediately give the limited partners their interests without triggering income tax.
- You cannot transfer land with a mortgage or trust deed that has a due-on-sale clause without the consent of the lender.

- A transfer of property to an FLP may be subject to a transfer tax in some jurisdictions (e.g., the state of Washington).
- Transfer of property into an FLP may cause a revaluation of the property for property tax purposes.
- Capital, as distinguished from personal services or labor, must be a material income-producing factor within the FLP in order for it to be recognized for income tax purposes.
- You should not transfer annuities to an FLP unless the partnership will hold the annuities as a nominee for the benefit of the annuitant under a nominee or special allocation agreement that allocates all tax attributes of the annuity to the annuitant.

What kinds of assets should *not* be transferred to the family limited partnership?

You should not transfer your residence, your retirement plans, or your subchapter S stock into an FLP.

Why shouldn't I transfer my residence into an FLP?

It is not advisable to transfer your primary residence to an FLP because you could lose valuable income tax benefits:

- If you are over age 55 and you sell your house, you can exclude up to $125,000 of realized gain on the sale. This exclusion can be lost if your home is transferred to an FLP.
- If there is a mortgage on the house and it is transferred to the FLP, the income tax deduction for interest payments could be lost or that deduction could be converted into an investment-interest deduction and limited under the investment-interest deduction rules.
- You have a general right to postpone paying tax on any gain realized from the sale of your principal residence provided that you purchase another principal residence within 2 years before or after the sale of the old residence and that the purchase price of the new home is equal to or greater than the adjusted sale price of the old home. This benefit can be lost if you transfer your home to an FLP.

Why shouldn't I transfer my pension, profit-sharing, and IRA accounts into my FLP?

Under federal law, an IRA must be owned only by an individual, and a qualified retirement plan must be owned only by a qualified retirement plan trust.

Why shouldn't I transfer my S corporation stock into my FLP?

If you transfer S corporation stock to an FLP, the transfer will terminate the "S" election.

GIFTS

Should I utilize my exemption equivalent during my lifetime or upon my death?

Many people have the misconception that it is best to "save" their exemption equivalent until their death. However, a more powerful leveraging technique is to utilize it during your lifetime. If you use your $600,000 exemption equivalent by making lifetime gifts, the $600,000 will appreciate in the recipients' hands and not in your taxable estate.

Between real investment growth and inflation, the value of the gift at your life expectancy should be substantial: a $600,000 gift will double every 7.2 years at 10 percent; if your life expectancy is 21 more years, the $600,000 will be worth $4.8 million in the hands of the recipients at the end of that time. Assuming an applicable 50 percent federal estate tax rate, you would have to leave $9.6 million to provide your heirs with the same value.

Can a gift program really save me meaningful federal estate and gift tax?

The gift tax law has three special features which appear to encourage people to make lifetime gifts:

- The annual exclusion.
- The removal from your taxable estate of after-gift appreciation.
- The computation of the gift tax only on the value of the prop-

erty given ("tax exclusive"). The estate tax is computed on the value of the property from which a transfer is made at death, including the tax ("tax inclusive").

To optimize your tax-saving possibilities, you should make maximum use of your annual exclusion and seriously consider using your exemption equivalent amount while you are alive.

The annual exclusion provides you with a golden opportunity to reduce your taxable estate—particularly if you begin as early as possible and follow through on a regular basis. For example, assume you and your spouse have cash in a money market account, stock, or other property which grows at 5 percent per year and the two of you give $20,000 in value per year from these assets to each of your three children. In 10 years you will have removed more than $792,000 from your taxable estate without paying a cent of gift tax or estate tax, saving between $293,000 (at a 37 percent rate) and $435,000 (at a 55 percent rate). There is no more tax-efficient device for reducing gift and estate taxes than a program of annual tax exclusion gifts.

Is it true that, dollar for dollar, it's 33 percent more expensive to leave property to certain people at death than it is to give it to the same people during my lifetime?

Gift tax rates are effectively lower than estate tax rates if you've already used up your $600,000 lifetime estate and gift tax exemption equivalent and you are making a taxable gift (a noncharitable gift over the $10,000 annual exclusion which is not being made directly to an educational institution or health care provider for a beneficiary's tuition or medical care). How much lower depends on your nominal tax bracket: the higher the nominal bracket, the greater the gift tax advantage over estate tax. Let's assume a 50 percent nominal tax rate applies. (Actually, there is no 50 percent bracket today, but this percentage simplifies the example.) At this level the effective gift tax rate is 33⅓ percent lower than the effective estate tax rate.

You also have to live 3 years after the gift is made to realize the gift tax advantage. If you don't, the gift tax paid (or payable) by reason of the gift is added to the tax base on which the estate tax is calculated; thus, except for any appreciation in the asset, the gift tax advantage is neutralized.

How can estate taxes be 33 percent higher than gift taxes if they both use the same rate schedule and the taxes are supposed to be "unified"?

The estate tax is calculated on the amount of property in the decedent's estate *before* bequests are paid, that is, before taxes are taken out. Thus, estate taxes are said to be *tax-inclusive;* they are calculated the same way the income tax is calculated. The gift tax, on the other hand, is calculated on the amount received by the recipient *after* taxes are taken out. For this reason, the gift tax is said to be *tax-exclusive.*

For example, assume you have used up your exemption equivalent amount, you've made your $10,000 total annual exclusion gifts for the year, and you have an additional $150,000 available to give away to children either by gift during your life or by bequest upon death. If you wait until death, your estate will have to pay 50 percent of the total $150,000 to the government, leaving only $75,000 for your children. By making a gift to your children now, however, you can give them $100,000, paying a 50 percent gift tax, that is, $50,000, calculated only on the amount the children receive. In either case, the full $150,000 is used up, but by lifetime giving, you're able to give your children one-third more than they will receive if they have to wait for a distribution from your estate.

For the mathematically inclined, the following discussion may help. For a tax-inclusive tax, like the estate tax and the generation-skipping transfer tax (GSTT) on taxable distributions and taxable terminations, the following expression shows the relationship of V_e (the value under the estate tax received by the donee), C_e (the cost of the bequest to the donor under the estate tax), and T (the marginal unified gift and estate tax rate):

$$V_e = C_e(1 - T)$$

For tax-exclusive taxes, such as gift taxes and the GSTT on direct skips, we have

$$C_g = V_g(1 + T)$$

where C_g is the cost of the gift to the donor and V_g is the value received by the donee.

To find the relative costs of giving under the two systems (estate tax and gift tax), let's see what we must do to get the same value, V, to the donee. To do so, we set $V_g = V_e$, which yields

$$C_e(1 - T) = C_g/(1 - T)$$

or

$$C_g/C_e = (1 - T)(1 + T)$$

So at a 50 percent marginal rate, the cost of giving as a fraction of the cost of bequesting is (1 – 0.5)(1 + 0.5) = (0.5)(1.5) = 0.75. That is, it costs only 75 percent as much to make the gift as to make the bequest. At a higher rate, the gift tax advantage is even greater.

Now, most people don't have a variable amount of property to give, so it may be more useful to determine, given a fixed amount of property available to give, how much we can get into the donee's hands by gift versus bequest. Here, we let the cost of the gift/bequest to the donor be the same under the two tax systems, or $C_e = C_g$, which yields

$$V_g(1 + T) = V_e/(1 - T)$$

or

$$V_g/V_e = 1/[(1 - T)(1 + T)]$$

So at a 50 percent marginal rate, we find that we can get 33 percent more property into the donee's hands by gift than by bequest.

Should parents always give property away instead of dying with it?

No. Whether to give property away or bequeath it depends on a family's specific situation, assumptions about future facts and law, and the form of the gift. Nontax considerations may very well be much more important than tax-saving considerations. Serious gifts should be made only with the advice of a qualified estate planning attorney.

What are the assumptions I should consider before making a gift?

Let's look at some of the tax issues first. If you want to make gifts, begin by maximizing your annual exclusions. They're as "good as gold" because they're free of gift and estate tax; and if you don't use them, you'll lose them. Next, remember that gifts exceeding annual exclusions will be sheltered from gift tax by your exemption equivalent; this permits you to transfer future appreciation without additional transfer tax. Ask yourself if the property you are considering giving is highly appreciated, and remember that you will be paying gift tax on the built-in gain on the property's value if you give it away. If you leave the property to your heirs on your death, they receive a step-up in basis, which they do not receive if you give them the property outright. Do you expect the asset to appreciate substantially in the future or throw off substantial ordinary income, or neither? What do you assume marginal estate and income tax rates will be? All of these factors are important in determining whether the tax consequences of giving will be greater or less than the tax consequences of leaving your property to your heirs by will or trust.

You should also consider the opportunities available to leverage your credit in lifetime giving that are not available at death: ILITs, FLPs, and QPRTs are all effective in this regard.

How can I make gifts to my children and not lose control over them?

When making gifts, you can make the gift outright, in trust, or in the form of a family limited partnership. If you make outright gifts, you lose all control. If you make gifts in trust, you maintain control of the assets but they will normally be gifts of a future interest and will not qualify for the annual exclusion unless you give a demand right to your beneficiaries when you make the trust gift.

A family limited partnership offers you the ability to make gifts to your children and control the gift under your own terms without worrying about demand rights and the annual exclusion. As a general partner, you maintain management and control of the assets and how they are distributed during your lifetime.

Is there any way I can protect my estate from changes in the exemption equivalent?

If you use your exemption equivalent now by making gifts, you will not be affected by any future decrease in the equivalent amount. If it should be increased in the future, you will undoubtedly have the right to give the difference at that later time.

Do I have to file a gift tax return when I use any part of my exemption equivalent?

You must file a federal gift tax return, but no payment will be due.

Is there a way to hold my assets in a revocable trust and continue my gift planning in the event of my disability?

Through special drafting in your revocable living trust, you can provide that, in the event of disability, your trustees may make distributions to your agents under a *limited durable power of attorney* specially designed for gifts. When a distribution is made from your trust to your agent, no gift occurs. The 3-year rule does not apply to gifts made under a power of attorney which contains specific authorization to make such gifts.

Your limited durable power of attorney should be drafted to be effective only upon your disability. It generally should restrict the power to give to favor only the persons and organizations you want to receive your assets. Your power of attorney should specifically authorize various formats under which gifts may be made (e.g., outright or in trust).

In addition, if you envision large transfers, as may be the case if you desire to use your exemption equivalent during your lifetime, care should be taken to require a *special independent agent* (usually a certified public accountant or corporate fiduciary) to approve any transfers before the gifts are made. This protects your agent from potential adverse tax consequences and assures you that an independent party will review your situation and determine whether the transfers are, in fact, a good idea under the circumstances.

Since there is an unlimited gift tax exemption for tuition and health care in addition to the $10,000 annual exemption and there is no present-interest requirement, can't I set up a trust to be used only for those purposes and contribute any amount to it I want, free of gift tax?

Unfortunately, the IRS nixed this idea in its regulations, on the grounds that because the transfer is not directly to the educational institution or health care provider, it does not qualify.

I don't have much to give now, but I want to do something special for my church. What can I do?

You can make a gift of life insurance and tailor the amount of the death proceeds to the amount of monthly premiums you can pay. To accomplish this, you would name your church as the beneficiary of the life insurance policy. If this is done properly, you will be entitled to deduct the premium payments on your federal income tax return.

Planning for Spouses: QTIP Trusts

What is a QTIP Trust?

"QTIP" stands for "qualified terminable interest property." In a nutshell, a *QTIP trust* is an estate planning device which allows you to obtain an estate tax marital deduction while providing your surviving spouse with full income and limited principal rights in your property.

How does it work?

You can provide that your property will continue in or be transferred to a trust for the benefit of your spouse (assuming your spouse survives you). If the trust meets certain requirements and if the person filing your estate tax return makes the election on the return, then the property in the trust will qualify for the estate tax marital deduction.

There will not be any estate tax on property transferred into the QTIP trust at the first spouse's death. While your spouse is still alive, the trustee of the QTIP trust must distribute the income from the trust to your spouse. Your spouse will have access (either partial or complete) to the trust principal during his or her lifetime under the standards that you set forth in your trust instructions.

When your spouse dies, the property which is then in the QTIP trust will be taken into account in computing your spouse's estate taxes. The remaining trust property—after estate taxes are paid—is then distributed to whomever you named as the remainder beneficiaries in the trust document.

How do I qualify my spouse's trust for QTIP treatment?

Four requirements must be met in order for a trust to qualify as a QTIP trust:

- The trustee of the QTIP trust must be required to distribute the net income of the QTIP trust to your spouse at least annually.
- The QTIP trust must be invested in income-producing property, or the spouse must have the power to require the trustee to convert non-income-producing property to income-producing property.
- During your spouse's life, your spouse must be the only current beneficiary of the QTIP trust.
- The executor of your estate must make the appropriate election on your estate tax return.

An examination of the QTIP's name reveals a lot about what it does. "Qualified" means that assets left to such a trust qualify for the unlimited marital deduction from federal estate taxes. This is a critical provision because no estate taxes are due if the marital deduction applies. "Terminable interest" means that the trust will dictate who ultimately receives the property after both spouses pass away. This feature ensures that your intended ultimate heirs, usually your children, are protected. If your surviving spouse remarries, his or her spouse could otherwise be entitled to a portion of your estate. Furthermore, since the assets are controlled by the trustees, there is less danger that an elderly person will be talked out of his or her inheritance by predatory persons.

Why must the QTIP trust be invested in income-producing property?

Without this requirement, one spouse could defer taxation without giving the surviving spouse any real benefit from the property. Investments in non-income-producing property are permitted only with the approval of the beneficiary spouse.

Are QTIPs appropriate for every married estate?

Although QTIP trusts are popular, they are not appropriate for every estate. Some people prefer QTIP trusts over other marital deduction devices because a QTIP trust provides the surviving spouse with income during his or her life and can still restrict that spouse's ability to get to the trust principal. Many people will not wish to restrict that right when planning for a spouse.

Why might I want to restrict my spouse's right to principal?

There are many reasons why a spouse might not want his or her surviving spouse to have access to the trust principal. For example, you may be concerned that your surviving spouse might remarry a person who is after his or her inheritance. A QTIP trust can ensure that your spouse will be taken care of during his or her lifetime and, after your spouse's death, that your children or grandchildren will receive an inheritance that was not depleted by a new spouse. The specific terms would be something like the following:

1. Pay all of the income to my surviving spouse for the rest of his or her life. (In order to qualify for the unlimited marital deduction as set forth in the Internal Revenue Code, the surviving spouse *must* have the right to receive all of the income at least annually from a regular marital trust or from a QTIP trust.)
2. My trustee has the discretion to make the principal available to my surviving spouse if my spouse needs it for health, education, maintenance, and support.
3. If my surviving spouse remarries, he or she will continue to receive the income from the QTIP trust but will lose all right to principal during the period of the remarriage.
4. If my spouse becomes single again, go back to my instructions in paragraph 2 above.
5. On my spouse's subsequent death, my children will receive whatever is left in my spouse's QTIP trust.

Can I give my spouse discretion regarding distribution of the QTIP property on his or her death?

A QTIP can give a spouse a limited power of appointment to decide who gets the principal, or it can provide that the assets pour over into another trust (created on the death of the spouse) to be held for other beneficiaries such as children or grandchildren.

How does a limited power of appointment work?

The QTIP provides that your spouse can leave the property to a class of beneficiaries—such as children, grandchildren, descendants—in whatever amounts or proportions that he or she chooses. This enables your spouse to monitor the behavior of members of the class and make decisions based upon that behavior that will affect their inheritance.

When is this device most useful?

A limited power of appointment is especially helpful when there are young children, whose adult behavior and personalities are not yet known, or mature children whose behavior and relationships to their parent or stepparent are in question.

QTIPs are most frequently used in second marriages. In the classic example, one spouse of the second marriage wants to take care of the other spouse on death but also wants to make absolutely sure that the children from his or her first marriage inherit the estate. The QTIP ensures that the hoped-for result will become a reality.

Our marriage is the second marriage for both of us, and each of us has children by former marriages. How can we protect each other while making sure that each of our estates goes to our respective children from the previous marriages?

Each of you should prepare a testamentary QTIP in your living trust. The income from that trust will be paid at least annually to the survivor for his or her life, and principal may be applied for the health, education, maintenance, and support of the survivor as well. There will be no estate tax until the surviving spouse's death, and each of your estates will then pass directly to your respective children by the prior marriages.

Can my children receive principal distributions while my spouse is receiving the income?

The marital deduction will be disallowed if any part of the principal benefits anybody other than the surviving spouse during that spouse's lifetime.

Are there any problems with QTIP planning?

When property passes to a QTIP trust for a surviving spouse, he or she may want as much income as possible, while the remainder beneficiaries want to inherit as much principal as possible. This situation can put the stepchildren and the stepparent at odds with each other.

How does the trustee resolve this conflict in interests?

The trustee must be fair to both the surviving spouse and the remainder beneficiaries in exercising his or her fiduciary responsibility and must invest the trust funds for both reasonable income and capital appreciation requirements.

What is the number-one problem with QTIP planning in second marriages?

If the QTIP provides for the needs of a stepparent from trust principal, any such distribution will come directly out of the pockets of the stepchildren and they will have a strong interest in obtaining, reviewing, questioning, and even challenging the distributions made to the surviving spouse.

If the surviving spouse is a trustee, this fiduciary duty will place the spouse in an awkward position and exacerbate the conflict. This planning arrangement may not be good for family dynamics.

Are there other problems with QTIP planning in second marriages?

In a remarriage situation, the spouse and the children may be of the same generation, so the likelihood that the children will predecease their stepparent is statistically very realistic. In effect, this disinherits the children of the first marriage if they do not survive the stepparent.

What alternative do I have for taking care of both my current spouse and the children I have from a prior marriage immediately upon my death?

You can use the unlimited marital deduction through a QTIP to pass property tax-free to your spouse upon your death if you predecease your spouse, and you can provide life insurance coverage through an ILIT for the benefit of your children. In this way, your children will not have to wait until your spouse dies to receive their inheritance; your gift of life insurance will pass upon your death directly to the children from your irrevocable life insurance trust.

Planning for Minors

How can I make gifts to my minor child?

Under the Uniform Gifts to Minors Act (UGMA) and the Uniform Transfers to Minors Act (UTMA), you can set up an account at a bank for the benefit of your minor child and make various irrevocable gifts to the account while your child is a minor. Gifts to these types of accounts automatically qualify for the $10,000 annual exclusion for gifts. During the lifetime of your child, monies from the account can be used for the child's health, education, maintenance, and support. However, you cannot use the funds in the account to relieve your obligation to support the child.

Depending upon what state you live in, your child will automatically have legal access to the account upon reaching the age of 18 or 21. This can be of concern to parents because the child may not be mature enough to properly deal with a large sum of money at that age.

How can I qualify my property for the annual exclusion?

In order for a gift to qualify for the $10,000 annual exclusion, the gift must be a gift of a present interest. That is, the recipient must have the immediate use of the gift; otherwise, the gift is deemed a gift of a future interest and will not qualify for the annual exclusion. Since minors cannot control property, a problem arises when parents and grandparents try to give property to them and still have their gifts qualify for the annual exclusion.

Internal Revenue Code Section 2503(c) provides a means by

which parents and grandparents can give property to minors in trust and still have the entire gift amount qualify for the annual gift exclusion. Such a gift is called a *2503(c) trust.*

How does a gift in trust to a minor qualify for the annual exclusion?

For a gift to conform to Code Section 2503(c), three requirements must be met:

- The trust property and the income derived from it can be spent by or for the benefit of the minor child prior to the minor's reaching the age of 21.
- When the minor reaches the age of 21, all remaining property must pass to him or her.
- If the minor dies before age 21, all remaining property must pass to the minor's estate or be subject to the minor's power to appoint the property (to himself or herself, his or her estate or creditors, or the creditors of his or her estate).

You can create a trust, subject to the above requirements, that can receive your gifts, hold the property for the benefit of your minor child, and still qualify for the annual gift exclusion.

My state has enacted a gifts-to-minors law which provides for distributions at age 18, not 21. How does this affect Code Section 2503(c) gifts?

If your state's law sets majority at age 18 rather than 21 and its gift statutes are modeled after either the Uniform Gifts to Minors Act or the Uniform Transfers to Minors Act, the gift will be treated as a gift of a present interest under Section 2503(c).

Can gifts made to a child's 2503(c) trust remain in trust past the child's twenty-first birthday?

Yes. There are two ways that a 2503(c) trust can continue after the child turns 21. The trust will still qualify for the exclusion as long as the child has the right to compel the distribution of the trust under either of the following terms:

- At any time after reaching the age of 21.
- During a limited period after reaching 21. After this period, if the right is not exercised, the trust continues under the terms set forth by the trust maker.

Generally, if the trust maker wants the trust to continue past the child's twenty-first birthday—which is almost always the case—the latter approach is used.

What are the instructions in a 2503(c) minor's trust?

Almost all 2503(c) minor's trusts provide the following instructions:

> Use both the income and principal of the trust for the health, education, maintenance, and support of my child.
>
> Before making any distributions to my child, see if my child has any other sources of income or support, such as grants, scholarships, or other forms of income.
>
> My primary objective in establishing this trust is to provide a college education for my child. If my child does not immediately attend college after graduation from high school, my trustee may withhold the distribution of both income and principal in my trustee's sole discretion, until my child elects to further his or her education.
>
> When my child obtains a college degree, my trustee shall distribute the remaining trust income and principal to my child. If my child does not obtain a college degree, my trustee shall hold both income and principal until my child reaches age 35. My trustee shall, however, have the power to make discretionary payments of both income and principal in the event of an opportunity or expense deemed by my trustee to be in the best interests of my child.

Can I create a 2503(c) trust for multiple beneficiaries?

No. You must create a separate 2503(c) trust for each intended beneficiary. Each trust is a separate taxpayer and must have its own tax identification number and file a separate tax return.

Is there any reason I should choose a 2503(c) trust over a simple UGMA or UTMA custodial account?

If you are custodian of the account, all of the assets in the account will be includable in your estate if you die before they are distributed to your child. In a properly drafted 2503(c) trust, the assets are totally removed from your estate.

Is there some other way I can create a trust for my minor child and still qualify for the annual exclusion?

You can create a *demand-right trust* for your minor child. This is essentially an irrevocable trust created by one or both parents for the benefit of their minor child.

There is a strict procedure for making gifts to a demand-right trust that must be followed in order to qualify the gifts for the $10,000 annual exclusion: The trustee must immediately notify the minor beneficiary—through the child's legal guardian—that a gift has been made to the trust and that the beneficiary has a specified period of time (typically 30 to 45 days) to demand a distribution from the trust in the amount of the gift. If the specified number of days lapses, the gift made to the demand-right trust will stay inside the trust and continue to be governed by its terms.

An irrevocable trust with a demand-right provision is an important part of proper estate planning for anyone who wants to put money aside for a minor child, does not want the property to be taxable in the giver's gross estate, yet wants to retain some control over the child's use of the property after the child reaches the age of 21.

Are there income tax benefits to 2503(c) or demand trusts?

These trusts were traditionally used to shift income to children or grandchildren in lower income tax brackets. However, under the kiddie tax provisions of the Tax Reform Act of 1986, this is no longer allowed for children under the age of 14.

Planning for Grandchildren

What is the generation-skipping transfer tax?

A basic premise of the federal estate tax is that wealth will be taxed as it passes from one generation to the next. In transfers from parent to child, from child to grandchild, and from grandchild to great-grandchild, the federal estate tax is imposed upon each transfer.

To avoid the consecutive imposition of the federal estate tax, affluent persons established trusts for the benefit of successive generations. These trusts paid income to the intermediate generation and distributed principal to the successive generation. Historically, the federal estate tax was avoided if the lifetime beneficiaries did not have sufficient rights which would cause inclusion of the property in their estates.

In order to stop persons from circumventing the federal estate tax by such devices, Congress established the *generation-skipping transfer tax (GSTT)* in 1986. This tax is imposed on many transfers which avoid the normal parent-to-child-to-grandchild transfer of assets.

How is a generation-skipping transfer determined?

A generation-skipping transfer is a transfer to a *skip person,* that is, a person who is more than one generation below that of the transferor. It is easiest to determine a skip person within the family tree. A transfer to a grandchild is a transfer to a skip person, because the child of the transferor is omitted, or "skipped."

How are transfers measured when they're not going to grandchildren?

When transfers are made outside of the family, generations are measured in years, using the transferor's age:

- Persons who are less than 12½ years younger than the transferor are in the transferor's generation.
- Persons between 12½ and 37½ years younger than the transferor are in the transferor's children's generation.
- Persons more than 37½ years younger than the transferor are skip persons.

Upon what transfers is the GSTT levied?

It is levied on any transfer which is made to a skip person and which is either a taxable termination, direct generation skip, or taxable distribution.

What is a taxable termination?

A *taxable termination* occurs when a beneficiary's (typically a child's) interest in a trust expires or terminates and thereafter only skip persons will have an interest in the property.

What is a direct skip?

A *direct skip* is any transfer which is made directly to a skip person and which is subject to federal gift or estate taxes.

What is a taxable distribution?

A *taxable distribution* from a trust is any distribution which is not a direct skip or taxable termination and is made to a skip person.

Don't I receive a tax-free amount that I can leave to my grandchildren?

The law provides that each grandparent can leave up to $1 million of property directly or indirectly to grandchildren and other descendants at or below his or her grandchildren's generation without having to pay GST tax. If your generation-skipping transfers exceed $1 million, GST tax will be owed. Generally, the tax imposed is equal to the highest applicable federal estate tax, which is currently 55 percent.

How can I get a $1 million exemption and still have to pay federal estate tax?

If you left property directly to a grandchild and there wasn't such a thing as the GST tax, you would pay estate tax on the transfer—just like you would on the transfer to a child—from 37 to 55 percent. This is exactly what happens when you leave property to a grandchild and qualify for the GSTT exemption.

If you did not qualify for the GSTT exemption, you would pay GST tax at the top marginal bracket of 55 percent and then pay another estate tax on the transfer to your grandchildren.

I intend to leave one-third of my property to each of my two

living children and the remaining one-third to my deceased son's two children (my grandchildren). Do I have to pay GST tax?

Since your son is deceased at the time you make the transfer, your grandchildren will be moved up to the generation of your deceased son and the transfer will not be subject to the GST tax.

Are there ways to soften the harshness of the generation-skipping transfer tax?

Your estate planning attorney can explain a number of softening techniques, including:

- Allocation of the $1 million-per-person GSTT exemption
- Early allocation of that exemption to a trust so that the appreciation or increase in the value of trust assets will magnify the benefit of the exemption
- Careful use of a general power of appointment
- Careful use of a special power of appointment
- Careful use of sequential powers of appointment

Is the GSTT exemption available for gifts as well as for federal estate tax?

Yes, it is available for lifetime gifts as well as for gifts at death.

How is the GSTT exemption allocated?

For lifetime transfers, the allocation is made by an election on the federal gift tax return for the year in which the transfer was made. With respect to transfers at death, the allocation is made on the federal estate tax return.

What are the tax advantages of utilizing the GSTT exemption?

While generation skipping was historically a tool only for the very wealthy, the Tax Reform Act of 1986 has created an opportunity for everyone to utilize this technique to save substantial taxes. With proper planning, once you transfer assets and designate them as exempt under the generation-skipping exemption, the assets plus all income and appreciation attributable to them are not taxed in the estate of your child.

What planning should a couple do to ensure that each spouse can take advantage of his or her individual exemption from the GST tax?

If one spouse has assets worth less than $1 million and the other has assets worth more than $1 million, steps should be taken to increase the size of the less wealthy spouse's estate to ensure that his or her estate can also utilize the full GSTT exemption. A transfer of assets may be made by outright gift or by trust.

Where can I create my GSTT trust?

You can create a trust specifically for GSTT purposes in your will or living trust or as a separate irrevocable trust.

How can my spouse and I utilize both our $1 million generation-skipping exemptions?

A person must be deemed the "transferor" of property to qualify for the $1 million generation-skipping exemption. This may pose a problem with the typical estate plan created by a married couple. Such a plan generally allocates $600,000 to a family trust, with the remaining balance to a marital trust. The property in the family trust is deemed that of the decedent, and thus the decedent qualifies as the "transferor." However, the assets in the marital trust are deemed those of the surviving spouse, so he or she is now the "transferor." The decedent's remaining $400,000 exemption may be lost, and on the surviving spouse's death the maximum generation-skipping exemption would be $1.6 million ($1 million from the surviving spouse as transferor and $600,000 from the decedent's family trust with decedent as transferor).

To fully utilize both exemptions, a special election may be made as to part of the marital trust. In our example, the $400,000 is placed in its own trust, called a *reverse QTIP.* The property in the reverse QTIP is treated as belonging to the decedent rather than the surviving spouse for GSTT purposes but as belonging to the surviving spouse for estate tax purposes. Thus, the decedent remains the transferor of the property for GSTT purposes and, by making the proper allocations, can utilize his or her entire GSTT exemption of $1 million. On the death of the surviving spouse, both spouses have utilized their maximum exemptions, totaling $2 million.

Can a trust which is separate from the living trust qualify for the GSTT exemption?

Practitioners often create a separate irrevocable life insurance trust for GSTT purposes. If the trust is funded with life insurance, only the insurance premiums apply toward the $1 million exemption. Note that a spouse should not be named as a beneficiary of a GSTT trust that is created to own life insurance on the life of the other or both spouses.

Can I use a GSTT exemption with my revocable living trust and still allow my children to use the property?

Yes, you can. One commonly used technique is to divide the transferor's property into equal shares for his or her children. Each child's share is then divided into exempt and nonexempt trust shares. The exempt portion of each share represents the transferor's pro rata proportion of his or her generation-skipping exemption amount of $1 million.

The trustee can be directed to sparingly use the property in each child's exempt share for the benefit of that child whenever the assets in the nonexempt share are not sufficient to adequately provide for the child. Whatever assets are left in the child's exempt share at that child's death can pass to that child's children without being subject to estate tax or generation-skipping tax.

Are there any nontax advantages to using generation-skipping trusts?

Placing property in trust for children and grandchildren provides several nontax benefits for your children and grandchildren. These include:

- Your descendants' trust property will not be distributed to their spouses on divorce or death.
- The trust property is not subject to the claims of the beneficiaries' creditors.

What is a dynasty trust?

A *dynasty trust* is a trust designed to remain in existence for multiple generations without the imposition of an estate tax or generation-skipping tax as the property passes from generation to generation. In many states, the creation of a dynasty trust is, in effect, the creation of a nest egg or protective shield for each generation: the trust not only is protected from federal estate taxes but also may be protected from the claims of beneficiaries' creditors and, in the event of divorce, of their ex-spouses.

Typically, affluent persons place property in trust and create life estates for the benefit of successive generations. At each generation, the beneficiary may be a single descendant or may be a class of descendants among whom the trustee, if given the power to do so, "sprinkles" the principal and income. Most dynasty trusts provide for the distribution of income and for no distributions of principal or very limited principal distributions.

On death, a descendant beneficiary may be granted a limited power of appointment to reallocate the remainder in the trust among his or her descendants.

How long can a dynasty trust last?

State statutes generally provide that a transfer of a property interest in trust will not be valid unless it vests within the time of a life or lives in being plus 21 years. This is the classic *rule against perpetuities.*

Can the limitations of the rule against perpetuities be avoided?

A dynasty trust can be drafted so that the class of beneficiaries is so large as to maximize the applicable period. For example, the class could be all the descendants of John D. Rockefeller living at the time the trust becomes irrevocable.

Three states—Idaho, South Dakota, and Wisconsin—have abolished the rule against perpetuities. If a dynasty trust is established in one of these states, it can last until the principal is exhausted. If you wish to take advantage of these states' laws, you should name a corporate fiduciary within their borders as trustee of your dynasty trust.

What types of trusts can be utilized as dynasty trusts?

Generally, a dynasty trust can be created as an irrevocable trust or as part of a revocable living trust, which will become irrevocable upon the death of the trust maker.

How do I create a dynasty trust within my revocable living trust?

Your revocable living trust can provide that at your death an amount equal to your available unused GSTT exemption is to be segregated into a dynasty trust for the benefit of your descendants. The portion of your estate in excess of the available exemption will be transferred to beneficiaries using traditional estate planning concepts.

What is the procedure if I use an irrevocable trust as a dynasty trust?

If you establish an irrevocable trust as a dynasty trust during your lifetime, you will file a gift tax return and allocate part of your available GSTT exemption to your gift to the dynasty trust. However, if your spouse is a beneficiary of the trust during your lifetime, no allocation of the GSTT exemption may be made to the trust until the death of either you or your spouse.

What are the advantages of an international dynasty trust?

The benefits of creating dynasty trusts internationally are greater flexibility, more efficient income tax treatment, and the ability to accommodate several nationalities of trust makers and beneficiaries.

What does "leveraging the exemption" mean?

Affluent persons often desire to transfer more than their combined gift and estate tax exemption equivalent amount of $1.2 million and their combined $2 million GSTT exemption by "leveraging" their gifts.

Leveraging devices permit the value of a gift to a trust to be discounted for federal gift tax purposes. Such devices include transfers of fractional interests, transfers through entities such as family limited partnerships, and other devices which reduce the value of the property for purposes of federal gift tax valuation.

Often, life insurance policies are purchased as a leveraging device. If an irrevocable life insurance trust is created as a dynasty trust, only the trust maker's annual contributions for the premiums reduce his or her GSTT exemption. To the extent that the death

TABLE 3-1 Appreciation of $1 Million Trust Estate

			Value in 100 Years*	
Interest Rate, %	Years to Double	Number Doubles	With No Tax	With Tax†
10.0	7.2	14	$13,780,612,340	$565,091,240
7.2	10.0	10	1,045,871,999	42,887,289
5.0	14.4	7	131,501,258	5,392,373
3.6	20.0	5	34,353,860	1,408,723

*Assumes four generational deaths in 25-year intervals and no income taxes for either calculation.

†Assumes 55% federal estate tax rate.

benefit of the policy in the dynasty trust exceeds the aggregate premiums paid by the trust makers, leveraging has occurred.

Do dynasty trusts generally appreciate or depreciate in value over the generations?

Let's assume that you purchase a $1 million life insurance policy and successfully qualify it for GSTT treatment to keep it federal estate tax–free intergenerationally. Under the Rule of 72, your trust estate would compound and grow in both tax-free and taxable environments. The comparative values in 100 years are shown in Table 3-1.

4

Asset Protection Planning

Of all the areas of estate planning, the one that piques the interest of most people is asset protection. In today's litigious climate, everyone worries not only about death, disability, and taxes but also about the odds of being a part of a lawsuit. Most people do not want to deliberately avoid their fair obligations, but they do want to protect their assets from a possible unjust and unduly large judgment stemming from an obviously ridiculous lawsuit. It is only prudent to provide for such a circumstance.

A number of our contributing authors submitted questions and answers concerning asset protection. The material covers almost every aspect of this complex area of planning.

This chapter presents a great deal of practical information that will help you decide if, and to what extent, you would like to engage in asset protection planning. After reading and studying this chapter, you may be motivated to learn more from your attorney about how you can protect your assets before you are ever sued.

The Purpose of Asset Protection Estate Planning

What is asset protection estate planning?

Asset protection estate planning is the process of organizing one's assets and affairs within an estate plan that protects assets not or from liabilities and litigation but also from living and death probates and death taxes.

What is the objective of asset protection estate planning?

Your primary line of defense for protecting your assets is and always should be your personal liability insurance coverages, including malpractice insurance if you are a professional such as a doctor or a lawyer. Your insurance provides you not only with liability coverage but also with competent legal representation coverage.

Just because someone is competent and careful doesn't mean that he or she will not be sued. We live in a litigious society where a person's competence is no longer as important as who can be blamed for someone's misfortune. Typically, juries like to blame the professional or businessperson because he or she has wealth, income-producing capacity, and insurance.

We spend a lot of time on building and learning how to build our fortunes; unfortunately, we spend very little time—and very little is ever taught—on the subject of protecting our fortunes from creditors. Asset protection planning has as its objective the protection of a family's property and income from the attacks of gold-digging plaintiffs or creditors.

Why should I engage in asset protection estate planning?

Besides the obvious reason—to protect the assets that you have worked so hard to earn—you should engage in asset protection estate planning for the following reasons:

To Achieve Peace of Mind You can practice your chosen occupation or profession without the constant worry of losing everything if you are sued. With a clear mind you can do a much better job and be less likely to make mistakes.

To Avoid Probate and Estate Taxes A by-product of a well-designed asset protection estate plan is an estate plan that is also designed to avoid living or disability probate (guardianship), death probate, and estate taxes through the use of various trusts and other traditional estate planning tools.

To Save on Liability and Malpractice Insurance With your assets protected from the reach of creditors, you will not need to carry as much insurance coverage. You could probably reduce your coverage to the minimum amount necessary to retain your privileges and still maintain the legal representation coverage. The cost of obtaining the asset protection estate planning can, in most cases, be recovered in the first year or within a few years by the savings in premiums. A further bonus is realized when such insurance premium savings continue year after year. It is never advisable to go completely bare of any liability coverage.

To Reduce Settlements and Numbers of Suits By judgment-proofing your assets and reducing your liability coverage, you will cause potential plaintiffs to either terminate plans for litigation or settle within your reduced liability coverage. Just think, if we all made ourselves judgment-proof and reduced our liability coverage, the number of lawsuits and the dollar amount of settlements could decline and liability insurance rates would perhaps be more affordable again.

To Protect against Exemplary Damages Exemplary, treble, or punitive damages are not covered by your liability insurance. The theory is that a person who commits a wrongful act should be punished and made an example of; as a practical matter, some juries like to take from a rich defendant and give to a poor plantiff. This is what is commonly referred to as the "deep-pocket" or "Robin Hood" syndrome!

To Protect against the Bankruptcy of Insurance Carriers There is no guarantee that your liability insurance is going to be there when you need it. People all over the country are realizing this unfortunate fact as more and more liability insurance carriers are filing for bankruptcy. What is even more unfortunate is that some people learn this fact after they have had claims filed against them. If your liability insurance is presently your only asset protection, you should do some serious thinking. We're experiencing a trend in the insurance industry that indicates that not only is liability coverage becoming unaffordable but some day such coverages may not even be available at any cost.

To Gain Strategic Bargaining Power An asset protection estate plan increases the likelihood of negotiating a favorable settlement.

Vince Lombardi, the famous football coach of the Green Bay Packers, was a great believer in running the ball rather than passing it. It is said that he believed that only three things could happen when passing the football—and two of them were bad. The same can be said for creditors when they are faced with a proper asset protection plan: four things can happen—and three of them are bad for the creditors:

1. They could settle for the amount offered.
2. They could lose and get nothing.
3. They could win, but the award could be less than the amount offered by the insurance carrier as a settlement.
4. They could win, and the award could be equal to or greater than the insurance coverage; however, due to the unavailability of leviable assets, they will probably be able to obtain only the amount of the insurance coverage and then only after a long, drawn-out court battle months or years down the road. Furthermore, the contingent percentage fee the creditor's attorneys charge will usually be a higher percentage if they have to pursue litigation.

By settling for the amount offered, creditors will be the winners, and they will get their money a lot sooner, especially in light of the time value of money. This strategy enhances the defendants' bargaining position, in effect leveling the litigation playing field. It works best if liability insurance can be used as the proverbial carrot at the end of the stick to entice the plaintiffs to settle for the amount offered by the defendants.

The concept of the contingent fee gives plaintiffs the "I've got nothing to lose" attitude. This attitude makes for an unbalanced litigation playing field against defendants, who start off as losers since they must pay hourly fees and retainers to their lawyers. Asset protection estate planning creates an incentive for plaintiffs to settle early to save litigation costs and time and to ensure at least some settlement amount.

Are lawsuits a legitimate concern for anyone who has assets?

Most definitely. Whenever anything bad happens to anyone in America, the typical first response is to figure out who to blame for the misfortune and, more importantly, who to sue. Often, defendants are sued simply because they have deep pockets. If there was no money to be had, many lawsuits would never even start.

Some would respond by saying, "That's what insurance is for." However, because of the litigious nature of our society, insurance becomes less and less affordable. Also, many people find out the hard way that their policies do not cover "gross negligence" and do not pay punitive damages. Punitive damages are amounts awarded by juries beyond the actual damages to the plaintiff. Punitive damages may be many times the award for actual damages and sometimes make up the largest part of the award in a personal-injury lawsuit.

Finally, even if defendants win their court cases, they really lose: They spend lots of money on legal fees, devote much time to the lawsuits, and experience the stress caused by being "targets" in the legal system.

Are there any assets that are exempt from claims of creditors?

Some of your assets are protected from creditors by state or federal law. These are what are known as *exempt assets*. Assets which have historically enjoyed at least some protection in some states are your homestead, tangible personal property (up to a maximum limit), automobiles, life insurance cash value, qualified retirement plan benefits, annuities, and even wages and salaries. The laws in every state are different, so you must ask your estate planning attorney about the types of property that are exempt in your state.

As you probably can see, if you have any degree of wealth, your nonexempt assets have exposure to creditors even in states that have the most favorable laws protecting debtors. That is why asset protection estate planning is so important for most Americans.

My uncle tells me that the best way to protect money from the Internal Revenue Service and from creditors is to put it in a can buried in the backyard. What do you think?

The law imposes a duty on your executor (personal representative), trustee, or other agent on your death to make a diligent search for all assets that would be included in your taxable estate. An attorney assisting your death agent will insist on being informed about assets such as the money in the can. Whether it will be necessary to file a death tax return will depend upon the total amount of your taxable estate.

Under the laws of most states, your death agent is required to see that your debts are paid. Therefore, the death agent cannot escape paying creditors by ignoring the presence of the buried money.

Money in a can is a foolish "investment" for a number of reasons. First, money buried in the backyard could easily be forgotten and go undiscovered for years or perhaps forever. Second, the money earns no current return as an investment. Third, the money provides no protection against inflation. Fourth, the money could wind up being owned by a stranger, either because of chance discovery by the stranger or because of transfer of legal title to the land on which the money is buried.

The essence of planning is to be able to control your property. By hiding assets and hoping for the best, you are not planning but only thinking wishfully. There are numerous methods for protecting your assets from taxes and creditors while controlling how those assets are used.

Life Insurance Policies and Annuities for Asset Protection

Are life insurance proceeds, disability proceeds, and annuities protected from creditors?

In virtually all states, proceeds paid at death to named beneficiaries of life insurance or annuity policies are protected from the claims of the insureds' creditors. Some states also exempt life insurance proceeds from the claims of the beneficiaries' creditors. Disability insurance benefits are likewise protected.

Although the states vary on this issue, the cash value of life insurance may also be exempt from creditors. The theory behind this exemption is that if cash values could be taken by creditors, the insurance companies would reduce the death benefits payable by the cash values removed. Since the proceeds of the death benefits are exempt, the cash values should also be exempt to protect the full payment of the proceeds by the insurance companies.

Generally, exemption of the cash value of life insurance applies only if the insured owns the policy. A trap for the unwary can be cross-owned life insurance between spouses: if a husband owns life insurance on his wife and the husband is successfully sued, his creditor could take the cash value of the life insurance he owns on his wife. Often, attorneys recommend an irrevocable life insurance trust (ILIT) to avoid this situation. An ILIT will protect the cash value from creditors and from a divorce action and protect the death benefit proceeds from estate taxes.

States specifically disallow protection of the cash value of policies purchased to defraud existing creditors. In other words, if a person purchases a large life insurance policy in an attempt to put cash out of the reach of creditors who are seeking to recover mature claims, the statute will not protect the cash value.

In a few states, including Florida and Texas, the cash value of annuities, variable life insurance, and variable annuities now enjoys the same full creditor exemption as the cash value of life insurance.

Qualified Retirement Plans and IRAs for Asset Protection

Are qualified retirement plans and IRAs protected from claims of creditors?

One of the best places to shield assets is within your own retirement plan or plans, such as a corporate pension or profit-sharing plan. Qualified plans are exempt from the claims of creditors under a 1992 Supreme Court decision. The Court held that state laws exempting qualified plan assets from claims of creditors in bankruptcy are valid. The Court also held that the provision of the Employee Retirement Income Security Act (ERISA) of 1974 exempting qualified plan assets and IRAs from creditors' claims in bankruptcy is also valid. State law is also a factor in protecting qualified retirement plan, as well as Keogh (HR-10) plan, proceeds from creditor claims.

As long as assets remain in a qualified retirement plan, they are exempt; but as benefits are paid, they can be subject to claims. A court cannot, however, force you to take a lump-sum distribution at retirement; therefore, the creditor has to wait until you retire and until each installment is paid. It is arguable, however, that installment payments from a qualified plan are a substitute for wages and salary and that those states prohibiting garnishment of wages or salary might give the same protection to these installment payments.

Additionally, if a judgment has been rendered against an individual, that individual can continue to contribute to the plan; however, if the sponsoring corporation is also liable, the courts may be able to limit future contributions.

If a plan participant dies before retirement, will the benefits paid to a beneficiary be exempt from the participant's creditors' claims?

If a retirement plan provides for a preretirement death benefit, then the plan is akin to a life insurance policy, and like life insurance proceeds, the retirement plan death benefit proceeds will be exempt.

What is the best way to provide creditor protection for my IRA and Keogh plan?

The issue of whether IRA and Keogh plan assets are subject to creditors' claims is, to a great degree, state-specific and, to a lesser degree, unsettled. While public and private pension plans are exempt from creditors' claims (with the notable exception of court-ordered alimony or child support claims), IRAs and Keogh plans are not always exempt under state law.

If you live in a state that does not provide protection, here are a few things you can do for added safety:

- Make another person, even your spouse, a cotrustee of the plan.
- Be sure that your plan has clear spendthrift language, that is, language that prohibits creditors from taking plan assets.
- Consider joining with other, similar small businesses in your area to create a group pension plan with several principals. This action could provide your Keogh with the same protection as an ERISA plan.
- Avoid unreasonably high balances—those which may be considered in excess of what is reasonably needed for retirement.
- Avoid frequently using the account for personal loans.
- Avoid exercising individual, unlimited, and complete control over the fund.

Title to Assets for Asset Protection

If I title all my property in my name and also state that the property is payable on death to my nephew, can I keep my creditors from reaching the property during my life and from reaching it in the hands of my nephew after my death?

The law of your state should be considered before you use the payable-on-death (POD) technique. Some states allow only certain kinds of property (e.g., bank accounts or investment securities) to be titled in your name and designated POD to another person. POD titling does not protect your assets from your creditors while you are alive, and you should not be surprised if creditors follow POD-titled assets into the hands of your nephew after your death.

If my spouse and I place our assets in a revocable living trust, does that protect our assets from our creditors? What about after one or both of us dies?

If you and your spouse place your assets in a revocable living trust, your creditors will be able to attach your assets just as if the assets were not held in a trust. If you look at things from your creditors' point of view, it is easy to see why the law so provides.

You and your spouse, as makers of the revocable living trust, retain the power to alter, amend, or completely revoke the trust at your leisure. You can even serve as the trustees of your own trust. In short, you can do anything with the trust property after you put it in the trust that you could have done before you put it in the trust. Because you retain so much control over the property in the revocable living trust, the trust is ignored and you and your spouse are still considered the "owners" of the property for creditor purposes. It would be unfair for the law to allow debtors to hold large amounts of property in trusts over which they retain complete control and yet deny creditors access to that property.

Most well-drafted revocable living trusts provide that, if the maker of the trust dies, the trust becomes irrevocable. Most states' statutes and case law provide that once the trust becomes irrevocable, the rules applicable to revocable trusts no longer apply and assets in the trust can then be protected from creditors. There are laws with respect to fraudulent transfers and laws with respect to transferee responsibility as related to tax and certain other liabilities, and these should be taken into account to determine how much protection the then irrevocable trust provides.

After the death or deaths of the makers, a revocable living trust can help protect assets in a majority of states. You should seek competent legal advice about the law in your state as it relates to using a revocable living trust for protection of assets after your death.

I understand that in my state real estate that is held by my spouse and me in tenancy by the entirety is not subject to the claims of our creditors and we thereby have some protection for our home or other real estate. Is this true?

In most states a home or other real estate held by spouses as tenants by the entirety is protected from the claims of each spouse's separate creditors but is *not* protected from the claims of both spouses' joint creditors. Therefore, if you alone are the debtor or if your spouse alone is the debtor, then your tenancy by the entirety real estate is protected. But if both you and your spouse are liable for the same debt or if you and your spouse grant a mortgage or other interest in the real estate, then your jointly held property is not protected.

This protection is only available to property held jointly by a husband and wife. If you hold property jointly with a person other than your spouse, this protection is not available. Also, in some states, you must clearly show that you and your spouse intend to own property in tenancy by the entirety. If the title to the property merely states that you and your spouse own the property as joint tenants with right of survivorship, then the protection given to tenancy by the entirety ownership may not apply; if one spouse has a creditor, that creditor may be able to seize all or part of the property.

If my spouse and I transfer our home or other real estate to a joint revocable living trust or to separate revocable living trusts for each of us, will we lose the protection of tenancy by the entirety?

A revocable living trust has many advantages, including probate avoidance and full use of your two $600,000 exemption equivalent amounts for federal estate tax purposes. However, if you and your spouse transfer tenancy by the entirety property to a joint revocable trust or to two separate revocable trusts, then, in some states, the creditor protection offered by tenancy by the entirety might be lost.

In many states, whether or not real estate is available to a creditor is determined by how the property is recorded in the office which maintains real estate title and other records. So if real estate is recorded in the name of husband and wife as tenants by the entirety, the rights of the creditor might be hampered or possibly totally cut off with respect to that real estate. This may not be so with property titled in the name of a revocable living trust.

One way to have your cake and eat it, too, is to leave the title recorded in your names as tenants by the entirety and to formally execute either a deed that is not recorded in your county or, better yet, a joint declaration of trust ownership, which is then available for recording when appropriate. However, the mere existence of the unrecorded deed or joint declaration of trust ownership may technically eliminate the creditor protection created by tenancy-by-the-entirety ownership. You must analyze your particular state's laws and use the best arrangement to accomplish your specific needs.

Fraudulent Conveyances

Why is planning *in advance* so important? What is a fraudulent conveyance?

You might compare planning for asset protection to buying insurance on your boat. You cannot legally insure the boat after it has sunk. In fact, you can't buy insurance after the engines have quit and you are taking on water. To carry the analogy even further, you can't even buy the insurance when the boat is fine if you are out on the ocean in the midst of a raging storm. You need to insure your boat while your boat is ship-shape, the seas are calm, and there is no storm on the horizon.

Fraudulent conveyance laws vary from state to state, but they always have the same general goal: to prevent people from making transfers with the intention of hindering, delaying, or defrauding present or subsequent creditors. Present creditors are pretty easily ascertained. Questions usually arise about which "subsequent," or future, creditors are protected by fraudulent conveyance. Did the individual doing the estate planning make the transfers with the intent to hinder, delay, or defraud future creditors?

Fraudulent conveyance laws are not designed to protect everyone who could someday be a person's creditor. They pertain only to those creditors that a person harbored an actual fraudulent intent against on the date of the transfer or those creditors whose rights a person acted against with reckless disregard after conveying assets. For example, an attorney who conveys all of his assets to an offshore asset protection trust, cancels his malpractice insurance, and then constantly practices law while in a drunken stupor has probably made a fraudulent conveyance as to those clients he harms with his legal advice.

It clearly is *not* a fraudulent conveyance when a transfer is made by a person who has no pending or even threatened claims or has no reason to believe that legal problems will develop in the future, but simply wants to plan for his or her family's future well-being. It clearly is a fraudulent conveyance when an individual makes a transfer just before filing for bankruptcy or divorce or immediately after being sued for malpractice. In between these two extremes lies a large gray area of interpretation.

Our common law seems to favor the free alienability of property, which means that a person can dispose of his or her property as he or she sees fit, including selling it; giving it to children, spouses, charities, or trustees; or burning it.

The fraudulent conveyance laws do not pertain so much to who receives the property but, rather, to the intent of the person who is making the transfer. In one of the most famous cases in this area, the court stated that planning for a future "what if" is permissible so long as the "what if" is a mere possibility rather than a probability.

If a transfer or conveyance is found to be fraudulent, the remedy serves to "unwind" the transfer so that the asset is again available to the judgment creditor.

What is the difference between fraudulent conveyance and fraud?

As explained above, fraudulent conveyance laws provide remedies to creditors to recover a debtor's assets from some third party such as a trustee. Fraud, on the other hand, is defined by *Black's Law Dictionary* as an "intentional perversion of the truth for the purpose of inducing another in reliance upon it to part with some valuable thing belonging to him." Although both contain the root word "fraud," there is typically little relationship between the two offenses.

Family Limited Partnerships for Asset Protection

What is a family limited partnership?

The term "family limited partnership" does not appear anywhere in the state statutes or anywhere in the Internal Revenue Code, but such partnerships are formed under the same statutes and same requirements as those governing any other limited partnership. A *family limited partnership (FLP)* is a limited partnership that is owned by and consists predominantly of family members or family-controlled entities, such as trusts, corporations, or LLCs, that serve as the general partner and the limited partners. An FLP is used to restructure the ownership of a person's assets in a manner that maximizes the preservation and use of the assets during the person's lifetime. It also maximizes the value of what an individual can leave to his or her heirs or other beneficiaries.

Does an FLP provide any creditor protection?

Yes. Since assets transferred to an FLP are no longer owned by the family members but are owned by the FLP, these assets are no longer available for satisfying claims of any creditors of a family-member partner.

Under the laws of most states, a creditor can obtain a court-issued *charging order,* which requires that *if* and *when* a general partner makes cash distributions from the partnership, the distributions which would have been made to the partner against whom a judgment has been obtained must, instead, be paid to the creditor. The creditor may not prevail upon the assets of the partnership or obtain the debtor partner's interest in the partnership.

A charging order is an "exclusive" remedy of a creditor. The creditor has only the right to receive cash distributions that the debtor partner would have received if and when the general partner decides to make such a distribution. The creditor may not force the general partner to make any distribution because to do so would cause a disruption of the partnership and would punish and adversely affect the interests of the other partners against whom the creditor has no claim.

Are there any income tax effects of a charging order?

In 1977, the Internal Revenue Service was asked to rule upon the income tax consequences to a creditor who obtains a charging order. In Revenue Ruling 77-137, the IRS said that partnerships do not pay income taxes but partners do on the basis of their pro rata shares of the income of the partnership. This is true whether or not the general partner makes actual distributions of the income to the partners. The IRS then said that if a creditor obtains a charging order, the creditor is an *assignee* of the partnership interest subject to the charging order. As a result, the creditor, not the debtor partner, pays the income tax upon the debtor partner's pro rata share of the income whether or not the general partner made any actual distributions of such income.

Because a charging order carries with it this potentially serious tax consequence, it makes the FLP a powerful asset protection tool. It gives a debtor partner a negotiating edge against a creditor: the creditor almost always considers it better to settle a claim early and within the partner's liability insurance limits than to pay taxes indefinitely on money he or she has not even received. An FLP offers an obstacle that is typically not worth the creditor's effort to try to overcome.

Family limited partnerships are discussed in detail in Chapter 3.

Isn't an FLP just a form, available to anyone?

An FLP, as a limited partnership, is expressly authorized by Subchapter K of the Internal Revenue Code. Every state has a Limited Partnership Act that regulates the operation of limited partnerships established within its borders. Like all partnerships, an FLP must obtain a federal ID number and must file a partnership income tax return (Form 1065) each year.

To be effective, an FLP must be carefully drafted by an attorney who is very knowledgeable not only about partnership law but also about partnership income tax and estate tax issues. Specialized language is essential to ensure the effectiveness of an FLP. If not drafted correctly, an FLP will not offer any creditor protection or accomplish any other estate planning objectives.

In addition to partnership law, an attorney engaged in creating FLPs must also understand *fraudulent conveyance laws.* These are laws that exist in every state to give creditors rights in property that is conveyed with the intent of defrauding, hindering, or delaying legitimate creditor claims. If these laws are not followed, it is possible for a creditor's attorney to reach partnership assets in spite of the protections offered by an FLP.

An FLP is a complex planning strategy that should be initiated and implemented only by a qualified attorney.

Corporations for Asset Protection

Can corporations be used as an effective asset protection tool?

Yes. A corporation is often a very practical and usable asset protection tool.

If one or more individuals establish a legal corporation according to the laws of the state of their residence or the laws of the domicile of the corporation, the corporation forms a legal barrier between the assets owned by the individuals and the corporation's creditors. If the corporation is sued, the individual stockholder's personal assets are not reachable by the corporation's creditors.

To be effective, this strategy may require the creation of several corporations in combination with trusts to create multiple legal barriers. Doing business with the public as a corporation is far more preferable than conducting business as a sole proprietor or as a general partnership as far as asset protection is concerned.

All factors, both tax and nontax, must be considered when deciding whether to use one corporation or multiple corporations to provide asset protection. It is important that you seek advice from your tax attorney as well as your other advisors before establishing a corporation.

Since I have a good business liability insurance program, why do I still need to incorporate my small business for asset protection?

Liability insurance is a must in these litigation-happy days, but no amount of insurance can protect against all possible claims. The corporate structure is a separate entity, or person, which simply provides an extra blanket of protection for your assets. You should remember, however, that if you create the liability personally, even if you were conducting your corporation's business, your corporation will not protect you against a personal judgment. That is why it is simply good business to have the protection of both personal liability insurance and a corporation.

Furthermore, the limited liability of a corporation extends to matters involving contracts and creditors' claims. New technology or discoveries could make your product or service obsolete overnight, leaving your business in financial difficulty. There could also be a significant downturn in business which might affect the value of your inventory. Every business owner should consider some form of limited liability coverage for his or her small business.

My friend and I want to go into business together. We want to form a corporation. The business will either make it big or totally fail and go bankrupt due to the nature of the proposed business. In order to get started, I intend to contribute some real estate to the new corporation and my friend will be contributing some fairly valuable equipment. Is there a way that we could protect these assets from the corporation's creditors in case the business fails?

Yes, there are several ways that you can protect the valuable assets you and your friend intend to contribute to your new business. First of all, you and your friend could simply lease the land and equipment to the corporation. If the business fails, it will stop making lease payments, thereby entitling you and your friend to reclaim your property.

Additionally, other corporations could be formed to own the property, and those corporations could lease the land and equipment to the corporation under which you will be conducting your business. Various types of trusts, limited partnerships, and limited liability companies could also own the valuable assets with leases going to the new business venture.

No matter which of these scenarios you choose, if you structure them properly and follow the legal formalities required by state law in maintaining the entities as totally separate, the assets you and your friend now own would not be reachable by creditors of the new venture if it fails.

If I create a revocable living trust, will it still be necessary for me to keep my corporation for personal liability purposes? Won't my living trust protect my assets from creditors?

No. Your revocable living trust offers you, as the maker, virtually no personal liability protection because the trust is revocable and totally in your control. If it is under your control, then creditors can ultimately control the property in your living trust.

You should keep the corporation, but you should talk with your estate planning attorney about the possibility of having a revocable living trust for estate planning and a separate, irrevocable trust for other assets you care to protect, not so much for yourself but for others.

Using Gifts for Asset Protection

Can I protect my assets by giving them away?

Giving your assets away is one of the quickest and easiest ways of disposing of assets and protecting them from your creditors. However, the transfers should occur prior to any claim or possible claim, or you risk having the transfers considered fraudulent. If they are deemed fraudulent conveyances, the recipients can be forced to give the gifts to your creditors. Thus, if you have no liability or malpractice claims or alleged claims against you, right now is the best time to make gifts.

There are, however, several problems associated with giving property away through a direct gift:

- You lose control and, perhaps, enjoyment of the asset you give away.
- If the value of the gift exceeds the $10,000-per-recipient annual exclusion, then you must file a federal gift tax return and claim a portion of your lifetime unified estate and gift tax credit. The unified credit exempts $600,000 of assets from estate and gift tax. If the unified credit is exhausted, then you will have to pay a gift tax.
- There is a risk that the recipient of your gift might lose the asset to his or her creditors or to his or her spouse in a divorce action.
- If the recipient of your gift is a minor, he or she cannot own or control property. This makes it very difficult for anyone to do anything with such property.

The solution to all of these problems is to make gifts through a well-drafted trust.

Can I use an irrevocable life insurance trust for asset protection?

An irrevocable life insurance trust (ILIT) is a very effective asset protection tool. Assets that you place into the trust during your lifetime will be protected from your creditors as long as you have not violated any applicable fraudulent conveyance statutes. Additionally, since the life insurance policy death proceeds will be payable to your ILIT instead of outright to individuals, the ILIT, if drafted properly, will provide excellent asset protection for the beneficiaries of the ILIT during their lifetimes.

I want to establish a college fund for my children, but I also want to make sure that, if I am sued or go bankrupt, those funds I set aside for my children cannot be reached by my creditors. Any suggestions?

One of the best estate planning tools to accomplish your objectives is a lifetime irrevocable trust for each of your children. After you create the trusts, you can make gifts of cash or other assets to the trusts subject to the $10,000 annual gift tax exclusion.

It is best, for purposes of asset protection, to appoint a disinterested, nonfamily third party to serve as trustee of these trusts while your children are minors. The assets that you place in the children's trusts will be totally protected from your creditors and even from a bankruptcy court provided the trusts are properly drafted and you do not make transfers of gifts to the trusts that would violate your state's fraudulent conveyances act.

Leasebacks

What is a sale-and-leaseback arrangement?

In a *sale and leaseback,* an individual transfers ownership of an asset such as an office building or equipment to other family members or to a trust and then leases the asset from the family members or the trust. The initial transfer can be the result of either a sale or a gift.

If it is a sale, the buyer pays in cash or in installment payments, and the prior owner, or his or her business, pays rent to the buyer. For this technique to be effective, the sales price must be a fair market value and the rent must be a fair rental value. Since the prior owner no longer owns the asset, his or her creditors cannot reach it.

There are problems associated with this transaction. Upon the sale of the asset, recapture of depreciation can result. Also, the IRS may contend that the transaction has no business purpose; if it does, the IRS will treat the transaction for tax purposes as if it never occurred. Therefore, the original owner will not get a deduction for the lease payments, and the trust will not be able to take depreciation and other deductions. In the past, the IRS has been eager to litigate these transactions, but it has lost in Tax Court as well as in a majority of the U.S. Courts of Appeal.

There is a single solution to both these problems: the owner gives cash *and* his or her borrowing ability (by personally guaranteeing loans) to an irrevocable trust, such as a children's or grandchildren's trust. The trust can then purchase new assets needed for the business; the business can then lease these assets from the trust. The key here is to buy new assets from an independent third party.

The business can deduct the rent, and the trust will have rental income, which may be offset by depreciation and operating expense deductions. The trust can use the rental income to repay any funds borrowed to purchase the assets.

Can I put corporate assets into a children's trust to protect those assets?

Yes. You can achieve excellent results by having irrevocable children's trusts own valuable patents, trademarks, copyrights, licenses, and distribution agreements, as well as any other type of valuable asset that you want to protect.

With this strategy, the children's trust would lease the needed assets to the corporation.

Are there any income tax benefits with this leaseback arrangement?

Yes. Income earned on the assets would go to the children's trust and be taxed at the children's income tax rate as opposed to the corporate income tax rate or that of the stockholders if the operating entity is a subchapter S corporation. The use of a children's trust for shifting income is viable only if the children are 14 years of age or older. You should thoroughly discuss this strategy with your tax advisor before you use it.

Community Property Considerations in Asset Protection Planning

What is community property?

In the nine community property states, spouses own most of the assets of their marriage as community property. *Community property* is all property of a marriage other than separate property. *Separate property* is any property acquired before the marriage, or any property acquired during the marriage through gifts, inheritance, bequest, recovery for personal injuries, or partition of community property. The community property system has far more tax and nontax planning advantages than the common law property systems found in the forty-one noncommunity property states, which are called common law property states.

Unfortunately, community property ownership does not protect assets from the claims of either spouse's creditors. The *separate* property of the nonliable spouse is, however, exempt from debts and tort claims of the liable spouse's creditors.

How can we protect assets in a community property state?

Because community property is subject to the claims of creditors of either spouse, in some instances it may be a good idea either to partition community property into separate property before a claim arises or to have one spouse give his or her property to the other spouse, thereby making the property the other spouse's separate property. Remember, separate property includes property acquired by gift.

Partitioning property is accomplished by a written document which identifies the asset being partitioned and which states the mutual intent of the husband and wife to partition the property. After the partition agreement has been signed, the husband owns his part of the asset as his sole separate property and the wife owns her part of the asset as her sole separate property.

This technique cannot be used in all community property states, so always confer with your attorney before partitioning community property.

Are there any problems with partitioning or giving away community property?

There are potential problems associated with both of these strategies:

- A surviving spouse's separate property will not get a step-up in basis to fair market value at the death of the first spouse to die. (Only the deceased spouse's property gets the step-up in basis.) A surviving spouse's interest in community property will get a step-up in basis on the death of his or her spouse.
- Once given away or partitioned, the property is the separate property of each spouse. A divorce court cannot order a spouse to transfer this separate property back to the spouse who gave it away or convert the property back to community property.
- If one spouse dies and leaves his or her separate property to the surviving spouse in a will, the surviving spouse becomes the full owner of the property and that property is then subject to his or her creditor claims.
- If there are too many assets in one spouse's name, creditors can easily argue that the "rich" spouse is really just holding those assets as the trustee of a *constructive,* or *resulting, trust* for the benefit of the "poor" spouse. Since a resulting or constructive trust is an unwritten revocable trust created by a person's actions, such a trust does not protect the assets of its maker. The debtor spouse's creditors may break this trust and have access to its assets.

Can these problems be overcome?

While the loss of a 100 percent step-up in basis on the death of the first spouse to die cannot effectively be overcome, the other problems can be by using an *asset protection trust.*

In an asset protection trust, one spouse, as trust maker, transfers legal title to some or all of his or her separate property assets to an irrevocable trust. These separate property assets may be separate assets that were previously acquired or separate assets that were recently acquired by a partition of community property or by a gift from the other spouse.

Either spouse (or both) may be named as the trustee of the asset protection trust. The trustee owns and controls the legal title to all trust assets. The nontransferring spouse is then named as the life beneficiary of the trust and, as such, will own a life estate or beneficial title to the assets for life. Beneficial title is the right to use and enjoy the property.

After the beneficiary spouse is deceased, children or others (the remainder persons) become the beneficiaries. Their beneficial title can remain in trust for their lives or can be distributed to them upon their attaining a certain age of maturity. The surviving spouse can remain as trustee and continue to be in control of the assets of the trust.

Assets can be added to the trust by any person at any time through lifetime transfers or by a will or a trust at death.

The key provision which protects assets in an asset protection trust is a *spendthrift provision.* However, the spouse who owns the separate property assets will not qualify for protection from creditors under the spendthrift provision of the trust. This is why the spouse transferring the separate property is not a beneficiary of the asset protection trust. Trust assets are, however, protected from the creditors of the other spouse, who did not own or transfer the separate property assets to the trust and who is the life beneficiary of the trust.

Both spouses can be trustees of the asset protection trust provided successor trustees are named in the trust document. If a potential liability suit arises, then the spouse who transferred the assets to the trust can resign as trustee in favor of the other spouse or a successor trustee.

Are there any solutions to the problem of divorce when giving or partitioning assets?

This problem can be mitigated by having the spouses enter into an *option agreement:* each spouse agrees to exchange 50 percent of his or her assets for 50 percent of the other spouse's assets in the event of a divorce. This at least helps to equalize the property of the spouses. If the spouses have a solid marriage, an option agreement is usually not necessary.

Offshore Planning for Asset Protection

What is offshore planning?

In its simplest form, offshore planning is simply one more method of asset protection. Asset protection is maintaining control of what you have accumulated and ensuring that your family and loved ones will benefit from it in the long run. Its purpose is to avoid losing your hard-earned wealth to a catastrophic creditor, an irate troublemaker, an unplanned business reversal, or the IRS or some other government regulatory bureaucracy. It is planning in advance against a future catastrophe.

Buying insurance is one form of asset protection. So is proper estate planning through various trusts or a family limited partnership. By definition, *offshore planning* is international estate, business, tax, and investment planning under the laws of a jurisdiction that you find to be more advantageous than your own country's laws. People in Europe, the Middle East, or Asia who plan under the laws of the United States are doing offshore planning. For U.S. citizens, offshore planning means making use of the laws of a country other than the United States.

Why do people use offshore planning?

The motivations for going offshore are as many and varied as the people who choose to do so. Some people have chosen offshore planning because:

- They live in a country with an uncertain political future.
- They live in a country with forced heirship laws that would prevent them from distributing their wealth the way they choose.
- Their professional liability insurance has become more and more expensive for less and less coverage.
- They are general partners and therefore liable for the mistakes of all the other partners.
- They want to protect an expected inheritance.
- They are afraid of becoming targets of new legislation and

some of the arbitrary and capricious decisions of environmental or other regulatory agencies.

- They prefer to avoid asking their future spouses for a premarital agreement, or they would like to supplement such an agreement with added protection.
- They want to lower their high financial profile by using the confidentiality afforded by offshore planning.
- They want to protect their assets from litigious predators.
- They want to take advantage of certain offshore financial instruments that will afford them additional avenues of income tax deferral and estate tax avoidance.

Who uses offshore planning?

Offshore planning is widely used by many prestigious U.S. corporations and banks. Some of the best-known names in the Fortune 500 do much of their business and banking outside of the United States. Sears, McDonald's, IBM, Boeing, and Dow are among the hundreds of overseas players. Banks as large as Chase Manhattan and Citibank make a good share of their profits outside the borders of our country.

Some corporations, such as Dow, have their own offshore banks which provide another profit center, as well as allow them to obtain favorable interest rates on loans and protection from currency fluctuations. Business enterprises from manufacturers to medical schools find it advantageous to locate on foreign soil. An inordinate number of ships, for example, are registered in Liberia and Panama.

Noncorporate users are often individuals of high net worth but not always. Different people have different motivations for "going offshore." In spite of the "jet-set" image of offshore planning, many middle-class professionals and businesspeople make use of it as well.

What are the advantages of offshore planning?

One of the big benefits of offshore planning is confidentiality. Many people are simply tired of the lack of privacy in one's business and financial affairs in the United States. If you know where and how to look, you can find out dozens of things about someone through a simple search of public records. However, in many of the popular offshore financial centers, there are strict privacy laws that protect the customers of offshore institutions. Many of these jurisdictions make it illegal for an employee or officer of the bank, for example, to reveal that someone even has an account there, let alone any of the details of that account. Many jurisdictions back up their laws with criminal penalties for any institutional employees who violate them. This prevents information from getting to government agencies, competitors, and predators.

For many people, protection of their assets from the groups just mentioned is more important than privacy concerning the assets. They find themselves in positions of vulnerability and high liability and fear losing the nest egg that they have worked a lifetime to earn. They go offshore to build a hedge of protection around the things they own to preserve them for the ones they love.

JURISDICTIONS FOR OFFSHORE PLANNING

What countries are commonly used for offshore planning?

The United States is used as an offshore center for citizens of other countries. For U.S. citizens, there are a number of offshore choices: Andorra, Anguilla, Antigua, Aruba, Australia, Bahamas, Barbados, Barbuda, Belize, Bermuda, British Virgin Islands, Cayman Islands, Cook Islands, Costa Rica, Cyprus, Gibraltar, Grenada, Guernsey, Hong Kong, Ireland, Isle of Man, Jersey, Labuan, Liechtenstein, Luxembourg, Madeira, Malaysia, Malta, Marshall Islands, Mauritius, Monaco, Montserrat, Nauru, Netherlands Antilles, Nevis, New Zealand, Niue, Panama, St. Kitts, Seychelles, Singapore, Switzerland, Turks and Caicos, and Vanuatu.

You can see that offshore jurisdictions are in all parts of the globe including the Americas, Europe, Asia, the Far East, the South Pacific, and especially the Caribbean.

A few of these have become more popular because of legislation which serves to clarify their rules of asset protection and provide certainty about what to expect within their jurisdictions. For these reasons, some of the most popular countries include the Bahamas, Belize, Bermuda, the Cayman Islands, the Cook Islands, Cyprus, Gibraltar, Mauritius, Nevis, and the Turks and Caicos Islands.

What factors should I consider in choosing an offshore financial center?

You should consider the following factors:

- The extent of and the protection offered in the financial center's offshore asset protection trust law (Is it well defined, established, protective, and favorable to what you want to accomplish?)
- The offshore center's reputation in the business world generally
- The common language of the offshore center
- The availability of support services such as attorneys, accountants, and financial advisors
- The tax laws of the offshore center
- The economic and political stability of the offshore center
- The state of the offshore center's telecommunication facilities (ready availability of telephone, television, fax, wiring services, etc.)
- The physical accessibility of the offshore center
- The currency of the offshore center and its relationship to the U.S. dollar
- The desirability of the offshore center as a place to visit for you and your family

THE COST OF OFFSHORE PLANNING

What costs should I expect to encounter in offshore planning?

Depending upon your choice of planning tools, you should expect to pay between $15,000 and $50,000 (or a small percentage of the assets) for legal fees and setup costs, along with annual maintenance fees of approximately $2000.

The Offshore Trust for Asset Protection

What is an offshore asset protection trust?

An *offshore asset protection trust* is typically an irrevocable, tax-neutral grantor trust. It is considered by many specialists in the field to be the most powerful strategy available for protecting assets from judgment and tort creditors.

A creditor who obtains a U.S. judgment has several hurdles to overcome to attach the assets in the trust. Procedurally, the creditor has to file a brand new lawsuit, since the foreign trustee or court does not have to honor U.S. judgments. Also, the creditor has to prove that the statute of limitations did not expire (usually 1 to 2 years from trust creation) and that the creditor has standing to sue.

There are other difficulties, since the creditor has to retain a foreign, non-contingent-fee lawyer and post a large cash bond and legal fee retainer. It will likely take several years for the creditor to get the case to trial. Even then, should the creditor overcome these hurdles, the foreign trustee could change the *situs* of the trust (the trust's jurisdiction and where the assets are held), so the creditor might have to start all over again in another jurisdiction.

What are the objectives of an offshore asset protection trust?

An offshore asset protection trust has a number of objectives, including:

1. To separate an individual from assets that creditors could take under the laws of the United States
2. To ensure that the assets are safe and secure and are under competent and reputable management
3. To allow assets to revert back to their owner when creditor exposure has subsided
4. To prevent additional estate, gift, income, and excise tax exposure
5. To be free of any violation of criminal laws, tax laws, or bankruptcy laws
6. To allow the maker to direct investments and change trustees
7. To be part of an overall comprehensive estate plan which is coordinated with the maker's other assets and estate planning
8. To put the maker in a position that allows him or her to honestly inform a court of law that the maker has no power or authority over the trustee and, because of this lack of authority, possesses no legal ability to comply with the court's orders
9. To create a situation in which assets can be moved, sold, invested, managed, or distributed by the trustee even though the

maker is under court order or other constraints that prevent the maker from doing so personally

10. To allow the trustee to easily change the situs of the trust in the event of the commencement of litigation in the foreign situs or for any other legitimate reason

Is this type of offshore planning legal?

Of course it is. There are places on your tax return to report income from foreign trusts. But engaging in offshore planning does require that you broaden your thinking. You must stop seeing estate, business, tax, and financial planning parochially and start acting as an international person. Just as you can travel to other countries, work in other countries, carry on business in other countries, buy things from other countries, and vacation in other countries, you can also do planning in other countries.

A person doing offshore planning is much like a business located in Illinois deciding to incorporate in Delaware because advantageous laws exist there for corporations.

That's not to say that no one has ever used international planning in an illegal way. But international treaties and agreements are making it harder and harder to do so. Offshore planning does have an exotic mystique about it, brought on by books and movies about drug runners, smugglers, money launderers, and mob guys. Even though these are the types of people who get all the press (when they get caught), international finance and planning is a completely legitimate multibillion-dollar industry that quietly goes about its business 365 days per year, year after year.

In the real world of international planning, the offshore institutions that you work with are as likely to check you out before accepting you as a client as you are to check their references. They are very careful to involve themselves only with legitimate businesspeople and investors and to avoid any contact with the criminal element.

What are some of the laws I should be aware of in using offshore planning?

There are a few federal laws that pertain to offshore planning, most of which carry criminal penalties of fines and jail time if violated. Your best prevention against violating any of the laws mentioned below is to use a qualified estate planning attorney and other qualified advisors who are conversant with the laws and experienced in their application.

- *Bankruptcy Reform Act of 1994,* revised Section 152 of Title 18 U.S.C. and added Section 157 entitled "bankruptcy fraud": Under these sections, a person who individually or on behalf of a corporation makes false or fraudulent representations, or knowingly and fraudulently transfers or conceals any of his or her property or that of the corporation, is subject to fine and/or imprisonment.
- *Crime Control Act of 1990:* This act provides for criminal penalties for any person trying to place an asset beyond the reach of the FDIC or the RTC.
- *Money Laundering Control Act of 1986:* Enacted to help fight the war on drugs and drug traffickers, this act was broadened, in 1988, to also include financial crimes. It provides for severe fines and/or prison terms for people who conduct a financial transaction designed to evade the payment of federal income taxes, to conceal the nature, source, ownership, or control of the proceeds gained from an unlawful activity, or to avoid federal currency reporting laws.
- *Internal Revenue Code Section 7206(4):* This section provides that a person who conceals property to defeat the assessment or collection of a tax is subject to fine and/or imprisonment.

Are offshore asset protection trusts guaranteed to work every time?

There are very few guarantees in life. The same is true for offshore asset protection planning. Such variables as a person's individual situation, the types of assets held by the offshore asset protection trust, the quality of the drafting of the trust document, the skill of the attack and the defense of the trust, the quality and soundness of the law of the particular foreign jurisdiction, and many other factors affect the viability of any offshore plan using an asset protection trust.

Most offshore planners agree that offshore planning "works" if it leaves their clients better off than they would have been without the planning. That standard is virtually always met.

What if I'm already involved in a lawsuit?

Under the fraudulent conveyance rules, if you are currently involved in a suit, you will not be able to set up an offshore asset protection trust. This is the general rule unless the maximum potential of the claim is less than your entire net worth. In this situation, it may be possible to transfer some of your assets while still leaving enough to honor the existing claim.

This can be a very tricky issue, so you should obtain proper legal advice.

If an offshore asset protection trust is truly irrevocable, how do I ever get the assets back?

Offshore asset protection trusts are designed in such a way that you and your beneficiaries may receive the assets back at any time. The irrevocable nature of the trust is for your protection. Depending on the jurisdiction used, both the maker and the heirs may be allowed to be beneficiaries of the trust. Trust laws do vary, so a proper investigation of a specific jurisdiction's treatment of this issue should be made.

USING AN OFFSHORE ASSET PROTECTION TRUST

How does an offshore asset protection trust work?

The key to an offshore asset protection trust is that, once ownership has been transferred, neither the trust maker nor the trustees can be forced to repatriate assets for the benefit of creditors. Therefore, a properly drafted offshore asset protection trust should contain language requiring that the trustee ignore instructions that are given to the trustee under duress, such as under a court order from a foreign jurisdiction.

Any asset can be transferred into an offshore asset protection trust, either directly or by transferring shares of a limited partnership which owns the asset. However, liquid assets which can be physically relocated are best. That is because courts are unlikely to give up control over a fixed asset, such as real estate, that lies within their jurisdiction.

The main reason the offshore asset protection trust works is that it places assets under the control of a trustee in a jurisdiction that does not recognize judgments awarded in the United States by U.S. courts. It works because of legislation and statute, not because your assets are "hidden." If a judgment is entered against you in a lawsuit, you will be asked under oath to disclose your assets. If you attempt to "hide" your assets, you will likely be committing perjury. Indeed, if you attempted to hide assets from, say, the IRS, you could be faced with criminal charges. Offshore planning works, ultimately, because it is based on sound legal principles. It serves to discourage a litigant from filing suit in the first place, and if a suit is filed, it encourages early and fair settlements.

Can you give me an example of a situation in which an offshore asset protection trust would be effective?

To demonstrate why the offshore asset protection trust encourages settlement or avoids litigation altogether, let's look at a typical lawsuit against a person who has used offshore planning in the Bahamas. The Bahamas is a very popular offshore center because of its proximity to the United States and easy access via a short flight from Florida.

In our example, George Upright, a prominent businessman, has fired an employee for dishonesty. An overzealous attorney has convinced the employee to sue her former boss for discrimination, with one-third of the settlement to be given to the attorney in fees. The jury compares the poor, unemployed worker to the successful business owner and decides George deserves to pay because he has more. In spite of any evidence to the contrary, the jury finds for the plaintiff and awards $20,000 in actual damages and $3 million in punitive damages.

George carries $1 million of liability insurance coverage in an umbrella policy, but finds out it does not include punitive damages. George mumbles something about being covered when you fall off the roof but not when you hit the ground. After the judgment is handed down, the opposing attorney takes George's deposition, under oath, to determine where all of George's personal assets are located. George states that he has a checking account containing approximately $5000 and a savings account containing approximately $50,000 in the name of his revocable living trust. He also has a car and some personal effects. The lawyer finds out that the home George lives in is owned by his wife's revocable living trust, so it is unavailable to satisfy the judgment. Everything else, totaling approximately $2 million, is owned by an offshore asset protection trust in the Bahamas which George established about 3 years ago.

The aggressive plaintiff's attorney decides to go after the offshore asset protection trust. When he does, he trips over a whole series of barriers:

- First, the attorney finds out that Bahamian courts will not recognize a judgment handed down by a foreign court, so he must initiate new proceedings in the Bahamas.
- Since the attorney is not licensed to practice law in the Bahamas, he must retain Bahamian counsel. He wonders if the client can foot the bill for the Bahamian attorney since he is being paid on a contingency basis and hasn't been paid himself.
- The Bahamian attorney points out that the Bahamian court is unlikely to find that the plaintiff has a jurisdictional basis to bring the suit because neither George nor the assets he owns outside the offshore asset protection trust are within the Bahamian jurisdiction.
- Next, the attorney decides to sue the trustees, which would allow the Bahamian court to have jurisdiction. However, he finds there are no filing, registration, or disclosure requirements for trusts established in the Bahamas.
- George Upright, the defendant, is very cooperative and tells the attorney the name of the trust company which is acting as trustee of his offshore asset protection trust. However, because of very strict secrecy laws which apply to banks and trust companies and their employees, officers, lawyers, and accountants, the attorney is finding it very hard to gain enough information upon which to formulate a claim.
- The U.S. judge issues a court order requiring that George Upright instruct the trustee to disclose all requested information about his offshore asset protection trust. George complies with the court order. The only problem is that the trust says that the trustee cannot obey any instructions from the trust maker that are given under duress. The trustee is bound by fiduciary law, a law higher than the court's order, to follow those instructions in the offshore asset protection trust.
- Then the attorney finds out that because he represents a foreign plaintiff with no Bahamian assets, the court will require

a substantial cash payment to George as a security deposit in the event George prevails in the case.

The litigant has to overcome all of these barriers before she can even bring a case against George in the Bahamas. Now, if the plaintiff were a large corporation with lots of money and a very emotional CEO who was out to get George (instead of a person with few resources), it might actually be able to clear all of these hurdles with money, patience, and persistence.

If the plaintiff does clear all the preliminary hurdles to bringing a lawsuit against the offshore asset protection trust, she is still met with some final barriers such as:

- Actions can be brought only by actual creditors who had claims that existed at the time George set up his offshore asset protection trust and that were known about by George.
- The creditor has the burden of proving that the claim existed and that George knew about it when he established his offshore asset protection trust.
- Regardless of the above, the action has to be brought within 2 years of the date that the offshore asset protection trust was set up.

So even after clearing the preliminary hurdles, the litigant still fails to reach the offshore asset protection trust because George established his offshore asset protection trust more than 2 years ago. Also, even if the trust was set up less than 2 years ago, the creditor could never establish that she had a claim against George at that time and that he knew about it. Finally, even if all the above factors are met and the creditor is successful, the transfer of assets to the offshore asset protection trust can be set aside only to the extent necessary to satisfy the claim. The balance of the assets in the offshore asset protection trust remain intact.

It is easy to see why the plaintiff's attorney in George's case would recommend a reasonable out-of-court settlement when faced with the daunting prospect of litigating the case (especially on a contingent-fee basis) in a foreign jurisdiction.

I have been wrongly sued by a former business partner. My insurance carrier says that I do not have insurance to cover the claim, and I am afraid that the litigation is going to be very expen-

sive. In addition, the IRS has recorded a tax lien against me as the result of an audit of a limited partnership in which I was an investor. I just received a $1 million inheritance from my mother, and I want to protect it by placing it into an offshore trust. Do you see any problems with this?

Yes. The transfer you are contemplating would be fraudulent both as to your former business partner and as to the IRS. The Uniform Fraudulent Transfer Act, adopted in one form or another in every state in the United States, provides that a transfer made by a debtor is fraudulent as to any creditor

> if the debtor made the transfer either (*a*) with the actual intent to hinder, delay, or defraud the creditor, or (*b*) without receiving a reasonably equivalent value in exchange for the transfer, when the debtor was engaged or about to engage in a business or transaction for which the remaining assets were unreasonably small or when the debtor intended to incur debts beyond his or her ability to pay them as they became due.

A transfer may also be considered to be fraudulent if the debtor did not receive a reasonably equivalent value for the transfer and if the debtor was insolvent at the time of the transfer or became insolvent as a result of the transfer.

As you can see, since your contemplated transfer to an offshore trust is done for the purpose of hindering future collection actions by your former business partner and by the IRS, the transfer would be fraudulent as to them and, thus, your transfer to an offshore trust would be voidable by them. The only appropriate and defensible time to engage in asset protection planning with the use of an offshore trust is at a time when no substantial debts or obligations are owing by you. If you wait until potentially devastating claims are already brought against you, your available options will be severely limited.

TAX ISSUES OF AN OFFSHORE ASSET PROTECTION TRUST

What are the income tax ramifications of an offshore asset protection trust?

A properly drafted offshore asset protection trust is a *grantor trust* under the Internal Revenue Code. A grantor trust is a trust whose income, loss, deductions, or credits are reported on the maker's income tax return rather than on a return filed by the trust itself. This means that the asset protection trust is income tax–neutral; it does not change the income taxation of the assets within it.

Can an asset protection trust own S corporation stock?

Subchapter S elections are available for any domestic corporations whose stock is owned by an offshore asset protection trust that is a grantor trust.

If my business is involved in international operations, can I save taxes by having it held in an asset protection trust?

The simple ownership of an international business corporation (IBC) within an asset protection trust will provide no tax benefit to an individual. Congress has enacted several antiavoidance rules that specifically address the ownership of foreign corporations. These corporations, generally known as *controlled foreign corporations,* are fully taxed on their worldwide operations. Therefore, except at the corporate tax level, there are no major tax advantages of holding an IBC within a typical grantor-type asset protection trust.

There are several variations of the foreign corporation rules, so before you initiate any type of foreign business operations, regardless of their purpose, a complete analysis of the issues should be done by a competent international corporate tax attorney.

What are the estate and gift tax consequences of an asset protection trust?

Because the trust's assets revert to the maker at the maker's death or under certain other circumstances, the trust assets will be included in the maker's gross estate for federal estate tax purposes. All of the assets in the trust receive a step-up in basis upon the maker's death. For these reasons, there is no gift tax consequence when the maker contributes assets to the offshore protection trust.

Isn't there an excise tax for transferring appreciated assets into a foreign trust?

There is a 35 percent excise tax for contributions of appreciated assets into an international trust. However, if the transfer is made to a grantor trust, there is no 35 percent excise tax, since the trust is fully taxed to the grantor. If the trust becomes a nongrantor trust, the excise tax will be triggered.

Do I have to report the creation of my trust to the IRS?

Yes. When you create any foreign trust, you are required to file certain IRS forms within 90 days of creating the trust. In fact, for contributions of appreciated assets to the trust, you are required to file another form on the day of the transfer. Failure to file these forms can subject you to fines, penalties, and/or imprisonment.

You say that I have to notify the government if I create an offshore trust. What happens if the government is my creditor?

Asset protection trusts work against government agencies as well as private creditors. However, they must work within the rules, just as U.S. citizens must. Asset protection trusts cannot be used to avoid current tax liens, current EPA liabilities, or any other government claim against you. The government has worked closely with foreign jurisdictions, so you should not assume that all assets will be out of the reach of the U.S. government. It does have a substantial amount of power to seize your assets.

Most people who initiate asset protection planning are not concerned about normal governmental interference in their lives. They are usually more concerned with frivolous lawsuits and other miscellaneous legal actions against them.

OFFSHORE TRUST PLANNING AND REVOCABLE LIVING TRUST PLANNING

It sounds like an offshore asset protection trust is much like a revocable living trust. Is that true?

In many ways an offshore asset protection trust is much like a revocable living trust. For example, both can avoid the costs and time delays of probate, both can provide for administration in the event of the trust maker's disability, both can maintain confidentiality, both can aid in planning for estate taxes, and both can contain specific provisions about distributing assets to heirs. One big difference between the two trusts, however, is that the offshore asset protection trust can offer creditor protection for the trust maker during his or her lifetime, while the revocable living trust cannot.

An offshore asset protection trust should always be integrated with the trust maker's overall estate planning. A person should have an offshore asset protection trust and a revocable living trust, plus other planning tools, for a truly effective estate plan.

While the two types of trust are similar, they have different estate planning functions. An offshore asset protection trust's main objective is to protect assets from egregious creditors; a revocable living trust's primary objectives are to care for the maker if he or she is disabled, to reduce federal estate taxes, and to ensure that after the death of the maker the trust property will be managed, administered, and distributed according to the instructions in the trust.

TRUSTEES OF AN OFFSHORE ASSET PROTECTION TRUST

Who should be the trustee of my offshore trust?

You should name both a U.S. individual or corporate trustee and a reputable foreign professional corporate trustee. You can name one or more foreign trustees, but most people are more comfortable with having at least one U.S. trustee.

How do I choose an international trustee?

After choosing the offshore jurisdiction you prefer, you should interview different trustees to determine what services they can provide. Many are very sophisticated and assist their clients in almost any financial transaction. On the other hand, some trustees only passively hold their clients' assets and provide very few managerial services. Although you may pay a bit more for the services of the former, the money is well spent, especially if the latter type of trustee would constantly refer you to more "experienced" institutions. Just as in the United States, you get what you pay for; the cheapest trustee is not necessarily the best one for your situation.

How are my assets protected from the trustee?

Many individuals appoint a *trust protector* to oversee the activities of the trustee. The trust protector can be either an individual or a group of individuals and corporations. The trust protector is often authorized in the trust document to fire the trustee if the protector deems it necessary. Most jurisdictions have specific legislation addressing this issue. In fact, in several jurisdictions, you can give the trust protector almost any power. This allows you to provide several layers of safety regarding your foreign trustee.

In general, you must feel comfortable about dealing on an international basis. If you are more concerned with the credibility of the trustee than the threat of a lawsuit, you shouldn't proceed with this type of planning. In the worst-case scenario—a lawsuit in the United States—it may be necessary that the foreign trustee hold title and have full control of the assets within the trust. If you are not comfortable with this, you should, once again, not initiate this type of planning.

I would like to have a little more control over my offshore trust and my trustee. How can I accomplish this?

Some offshore asset protection trusts provide for a *trust advisory committee.* The maker will usually be the chairperson of the committee. The committee may:

- Render nonbinding investment advice
- Change the foreign trustee and U.S trustee as long as a replacement foreign trustee is named
- Name replacement committee members and remove members

Your participation on this committee should be suspended any time a creditor is a threat. In addition, international trustees are often directed by your instructions as set forth in a document sometimes known as a "letter of wishes." In it, you can request that the trustee invest the trust assets in a certain way or make distributions in a particular manner consistent with the terms of the trust. If the trustee does not want to follow these instructions or desires, he or she can be removed by the protector or trust advisors, or both.

An Offshore ILIT

Is there a vehicle that can serve to protect my wife's and my

assets from judgment and tort creditors and at the same time afford us considerable estate tax savings?

You can create an offshore asset protection trust which will also serve to own and be the beneficiary of a second-to-die life insurance policy on both of your lives. This policy will fund the trust on the death of the surviving spouse. The proceeds will be used to provide the liquidity to pay any estate taxes due at that time. This trust, known as an *offshore ILIT,* is useful for several reasons:

1. It allows you to obtain favorable insurance rates from reputable offshore insurance companies.
2. It saves you costs by combining the benefits of two planning tools (the offshore asset protection trust and the ILIT) in one vehicle.
3. It allows you to obtain optimum asset protection benefits for all noninsurance assets that are transferred to the trust (usually not to exceed your exemption equivalent) and for all remaining assets even if a portion of the trust's funds are used to finance the payment of the taxes. (*Note:* The payment of taxes is achieved by purchasing illiquid assets or by lending to the estate or trust.)

Foreign Bank Accounts

Can't I just establish a foreign bank account to provide asset protection?

Foreign bank accounts may seem to be an exotic way of protecting assets, especially if the account is in a country which jealously protects the secrecy of its depositors. The big problem with this method is that a judge can easily order you to return the funds to the United States if a creditor learns of the foreign account.

To maintain the privacy of a foreign account, you must cheat and lie and even commit tax fraud to protect the secrecy of the assets in the account. While it is not a crime to have a foreign account, it is a crime to lie about its existence, especially to a court or to the IRS. In fact, Form 1040 of the federal income tax return requires that foreign bank accounts be disclosed on its Schedule B.

As Sammy Davis, Jr., used to say, "Don't do the crime if you can't do the time." Therefore, you should rule out this method as a legal means of protecting your assets from creditors.

Offshore Annuities

Is there a way that a U.S. citizen can utilize offshore planning to gain current income tax benefits?

A nice way to obtain international diversification and tax-deferred benefits is through the use of an offshore annuity. Offshore annuities have essentially the same advantages as their U.S. counterparts. You obtain tax deferral on the income earned until you start withdrawing the funds. In addition, offshore annuities provide privacy, international diversification, the flexibility to choose which investments are subject to the annuity, and protection from judgment creditors.

Expatriation

What is expatriation?

Expatriation is the process of giving up citizenship in one's native country and becoming a citizen of some other country.

How does someone give up his or her U.S. citizenship?

The person first finds another country that will accept him or her as a citizen, based upon the person's ancestry or willingness to contribute to the local economy through business or investment. When all the arrangements are made, the person simply walks into the U.S. consulate, turns in his or her passport, and formally renounces his or her citizenship.

Why would someone give up his or her U.S. citizenship?

The primary nonpolitical reason that people give up their U.S. citizenship is to avoid what they consider confiscatory tax policies of the government. In spite of all the offshore and domestic tax and estate planning that can be done, the United States is still one of the few countries in the world that taxes its citizens on everything they own and earn worldwide, regardless of where they live.

The only way to avoid global taxation is to *not* be a U.S. citizen. Just living abroad will not make any difference.

Most people who take this step are, naturally, individuals who have a lot to lose because of the size of their wealth. Some pay so much in income taxes that they can't enjoy the lifestyle they prefer. Others cannot bear the thought that the government's estate taxes will take more than half of what they have worked so hard to accumulate, especially after it was already taxed once at the income tax level. Others see property ownership rights diminishing under U.S. law and fear an uncertain economic future.

One of the most famous expatriates is John Templeton, the mutual fund manager. He gave up his U.S. citizenship and moved to the Bahamas, where there is not only no income or estate tax but no tax of any kind! It is estimated that when he sold his company in 1992, he saved more than $100 million in capital gain taxes.

Another well-known example is John Dorrance III, an heir of the Campbell Soup fortune. Because he became a citizen of Ireland, his heirs will be subject to only a 2 percent estate tax instead of the 55 percent U.S. estate tax. Since his estate is estimated at over $1 billion, the savings for his family could amount to over half a billion dollars!

Obviously, these expatriates and others who move to countries that have no taxes are also saving a fortune in income taxes over the years. If they were to keep investing in the United States through normal channels, they could pay more each year in their 39.6 percent federal income tax bracket than many people earn.

What are the disadvantages of giving up my U.S. citizenship?

Besides the emotional concerns inherent in severing patriotic allegiance and moving far from friends and family, there are a few practical disadvantages of giving up your citizenship. Unless you can convince the IRS that tax avoidance was not a "principal purpose" for expatriating, it will continue to tax you for another 10 years on U.S. income, including capital gains from U.S. real estate and stocks in American companies.

Also, as a noncitizen, you may not come back to the United States for more than 30 days in the first year. After that, you are limited to 100 to 120 days per year. So don't think you can give up your citizenship and continue to live exactly where you do now!

Finally, once you give up your U.S. citizenship, it is hard to get it back. Like any other nonresident alien, you will have to get a green card and go through the entire naturalization process. Expatriation is certainly not a step to be entered into lightly or without legal counsel. It is still considered by most to be a planning strategy of last resort.

5

Charitable Planning

Charitable giving has always been a fundamental aspect of estate planning. Most people who plan have a strong sense of family and community and are therefore inclined to make charitable gifts a part of an overall estate plan.

This sense of charity was reflected in the questions and answers provided by a number of our contributing authors. They addressed a broad spectrum of charitable planning, with the emphasis placed on charitable remainder trust planning.

It has been our experience that better estate planning attorneys have a good deal of knowledge about charitable planning. This knowledge is extremely important given the complex nature of the charitable giving provisions of the Internal Revenue Code. Charitable planning is not an area that should be approached lightly, as you can see from reading this chapter. There are a myriad of issues that must be considered, including control; income, gift, and estate tax ramifications; current finances; future income and principal needs; the extent of your charitable inclination; and the types of property you own.

This chapter gives an excellent overview of all of those issues and how to deal with them. It also has a number of examples which will help you visualize the concepts included in the broad topic of charitable planning.

Charitable Giving

Why does a person give to charity?

Many people give to charity because they are philanthropic. They feel they can benefit society by giving to organizations in which they believe.

What is the simplest and most common way to make a gift?

The simplest way to give to a charity is by making an outright gift. Outright gifts can be made either during a person's lifetime or at death. *Donors* of charitable gifts generally receive tax benefits. The availability and amount of those benefits depend on several factors, and the charitable gift must be properly structured to maximize the tax advantages. Some of the factors to be considered are:

- The type of property given (e.g., cash, stock, real estate, short-term or long-term)
- The nature of the charitable organization
- The value and tax basis of the gift
- The potential giver's contribution base (adjusted gross income, without regard to net operating loss)
- The charitable deduction interplay between or among other charitable gifts made in the same year or "carried over" from prior tax years

Can I actually "make money" by giving to charity?

If you have any charitable interest—and most people really do have a strong charitable impulse to help, for example, the church they attend, the school or college from which they or their children graduated, or the hospital where loved ones have been cared for—then you can "profit" from the pleasure you'll derive by helping a charitable organization you believe in to carry out its worthwhile mission. And if you plan your charitable gift wisely, the combination of tax savings and financial benefits can make your sacrifice almost painless. In fact, you'll probably feel you've come out ahead, all things considered.

The key is proper planning.

I would like to make a charitable contribution, but I do not have the financial means available to me. Are there any alternatives?

Outright gifts during life can be made only by persons who can afford to do so. However, charitable giving can include *split-interest trusts.* These are special trusts which provide both a benefit to a charity and a benefit to a "noncharity." This noncharity is generally the donor and the donor's family.

Split-interest trusts have gained popularity because they can satisfy personal financial needs as well as philanthropic desires. The most commonly used split-interest trust is the charitable remainder trust. A less frequently used split-interest trust is the charitable lead trust.

Charitable Remainder Trusts

What is a charitable remainder trust?

A *charitable remainder trust (CRT)* is an irrevocable trust created for the purpose of holding assets given to the trust by a donor during the donor's lifetime or upon the donor's death.

A CRT is a split-interest trust in that its donated assets are shared between noncharitable beneficiaries and charitable beneficiaries. Typically, a CRT is designed to pay income to one or more trust noncharitable beneficiaries (usually the donor and the donor's spouse) for life or for a term of years, after which the trust assets are paid to or held for qualified charitable beneficiaries.

The percentage of income that must be paid annually to the income beneficiaries cannot be less than 5 percent of the value of the trust assets. There is no limit as to the number or type of income beneficiaries (individuals, corporations, trusts, etc.), except that at least one income beneficiary *must* be a taxable entity and that unborn individuals (such as grandchildren not yet born when the trust is created) do not qualify unless the trust's duration is limited to a term of years.

A CRT can continue for the lifetimes of the persons selected as income beneficiaries or for a term of years not to exceed 20. When the last income beneficiary dies or the term of years expires, all assets remaining in the trust must be distributed to one or more charities, called *charitable remaindermen.*

How does a CRT work?

To understand how a CRT works, let's look at an example of a typical situation in which a CRT is used:

Mr. and Mrs. Hastings have stock for which they paid $10,000. The stock has grown in value over the years and is now worth $110,000. The stock pays them a dividend of $1500 per year, which is a 1.36 percent return. Mr. and Mrs. Hastings are each 61 years old. Their total estate is large enough for this stock to be taxable in their estate at a 50 percent marginal tax rate.

If the Hastings sell the stock, they will have a capital gain of $100,000 ($110,000 sale price – $10,000 basis). Their federal capital gain tax rate is currently 28 percent. Accordingly, if the Hastings sell the stock, they will pay a $28,000 capital gain tax, leaving them with only $82,000 ($110,000 sales price – $28,000 tax) to invest. If they invest the $82,000 and receive a 7 percent return, they will receive $5740 in income.

Instead of selling the stock, the Hastings can create a CRT and donate their stock to it. The CRT then sells the stock. Since the CRT is charitable in nature, it pays no capital gain tax. Accordingly, the trust now has $110,000 to invest.

The Hastings can write into the trust that they want a 7 percent annual income from the trust. They will then be receiving $7700 per year in income. This income will continue to be paid to the Hastings or, after one of them dies, to the surviving spouse for life. Upon the death of both Mr. and Mrs. Hastings, the balance of the funds in the CRT will be paid to a charity which Mr. and Mrs. Hastings designate.

When the trust is signed and the Hastings contribute their stock to it, they are making a charitable contribution of a portion of the value of the stock. The value of the charitable deduction that the Hastings receive is the original value of the gift less the present value of the income going to the Hastings on the basis of their actuarial life expectancies. In the case of the Hastings, they receive a charitable deduction of $23,770 (based on a 7 percent rate from IRS tables for the month of contribution), which will save income tax of $9508 (assuming a 40 percent tax rate).

Since the stock is now in an irrevocable trust, the $110,000 has been removed from the Hastings' estate for estate tax purposes, thus saving $55,000 in estate taxes ($110,000 × 50 percent marginal estate tax rate). Upon the death of both Mr. and Mrs. Hastings, the balance of the proceeds in the trust will go to the charity or charities of their choice.

PROPERTY USED TO FUND A CRT

What types of assets are the best to give to a charitable remainder trust?

The best assets to give to a CRT are highly appreciated assets in which the maker has a low basis. If an individual sells these assets without using a CRT, the gain on the sale will be subject to a capital gain tax, which at this time is 28 percent.

An additional advantage of transferring to a CRT highly appreciated assets which comprise a major portion of an individual's estate is that it allows the tax-free diversification of a person's portfolio (so that all his or her eggs are not in one basket) and, at the same time, often permits an increase in the level of income produced.

I have highly appreciated assets I would like to transfer to a CRT. They are, however, mortgaged. Can I still transfer them to the CRT?

The short answer is no. Mortgaged assets are not generally suitable, especially if you are liable for the mortgage debt. You may realize taxable income and at the same time disqualify the CRT from the tax-exempt status you are hoping to give it. You can, however, consider partitioning the property or paying it off by using a swing loan. Partitioning property means that you divide the property into pieces, keeping the mortgage on the piece that you do not put into a CRT but freeing up another piece that can be contributed to your CRT free from the mortgage.

I do not have highly appreciated assets to transfer to a CRT. I do, however, have a taxable estate. Will a CRT still be of assistance to me?

Assuming your estate consists primarily of cash, a CRT may not be quite as valuable to you as it would be to the owner of highly appreciated property. You have no concerns about capital gain tax avoidance. Do not, however, rule out a CRT.

Every cent of your net estate over the federal estate tax thresholds ($600,000 for an individual and $1.2 million for a married couple with a properly drafted estate plan) is going to be taxed starting at 37 percent and going up to 55 percent. If your state has an estate tax, the figures are even higher.

The federal estate tax is an everything tax. It taxes you on everything you own or control. If you take no action to avoid this tax, you will be making a "charitable" contribution. The only question is who the "charity" will be: the U.S. government or a charity of your choice.

A CRT can provide great assistance in reducing or eliminating estate tax, as well as creating an immediate income tax deduction that you would otherwise not have. In other words, you benefit now and the charity of your choice benefits later.

You should consult with your estate planning attorney and your other tax advisors to find out if CRT planning will help you. By reviewing the possible benefits with your advisors, you will be able to make an informed decision that may well mean substantial benefits for you and your family.

Can I transfer my qualified retirement plan or IRA into a CRT?

You may not transfer your interest in a qualified retirement plan or an IRA or its income stream into a CRT during your life. However, a qualified plan or an IRA are excellent assets to make payable to a CRT at your death (a *testamentary transfer*) because the CRT can receive distributions from the plan or IRA free of estate or income taxes.

Qualified plans and IRAs are unique assets that may be taxed at over 80 percent at the highest tax brackets. When the owner of the plan or IRA dies, the value of the assets in the plan or IRA is subject to estate tax and the noncharitable recipient of income from the plan or IRA is subject to income tax on the distributions received. People are invariably shocked when they discover that what they viewed as a significant asset in their estate will be decimated by taxation and, consequently, that very little of this asset will ultimately be passed on to their heirs.

A testamentary transfer of the benefits from a qualified plan or from an IRA into a CRT allows you, as the trust maker, to direct where and how your *social capital* (the substantial amount which would have gone to the IRS as taxes) will be spent. It allows your surviving spouse to receive a fixed percentage of the CRT for his or her life, with income tax payable only on the amounts actually distributed to your spouse.

Before designating a CRT as the beneficiary of your qualified plan or IRA, you must consider that your surviving spouse will lose the right to principal from the plan or IRA after it is transferred. Your surviving spouse's financial needs, security, and level of comfort must all be considered in determining if qualified plan or IRA benefits should be contributed to a CRT.

If the property which I contribute to my CRT loses value or becomes worthless, what happens to my income? Will the charitable organization pay me in any case?

The trustee of your CRT is required to pay you the required income amount as long as it can be generated from the property in the CRT. The trustee will do everything possible, including selling the property in the CRT, to produce the required income. However, if the assets become totally worthless or are totally used to pay the income, the charitable organization itself has not guaranteed and is not required to pay you the annuity from its own assets. The CRT has "guaranteed" to pay the annuity, but the trust's guarantee is limited to the CRT's assets. But remember, if you never set up the CRT but continued to own the property yourself and the property became worthless, there would be no one to guarantee you any continued income from the property.

If the charitable organization you want to make a contribution to is quite substantial, you may want to consider a gift annuity instead of a CRT. Gift annuities are discussed below.

THE BENEFITS OF A CRT

Are CRTs just for the wealthy, or can someone with a modest estate benefit by creating a CRT?

A CRT can provide substantial benefits to persons with modest estates. Generally, individuals with smaller estates desire to maximize the income provided by their investments, and they can do so by using a CRT to convert highly appreciated but low-income-producing assets into investments which will provide a substantially greater income. At the same time, they will not lose a significant portion of the investments to capital gain taxes.

Can you summarize the benefits of a CRT to me, the donor?

You must want to make gifts to charity. A CRT is not a tax shelter that you invest in to make a return. A CRT is first and foremost a method to benefit charity. If that is your intent, a gift to a CRT gives you, as the donor, the following benefits:

- You receive a current charitable income tax deduction for the present value of the remainder interest, that is, the portion which will go to the charity.
- Your assets are transferred to the CRT and may be subsequently sold without the imposition of federal income tax on any gain realized.
- The noncharitable beneficiaries may receive more income after the transfer than the asset was earning before the transfer.
- You can retain control over the designation of the ultimate charity to receive the remainder.
- If you are the trustee, you may control the investment of the CRT's assets.
- You can receive recognition during your lifetime for a generous gift to charity.

Types of Charitable Remainder Trusts

Are there different types of CRTs?

Yes. There are three primary types of CRTs: the charitable remainder unitrust (sometimes called a CRUT), the charitable remainder annuity trust (sometimes called a CRAT), and the charitable remainder unitrust with net income makeup provisions (sometimes called a NIMCRUT).

CHARITABLE REMAINDER UNITRUSTS

What is a charitable remainder unitrust?

A *charitable remainder unitrust (CRUT)* is a type of CRT in which the income paid to the income beneficiaries of the trust is equal to a fixed percentage of the annual fair market value of the trust. This percentage (which must be 5 percent or greater) is chosen by the trust maker before the trust is drafted. There is no maximum percentage amount.

Although the percentage chosen by the trust maker remains fixed, the amount to be paid to the income beneficiaries, called the *unitrust amount,* will vary depending on the fair market value of the trust each year. As the fair market value of the trust assets increases, so will the income (unitrust amount) paid to the income beneficiaries. Likewise, as the fair market value of the trust assets decreases, so will the unitrust amount.

Here is an example of how this works: If a trust maker creates a $100,000 CRUT and chooses an 8 percent payout rate, the unitrust amount for the first year is $8000. If the value of the trust in the second year rises to $110,000, the unitrust amount will be $8800. If the value of the trust in the third year falls to $90,000, the unitrust amount will be $7200.

If the trust does not earn enough income in a year to pay the unitrust amount, capital gains or principal must be used to make up the difference.

Do the assets of a CRUT have to be valued each year?

Because a CRUT pays the unitrust amount to the income beneficiary on the basis of a fixed percentage of the value of the principal determined annually, the assets need to be valued annually. If the value is readily ascertainable, such as with publicly traded securities, no appraisal is required. For hard-to-value assets such as real estate or closely held business stock, a qualified appraiser must value the assets.

CHARITABLE REMAINDER ANNUITY TRUSTS

What is a charitable remainder annuity trust?

A *charitable remainder annuity trust (CRAT)* is a type of CRT in which the income paid to the income beneficiaries of the trust each year, called the *annuity amount,* is equal to a fixed amount. This amount, which can be expressed as either a specified dollar amount or a percentage of the initial fair market value of the trust, is chosen by the trust maker before the trust is drafted. The annuity amount for a CRAT must be at least 5 percent of the initial fair market value of the trust.

Because the income paid to an income beneficiary is based upon the initial value of the trust, the income paid remains constant regardless of whether the value of the trust increases or decreases. For example, if a trust maker creates a $100,000 CRAT and chooses an annuity amount of $8000 (whether expressed as an actual dollar amount, $8000, or as a percentage, 8 percent, of the initial fair market value of the trust), the annuity amount remains a constant $8000 per year.

Also, if the CRAT does not earn enough income in a year to pay the annuity amount, capital gains or principal must be used to make up the difference.

I'm 70 and I am caring for my elderly mother and aunt. My major asset is a piece of farmland that is appreciating quickly. I would like to leave this land to a charity when I die, but I have to count on a certain amount of income for the remainder of my life. Would a CRT be right for me?

If you are interested in the advantages of a CRT but need a guaranteed income, you might want to consider a CRAT. Here is an example of how a CRAT could work for you:

> You establish a CRAT by placing the farmland with a fair market value of $1 million into a CRAT. The trustee sells the land and invests the proceeds in income-producing bonds.
>
> Your CRAT provides that 6 percent of the initial value of the trust amount will be paid to you annually for your life. You will receive $60,000 per year for life even if the principal of the trust decreases in value.
>
> The trust avoids paying capital gains when it sells the farmland; you have generated guaranteed income that the farmland would never have provided; you have an immediate income tax charitable deduction; you have reduced the size of your estate thus saving estate taxes; and you have fulfilled your charitable desires.

What is the difference between a charitable remainder unitrust and a charitable remainder annuity trust?

The primary difference between a CRUT and a CRAT is the method used to calculate distributions to the income beneficiaries.

With a CRUT, the unitrust amount (the annual distribution to the income beneficiaries) must be based upon the value of the trust assets determined annually, usually at the beginning of the year. Consequently, the amount of the distribution to income beneficiaries can fluctuate depending on the value of the trust assets.

Under a CRAT, the annuity amount (distribution for the first year and each successive year) is based upon the initial value of the assets contributed to the trust. Since revaluation of the trust assets is not allowed, no gifts can be made to the CRAT after the date of the initial contribution.

I always like to know exactly what I'm getting, so I think I prefer a CRAT. Can I specify as high an annual payout as I want?

No. There is an upper limit on the percentage payout that you as the maker may specify. You are not free to specify as high a percentage payout as you happen to want on the assumption that a reduced income tax is the only price you'll pay.

A CRAT is not valid if there is a greater than 5 percent probability that the payments to the noncharitable beneficiary (usually you and your spouse) will exhaust the CRAT assets before the deaths of those noncharitable beneficiaries. This probability is calculated based on the annuity amount, the age or ages of the noncharitable beneficiaries, and an assumed rate of return (geared to the federal government's borrowing rates).

For example, if you contribute $100,000 to a CRAT, specifying a 6 percent annual payout to you or your spouse as long as one of you is living, and both you and your spouse are age 60, your income tax deduction (under an assumed 7 percent rate from IRS tables for the month of contribution) would be $31,863. However, if you were to specify an annual percentage rate of 8 percent, your charitable contribution should be $9151, but under current IRS rulings, since there would be a greater than 5 percent probability that the fund would be exhausted before you and your wife have both died, the IRS would not allow any deduction.

Your advisors should determine that the percentage payout meets this 5 percent probability test when designing your CRAT.

I'm 60 years old. Which is the "best deal" for me, a CRUT or a CRAT?

The "best deal" for you depends on your needs and objectives, as well as on your assessment of the future of the economy.

If you're optimistic and believe that the economy and the stock market will continue to grow in the future as they have historically and that future inflation will reduce the value of today's dollar, you might decide that your best choice is a CRUT. For example, let's assume that you make your charitable gift by transferring stock that you purchased for $100,000 and that is now worth $500,000 to a CRUT, and you specify in the trust document that the trustee will pay you or your spouse a unitrust amount of 6 percent from the trust's assets once every year as long as either of you is living.

If the value of the stock never changes (highly improbable), you will continue to receive $30,000 per year (6 percent of $500,000). If the assets in the trust rise to $600,000 in value, your annual income will also rise, to $36,000 per year. But if the assets in the trust decline in value to $400,000, your annual income will be reduced to $24,000 per year.

Your contribution will have these economic and tax effects:

- The trustee can sell the stock and reinvest 100 percent of the proceeds without the burden of a capital gain tax either to you or the CRT. In contrast, if you were to sell the stock yourself to reinvest in higher-yielding investments or assets that you feel have better future prospects, your $500,000 stock would shrink by $112,000 after you pay the capital gain tax (at the current 28 percent rate) on the $400,000 appreciation, leaving you with only $388,000 to reinvest.
- Your 6 percent unitrust amount is twice as high as the dividends you're now receiving from the stock. Your income from the CRUT may be higher yet in the future if your optimistic expectations for the economy and stock market are accurate (or, of course, lower if the assets decline in value).
- Assuming you create and fund the CRUT during your lifetime, you'll be entitled to an income tax deduction for the year you make the contribution for the value of your charitable gift of the remainder interest to the charity. The exact amount of the deduction depends on interest rates published monthly by the IRS (which are based on how much the government has to pay on its borrowings). If the published inter-

est rate is 7 percent and your spouse is also age 60, you'll be entitled to an income tax deduction this year of up to $126,940, which translates into $50,776 of potential income tax savings if your combined federal and state income tax effective rate is 40 percent. There are limits on how much deduction you can take in a given year. These limits are geared to your income level and deductions in excess of the annual limit can be carried over to the next 5 years.

- The assets in the CRT will not be subject to federal estate or gift tax at any time.

If you're not so optimistic about the economy and the stock market, or you simply want to assure yourself of a fixed, never-changing, annual payment, then you may prefer the CRAT. If you contribute your stock to a CRAT, specifying a $30,000-per-year annuity amount (6 percent of the $500,000 initial value of the stock), the trustee of the CRAT must pay you or your spouse, as long as either of you is living, a fixed annual payment of $30,000 regardless of what happens to the value of the trust's assets or the income they generate. You'll forgo the possibility of increasing annual payments with rising stock levels and inflation, but you'll lock in the fixed payment rate you specify in the CRAT document.

You'll also get a larger income tax deduction from a 6 percent CRAT than you would from a 6 percent CRUT under current interest rates. By contributing your stock worth $500,000 to a CRAT and specifying a fixed 6 percent annuity amount as long as you are living, you'll be entitled to an income tax deduction in the year of the gift of up to $159,317, which translates into a potential income tax savings of $63,727 (assuming a 40 percent combined federal and state effective rate). At your age, the CRAT will provide almost $13,000 more in tax benefit than the CRUT. The result would be different at any other age, payment level, and IRS rate applicable at the time you make your contributions. (For example, with a 7½ percent payment at your age under the current IRS rate, the tables are turned: a CRUT would produce a larger deduction than a CRAT.)

Since your contribution is appreciated stock, your tax deduction will be limited to 30 percent of your adjusted gross income. If your adjusted gross income is $150,000 in the year you make the gift, you can deduct $45,000 on your tax return for that year and carry over the balance for up to 5 more years.

With the help of your estate planning team, you should weigh the flexibility and probable (based on historical results) economic advantages of a CRUT against the fixed income of a CRAT, consider the estimated income tax deduction that will be available and usable by you if you create and fund your CRT during your lifetime, and decide which arrangement will be best for you.

CHARITABLE REMAINDER UNITRUSTS WITH NET INCOME MAKEUP PROVISIONS

Are there any types of CRTs other than the CRUT and CRAT?

Yes, there is a third type of CRT: the *charitable remainder unitrust with net income makeup provisions,* often referred to as a *NIMCRUT.* A NIMCRUT is a special form of CRUT. The unitrust amount of a NIMCRUT is calculated by the trustee in the same manner as that of a CRUT. However, if the NIMCRUT does not earn enough income in a year to pay the unitrust amount, because the payment is limited to the income actually earned by the CRT, then principal is not used to make up the difference. Instead, with a NIMCRUT, the trustee keeps track of any income shortage which occurs in one year and makes up that shortage by distributions in future years when trust income exceeds the unitrust amount. This is called the *makeup provision* of the NIMCRUT.

The makeup portion of a NIMCRUT works similar to an IOU. There are two situations that generate a "makeup account." The first occurs when the trust earns less income than the payout rate. When this happens, the trust owes the income beneficiary more than it can pay. This shortfall is accounted for as part of the makeup account.

For example, let's assume a trust maker creates a $100,000, 8 percent NIMCRUT. In year 1, the trust earns $8000 and pays $8000 to the beneficiary. In year 2 (assuming the $100,000 does not change in value), the trust earns $7000 ($1000 less than the required payout rate of 8 percent) and pays $7000 to the beneficiary. In year 3, the trust earns $7000 (again $1000 less than the required payout rate) and pays $7000. The makeup account at the end of year 3 equals $2000. In year 4, the trust earns $10,000, and the payout to the beneficiary will be $10,000: the $8000 unitrust amount plus the $2000 makeup from years 2 and 3.

The second situation that generates a makeup portion of the trust is a deferral of earned income. An advantage of the NIMCRUT is that it allows an income beneficiary to defer trust income until he or she needs it. The deferred income can grow inside of the NIMCRUT on a tax-deferred basis.

One method used to achieve this deferral of income is to have the trustee invest in a variable annuity, because a NIMCRUT does not recognize income produced in a properly designed variable annuity until the annuity income is actually distributed to the trust. The income beneficiary's ability to defer income inside a NIMCRUT while it grows on a tax-deferred basis, and the trust's ability to avoid recognizing undistributed annuity income as trust income, makes a NIMCRUT a very powerful retirement planning vehicle.

I like the idea of limiting the CRUT payment each year to the income actually earned. I don't need the extra income, and I think I'll be better off with the increasing value of the assets. However, I expect to retire in 10 years, and at that time I may want a larger income. Is it possible to provide for the CRUT payout percentage rate to increase when I reach retirement age?

No. The annual CRUT payout percentage rate is specified in the document, and that percentage cannot be changed. Nevertheless, a NIMCRUT may still give you the result you want. A NIMCRUT offers important planning possibilities if you do not require substantial income return from the CRUT presently or in the near term but anticipate having a more substantial income requirement in later years.

If you establish a NIMCRUT, your trustee could invest in a variable annuity to provide for your deferred income requirements. Alternatively, during the next several years before you reach retirement age, your trustee could invest in growth assets, typically paying low dividends, and you would receive only the net income actually generated by the trust. As you reach or approach retirement age and have a greater need for income, the trustee could then shift the investments in the NIMCRUT to high-income investments and pay you this enhanced income in your retirement years. Here is an example of how this works:

> You own $500,000 worth of stock, producing $15,000 in annual dividends. You contribute the stock to a NIMCRUT, specifying a 6 percent unitrust amount. Your NIMCRUT limits the trustee's payment distribution to the trust's actual net income. Since the stock you contributed pays only a 3 percent dividend, the trust at the outset would be generating a payment deficit to your

makeup account at the annual rate of $15,000. In 10 years the value of the trust assets might increase to $750,000, resulting in a $22,500 actual annual income to you (assuming the assets continue to earn a 3 percent dividend rate). Over this 10 years, the NIMCRUT may have built up a deficit, or "IOU," of around $187,500 in the makeup account. By converting the trust assets into bonds producing 8 percent on the $750,000 of trust assets, the trustee could "pump up" the payout to you to $60,000 per year in your retirement years, until the deficit is paid off (in perhaps 12 years), after which the annual payout would be reduced to the specified 6 percent of the trust's asset value at that time ($45,000 per year if the value remains constant).

I have heard that I can use a NIMCRUT as a strategy to provide for my retirement. How do I do that?

Let us assume that you have been setting aside money in your qualified retirement plan, and you are concerned that this will not give you enough income at retirement. You are comfortable putting aside an additional amount per year over and above what you are contributing to your qualified retirement plan. You would like in some way to give something back to your community after the deaths of you and your spouse.

You should consider establishing a charitable remainder unitrust with net income makeup provisions so that you will be able to create a source of additional retirement income. You can then make contributions each year to the NIMCRUT, and you will receive an income tax deduction based on the amount contributed each year to the trust. The deduction is calculated using your life expectancies, the payout rate you specify, and the IRS rates that apply each year you make your annual contribution. The charitable remainder unitrust is not a qualified retirement plan and, therefore, not subject to the ERISA rules, such as the limits on annual additions to qualified plans, the pre-59½ penalty tax on withdrawals, or the minimum required distributions beginning after age 70½.

CRT Planning

What type of CRT is best for me?

There is no "one-trust-fits-all" CRT. The type of trust a particular individual needs depends on his or her financial needs, objectives, and goals, including current and future income requirements.

It is very important to "crunch the numbers." Your planning team should carefully analyze these considerations, and advise you regarding the type of CRT that best effectuates your planning goals. Although the type of trust you choose will depend on your particular situation, the characteristics of each of the major types of CRT (CRAT, CRUT, and NIMCRUT) generally lend themselves to different planning objectives. For example:

- A CRAT is often used by trust makers who are concerned about the possibility that the principal of their trust might decrease and who want to guarantee that they will receive a certain amount of income from the trust. The disadvantage of a CRAT is that it is not "inflation-proof." A $2000 distribution from a CRAT 10 or 20 years from now will almost certainly be worth much less than a $2000 distribution today.
- Trust makers who are concerned about inflation often use a CRUT, since the distributions from a CRUT are based on a percentage of the trust, valued annually.
- Trust makers who wish to defer income use a NIMCRUT. A NIMCRUT, especially when invested in a well-designed variable annuity, allows the trust makers to defer income until they need it. A NIMCRUT can also maximize the amount of the ultimate charitable distribution because it allows tax-deferred accumulation of value.

In some situations, a person may be better off with more than one CRT. A CRAT might be used to guarantee an income flow; a CRUT may be used to shelter capital gain and provide an inflation hedge; and a NIMCRUT may be used to defer income until retirement.

CRTs are versatile planning techniques that can address a number of different, even conflicting, needs.

If I transfer assets to a CRT, am I not really giving away assets that my children would have ultimately received?

CRT planning often focuses on giving away that part of a person's capital that would not have been passed to his or her heirs. There are two types of individual capital: personal capital and social capital. *Personal capital* is the portion of your estate that you control and can pass to your heirs. *Social capital* consists of the assets you cannot pass on to heirs, capital which will be paid in taxes unless you direct it instead to charities of your choice. Many families who engage in charitable planning are not giving away their personal capital but, instead, are controlling and redirecting their social capital, which will otherwise go to the state or federal government.

Traditional estate planning has focused entirely on personal capital and ignored social capital. With inadequate or no planning, as much as 55 percent of a family's assets may be lost to taxes; this means 100 percent of the planning effort is focused on only 45 percent of the assets.

Few people believe the government is doing a good job of directing how our taxes—our social capital—is being spent. Unfortunately, few people know that, through creative estate planning, it is within their power to control how their estate tax dollars will be spent. It is possible for people to keep all of their social capital in their own community, to be spent according to their own values, instead of sending it to the government.

Quite often, by focusing some attention on controlling social capital, you can significantly improve your financial well-being, increase the capital being passed on to your heirs, and guarantee that 100 percent of your social capital is spent on causes and organizations which you believe are worthwhile. Furthermore, you have the option, if insurable, of creating a wealth replacement trust to purchase life insurance on your life that will replace the wealth you redirected to charity (which otherwise would have gone to the government).

Planned charitable giving can—with tax benefits—generate additional spendable income which you can leverage by purchasing life insurance through an irrevocable life insurance trust, replacing the value of the assets you give to charity and passing those assets on to your heirs completely free of estate and gift taxes.

CRTs and Taxes

CAPITAL GAIN TAXES

If I give appreciated assets to a CRT, can I avoid paying capital gain taxes when those assets are sold by my trustee?

Yes, although in a technical sense you are not avoiding capital gain tax but deferring it. A CRT must *recognize* capital gains when selling appreciated assets. This means that the trustee has to maintain records that track any gain on the sale of assets by the CRT, but the gain is not taxable to the CRT since the CRT is exempt from income tax (as long as it doesn't have "unrelated business" income).

However, the CRT's untaxed gain may in the future be taxed to you, as the income beneficiary of the CRT, but only to the extent that the required income distributions to you from the CRT exceed the ordinary income earned by the CRT, and then only at capital gain rates. However, the benefit you derive from delaying the taxes that you would have paid had you sold your appreciated assets and been subject to an immediate tax is considerable.

My stock presently pays a 3 percent dividend, and my proposed CRUT will pay me 6 percent. How will I be taxed on my annual income from the CRUT?

How you'll be taxed on your annual income depends on how the trustee generates the funds to make the payment. In the worst case, you'll report the income you receive as ordinary income and pay tax based on the amount you're paid. Alternatively:

- If the trustee sells the stock you contribute and reinvests it in U.S. bonds paying exactly 6 percent, you will be taxed on the 6 percent rate you actually receive. The CRUT is income tax–exempt and won't have to pay income tax on its capital gain, so it can reinvest the full current value of the stock.
- If the trustee reinvests in corporate bonds paying 7 percent, you'll still be taxed only on the 6 percent annuity payment you actually receive.
- If the trustee keeps most of the stock you contribute to the CRUT but sells just enough to generate the difference between the stock's 3 percent dividend and your 6 percent payment, your actual tax burden will be somewhat reduced because your 6 percent annual payment will then be part ordinary income (3 percent) and part capital gain (3 percent).
- If the trustee sells your stock and reinvests in tax-exempt bonds, some of your 6 percent annual payment will be reported and taxed as ordinary income (to the extent that the trust received dividends or other ordinary income), some will

be taxed as capital gain (until the gain is "used up"), and the balance will be tax-exempt income.

As you can see, in no case can you be worse off than being taxed on the amount you receive as ordinary income, and in some cases you'll be better off.

FEDERAL ESTATE TAXES

What are the federal estate tax consequences of creating a CRT during my lifetime?

If you create a CRT during your lifetime and direct that the income payments be made to you for life and to your spouse for life if he or she survives you, with the remainder passing to a specified charitable organization, then, in addition to the income tax deduction, there are beneficial gift and esate tax consequences:

- You have made two gifts: a gift of the survivor income interest to your spouse, which qualifies for the gift tax marital deduction (assuming you did not retain a power during your lifetime or through your will to revoke the income interest), and a gift of the remainder interest to charity, which qualifies for the gift tax charitable deduction.
- The value of the trust assets will be included in your estate, but your estate will have both a marital deduction for the value of your spouse's survivor income interest (if he or she survives you) and a charitable deduction for the value of the remainder passing to charity, so the trust assets will not be subjected to estate tax.

What if I make my CRT part of my will or trust so that it is funded only at my death?

If you fund the CRT at your death and instruct that your spouse is to receive income for life from the trust, the assets passing to the trust will be included in your estate for tax purposes. However, your estate will have a marital deduction for the value of your spouse's income interest and a charitable deduction for the value, at your death, of the remainder interest, which will ultimately pass to charity. The result is that the assets included in your taxable estate are offset by the marital and charitable deductions: no tax will be due.

Can I name my spouse and children as income beneficiaries of my CRT? If so, what tax consequences will there be?

In addition to naming yourself, you can name your spouse and children as income beneficiaries of the trust. If you name only your spouse and not your children as income beneficiaries, there will be no gift tax due because of the unlimited marital deduction.

Choosing to name your children as income beneficiaries subjects the transfer to the trust to gift taxation. The value of a child's income interest is a gift which does not qualify for the annual exclusion. You can keep your options open by having language in the CRT that allows you to retain the right through your will to cancel the gift to the children. By doing this, you have the option of canceling the gift to your children by changing your will prior to your death (and paying no gift tax) or of allowing the gift to take place on your death by taking no action.

There is one caution here: If you name your spouse *and* children as income beneficiaries and you die prior to your spouse without revoking your children's income interest, some part of the CRT will be included in your estate for federal estate tax purposes. Even though your spouse is then living, his or her interest in the CRT does not qualify for the unlimited marital deduction. This will cause federal estate tax to be due on your death, computed on all but the value of the charitable remainder interest.

You should contact your estate planning attorney and have him or her run the numbers so that you understand the gift and estate tax consequences of naming children as income beneficiaries in addition to your spouse.

INCOME TAX DEDUCTIONS FOR CRT CONTRIBUTIONS

Do all charitable organizations qualify for income tax deductions for charitable gifts?

Only certain charities qualify as charities under the Internal Revenue Code, so it is important to determine whether or not the organization you are interested in qualifies as a charity for income tax purposes. To do so, you should contact the charity and ask if it is qualified under the Internal Revenue Code and has received confirmation of its qualification from the IRS. You should also ask the charity to send you a copy of its latest IRS qualification letter.

You can also examine IRS Publication 78, *Cumulative List of Organizations,* which lists most qualified organizations and is updated annually. You can find this publication in your local library's reference section or call the IRS tax-help telephone number for your area.

Is there a limit to the amount of the tax deduction that I can claim in any year?

Yes. The limit is usually determined by three factors:

1. The type of assets you give to your trust (i.e., cash, long-term or short-term appreciated property, property having recaptured depreciation or depletion, or ordinary-income property)
2. Your adjusted gross income
3. The type of charity that is the charitable beneficiary of the CRT (i.e., public charity or private foundation)

If a charity is a *public charity,* such as a nonprofit school, church, or hospital, and you are making an outright lifetime gift of cash, you may deduct up to 50 percent of your contribution base (your adjusted gross income, without regard to net operating loss carrybacks). Thus, if you have a contribution base of $50,000, and make a $25,000 cash gift to a public charity, you may deduct the entire amount in the year of the gift. If you give $30,000, you may deduct only $25,000 in the year of the gift and carry over the additional $5000 for up to 5 more years. For short-term capital gain property, recapture or depletion property, or property that has ordinary income attributable to it, the amount of the tax deduction is also limited to 50 percent of your adjusted gross income. Because of the 50 percent limit, public charities are often referred to as "50 percent–type organizations."

However, even when you are making a contribution to a 50 percent–type organization, if your gift consists of stock, real estate or other capital assets you've owned for more than a year (long-term capital gain property), your deduction is, in general, limited to 30 percent of your contribution base.

In general, a charity that does not qualify as a public charity is labeled a "30 percent–type organization"; a private foundation is the most prominent example of this class. The ceiling on deductibility for gifts to such organizations is 30 percent of your contribution base. Thus, if you have a contribution base of $50,000 and give a $25,000 cash contribution to a private foundation, you can deduct only $15,000 in the year of the gift and carry over the remainder for up to 5 additional years.

Deductions for gifts to 30 percent–type organizations, including private foundations, are further diminished when the property given is something other than cash or ordinary-income property. For example, if you give stock or real estate you've owned for more than a year to a private foundation, your deduction is limited to 20 percent of your contribution base and may be further limited to your tax basis (typically, what you paid for the property).

There are a few exceptions to the above classifications. For example, some private operating foundations, supporting organizations, pass-through foundations, and pooled-fund foundations are 50 percent–type organizations for some income tax deduction purposes.

The deduction rules are complex and interrelated. Only the highlights have been touched on here. It's extremely important to consult with a knowledgeable professional prior to making any substantial charitable contribution.

When I give assets to my CRT, how will my income tax deduction be calculated?

The amount of your tax deduction for gifts made to your CRT is determined by calculating the present value of the remainder interest that your CRT will distribute to charity. The calculation of the present value of a future interest is somewhat complicated and takes into account the following five factors:

1. The fair market value of the property you are giving to the trust (adjusted for the amount of any ordinary income, short-term gains, or recapture attributable to the property)
2. The type of trust you've created, that is, an annuity trust or a unitrust
3. The number of years before the charity will receive its remainder interest, based upon actuarial tables if the trust was created for

the lifetime of the income beneficiaries or upon the term of years specified in the trust

4. The payout rate which you've established to provide for the income beneficiaries
5. A monthly, floating interest rate published each month by the IRS

What if I can't use all of the tax deduction in the year I make the gift to the trust?

If the full amount of the tax deduction cannot be used in the year you make the gift to the trust, you can carry it forward and deduct it in the 5 years following the year of your initial gift.

CRTs and Creditor Protection

What about creditor protection? Can a CRT help me there?

Although seeking creditor protection is usually not a primary reason for creating a CRT, this type of trust does provide the same type of creditor protection as any irrevocable trust provides. Since you have irrevocably transferred your property out of your name to another legal entity, a creditor cannot take that property. However, in most states, a creditor can take your right to the income from your CRT.

There are some methods that can be used to decrease the exposure of your income interest to creditors. One is using a NIMCRUT. In a NIMCRUT, since income can be deferred, it is possible to invest in assets that create no income for the creditor to take. You can then negotiate with the creditor and perhaps settle for pennies on the dollar while your IOU makeup account continues to build. After you have settled, you can have access to the amounts owed to you by the NIMCRUT when the NIMCRUT can generate that income.

If creditor protection is of great importance to you in the utilization of a CRT, it would be prudent for you not to serve as your own trustee.

Trustees

Can I be the trustee of my CRT?

Yes. You can be the trustee of your CRT. Also, a spouse can serve as cotrustee of a joint CRT.

There are three instances when an individual or his or her spouse may not act as trustee. These are:

1. When an asset whose value is hard to determine or questionable is being transferred to the trust
2. When a determination is made to distribute income to the income beneficiaries (the trust makers) from a variable annuity within a trust
3. When the terms of the trust authorize the trustee to "spray" or "sprinkle" income to the trust beneficiaries at the trustee's discretion

In these circumstances, trust makers serving as trustee must name an *independent special trustee* to sell the hard-to-value assets or make the annuity distribution decisions. The independent special trustee, as the name implies, must be independent; this trustee cannot be related to or controlled (including employed) by the trust makers.

As to other assets and for other trust actions, the trust makers may continue to act as sole trustees. Once the special assets are transferred, sold, or valued by the independent special trustee or the withdrawals from the annuity are approved, the trust makers may again act as sole trustees.

Making Changes to a CRT

What if I want to change my CRT after I have signed it?

Since a CRT is irrevocable, there are limits on your ability to change it once you have signed it. You can, however, by appropriate language in the trust document, reserve certain rights such as the rights to fill trustee vacancies, change trustees, change the charity that will be the ultimate beneficiary, and revoke a noncharitable income interest.

Can the charitable remainder beneficiaries of my CRT be changed later?

Yes. Even though a CRT is irrevocable, your CRT can be drafted to allow you, your trustee, or even other income beneficiaries to change the charitable remainder beneficiaries of the trust at any time prior to the death of the last income beneficiary. A change in charitable beneficiary is made by a written document.

Wealth Replacement Planning

How can I take advantage of the benefits of a CRT without reducing my children's inheritance?

There is an often-used planning solution for those who want to take advantage of the significant tax savings that a CRT can provide but are concerned about leaving assets to a charity on death instead of to their children. The solution is to replace some or all of the value of the assets going to charity with life insurance owned in a wealth replacement trust.

A *wealth replacement trust* is an irrevocable life insurance trust which is created for the purpose of owning a policy insuring your life or a policy insuring the lives of you and your spouse (called a *survivor* or *second-to-die policy*). You can use the income tax savings from contributions to your CRT and the increased income produced by the CRT to pay a portion or all of the cost of the life insurance required to fund your wealth replacement trust.

Since the life insurance proceeds received by your children as beneficiaries of a properly created wealth replacement trust are not taxable to your estate, your children receive the full value of the proceeds.

I like the concept of a CRT, but I really do not want to disappoint my children by substantially reducing their inheritance. What can I do to maximize their inheritance, contribute to charity, and minimize taxes?

There are ways that you can achieve all of your goals. Let's assume that you own a $1 million piece of real estate with a cost basis of zero. If you sell the property outright and pay income tax on the capital gain at 28 percent, you have $720,000 left. If you reinvest that $720,000 in an investment that yields 10 percent interest, your income will be $72,000 annually. Let's assume that you live on that interest income every year. At your death, 20 years later, the $720,000 principal is included in your estate and your estate tax bracket is 55 percent. After payment of the taxes, your family reaps the benefit of $324,000 on your original $1 million piece of property.

Now let's assume you create a CRT and transfer your $1 million piece of real estate into it. You will receive a substantial income tax deduction for your contribution to the CRT, which may put money in your pocket immediately.

The property is subsequently sold for $1 million. Because the property is in the CRT, you do not pay income tax on the capital gain. You and your spouse are the income beneficiaries of the trust. As trustee of the trust, you reinvest the entire $1 million at 10 percent, yielding $100,000 annually. Your annual income has increased by $28,000 per year, and over the next 20 years you will have increased your income stream by $560,000. After the deaths of both you and your spouse, the charity receives the $1 million.

We know that the value of your estate will be diminished at your death. The question is whether your children will receive $324,000 from your $1 million property or receive nothing because the property went to charity.

In our example, you, as trust maker, increased your annual income stream by $28,000 annually and received a substantial benefit from the charitable income tax deduction. You can use a fraction of this increased income or use the funds generated by your income tax deduction to pay the premiums for a $1 million life insurance policy to be held in a wealth replacement trust. Because the wealth replacement trust, not you, owns the policy, at your death the entire $1 million will be distributed to your children—estate tax–free.

This is truly a win-win situation:

- You receive a substantial income tax deduction.
- You increase your annual income stream.
- Your children receive $1 million free of income, gift, and estate tax.
- The charity or charities of your choice receive $1 million.
- The value of the property is excluded from your estate.

Outright Gifts versus a CRT

Are there any advantages to using a CRT versus giving an outright gift to charity during my life?

Making outright gifts to charity during your life gives you the opportunity to generate tax deductions for income tax planning and, even more importantly, the joy of seeing your gift immediately put to use by the charity in ways you believe are worthwhile. On the other hand, you are parting with assets which you may need in the future.

A CRT provides a flexible alternative if you wish to give yet still have the assets benefit you. Although you are making an irrevocable gift with a CRT, you can provide yourself with an increased income for your life, maintain control over the investments inside the trust by acting as trustee, and have the benefit of federal estate tax planning while still giving the remainder of the assets to a charity at the conclusion of the trust. CRT planning will also generate an income tax deduction for you, although the deduction will not be as high as that with an outright gift, since the gift to the charity is not immediate but is delayed until some time in the future.

What are the advantages or disadvantages of outright gifts at death versus CRT planning?

Leaving your assets at death to charity gives you the ultimate control over your assets during life. Moreover, assets left to charity at death will be free of federal estate tax. However, a CRT may still offer some advantages over this type of planning, including:

- The conversion of non-income- or low-income-producing assets to higher-income-producing assets while avoiding capital gain tax
- Diversification of assets
- A current income tax charitable deduction

What is the tax difference between a charitable lifetime gift and a charitable gift at death?

A charitable gift made during life has greater tax benefits because the donor can take an income tax deduction and the full value of the property is excluded from his or her estate. If the charitable gift is made at death, the full value of the property is also excluded from the decedent's estate, but the decedent does not reap the benefit of the income tax deduction. However, the decedent did have the use of the property until death, which he or she would not have had once the lifetime gift was made.

Charitable Lead Trusts

What is a charitable lead trust? Is it like a CRT?

Like a CRT, a *charitable lead trust* is an irrevocable split-interest trust which is composed of an income interest and a remainder interest, divided between charitable beneficiaries and noncharitable beneficiaries. However, it is the mirror image of a CRT: In a CRT, income is paid to the noncharitable beneficiaries for a term of years or their lives, after which the remaining assets of the trust pass to the charitable beneficiaries. In a charitable lead trust, income is paid to the charitable beneficiaries for a term of years or for the trust makers' lives, after which the remaining assets of the trust pass to noncharitable beneficiaries, which are often the trust makers' heirs.

A charitable lead trust also differs from a CRT in other ways:

- There is no 5 percent minimum limitation on the amount of income paid to a charity.
- The trust maker does not usually get a charitable deduction for the present value of the income payments the charitable beneficiary will receive.
- The trust maker cannot change the charitable beneficiaries of the trust after they have been chosen.

A charitable lead trust is similar to a CRT in that it can be structured either as a charitable lead annuity trust (CLAT) or as a charitable lead unitrust (CLUT). Under a CLAT, a fixed percentage of the original contribution is paid to a charity or charities each year. Under a CLUT, a percentage of the value of the assets is paid to a charity each year, so the assets must be valued annually to determine the amount to be paid to the charity.

When might I want to use a charitable lead trust?

A charitable lead trust is a strategy that allows charitable gifts for a period of years and the transfer of assets to heirs with a reduced value for gift tax purposes. The advantage to the maker is that the value of the gift to his or her heirs for tax purposes is only a fraction of the actual amount of the gift, which allows the leveraging of the maker's unified tax credit.

If you have charitable desires but do not require income from the assets and do not want your heirs to receive assets until a specified future time, a charitable lead trust may be a perfect vehicle.

We regularly give substantial amounts to charity out of our current income. Is there a way that we can make these gifts more tax-efficient and make a gift to our children as well?

People who regularly make gifts to charity should review the options available in establishing a charitable lead trust:

- Under a *charitable lead annuity trust,* a fixed dollar amount is given to charity annually for the term or life specified. If the income from the trust is insufficient to make the annual charitable payment, then the shortfall is taken out of the principal of the trust.
- Under a *charitable lead unitrust,* a fixed percentage of the fair market value of the trust assets is paid to the charity each year. Even if the assets in the trust grow in value, the charity receives the same percentage of the increase in assets.
- At the expiration of the term of years or at the death of the trust maker (whichever was the time specified), all of the assets in the charitable lead annuity trust or unitrust will be returned to the donor or to some other person(s) specified in the trust when it was established.

Thus, with a charitable lead trust, you can continue making regular contributions to charitable causes and you can ensure that the trust assets remaining after the set term or at your death, whichever is applicable, will go to your children. In addition, you will be able to transfer significant sums to them at less than fair market value. Because the heirs have no immediate right to the assets in a charitable lead trust but, rather, are entitled to those sums only at the expiration of the term or the death of the maker, there is a substantial discount in the value of those assets for federal gift tax purposes. This discount represents the period of time that the assets are being used for charitable purposes and are not available to the heirs. The Internal Revenue Service publishes tables that show what the current fair market value of those assets might be, depending upon the age of the trust makers or the term of years of the charitable income interest, the income payment rate, and the federal interest rates in effect when the trust is funded.

Do you have an example of how a charitable lead trust works?

Let's use an example of a charitable lead annuity trust. The giver/trust maker is a 60-year-old male who contributes $1 million to a 15-year annuity trust. Assuming that the annuity rate is 8 percent per year, the charities will be entitled each year to receive the sum of $80,000. Based on government tables and current federal applicable rates, the present value of the gift of what's left of the $1 million, which the heirs will receive in 15 years, is $252,592.

Thus, if you were the person in this example, you would be able to transfer $1 million in assets (plus any growth or appreciation on those assets or less any advance of principal) to an heir and pay transfer tax based on only the $252,592 present value. If this taxable portion of the gift can be covered by your unified credit, there will be no out-of-pocket cost in making the gift to your heir. While the value of the gift will be added back for purposes of computing estate taxes on your estate (whether your death occurs during or after the 15-year trust term), only the value at the time the trust was created, $252,592, is added back, regardless of whether the $1 million of assets has appreciated since the time of the trust's creation. Further, any gift tax paid will be a credit against the eventual estate tax payable.

Charitable lead trusts are subject to the general tax rules governing the treatment of all trusts. The trust is taxed on all of its income, but it is entitled to all available deductions, including a deduction for any amount of gross income, without limitation, which is paid for the charitable purpose. Thus, the trust ordinarily would have little or no taxable income.

With a charitable lead trust can I name someone other than myself to receive the remainder?

Yes. In fact, in almost all cases, the recipient of the remainder of a charitable lead trust is someone other than the trust maker. One of the primary benefits of a charitable lead trust, after charitable giving, is that it removes property from the maker's estate and passes it to the maker's heirs at a future date. The value to the trust maker is that the assets are valued for gift tax purposes as the present value of the remainder interest to be transferred in the future (i.e., the present value of the assets minus the present value of the charitable income interest). It is always much less than the fair market value of the assets at transfer.

Gift Annuities

Is there a simpler way than using a CRT to receive an annuity and an income tax deduction?

You might want to consider a gift annuity. A gift annuity has many of the same tax and economic consequences as a charitable remainder annuity trust, without the trust.

The concept of a gift annuity is simple: You transfer cash or other property to a charitable organization, which promises to pay you an annuity. The annuity is expressed as a percentage rate of return on investment, that is, on the value of what you transfer to the charitable organization. Normally, the annuity is to be paid to you for your life or to you or your spouse for as long as either is living.

The amount you contribute or the value of the property you transfer is greater than what it would cost you to purchase a commercial annuity contract from an insurance company. The excess that you pay, as determined by IRS tables that place a value on the annuity you will receive, is a charitable contribution for which you are entitled to a charitable deduction for income tax purposes.

In addition to this benefit, the balance of the value of the cash or other property that you transfer, over the calculated amount of the charitable contribution, is treated as being invested in the annuity. A portion of each annuity payment that you receive is treated as a tax-free return of capital (until you have recovered all of your investment in the annuity contract).

If you use appreciated property to purchase the annuity, you realize a taxable gain which (assuming the annuity interest is not assignable, except to the issuing charitable organization) is prorated over the annuity payout period until the total gain has been recognized. Here is an example:

> You transfer stock that you bought for $100,000 and is now worth $500,000 to a charitable organization (such as a college) in exchange for the college's promise to pay a 6 percent annuity of $30,000 per year to you or to your wife if she survives you. You and your wife are each 60 years of age. You will (on the basis of current IRS tables) get an income tax deduction of $159,317 for the year you purchase the gift annuity—a potential income tax savings of $63,727 at a 40 percent combined tax rate.
>
> Each $30,000 annual annuity payment will be taxed as $18,330 ordinary income, $11,501.39 capital gain, and $168.61 tax-free return of principal.

It is important to realize that a gift annuity is an unsecured obligation of the charitable organization. The specific cash or other property you transfer in exchange for the annuity is not segregated in trust to pay the annuity; the organization and its general assets stand behind the annuity. Therefore, you should consider purchasing a gift annuity only from a well-established, financially solid charitable organization.

You can purchase gift annuities that defer the commencement of the annuity payout. You might want to purchase an annuity now; obtain an income tax deduction now when your income is high; and defer the beginning of the annuity payments until your retirement. The results may be surprising!

In terms of the example above, if your annuity were to begin 5 years after the date you purchase the annuity, your income tax deduction would increase to $260,816 (a potential tax savings of $110,970); and each $30,000 annual annuity payout would be taxed as $21,580 ordinary income, $8075.27 capital gain, and $1344.73 tax-free return of principal.

Gifts to Charities

LIFE INSURANCE

What are the pros and cons of gifts of life insurance to charities?

Making charitable gifts of life insurance is an excellent way for a donor to greatly leverage his or her ultimate charitable gift. There are three general ways a donor can give life insurance to a qualified charity.

First, in most states, a charity can own and be a beneficiary of a life insurance policy on a donor's life. The donor gives the yearly premium dollars to the charity so that the charity can pay the premiums. This method has the advantage of providing the donor with an income tax charitable deduction for the premium dollars. The disadvantage of this method is that the charity owns, and therefore controls, the insurance policy.

Second, a donor can own a policy and name a charity as beneficiary of the policy. The advantage is that the donor has full control of the policy. The disadvantage is that the premiums are not income tax–deductible. The proceeds payable to the charity on death will qualify for the estate tax charitable deduction.

Third, life insurance can be used in conjunction with a CRT. A trust maker can fund a CRT with an existing life insurance policy and receive a charitable contribution deduction based on the principal amount of the policy. A trust maker can also establish a charitable remainder unitrust and give the premium dollars to the trust each year. The trustee could use these contributions to purchase a life insurance policy on the trust maker's life. The trust maker will receive a charitable contribution deduction for the additional yearly contributions to the trust.

Although a CRT can be an excellent vehicle to effectuate charitable giving with life insurance, caution should be used when planning with life insurance inside a CRT. An individual should consult closely with his or her attorney and insurance professional to make sure that the use of life insurance inside the trust is a sound investment, that the insurance contract is properly funded to the trust, that the proper type of CRT is being used, that cash-value invasions or loans from the policy will not be needed or used, and that his or her state permits a trust or charity to be the owner and beneficiary of a life insurance policy.

I took out a lot of life insurance a number of years ago to be sure that my family would have enough to continue its standard of living in the event of my premature death. Now I've built up my estate by investment and accumulation of other assets. Can I give this insurance to a charitable organization and get a tax deduction?

Giving the life insurance to charity could be a smart thing to do:

- You will get an income tax deduction for the replacement cost of the policies (if paid up) or the "interpolated terminal reserve" (something more than cash surrender value), but the deduction cannot exceed your cost (i.e., the total premiums you've paid). Loans against the policy would of course reduce the amount of the value and therefore the amount of the deduction.

- In addition, you'll receive an income tax charitable deduction for any premiums you pay in the future.

To qualify for these charitable contribution deductions, you must be sure to properly transfer all incidents of ownership to the charitable organization.

If your employer has a group term life insurance plan under which the company pays all the premiums, the first $50,000 of coverage is provided to you income tax–free. You are taxed for any insurance coverage in excess of $50,000 on the basis of values published by the IRS. However, if you designate your charity as the beneficiary of any portion of the insurance in excess of $50,000, you will not be required to pay income tax on the value of that excess coverage. In addition, if your family needs should change, you can revoke the designation of the charity and restore your family as beneficiary.

DIRECT BEQUESTS

I want to remember my college when I die, but I don't want to get involved in any extra documents. Is there a simple way to do this?

The simplest way to remember an institution, whether it be an educational, a medical, or some other charitable institution, is to leave a bequest upon your death. The bequest can take several forms. A *cash bequest* provides that your college receives a specific dollar amount. You can also give tangible property such as a residence or a piece of artwork. A *residuary bequest* allows your college to receive everything after estate expenses and specific bequests have been made. You can leave the remainder of a retirement plan to your college. You might want to consider a *contingency bequest,* which would allow your college to receive your assets only in the event of the death of other beneficiaries. This is also called ultimate planning.

Foundations

Can I create my own charity to be the ultimate charitable beneficiary and name my children and their heirs as the directors and trustees of the charity?

Yes. You can create either a private operating foundation or a nonoperating foundation. Children or grandchildren can direct charitable distributions of income or principal. They can also receive reasonable fees for their services, as well as have their expenses reimbursed. This is an ideal way to "empower" children.

Sometimes it is best to give children control of wealth rather than giving them the wealth outright and immediately, which might harm more than help. Naming children or grandchildren as trustees of the family foundation creates family unity and fosters a disposition toward charity, thus raising their standing within their particular communities.

I've accumulated more than my family and I need. My children think they need more, but it's clear to me that I've got them pretty well provided for, and their living standards are already higher than mine were for most of my life. When my wife and I are gone, I want to leave a good portion of my estate to my family, but I also want to leave something behind that will benefit the community in the future. In addition, I would like to keep my children—and grandchildren down the road—bound together by a common interest. Finally, I want to have some control, personally, as long as I'm around and through my family's involvement after my death. What's the best way to accomplish this?

Control is important to a lot of people when they think seriously about charitable giving in relation to their estate planning. There are various ways of ensuring some degree of control over what you give.

Depending on the degree of control that is important to you, there are three arrangements that you might consider:

1. A private foundation
2. A supporting organization
3. A donor-advised fund of a public charity

Private foundations provide the greatest degree of ongoing control over the assets you give. You can establish a foundation by setting up a charitable corporation or a charitable trust; the most common form of private foundation is the charitable corporation, but the principles are the same in a charitable trust. Your attorney can prepare the private-foundation organizational papers to provide the requisite statement of charitable purposes which the foundation is to pursue and the requisite limitations on its activities.

You can provide the mechanics for appointing the governing board, generally trustees, all of whom can be family members if you so desire.

As long as your foundation is properly organized and operated for charitable purposes, it will enjoy tax exemption on its income and contributions to it will provide income tax, gift tax, and estate tax deductions for the contributor or contributors.

Should I establish a private foundation during my lifetime or after my death?

You can set up a private foundation during your lifetime, or you can provide in your will or living trust that it be established following your death.

If you establish your nonoperating private foundation during your lifetime, you can obtain an income tax deduction for contributions to that foundation of up to 30 percent of your contribution base (usually your adjusted gross income) in the year of contribution if your gift is made with cash or up to 20 percent of your contribution base if your gift consists of other property (stock, real estate, partnership interest, etc.) held for more than 1 year.

For a number of years prior to 1995, gifts of appreciated, publicly traded stock owned for more than 1 year were deductible up to their full market value (subject to the percentage limitations based on contribution base), but that provision of the tax law expired December 31, 1994, and gifts of such stock, as well as other long-term capital gain property, to a nonoperating private foundation are now limited for deduction purposes to the donor's cost. Contributions exceeding the deduction limits in any year may be carried over for up to 5 succeeding tax years.

While the income tax deduction limits that apply to gifts to most private foundations are more stringent than those that apply to gifts to public charities (such as most colleges and universities, churches, hospitals, community foundations), a nonoperating private foundation qualifies for estate tax and gift tax charitable deductions in just the same way as any public charity does. You can, for example, leave all of your estate at death to a nonoperating private foundation and receive a charitable contribution for the entire value of your estate, thereby reducing the estate tax to zero. You can make an unlimited amount of gifts during your lifetime to a nonoperating private foundation without incurring any gift tax or using up any of your gift and estate tax unified credit.

Does a private foundation pay income taxes?

A nonoperating private foundation is subject to an annual excise tax of 2 percent on its net investment income. It is also subject to a 15 percent excise tax on any shortage if it fails to make "qualifying distributions" (which include reasonable expenses of administering the foundation) each year equal to 5 percent of the fair market value of its assets (computed for the preceding year).

How does a private foundation get recognized by the Internal Revenue Service?

A private foundation must obtain recognition of its tax-exempt status by formal application to the IRS. It must also file an annual income tax information return and make its financial statements available for public inspection. In addition, it must furnish certain information to the attorney general of the state in which it operates.

It sounds like a private foundation creates a lot of administration without providing some of the significant tax benefits of a public charity. Are there different types of foundations that may make this administration worthwhile and increase my income tax deduction?

The combination of the administrative burden and the limitation on income tax deductibility tends to discourage widespread use of the private foundation for charitable giving, unless the amount of assets involved and the desire for control (and family involvement) are viewed as being significant to the would-be founder.

One variation of the private foundation is the *private operating foundation.* This is a foundation which directly conducts exempt activities rather than merely making payments to others for the conduct of these exempt activities. For example, a private operating foundation could be established to operate an art museum or a historic residence or to provide activities for elderly citizens of the community.

Since the operating foundation functions somewhat like a public charity, it qualifies for favorable income tax deductions for the contributor: 50 percent of contribution base and fair market value deductibility up to 30 percent of contribution base for long-term capital gain property. In a sense, it is also free of the 5 percent minimum distribution requirement because its distributions are made directly in carrying out its operating-foundation activities.

I'd like a larger income tax deduction than a private foundation will give me. Besides, I'm not sure my family will be comfortable with the administrative requirements of a private foundation. Isn't there anything simpler that will provide a better income tax deduction and still give me a degree of control?

A considerable amount of control, though less than that afforded by private foundations, can be achieved through use of a *supporting organization.* This is a separate organization (charitable corporation or charitable trust) established by a donor which is organized and operated "exclusively for the benefit of, to perform the functions of, or to carry out the purposes of" one or more specified public charities.

As the donor, you or you and your family can have a significant representation on the governing board of the supporting organization. However, your family members or other "disqualified persons" cannot directly or indirectly have 50 percent or more of the voting power of the governing board or a veto power over the actions of the organization. Also, you or your spouse cannot retain the right to specify who will receive the income or principal from a contribution.

While you may continue to have, directly or through your family or other persons, a very substantial influence in the affairs of the organization, a supporting organization is recognized as a public charity. Accordingly, it provides the higher income tax deduction limits (50 percent of contribution base for cash gifts, and fair market deductibility of gifts of long-term capital gain property of up to 30 percent of contribution base) that regular public charities (colleges and universities, churches, etc.) provide to their donors.

6

Elder Law Planning

Elder law is one of the fastest-growing areas of estate planning law. As America makes a demographic leap to a society consisting of more people in older age brackets and more people living longer, the issues of protecting, planning, and helping the elderly are taking on a greater and greater significance.

While many aspects of elder law have historically been of specific concern to lower-income, lower-net-worth individuals and couples, it is now becoming a planning concern among a larger segment of the public. One of the reasons for this attention is the realization by many people in their forties, fifties, and even sixties that they face the prospect of supporting their parents. Given this reality, they are more and more interested in determining the best courses of action for protecting their parents and their parents' assets, as well as qualifying for every government program that is available.

The other reason is that these same people are vitally interested in their own well-being and care as they age. With deficit reduction, fewer opportunities for people to retire with company pension plans, and the change in public sentiment toward welfare and other programs, planning for their own old age must begin earlier as opposed to later. By taking steps now, they can avoid a great deal of stress and financial strain in the future.

This chapter's questions and answers on elder law are detailed and informative. They clearly define many of the labyrinthine rules and regulations found in government programs. In addition, they provide some innovative planning solutions in an area that traditionally does not offer much maneuvering room for planners.

As you read this chapter, keep in mind that while Congress has created federal guidelines for the administration of many programs which may assist the elderly, each state and, in some instances, local community can alter the general rules and regulations as they see fit. Therefore, it is essential that you check with the law in your state and community to see how a particular program and its benefits would apply to you in your situation.

This chapter is must reading for anyone who has an aging parent or who feels the need to plan for himself or herself. It serves as an excellent primer in elder law and planning strategy.

Elder Law

What is elder law?

Elder law is a relatively new area of legal practice that combines the traditional areas of estate planning and trusts with issues such as age discrimination, Social Security, Medicare, Medicaid, and other state and federal assistance programs. Elder law also covers patients' rights, long-term care, right-to-die considerations, and other medical and lifetime concerns, including incapacity and disability.

Since 1988, a group known as the National Academy of Elder Law Attorneys has existed in support of this growing area of legal practice. Elder law is recognized by both the American Bar Association and many state bar associations as a viable area of the practice of law. Other organizations such as the National Network of Estate Planning Attorneys also provide leadership and education for attorneys in this specially recognized practice of law.

Whenever you are looking for an attorney who is experienced and informed in this area of the law, you should ask the attorney what state or national organizations he or she belongs to. This may be helpful, as many states still do not recognize certification or specialization in specific areas of law.

Who is generally considered elderly?

Generally speaking, a person who is age 65 or older can be arbitrarily classed as elderly. However, many people prefer the term "senior citizen" rather than "elderly" because the latter term has come to be popularly (but incorrectly) interpreted as meaning persons who are not only over 65 but also sick or frail.

Are our senior citizens being abandoned by their own government, and if so, what are the options?

The math is astounding—it is said that by the year 2025, more than one in every five U.S. citizens will be age 65 years or older. This means that between now and the year 2025, the 65-plus population will more than double.

Indeed, people are living longer and longer; it is now common for senior citizens to live at least into their upper seventies and in many cases into their eighties and beyond. While the general population may believe that the increase in life expectancy is a positive aspect of modern society, one of the tragic consequences is that there will be many more "living" senior citizens affected with incapacitating illnesses. So, the obvious question is, Who will take care of this large and upcoming segment of our population? And, as a by-product of this question, how many senior citizens will be abandoned, left alone and uncared for?

As to the question of who will take care of the increasing number of incapacitated senior citizens, the most obvious answer appears to be nursing homes. The purpose of a nursing home is to provide long-term custodial care for senior citizens who are incapacitated to the extent that they can no longer take care of themselves. There is a growing fear, however, that due to the increasing population of senior citizens, there are more elderly people who cannot afford nursing home care and, as a result, are not being cared for or are being abandoned by their families. At the same time, with the increasing number of law changes in relation to nursing home and Medicaid qualification issues, many senior citizens are of the opinion that the government is also abandoning the senior citizen segment of our population.

In short, the answer to who, exactly, will pay for long-term nursing home care is that there are very few options available. This issue and many others regarding senior citizens in the years to come are very important ones that will have to be dealt with—and ones which will have an impact on every segment of our society.

How does the legal code of professional responsibility relate to the representation of senior citizens?

According to the provisions of the Code of Professional Responsibility, an attorney owes several duties to his or her client, the most important of which include competence, diligence, and confidentiality. The rules of legal ethics require that all licensed attorneys maintain high ethical standards in all respects.

The client-lawyer relationship in which senior citizens are the clients is becoming an area of great sensitivity as to ethical issues. Perhaps the greatest reason for this increase in sensitivity is the increasing numbers of senior citizens. An attorney practicing in the area of elder law remains bound by the rules of ethics and more specifically the Code of Professional Conduct.

Because of the diversity of issues in the elder law area, a greater amount of expertise is required. An attorney should, at no time, undertake to represent a client in an area in which he or she is not competent, and an individual should be careful in choosing an attorney who is competent to practice in the elder law area. Further, attorneys who undertake representation of senior citizen clients must pursue the matters on behalf of the clients to their utmost abilities. Attorneys also owe senior citizen clients the duty to keep information received from them confidential, and this includes keeping it confidential from other family members including children or siblings.

Can a lawyer meet with other family members instead of the senior citizen (who is actually the client), and then proceed to complete various estate planning documents for the senior citizen client?

This is all too often the way elder law attorneys are initially contacted—not by the senior citizen client but by another member of the senior citizen's family.

An attorney's assistance is often sought after the senior citizen is already disabled or seriously or terminally ill. As a result, it is often another family member who not only makes the first contact with the attorney on behalf of the senior citizen but also thereafter meets with the attorney without the actual senior citizen client being present.

In most situations, the family member who initiates contact with an elder law attorney has only the best interests of the senior citizen in mind and wants nothing but the best in the form of care and legal guidance for him or her. However, there are situations in which the family member has other motives, such as gaining control over the elderly person's assets or being named as a sole or primary beneficiary of the senior citizen's estate.

Whatever the scenario, the attorney must ask himself or herself the essential question, "Who is my client?" To put it in its simplest form, the attorney must make a rational and conscious decision: "Do I represent the senior citizen or one or more of the other family members?" This question must be appropriately answered *before* the commencement of any actual preparation of documents. Once this all-important question is answered, the attorney has very clear-cut ethical standards to follow.

Assuming that the attorney chooses to represent the senior citizen, the attorney should create a working relationship with this individual and not with any other family members. While an initial consultation with family members outside the presence of the senior citizen is usually acceptable, the attorney should meet directly with the senior citizen client in a one-on-one setting. Obviously, certain situations arise in which other family members are crucial to the process of obtaining the data needed to complete an adequate and comprehensive estate plan, but all such information obtained through other family members should be carefully reviewed with the senior citizen client for its accuracy. This is best done between the attorney and senior citizen, alone, in the attorney's office, the home of the senior citizen, or a nursing home, for example. If it is necessary for another family member to be present for practical or logistical reasons, that family member should be asked, politely and kindly, to step into another room while the attorney meets with the senior citizen client.

When an elderly couple who have both been previously married and have children from prior marriages proceed to have their estate plans prepared, is it necessary or advisable for each of them to retain separate attorneys to prepare the documents?

It is not at all uncommon for an estate planning attorney to meet with both a husband and a wife regarding the completion of their estate plans. In fact, it is probably preferable to meet with both the husband and the wife, at least once, particularly in an initial consultation. At this initial consultation, assuming that the attorney asks the appropriate questions, it is then possible for the attorney and the clients to decide whether a potential conflict of interest exists in representing both the husband and the wife.

If a conflict of interest does exist, it will typically occur when the spouses are in their second marriage and each has children from the first marriage. Here, the interests of each respective spouse may greatly differ. For example, the husband may want to use his assets only for purposes of college planning for his own grandchildren. The wife may want her son or daughter to receive all of her assets to the exclusion of the husband's children or grandchildren.

When these potential conflict situations occur, it is often best for the attorney *not* to represent both spouses. If the attorney nevertheless decides to prepare estate planning documents for both spouses, then it is recommended that each of the spouses sign a document acknowledging that each has independently and freely chosen to utilize the same attorney and does not believe that utilizing the same attorney is a conflict of interest. Many attorneys who work with couples who have been previously married routinely utilize this type of acknowledgment as part of their written fee agreements, which are signed prior to commencing any legal work for the couples.

In terms of financial, estate, medical, and retirement planning, where do we start?

If financial planning focuses on building an asset base for a comfortable retirement and estate planning concentrates on the process of transferring wealth to the next generation or to charitable organizations in one's community, then elder law planning can be thought of as planning for the period in between retirement and death. It presents the challenge of protecting the assets of people who are living longer and thus have a higher risk of running out of health or assets. A level of 70 to 75 percent of preretirement income is considered by most financial planners as adequate for a comfortable retirement. With people living longer, this level needs to be maintained longer so as to prevent the depletion of one's assets.

To maintain this level of retirement income, asset allocation must be considered. The old rule of thumb of having a percentage of equity investments equal to 100 minus your age seems too conservative in the face of increasing longevity and exposure to the ravages of inflation. A different rule of thumb is beginning to take hold in which the number 120 is substituted for 100 in the formula, so a 65-year-old would maintain a level of equities of 55 percent (120 – 65) until age 75 before lowering the percentage of equities to, say, 50 percent or slightly less.

Running out of health presents a more difficult problem. Planning for it requires looking ahead to a time after age 85 when one will be as likely as not to have a physical illness necessitating long-term personal or nursing care and possibly will also be afflicted with an increasing mental incapacity. Once upon a time, when we were in our midteens, our parents said to us, "Look kid, what are your plans for college? It's not the end of the world if you don't go to college, but life goes better with college."

Today, the equivalent message to the person in his or her midsixties is, "Look, older kid, what's your game plan for getting older? You might be lucky and not need one, but life goes better with a plan."

I'm concerned about how the cost of care during a long-term illness or nursing home stay will affect my assets. Am I just being silly, or is this a legitimate concern?

It is a very legitimate concern. The most recent statistics indicate that one-half of all women and one-third of all men who live to age 65 will enter a nursing home at some point in their lives. A full quarter of these will remain in the home for over a year. Obviously, many others will choose to receive in-home care, which only increases the odds of high expenses.

Costs for nursing home care vary widely from state to state, but the average seems to be around $36,000 per year. In-home care can easily run more than $10,000 annually for only three nursing visits per week. And, as you might expect, these costs are increasing at a rate faster than the inflation rate.

Medicaid

What is Medicaid?

Medicaid is an outgrowth of Title XIX of the Social Security Act of 1965. It is, generally speaking, a medical assistance program for the aged, blind, or disabled and was promoted as a joint federal and state program. A recipient of Medicaid benefits does not actually receive direct cash benefits; rather, the recipient receives benefits by way of payments made directly to the recipient's health care providers, such as doctors, hospitals, nursing homes, medical testing facilities, pharmacies, and dentists.

What are some of the basics that I should know about Medicaid before I begin the process of "Medicaid planning"?

Every state is required to follow certain federal regulations with regard to Medicaid. However, each state may also legislate its own regulations in order to administer the Medicaid program within its borders. Many states follow the rules of the Federal Supplemental Security Income program. Several states actually have their own Medicaid eligibility criteria that are more restrictive than the federal criteria. Therefore, it is not enough for you to become familiar with just the eligibility criteria at the federal level; it is also necessary for you to learn the details of the eligibility criteria in your own state before you commence any Medicaid planning.

At the federal level, Medicaid is administered by the Health Care Financing Administration (HCFA), which is a part of the U.S. Department of Health and Human Services. At the state level, Medicaid is generally administered by the state agency which administers welfare programs, for which there is typically a county office. Each state issues its own set of regulations which are, in effect, interpreted at both the state and county levels. Thus, it is necessary to learn the methodologies and procedures utilized by your own county in addition to those required by the state and federal statutes.

If you think this system sounds like it could lead to a great deal of misinterpretation at the county and state levels, you are correct; therefore, taking on the goal of understanding some of the basics of the Medicaid program is no easy task. In this regard, it is best to remember that if you go into a nursing home and apply for Medicaid coverage, you will generally file the Medicaid application in the county where the nursing home is located. The criteria and forms required at the county level are perhaps the best starting point even though the county is nothing more than an "outreach" of the state and federal Medicaid statutes.

Who qualifies for Medicaid?

A person qualifies for Medicaid if he or she is determined to be categorically needy or medically needy. Persons who are *categorically needy* are eligible only because they meet requirements relating to old age, blindness, or disability and are below certain asset and income levels. *Medically needy* persons qualify for eligibility only because they have high medical bills and thus their remaining income and other resources are at, or below, applicable financial standards.

How is the Medicaid program administered?

Medicaid is administered by your state's welfare agency, such as the Department of Human Services. Approved care and services under Medicaid are funded almost equally by the federal government and your individual state. Specific services for which payment can be made and the proper payment rate are established by the welfare agency and are reviewed and adjusted periodically.

Isn't welfare for single parents and individuals who are out of work?

Yes, it is. However, most state welfare agencies are divided into three divisions:

1. Income maintenance (which provides food stamps and Aid for Dependent Children) as well as other financial need–based programs
2. Medical services.
3. Child support enforcement

The division of medical services is responsible for administering the Medicaid program. This division publishes and updates a *Medical Services Manual,* which contains the policies and procedures of the Medicaid program. It is also responsible for generating and distributing medical cards to those entitled to them, overseeing the payment and policies relating to payment of medical providers for services rendered, and determining what services are to be covered. Additionally, this state agency has the responsibility of developing plans for furnishing assistance and services to eligible individuals and for determining the general policies relating to Medicaid (and the other programs which your state's welfare agency directs).

SERVICES PROVIDED BY MEDICAID

What services are available to me if I qualify for Medicaid?

Medicaid provides adult care home or nursing facility care, including "custodial care," and health insurance as a last resort if there is no other coverage (including Medicare) to low-income, blind, or disabled persons of any age. Medicaid also provides payment to enrolled providers of comprehensive medical care for services furnished by them.

Also funded through Medicaid, your state welfare agency generally provides services under the Home- and Community-Based Services (HCBS) program as long as you sign a waiver relinquishing all rights to other services provided by Medicaid.

In addition to qualifying for Medicaid, you may be eligible for other programs which are available through one or more state agencies:

- Food stamps
- Commodity distribution
- Low-Income Energy Assistance Program (LIEAP), which provides assistance in paying utility bills (There is also a weatherization program available through the Department of Energy. Check with your utility company. Most rural electric cooperatives provide assistance in this area as well.)

Your state's Department on Aging may be able to provide you with assistance in the following areas (contact your area agency on aging or similar entity):

- Home care services (Senior Care Act): assistance with housecleaning and home chores to elderly and disabled persons free of charge
- Local senior center, transportation services, and nutrition sites
- SHICK (Senior Health Insurance Counseling): free counseling about health insurance issues for senior citizens

What is the Home- and Community-Based Services program?

Home- and Community-Based Services (HCBS) is a program of long-term-care services which include a variety of medical and nonmedical services funded by Medicaid. They are designed to provide the means of meeting your functional and medical needs in your own home and community when without such services you would be placed in a nursing facility, hospital, or institution. Services under HCBS will be provided only if they are cost-effective: the cost of providing home- and community-based services for an individual must be less than the cost of providing long-term care in a nursing facility for that individual.

Although this program is funded through Medicaid, HCBS is an exception to the Medicaid state plan in most states and provides services which are beyond the scope of services available to regular Medicaid recipients. Therefore, to receive services under HCBS, you must sign a waiver to the state Medicaid plan giving up your right to other services provided by your state through the regular Medicaid program.

What are attendant care services?

Attendant care services are a type of home- and community-based service for long-term care that may allow you to remain in your own home rather than in an institution or nursing facility. There are three classifications of attendant care services:

1. Class I services, known as *homemaker services,* are limited to the performance of nutritional and environmental support services.
2. Class II services include the performance of homemaker and nonmedical attendant care functions.
3. Class III services include the performance of homemaker, attendant care, and health-maintenance tasks.

When will Medicaid pay for home health services?

Medicaid pays for home health services only when a physician has established a written treatment plan and has certified the need for such services.

Who actually provides home health services?

These services are provided either by a qualified home health agency or, when the services of a home health agency are not available, by a registered nurse as long as he or she is licensed to practice in your state and has received written orders from your physician or is supervised by a local health department nurse.

Are medical supplies covered by Medicaid?

They are covered when they are part of a necessary treatment plan and are used in conjunction with visits from the home health agency or registered nurse.

What additional services provided by home health agencies may be covered by Medicaid?

Services that may be covered include skilled nursing services; psychiatric nursing services; physical, occupational, and speech therapy (when restorative in nature); rental of durable medical equipment; and certain home health aide services, up to one visit per day by an aide who is under the supervision of a registered nurse.

What are home health aide services?

Home health aide services may include such tasks as bathing, feeding, assisting with personal care, monitoring vital signs, and assisting with medication. These services are not required to be in the physician's treatment plan or certification.

What isn't covered as part of home health agency services?

Drugs and other medication (pharmaceuticals), purchases of durable medical equipment, and homemaker or other social work services are not covered. However, homemaker and other social work services may be provided by your state's welfare agency or Department on Aging.

What hospital care can be paid for through Medicaid?

Federal law mandates that the following inpatient services be covered:

- All inpatient services for Medicaid recipients unless not medically necessary (such as elective surgery)
- Alcohol and drug abuse detoxification
- "Swing-bed" accommodations (a hospital bed which can be used interchangeably as a hospital or nursing facility bed), but only if the individual needs skilled nursing care and the hospital's swing-bed accommodations have been approved

What limitations are there on these types of hospital services?

These services must be ordered by a physician and must be medically necessary. Television and personal items are not covered.

What if I'm outside my state of residence when I need these types of services?

Out-of-state services require prior authorization unless they are rendered in emergency situations.

What if I just need to see a doctor at his or her office?

Twelve office visits per year are allowed. If you visit a hospital and your condition is a nonemergency, the hospital visit is counted as one of the twelve office visits.

In addition, 32 hours of psychotherapy are covered. Concurrent care by two or more physicians is covered, if necessary, as well as certain physician extender services, such as adult care home visits, routine physical, annual medical history, subsequent day-hospital visits, and routine home visits. "Concurrent care" means that you are being cared for by two or more physicians for the same ailment.

What limitations are there on physician services?

Only medically necessary services are provided. Office visits for injections only are not covered. Also, experimental procedures are not covered.

Can I choose the physician I want to see?

The answer depends on where you live. Generally, you can choose the physician, but individuals who live in certain locations are required to participate in what is known as the Primary Care Network.

What is the Primary Care Network?

In certain locations, physicians contract with the state agency in charge of medical services to provide case management. They may be in general practice, family practice, internal medicine, or certain other areas of recognized expertise. You are allowed to choose from a list, provided by the welfare agency office, the physician or physicians who will provide you with your primary care when it is determined that you are eligible.

The physician you see manages your case, provides direct medical care to you, and makes a written referral for you when you need other specialized medical care. It is believed that this type of case management is cost-effective and reduces the need for unnecessary medical services.

If I need to be in a nursing facility, will Medicaid pay the cost?

Residential (custodial) long-term care is covered. *Residential care* is defined as supervised, nonmedical care in a residence which has been assessed and licensed or registered by the agency in your state which is authorized to do this.

The care provided by the facility is to match the individual's needs, limitations, and abilities. Care includes assistance with making and keeping appointments for regular or emergency medical care, meeting nutritional needs, taking medications, contacting and maintaining relationships with family and friends, and gaining access to recreational, social, religious, and other community activities. Also included are laundry services and necessary transportation. All of these services are in addition to assistance with necessary activities of daily living.

How does my state agency determine what services will be provided to me?

Your state agency is responsible for completing an assessment of your needs. The purpose of the assessment is to determine what services you need and, if possible, to refer you to home- and community-based services to avoid your having to enter a nursing facility, hospital, or state institution.

Your state's Department on Aging provides the assessment service if you enter a nursing facility from the local community. If you enter a nursing facility from a hospital, the hospital performs the assessment.

The assessment is a way of determining your medical needs and the level of assistance you need in performing activities of daily living. Although services are to be provided on the basis of personal need, priorities are based on a point system which rates your functional level, age, informal support system, and recent hospitalization and medical needs. Your state welfare agency or Department on Aging may be able to help you as a result of the Senior Care Act and may provide you with assistance in homemaking chores in addition to Medicaid's providing you with the medical services you may need.

Do I have to go to a nursing home if what I really need is assistance with some of my necessary daily activities but I can't afford to pay for the help?

No. If you are impaired due to disability, medical problems, or age, the state entity which administers the welfare programs will attempt to provide the services you need and allow you to remain in your own home if possible. Services vary according to your income and your needs.

Qualifying for Medicaid and Long-Term-Care Expenses

What are the rules for qualifying for Medicaid assistance with long-term-care expenses?

The rules regarding qualification for Medicaid assistance can differ greatly depending upon various factors in the applicant's situation. A special set of rules, known as the *spousal impoverishment rules,* apply to a married couple when one spouse is applying for assistance and the other spouse is not applying. (The nonapplicant spouse is called the *community spouse.*)

If both spouses need assistance, they are treated as single individuals under the rules.

Medicaid is a "means-tested" system under which a person must qualify financially to receive benefits. Although the rules vary from state to state, the Medicaid rules essentially require that an individual have no more than $2000 in cash assets and must use all of his or her income to pay for the cost of care before that person may qualify for assistance.

What are the special spousal impoverishment rules?

The goal of the spousal impoverishment rules is to allow the community spouse to stay at home and maintain some semblance of the couple's former lifestyle.

Until as recently as 1988, spouses had to spend down their assets in order to qualify the applicant spouse for benefits. Now, generally, the federal government sets a range of financial qualifications which limit the amount of assets the community spouse can retain and still have the applicant spouse qualify for benefits. The assets of both spouses are added together and divided by 2. The community spouse is allowed to retain an amount set by state laws within the range established by federal guidelines. This range was originally set by Congress at $12,000 to $60,000. The dollar limits for Medicaid qualification are indexed for inflation and adjusted each January 1 and May 1. The May 1, 1996, figures are $15,384 to $76,740.

In addition, the community spouse may continue to reside in the couple's personal residence and may retain a car of any value, as well as personal effects.

The government allows the community spouse to retain a particular level of income without forcing that income to be spent on the applicant spouse's care. Any excess over the allowable level of income must be spent on the applicant spouse's care. As of May 1, 1996, the base amount of income which can be allocated to the community spouse is $1295 per month. It can be greater than this under certain circumstances relating to the cost of housing.

If we entered into a second marriage with a prenuptial agreement in place and kept our assets completely separate at all times, will we be treated as single persons for eligibility purposes if one of us is placed in a nursing home and applies for Medicaid?

A prenuptial agreement is an agreement between a husband and wife prior to their marriage. Generally, the terms of a prenuptial agreement ensure that each spouse's assets are kept separate from the other spouse's assets, with the intent typically being to allow each spouse to leave the separate assets to his or her own children from a previous marriage.

As an estate planning tool, a prenuptial agreement can be very effective for the distribution of assets in accordance with one's wishes; however, the same does not generally hold true regarding Medicaid qualification matters! In most states, all assets held by married persons, even if those assets are retained separately between husband and wife at all times and are subject to the terms and conditions of a prenuptial agreement, are considered "joint assets" and are subject to the eligibility requirements for married couples under the Medicaid laws. Thus, as a general rule, the use of a prenuptial agreement will not be effective for Medicaid planning.

How long do we have to live together before we are considered married?

Time is not really a factor. There are three elements to a common law marriage:

1. You must have the legal capacity to enter into a marriage.
2. You must consider yourselves as married by expressing words of present intention to take each other as husband and wife.
3. You must hold yourselves out as husband and wife to the public or sign a document showing completion of item 2 above.

Not all states recognize a common law marriage, so it is important that you find out from your lawyer if you may be subject to the common law marriage rules, especially if either or both of you are thinking of applying for Medicaid.

INCOME REQUIREMENTS

What is a spenddown, and does it apply to income?

A *spenddown* is generally a requirement that applies to available assets or resources. However, if a person's income is in excess of the state-allowed maximum, that individual may still qualify for assistance for long-term care if the person spends the excess income for qualifying purposes, effectively reducing the amount of available monthly income below the limit established by law.

Is all income included in the income test for eligibility?

Yes, generally all income from any source must be reported, regardless of whether it is earned or unearned. This includes wages, self-employment income, investment income, property rental income, pension income, other benefit income, and certain contributions. The only requirement is that the income must be measurable and available to the individual producing it (this means having the legal ability to make it available).

The proceeds from the sale of property are not considered income unless they stem from an installment contract under which regular payments are received. Otherwise, such proceeds are determined and reviewed to determine eligibility under the provisions relating to available assets. The types of income that are not included in the income test for eligibility are referred to as *exempt income.*

Can the income of anyone else in the home be taken into consideration for the purposes of eligibility?

Yes. When an individual who does not have the legal responsibility to do so voluntarily and regularly contributes cash toward household expenses and maintenance needs of the individual in need, the net amount of income realized by the household is taken into consideration.

Who is a legally responsible relative?

A *legally responsible relative* is a person, such as a spouse, who has the legal obligation to provide support for the person who needs assistance. The income of a legally responsible person must be considered in determining eligibility for assistance.

If I am married and need assistance with long-term care, can income be allocated to my spouse, who will remain in our home?

Yes. Under federal law, spouses are allowed to protect a portion or all of their income when either the husband or wife requires care in a Medicaid-approved facility. All income of both spouses is taken into consideration. Depending on the total income, a portion of the combined income can be allocated to the community spouse.

What amount of income can be allocated to the community spouse?

Based on the total nonexempt monthly income of the couple, the community spousal allowance is determined as follows:

1. If the combined total nonexempt gross income of both spouses is $1295 or less per month, all of that income can be allocated to the community spouse.
2. If the combined total nonexempt gross income (or adjusted gross income for the self-employed) is more than $1295 per month, income sufficient to bring the community spouse's gross income up to $1295 per month can be made available.

Is $1295 all that the community spouse is entitled to have?

No. The amount to which the community spouse may be entitled can be increased to a maximum of $1871 per month if there is a monthly rent or mortgage payment that exceeds $369.

If a court order has been entered against the institutionalized spouse for the support of the community spouse, the income allowance for the community spouse shall not be less than the amount the court ordered, even if it exceeds the cap. Also, if there are significant financial needs that constitute financial duress, as determined by a fair-hearings officer, the allowance shall be increased to an amount determined by that officer.

What if other dependents are in the home?

A child, parent, brother, or sister of either spouse who lives with the community spouse can receive $430 per month of the income of the institutionalized spouse as long as that family member's gross monthly income does not exceed $1295.

Must income be allocated?

No, income allocation is not required just because an allowance could be provided. The institutionalized spouse has the choice of providing the full maximum allowance, a smaller portion of it, or nothing at all.

Can any of the income be protected for the miscellaneous needs of the institutionalized spouse?

Yes. A personal-needs allowance of $30 per month may be allocated out of that individual's income if the income is less than $1295 per month.

What if I have too much income to qualify for nursing home care but not enough to pay for it? What can I do?

For individuals who fall into this income gap, there is something that can be done to assist them in qualifying for Medicaid in order to have the ability to enter an adult care home. Since the average cost of nursing home care ranges from approximately $2000 to $4000 per month, it is very conceivable that an individual may have more than $1470 monthly income but less than what is needed to pay privately for the care that is required.

To get out of this income-gap trap, you can create an *income trust,* which is explained later in this chapter.

Is it true that I am not entitled to any assistance if my income exceeds the stated amount?

This isn't true. Although you will not be entitled to assistance with your cost of long-term care, such as in an adult care home, you may still qualify for medical assistance for coverage of other medical services, including temporary care in certain situations.

Once eligibility is determined, how must income be used to provide payment to the facility which is providing care?

Assuming the monthly income limit is met, the monthly patient liability is calculated by determining the amount of countable income in excess of the $30 personal allowance.

What expenses must be paid out of the patient's income?

If medically necessary, all expenses for medical services incurred by the individual beginning with the first month of eligibility can be paid out of a patient's income, including medical bills transferred to a collection agency for repayment. Such expenses can be applied to a future month's obligation when it is not possible to pay for expenses in the month they are incurred.

Also, Medicare premiums and medical insurance premiums are expenses that can be paid out of a patient's income. (Each policy must be looked at to determine if it is intended to cover the actual cost of care or to provide a per-diem amount, which is viewed as income replacement and not as insurance.)

AVAILABLE RESOURCES

Is there a spenddown requirement for available resources

There is a *spenddown* requirement that applies to available assets or resources. Under this requirement, an individual must reduce the amount of assets available by spending them for qualifying purposes until they have been spent down to a level that will allow the individual to qualify for assistance.

What are available resources?

Available resources include all property of whatever nature and kind, real or personal, except property that is exempt as a noncountable asset or inaccessible asset. Available resources do not include income.

What is the maximum amount of available resources that a person can have in order to qualify for Medicaid?

A person's available resources must be less than $2000 in value.

What are countable assets?

Countable assets are those available resources that count toward the $2000 amount. These assets are subject to the spending-down requirement of the Medicaid rules. They include the following:

- Cash over $2000 (in most states)
- Cash equivalents (certificates of deposit, notes, bonds, etc.)
- Annuities
- Whole life insurance (above $1500 face value in most states)
- Real estate other than the personal residence
- Automobiles in excess of one
- All other assets not listed as noncountable

What are noncountable assets?

Noncountable assets are assets that are safe from the spending-down requirement. They include:

- Cash under $2000
- One car
- Household furnishings and personal jewelry
- A prepaid funeral
- A burial account
- Term life insurance
- Whole life insurance with face value of $1500 or less
- Business property

Can countable assets be "transformed" into noncountable assets?

Yes, to some extent. Assume that countable assets amount to $300,000. The maximum amount retainable by the at-home spouse is $76,740 (this maximum may be increased after a fair hearing with the state Medicaid agency). The remainder must be spent down. Here are a few legitimate ways for the at-home spouse to transform countable to noncountable assets prior to applying for Medicaid for the institutionalized spouse:

- You are currently driving an old car which now requires a great deal of maintenance because of its age. Buy a nice, new car with all of the options. You are entitled to one car as a noncountable asset, and the purchase of such a car is a transfer for fair value.
- You have been putting off that new roof for a few years already, the house badly needs to be painted, the kitchen retains its 1951 style from when the house was built, and the house would be considerably more marketable with a garage (you always wanted one anyway). Go ahead and do all of those things—they are all perfectly legitimate expenditures for fair value!
- For years you have wanted to visit your sister in Budapest but never could afford it. Visit her now. Your payment for airfare is a transfer for fair value. If you do not use the funds for the visit to your sister, they will simply be consumed by the nursing home.

What are inaccessible assets?

Inaccessible assets are countable assets that you cannot access. If you cannot access them, Medicaid cannot access them either. Examples of inaccessible assets are:

- Assets held in certain irrevocable trusts
- Assets given to others
- Assets which, for one reason or another, cannot be accessed without the consent of a third party (other than a spouse)

What qualifies as a home?

A *home* is defined as real property in which the applicant is living or from which he or she is temporarily absent. This includes the tract of land and contiguous tracts of land upon which the house or other improvements essential to the use or enjoyment of the home are located.

Is my home always exempt from being considered an available resource?

Your home is exempt without regard to its value, but it may be subject to a redetermination of eligibility if you are absent for more than 12 months and no notice of intent to return has been filed. The statement of notice of intent to return is to be accepted without challenge regardless of whether or not it is realistic that you will actually return home.

If someone else is living in my home, such as a relative, is it necessary to have a notice of intent to return home on file with the state welfare agency?

No. If a spouse or other legal dependent continues to live in the home, it is not necessary to have a notice on file. Also, if your absence is due to a planned brief stay in the hospital (not to exceed 3 months), a notice does not have to be filed in order for the home to be treated as exempt in the determination of eligibility.

If I have transferred property to my children and reserved a life estate for myself, will the property be considered an available resource?

The holder of a life estate is entitled to the use and benefit of the property—and for real estate, the right to possession or to rents and profits—during the holder's lifetime. A life estate is, in a very real sense, ownership of the property for life, without the right to sell or dispose of the property. A life estate can be sold or transferred. Depending on when the property was conveyed and the reservation of the life estate was created, transfers of property within 36 months of applying for benefits may affect eligibility for assistance. The state agency will calculate the value of the life estate based upon your life expectancy according to a mortality table.

How is the market value for available resources determined?

Generally this is done by determining the equity value of the interest owned by the applicant (fair market value less encumbrances).

How is the determination of available resources made if I am married and my spouse and I both own property?

This is done initially by determining the total value of the available resources of both spouses at the time the institutionalized spouse first entered long-term care, unless one spouse has already been determined eligible for Medicaid or home care–based services under a Medicaid waiver.

The couple will need to provide documentary evidence of the resources owned at the time the first spouse entered the nursing facility, as well as of those owned currently, regardless of what has occurred to the assets since the first spouse began receiving long-term care.

If a person is single and has a qualified retirement plan (including IRAs), how much of the qualified plan assets must be spent before the person is eligible for Medicaid?

All of the qualified plan assets must be spent down, as with other countable assets.

If a person is married and has a qualified retirement plan (including IRAs), how much of the qualified plan assets must be spent down before the institutionalized spouse is eligible for Medicaid?

The qualified plan assets are added to the other countable assets and then the total value is allocated one-half to each spouse provided that the at-home spouse has at least $15,384 (the "floor") and not more than $76,740 (the "ceiling") in assets. The rest must be spent down.

Once there has been a determination of the available resources of both spouses, how is a division and transfer of resources between spouses accomplished?

If the institutionalized spouse is otherwise eligible and both spouses' combined resources are mostly joint-owned or primarily owned by the institutionalized spouse, the couple must then transfer sufficient resources to the community spouse to equal the allowance.

This is accomplished by first signing a notice of intent to transfer resources. The couple then has 90 days from the date the notice is filed to actually divide or transfer the assets. If the institutionalized spouse would not be eligible anyway and there would be no immediate eligibility, filing of the notice is not required and the couple can pursue the necessary transfers or division of assets prior to reapplying.

If the institutionalized spouse is unable to assist in the division and transfer of assets because of infirmity, a period of up to 1 year may be allowed for the community spouse to carry out the transfer. The community spouse must seek appropriate court action (through conservatorship or other approved methodology) to gain authority to complete the division and transfer of assets on behalf of the institutionalized spouse.

What specific actions are involved in the transfer of assets between spouses?

In order to accomplish the transfer of resources, the couple may be required to take such action as setting up separate savings accounts, changing ownership on titles and deeds, or liquidating property and dividing the proceeds. It is important that the spouses transfer resources in such a way that the resulting ownership interest of each spouse in the resources is clearly designated and separately identifiable. Once the property has been divided into separate shares, either spouse may have his or her name placed on the resource of the other for convenience purposes if their access to the property is limited to acting as agent for the other spouse.

Documentation of how the transfers have been carried out and any subsequent changes must be included in the agency case file.

Once the institutionalized spouse is determined to be eligible for Medicaid, what continuing review or assessment of the assets of the community spouse must be made?

Resources owned solely by the community spouse are not considered to be available to the institutionalized spouse beginning in the first month immediately following the month in which the institutionalized spouse is determined to be eligible. Resources transferred to the community spouse in accordance with his or her resource allowance are deemed to have been transferred during the 90-day or 1-year transfer period as set forth above.

Will the community spouse be required to spend down all of the assets owned by either spouse in order to assist the institutionalized spouse in qualifying for Medicaid?

No. There are limits on what the community spouse can be required to spend down. The community spouse will be allowed whichever is greater of the following amounts:

- $15,384
- one-half of the value, not to exceed $76,740, of the couple's nonexempt resources owned at the time the first spouse entered an institutional arrangement which began on or after September 30, 1989

These limits are reviewed and changed periodically based on increases in the consumer price index. Any increase will affect only those who apply or request an assessment on or after the effective date of the increase.

Is a spenddown required if eligibility is denied because of excess resources?

Yes. Once assets have been spent down to the appropriate level, either to $2000 in the event of an individual who is not married or to the level and amounts allowable under the spousal resource allowance, then eligibility will occur.

Applying for Medicaid

Can I request an assessment of available resources and eligibility without actually applying for the benefits?

Yes, but doing so may not be advisable or necessary. It would be better to request a determination after you have accomplished your planning for Medicaid and when you believe that a determination of eligibility will be made. If a request for an assessment is made, a "pseudo" application is filled out by the state agency and retained to track resources.

How do I apply for Medicaid?

Typically, you must apply in the welfare office in the county in which you reside. You will need to apply in person if you are legally capable of acting on your own behalf.

I'm not incompetent, but I have trouble getting around. Can't someone else apply for me?

If someone else is making the application on your behalf, that person must have your written consent to act as your authorized medical agent. A durable power of attorney for health care decisions may be sufficient, but it should specifically refer to the authority of your designated agent to act on your behalf in making medical decisions and dealing with governmental entities in regard to your qualifying for Medicaid. A broad general power of attorney is usually insufficient for this purpose.

Many people designate the acting trustee of their revocable living trust to be their agent for these purposes. The specific language designating the trustee as such should be contained within the trust document.

What are my rights in the application process?

You have the following rights as an applicant for medical assistance:

1. The right to information concerning the types of assistance which are provided and, upon request, information in pamphlet form regarding the various programs and eligibility requirements
2. The right to make application for assistance, even if there are concerns about your eligibility or ability to qualify
3. The right to a private interview
4. The right to individual determination, including the opportunity to present your request and explain your situation
5. The right to withdraw your application and to withdraw from Medicaid or any other program at any time

6. The right to a timely decision on your application
7. The right to the correct amount of assistance to which you are entitled
8. The right to written notice of the decision on your application regarding eligibility
9. The right to equal, nondiscriminatory treatment
10. The right to request a fair hearing on any agency decision or lack of action in regard to your application for or receipt of assistance.

What are my responsibilities as an applicant for Medicaid?

Your responsibilities as an applicant are as follows:

1. The responsibility to supply information essential to the determination and establishment of eligibility
2. The responsibility to give written permission for the release of information to the welfare agency when needed
3. The responsibility to report changes in your circumstances which would affect eligibility within 10 calendar days
4. The responsibility to comply with all Medicaid program requirements and supply required information
5. The responsibility to meet your own needs to the extent that you are able

What information must I provide?

In addition to basic biographical information, you must provide the following:

1. Your current living arrangement (Where and with whom do you reside?)
2. Whether you have been in the hospital in the past 45 days.
3. If your spouse is living, his or her Social Security number and source and amount of all income
4. If your living or deceased spouse is or was a veteran, his or her name, and VA claim number
5. Whether you are currently a party to a lawsuit or have a pending insurance claim

6. If you received a welfare payment or medical assistance from another state or county, when and how much
7. Detailed information about your real property and personal property assets (resources), including those in your spouse's name alone
8. Information about the medical insurance coverage you currently have, including Medicare
9. Whether you or anyone on your behalf has transferred property for less than its fair market value or you have given away property within 36 months of the date of the application
10. Detailed information about all of your sources of income, including Social Security and any other retirement or pension benefits
11. Information about every life insurance policy which you own and any burial insurance policy which you own

You must also consent to a home visit and to the release of information from employers, medical providers, financial institutions, insurance providers, and other business and professional persons or entities that may have information affecting your eligibility to receive benefits.

If you do not provide this information, the state agency may close the case until you comply.

How can I find out if incorrect information has been provided?

The agency should let you know when it believes that it is necessary to go to other sources for information. When a third party provides information that contradicts statements or information provided by you, you must be given the opportunity to resolve the discrepancy prior to a determination of eligibility.

What extent will the state agency go to in gathering information beyond what I provide?

The state agency administering the Medicaid program will allow you to clarify information when it finds that something is incomplete or inconsistent or when the circumstances indicate that a prudent person would investigate further and gather additional information. Your state agency will use, to the greatest extent possible, the information on the application form which you have provided for the purpose of determining eligibility. However, you should be aware that the agency administrative office will request additional substantiation of facts when the information you have provided is unclear, incomplete, or contradictory.

How long does the application process normally take?

Generally, action will be taken on your application within 30 days of the date you apply. The guidelines allow for up to 45 days, unless a determination of disability is being made, in which case it may take up to 90 days.

How private is the information that I provide during the application process?

The information that you provide is to be kept confidential by the welfare agency employee who is assisting you and by any other agency employee who must review the information to determine your eligibility for benefits. It may not be disclosed to anyone, with these exceptions:

1. The case record is to be made available to you, although the agency may not disclose to you information contained within investigative reports relating to alleged fraud, during the course of the investigation.
2. Disclosure of information may be made to nonagency employees, to the extent necessary, when the purpose relates to the administration of your case to provide you with the services to which you are entitled.
3. Information from your case record may also be disclosed to an official investigating the administration of welfare programs, if the information is reasonably necessary.
4. Information is to be disclosed when properly subpoenaed or ordered by a court of competent jurisdiction.

How is the determination of eligibility made?

Your application will be reviewed, as well as the intake record and any other forms used, such as a budget plan. Eligibility will be based on the facts of your particular situation as applied to the eligibility requirements of Medicaid under both state and federal law

An eligibility base period is established. It may be from 1 to 6 months, depending on what programs or assistance is being applied for. This base period is then used to determine financial eligibility for the individual for whom the application is being processed.

What factors determine when the period of eligibility begins?

The month in which the application is first received by the local agency office is the first month of the current eligibility base period, provided that all other eligibility factors, with the exception of a spenddown, have been met.

How will I find out what action has been taken on my application?

Written notice will be mailed to you.

If I am denied eligibility for Medicaid, how soon can I reapply?

Someone in the agency office should explain to you that you have the right to request a redetermination and have your case reactivated at any time if you have new information relating to your qualification for benefits. All factors of eligibility are to be reviewed, and this is to take place in a face-to-face interview with you, unless you waive your right to such an interview. The agency should review your situation as often as needed, but no later than every 12 months and no later than 6 months if you were initially within $300 of the resource level or if you were required to spend down a certain amount of available resources.

Once eligibility is determined, is it ever reviewed?

Yes, at least annually. Changes in income or in rent or mortgage payments must be reported within 10 calendar days of the change, and adjustments will be made at that time.

If my spouse is going into a nursing home, when should we apply for Medicaid?

It is generally advisable to apply for Medicaid immediately. When an application is made, a "snapshot" of your assets is taken to determine what you own and how much of that needs to be spent down. Assuming that you own no more than two times the ceiling amount which the community spouse can keep, this would allow the spouse at home to keep the maximum amount.

Often the spouse at home is mistakenly advised to spend down first and then apply for Medicaid. However, when the snapshot is then taken, you will have to spend down at least one-half of the amount remaining, without credit given for what you have already spent.

Medicaid planning is one of the most difficult areas not only because of the financial issues but because of the emotional issues as well. You should seek the advice of a competent professional as early as possible to determine what your planning options are.

The thought of having to choose a nursing home and apply for Medicaid is overwhelming. Are there any good sources of help and advice in the community?

A wonderful source of information and assistance for Medicaid is the Long Term Care Ombudsman. This organization often can supply quite detailed information on nursing homes, their track records, and names of other county or community resources. It helps people with problems and concerns about long-term care, and it is responsible for investigating and seeking resolutions to complaints about long-term care. The organization can advise you in selecting a facility and can answer questions about Medicare, Medicaid, and a patient's rights under the law. Many times the skills of a social worker are required for purposes of assessment of needs and availability of the appropriate services. Depending on your financial situation, that assistance may be available to you at no cost.

This type of organization is often a part of the state's Department of Aging.

Estate Recovery

What is estate recovery?

Congress has enacted a set of rules known as the *estate recovery rules*. Generally, under these rules the property included in an individual's estate after death can be reached by the government in order to "repay" medical expenses that have been paid by Medicaid.

The phrase "estate" is a term of art. The Omnibus Budget and Reconciliation Act of 1993 (OBRA) gives state governments the option to define assets owned by the deceased and passing to others through joint tenancy, a life estate, a revocable living trust, and various other means as part of the individual's "estate." You'll need to check with your attorney regarding your individual state law to see how you are affected by this legislation.

Federal and state law in most states now provides for the establishment of the Estate Recovery Unit, a division of the welfare agency administering Medicaid, for the purpose of recovering medical care costs from the estates of certain deceased medical assistance recipients. This law went into effect on July 1, 1993. It affects certain persons who were provided services subsequent to that date and were 55 years of age or older prior to their deaths or were receiving long-term institutional or HCBS care at the time of death.

The claim is normally filed against the recipient's estate. However, if there is a surviving spouse, no claim is filed. Instead, upon the death of the surviving spouse, a claim will be filed against that spouse's estate. A claim will not be established if any surviving children are under age 21 or are blind or permanently disabled under Social Security criteria.

A claim made by the Estate Recovery Unit is a first-class claim against the estate of the deceased person. Payment of funeral expenses is the only claim allowed to come ahead of an Estate Recovery Unit claim.

No liens are filed against the property of a Medicaid recipient or his or her spouse in order to establish a claim prior to the recipient's death. Claims are filed only against the property that is still available at the time of death. Agreements with heirs may be used for payment of claims.

What triggers estate recovery?

Notification of the death of the recipient will trigger a possible estate recovery process.

How does the Estate Recovery Unit receive notice that a death has occurred?

Notice may be obtained from newspaper obituaries, state Income Maintenance workers, the personal representative of the recipient's estate, governmental agencies, or any other reliable source. Then the Income Maintenance worker reviews any resource assessment information available. If there is a surviving spouse, recovery action will be suspended until the death of the surviving spouse.

How does the Estate Recovery Unit determine if there will be an estate recovery?

The determination of recovery action, if any, is a two-step process:

1. Resource assessment (Is there anything from which recovery can be made?)
2. Determination of the value of the claim for which recovery may be pursued

What property can be claimed against?

The primary assets considered are real property, financial accounts, and other liquid assets. Personal property—including, but not limited to, cars, furniture, clothes, jewelry and collectibles—is not considered, as no claim will be made against this type of property unless it is liquidated to pay creditors. If the property is liquidated, the estate recovery claim will then apply to all of the liquidated property.

Any estate recovery claim will be reduced by the amount of payments made by a long-term-care policy on behalf of a recipient.

What if there isn't a probate proceeding?

The agency will determine the appropriate action to be taken in regard to pursuing claims. Claims may be filed through one of several avenues, including, but not limited to, agreements with heirs, claims against financial accounts, and filing of a probate action.

If the family or heirs do not institute probate proceedings because the estate is too small or other planning was instituted such as a revocable living trust, the agency will determine whether to proceed with probate on the basis of the nature of the agency's claim, value of the estate assets, presence of other creditors, and any other relevant information. The claim may be made direct to any financial institution.

Medicare

What is the difference between Medicaid and Medicare?

Medicaid is the federal and state program of medical assistance used primarily to finance the costs of long-term care for elderly people. *Medicare* is the medical insurance program for persons over 65 years of age who require hospital (acute) care and skilled nursing care following acute care. Elderly people who do not have an illness triggered by a period of hospitalization cannot use the Medicare program to cover the cost of their long-term custodial care.

Doesn't Medicare cover the cost of nursing home care?

The misconception that Medicare covers all of the costs associated with long-term nursing home care is, unfortunately, a belief held by literally millions of Americans. Perhaps the basis of this misconception is the fact that Medicare provides federal health insurance for all persons over the age of 65 who are otherwise entitled to monthly Social Security or Railroad Retirement benefits. There are also other situations in which individuals under the age of 65 are eligible to receive Social Security benefits.

As for Medicare paying the costs of a nursing home, the reality is simple—don't count on it! Medicare will pay the costs of a nursing home, at best, for a limited period of time only: the first 20 days can be paid in full and, according to 1995 figures, an additional 80 days may be paid—after you pay $89.50 per day.

Even during the 100-day limited-coverage period, certain qualifications must be met in order to receive any Medicare benefits whatsoever. For example, the care received by the nursing home resident must be "skilled care"; the nursing home patient must have spent at least 3 days in a hospital, with similar treatments to those being received at the nursing home; the patient must be assigned to a bed that is Medicare-certified for reimbursement; and the nursing home must be Medicare-approved. To make matters worse, there are often disagreements as to the definition of "skilled care," which often result in disputes as to whether the patient qualifies for Medicare during the initial 20- and 80-day periods.

It cannot be overemphasized that, as a general rule, Medicare is not to be presumed to be an available resource for paying the costs associated with nursing home care.

How are long-term-care expenses usually paid?

Contrary to popular belief, Medicare pays very little of these expenses. Studies have consistently shown that the portion of such expenses covered by Medicare averages less than 2 percent. Private long-term-care insurance is covering a growing proportion of the expenses (an estimated 4 to 5 percent today). The two most common sources of payment, however, remain payment from individuals' own assets and payment by the Medicaid system. Medicaid has become known as the "payor of last resort."

In recent years, assisting clients with qualification for Medicaid benefits has been a growth industry. Through a strategy of planned transfers, a family can qualify for Medicaid benefits while preserving most, if not all, of its assets. Congress acted in 1993, with the passage of OBRA, to restrict many of these strategies, particularly those involving the use of trusts. In stark contrast, both Congress and the state governments have begun to develop incentives encouraging the use of privately purchased long-term-care insurance.

Medicaid Planning

What is Medicaid planning?

Medicaid planning involves studying and applying a complex set of rules to allow the maximum preservation of assets while qualifying for and receiving Medicaid payments. Congress has tried to impede the transfer of assets—typically to children—for the purpose of qualifying for Medicaid. These transfers can be risky for the parents because their assets become exposed to the children's own creditors or the terms of a property settlement during a child's divorce.

Generally speaking, who might benefit from Medicaid planning?

It is frequently said that Medicaid planning should become an ordinary part of preretirement planning. While this notion may seem a bit premature to some, all too often Medicaid planning does not occur until a person is either out of money or almost out of any other remaining assets. On many occasions, a senior citizen unnecessarily spends all of his or her money on nursing home care when other "estate planning" alternatives exist, particularly when the senior citizen is married and the other spouse remains in the marital residence.

Certainly, Medicaid planning becomes absolutely essential by the time an individual enters a nursing home and the other spouse is continuing to live in the marital residence. The goals of the spouse remaining at home should be not only to protect the residence but also to protect as many assets, and as much income, as possible. Medicaid planning is an essential ingredient in providing for the maintenance, care, and support of the spouse remaining at home.

Medicaid planning is also a possible alternative for senior citizens whose net worth is high. While the idea of preserving assets and, at the same time, becoming qualified to receive Medicaid benefits is offensive to many (including many of our elected officials in Washington), it is, nevertheless, incumbent upon the senior citizen with a higher net worth to at least examine the Medicaid planning options that are available under the current law.

For senior citizens who have relatively few assets and small amounts of liquidity, it is important to examine various Medicaid planning issues. For example, it is possible to utilize what little monies remain for preparing one's burial arrangements by purchasing an irrevocable burial or funeral contract which alleviates the need for other family members to incur this expense. An irrevocable burial or funeral contract is deemed under the current law to be an exempt, or noncountable, asset and thus is not included in the assets that may have to be spent to obtain Medicaid eligibility.

Despite a number of significant Medicaid law changes in August 1993 that minimized planning options, there still remain planning alternatives available to literally everyone at every level of net worth. Thus, as stated above, many people believe that Medicaid planning should be discussed as part of one's preretirement planning.

Why should I do any planning for my long-term care or disability?

The real issue is what will you do if you or your spouse becomes completely or partially incapacitated and needs assistance. More than that, where will you get the assistance and how will you pay for it? Additionally, you must face the moral or ethical dilemma of whether or not to make yourself indigent in order to qualify for public assistance through the various state and federal programs.

Let's start with some statistics to evaluate the likelihood that you may need assistance with long-term care and, further, the cost. Today, the average life expectancy for a man who reaches the age of 65 is 85 years. For women who reach the age of 65, the average life expectancy is 89 years. Men who reach age 65 have about a 30 percent chance of entering a nursing home, and women have a 50 percent chance. However, only 25 percent of the individuals who enter nursing homes stay longer than 1 year.

Home health care has been a burgeoning industry, primarily because home health care tends to be about one-half the cost of nursing home care. The effect this cost differential will have in coming years is hard to estimate, although it is likely that the numbers of people entering nursing homes will decrease as more and more people are provided assistance in their own homes.

The average cost of nursing home care in 1995 in the United States was about $36,000 per year, but in some areas the average is twice that. The best homes can cost up to $100,000 per year, and the cost is going up about 5 percent per year.

If you are destitute and qualify for public assistance through Medicaid, your alternatives are limited to making sure that appropriate exemptions have been provided and planned for. If you are among those who would not immediately qualify for benefits, you have the choice of divesting yourself of your assets in order to qualify or doing whatever you can to provide for your own care through financial planning and the acquisition of long-term-care insurance, if possible. Generally, the second option is the better one.

How do I begin in my Medicaid planning?

You should begin by analyzing your income and income-producing assets to determine whether or not you have sufficient income to provide for your own needs in the event you do need assistance. You need to determine your cash shortfall on a monthly basis in the event that you, your spouse, or both of you need assistance and then consider how to enhance income. Your planning options include long-term-care insurance (nursing home insurance), life insurance with long-term-care or loan/cash value provisions, annuities, and turning non-income-producing assets into income-producing assets

GIVING ASSETS AWAY

Is it possible to successfully give assets away, say, to my children, rather than spend them down?

Yes, it is possible, but you should be aware of the pitfalls of doing so. First, when you give away assets, you lose control of them. If those assets are to be made available for your benefit after you give them away, you must rely on the loyalty and integrity of the person to whom you gave the assets to carry through.

Once you transfer your assets to someone else, your assets are subject to that other person's exposure to liabilities, to a spouse looking for a divorce settlement, or to a bankruptcy court in the event of a bankruptcy petition, to name but a few.

When you file an application for Medicaid assistance, one of the questions you are asked is, "Have you made any transfers of assets for less than fair value within the last 36 months?" If your answer is in the affirmative, you will be ineligible for Medicaid assistance for a penalty period measured in months equal to the amount of the less-than-fair-value transfer divided by the average cost of nursing home care in your state of residence. This exercise is known as "looking back." For example, a transfer of $40,000 would create 10 months of ineligibility if the state's average cost of nursing home care was $4000 per month ($40,000 divided by $4000).

There is a degree of uncertainty about the length of this look-back period because of fiscal pressures on Congress and state legislatures. OBRA has already increased the look-back period twice, from 24 months to 30 months and then again to 36 months. This look-back period extends to 60 months for transfers of less than full value to irrevocable trusts.

When one spouse's health is declining and it is becoming clear that this spouse will have to enter a nursing home, is there any advantage to transferring assets to the well spouse while the declining spouse is able to make such transfers?

Yes, it is probably a good idea to do so. If the declining spouse enters a nursing home and later becomes unable to manage his or her affairs, the difficulty of transferring assets, such as the home, is substantially increased at that time. If assets must be spent down after one spouse is institutionalized, it will be much easier for the community spouse to transfer such assets before the health of the institutionalized spouse deteriorates further.

It may also be advisable for the community spouse to update his or her will or trust to change the beneficiary from the declining spouse to some other person. If this is not done and if the at-home spouse dies while the institutionalized spouse is alive, the family may find that the previously protected, noncountable assets (including the home) in the hands of the at-home spouse pass to the institutionalized spouse. If this occurs, the institutionalized spouse's countable assets may exceed the allowable amount, and upon the death of the institutionalized spouse, estate recovery may jeopardize even noncountable assets.

Isn't it somewhat immoral to spend down assets or give them away just to qualify for a government welfare program such as Medicaid?

Some people take the position that spending down their assets to qualify for Medicaid is immoral. They believe this even though agreeing with the law which requires that people must be prepared to pay for 3 years of their own long-term care if they do spend down their assets.

Others feel that they did not work and save all their lives to see all that effort lost. These people also point to the unfairness flowing from the "lucky" person who has an expensive long-term illness which requires hospitalization (covered by Medicare) and the "unlucky" person who slips into an Alzheimer's situation not covered by Medicare, thereby requiring that the person spend down his or her own assets before qualifying for Medicaid.

Increasingly, people are insuring their obligation to provide for 3 years of their own long-term care by purchasing long-term-care insurance. A few states have pioneered programs to let people buy a form of this insurance to protect a stated amount of nonexempt assets, for example, $50,000 or $100,000, from the spenddown requirement before qualifying for Medicaid.

Once we've qualified for Medicaid assistance, does this mean the government can never go back and place a claim on our assets in the future?

The answer is sometimes yes and sometimes no. Remember that assets transferred *before* the look-back period of 36 months are safely transferred. The government cannot go back to get those assets. Assets transferred within the look-back period will, in a sense, be "taken back" by the government because the applicant will simply not qualify for assistance until the value of these transfers is taken into account.

INCOME TRUSTS

What is an income trust?

An *income trust* is applicable only to individuals who require nursing home care and whose monthly income exceeds the amount necessary to qualify for Medicaid. It must be an irrevocable trust.

How does an income trust work?

The purpose of an income trust is to reduce an individual's income below that required to qualify for Medicaid. The sole beneficiary of the income trust is the individual, during life. All income received by the trust must be made available to pay for the individual's cost of care each month, with the exceptions of a monthly fee, not to exceed $30, as a trust maintenance fee for trustee compensation, maintenance of a bank account, and preparation of tax returns and $30 per month as a personal-needs allowance to the individual.

The state welfare agency and the Estate Recovery Unit are the beneficiaries after the death of the individual, and the trust must provide that the state's Estate Recovery Unit will be compensated for the amount of medical assistance paid on the individual's behalf from any amount remaining in the trust at the time of the individual's death.

LIMITED LIABILITY COMPANIES

If we create a limited liability company and place our personal assets into it, will this be an effective Medicaid planning tool?

The answer is a definite maybe.

Limited liability companies (LLCs) have been adopted as a separate form of legal entity in most states. The primary benefit of an LLC is that it acts as a protective device by shielding assets from creditors. If you create an LLC properly and place your assets effectively into the LLC, as a general rule your assets will be protected from creditors. This concept may be effective in protecting your assets, while also allowing you to qualify for Medicaid, presumably after having otherwise met the state's 36-month ineligibility period.

It may be possible in your state to create an LLC and then place all or selected assets into it. Your children could be the members, or owners, of the LLC interests and could receive most or all of the income generated by any of the assets placed into the LLC. Further, if properly designed, the children could receive the assets upon the death of the senior citizen who created the LLC.

One benefit of an LLC to a senior citizen is that it is possible for the senior citizen to retain control of the assets in the LLC yet retain no ownership interest.

Although still untested because of the relative newness of the LLC as a form of legal entity, assets placed into an LLC may be protected from nursing home costs after your state's ineligibility period has been met. However, one must also realize that LLCs have largely not been tested as Medicaid qualification vehicles, so you and your legal counsel should closely check the statutes and case law in your own state regarding this potential option.

REVOCABLE LIVING TRUSTS

I'm worried that as I get older, I may need to have someone who can handle my finances for me. But I'm afraid to give anyone that much power. What can I do?

Many older clients express this concern. The prospect of aging and perhaps reaching a point in your life when you simply cannot manage your affairs yourself can be frightening. *You* know what you want and need, but will anyone else know?

Do you really want to give up control of your personal affairs which you have handled quite skillfully for a lifetime? Probably not.

Giving a loved one or a friend your power of attorney may be the worst solution to this potential problem. Powers of attorney are very powerful documents. They typically give the holder (the agent) unlimited power and authority to do with your assets whatever *you* can do with them. There are typically no built-in safeguards to ensure that your assets will be used only for you and in accordance with your wishes.

Of course, if you have no planning in place and you become mentally unable to manage your own affairs, a court will appoint a guardian for you. That guardian may or may not be someone you would have chosen to handle your finances or make your personal decisions.

The safest way for you to handle the possibility that you may become unable to act for yourself is to do your planning within a revocable living trust. You can choose a disability trustee to take care of your finances and carry out your instructions as to how you are to be cared for, as well as how your loved ones should be cared for, should you become unable to make those decisions yourself.

You do not lose control, because you choose now whom you want to be in charge and then you give your trusted choice specific directions.

Will setting up a revocable living trust protect my assets and allow me to qualify for Medicaid?

As far as Medicaid is concerned, any assets in your revocable trust are considered your assets. As long as your trust is revocable, the assets in it are not "protected." Although a revocable living trust has many advantages, it is not a Medicaid planning tool.

How can I utilize a revocable living trust to hold my assets without increasing the "look-back" period?

In 1993, Congress decided to respond to those who were creating *irrevocable* trusts to put assets outside of their control in order to qualify for Medicaid. The action Congress took through OBRA was to extend the look-back period in the case of irrevocable trusts to 60 months rather than the 36-month look-back period for other gifts and transfers made at less than fair market value. However, this penalty provision does not affect revocable living trusts because the assets in a revocable living trust are taken into consideration to determine qualification for Medicaid. Thus, there is no reason to penalize someone for planning with a revocable living trust.

Can I still leave the door open for Medicaid planning if my assets are held by my revocable living trust?

Yes. This can be done through the use of a durable power of attorney for giving purposes. The revocable living trust should provide that the acting trustees can make transfers to the agent under the power of attorney. Generally, such a durable power of attorney should restrict the agent to making gifts only to those persons to whom you want to make gifts. It is best to utilize an independent agent (someone who is not potentially a donee or beneficiary). This protects your agent from potential adverse tax consequences and assures you that an independent party will review your situation and determine that the transfers are, in fact, a good idea under the circumstances. These gifts will still be subject to the normal look-back period of 36 months, but this approach allows planning to transfer assets and qualify for Medicaid after the 36-month period.

Long-Term Care

What is long-term care?

Long-term care is defined as a stay of more than 30 consecutive days in an establishment where food and shelter are furnished to four or more persons unrelated to the owner or operator and where some treatment or services are provided which meet some need beyond the basic provision of food and shelter. Such care may be provided by adult care homes, hospitals, psychiatric facilities, licensed nonmedical residential care facilities, and other facilities which meet the provisions in the definition of long-term care.

I have heard that there are three different asset levels that may affect my planning as I get older. What are these levels, and what do they signify?

There are three levels of assets that set in motion different kinds of planning. For couples at the first level, with assets valued at $250,000 or less (with a residence valued at about one-half of that), a long-term illness with a nursing home cost of $36,000 to $45,000 or more per year will soon deplete the Social Security, company pension, and interest and dividend income typically available to such couples. This would require that they spend down their assets before going on Medicaid. If both spouses require nursing home care, the inevitable will happen sooner. In this situation, some Medicaid planning may be helpful, as well as a possible restructuring of their investments, perhaps to buy an annuity that can cover the premium on long-term-care insurance. The insurance, however, will probably be too costly for the couple's modest income, given that they will typically have waited too long to buy it.

The second level of assets is the comfortable one, say, more than $1 million in liquid assets, sufficient at 4½ percent to produce the $45,000 needed each year to pay for the annual cost of a nursing home and leave normal Social Security and pension income to cover house upkeep, taxes, and other expenses. If both spouses need nursing home care, then the amount of investible assets should exceed $2 million if the goal is to keep principal intact.

Couples in the middle range of assets, between $250,000 and $1 million, which includes a substantial number of American families, have opportunities for creating a game plan which will allow them to look forward to leaving some property to their children and charity while they cope with the threat of "running out of health."

What is the best game plan for getting older if we have assets between $250,000 and $1 million?

Faced with the very real risk of running out of health, the well-advised client in the middle asset level, between $250,000 and $1 million, will take steps to defend against long-term-care costs. The first line of defense is to purchase long-term-care insurance while you are in your forties or fifties and while the cost is manageable. In your fifties or sixties, you will put your name on one or more waiting lists at an assisted-living center or assisted-care home (sometimes called a *continuing-care retirement community,* or *CCRC*) since, in any event, at the better communities there will be a wait involved.

The biggest mistake people make is not to put their names on a list or lists, just as if they were applying to one or more colleges. Applying is not a commitment to move to the facility. It simply is the deposit of a nonrefundable processing fee, typically $250, and a refundable deposit, typically $1000, which means that the cost of creating an option on a future residency is essentially the interest lost on the $1000 each year. It is smart, too, to put your name on all the internal lists you qualify for; for example, a married couple signs up on the one-bedroom as well as the two-bedroom lists. Time passes: the wait at an assisted-living center may be 2 to 3 years for a studio apartment, 4 to 5 years for a one-bedroom apartment, and 7 to 9 years for a two-bedroom apartment.

One day you receive a telephone call that the wait is over and an apartment is available. You then have three options: (1) Say, "No,

I'm not ready yet." (2) Say, "I'm ready, so go forward with the application." Or (3) say "I'm not interested; please give me my $1000 back."

If you choose option 1, most assisted-living centers will allow you to remain at the top of the list and will take the person next in line. That way, you can make a move on relatively short notice in the future without facing years of waiting at a stage of life when most people have more money than time.

If, during the waiting period, your health has deteriorated to the extent that admission is denied, there is still the protection afforded by the long-term-care insurance. If you are admitted to the CCRC but with a health care exclusion for the costs of care for a preexisting condition, not to worry: there is still the long-term-care insurance.

Even if issues of cost or preferred lifestyle at home may dictate consideration of the at-home plan, you should nevertheless get on a list and start "serving your time." After all, when you are much older, single, and lonely, you might decide that the community features of the campus-style assisted-living center better suit you. At that point, you will have the option to make a move and not the daunting prospect of a long wait.

One planning tip to keep in mind: If you are in a hurry to gain admittance, go for the unit with the shortest waiting time and get under contract with its health care guarantees. Once you are in the center, you can move to a larger unit when it becomes available. Meanwhile, your health situation is covered.

What are my options for remaining in my home and receiving care if I need it?

In response to the desire of many Americans to age at home, a new type of assisted-living center, sometimes called *continuing care at home,* has been developed. The similarities to a CCRC are many, although there is no waiting list because you provide your housing as well as meals. Consequently, the entry fee and monthly fee are much lower. A prospective member must meet health and financial requirements to gain admission. A type A contract is signed with the member. Care is provided in the member's home until the cost exceeds the cost of providing care in one of the nursing homes under the plan. At that point, the member must select and move to one of the nursing homes unless he or she wants to pay the excess cost, in which case the plan will keep the member at home.

LONG-TERM-CARE INSURANCE

Is long-term-care insurance a good solution for people who are concerned about the prospect of moving to a nursing home?

Long-term-care insurance is one of the few alternatives to self-paying the costs of long-term care. This type of insurance generally provides an amount of money per day for a fixed period of time or for the remainder of the insured's life.

A long-term-care policy can include an escalation feature which automatically increases the amount that will be paid annually so as to keep up with inflationary pressures. This escalation feature can provide for a fixed percentage increase each year or an increase that is tied to the consumer price index. A problem with many escalation clauses is that nursing home costs have risen steeply over the years and the future escalation in such costs may exceed the consumer price index.

What are some of the advantages of long-term-care insurance, and how does it work?

Long-term-care insurance is a product offered by insurance carriers to cover the cost of custodial care in a nursing home facility. Policies can be purchased which also cover the cost of home health care.

How you structure your policy will obviously affect its cost. Premiums are generally level, meaning a fixed amount per year. Most policies do not guarantee that the premiums will never increase but do provide that your premium can be increased only if rates are raised for everyone in your state carrying the same policy.

The major advantages of funding your potential long-term costs through insurance are simplicity and control. Having your own dollars to spend the way you want gives you power over your circumstances. You can let your loved ones know, and direct in your estate planning documents, how you want your affairs conducted if a major disability strikes. You will not be subject to the whims of government. You can go to the facility of your choosing, get the level of care you want and desire, and be certain that things will work as you require.

Because the Medicaid system does not reimburse nursing homes at the same rate that a private patient pays, there is always a risk that the quality of care received will not be the same if you rely on the Medicaid system to pay your way. By "paying the freight" yourself, you'll have better peace of mind that you'll get the care you expect and desire.

Paying for costs through long-term-care insurance allows you to budget for the cost of care. Once you've acquired the policy and established a relationship with a good agent, you can simply pay the premiums and not have to worry about where the money will come from if disability strikes.

What is the difference between long-term-care insurance and disability insurance?

Long-term-care insurance is the "flip side" of disability insurance. Disability insurance is typically purchased during one's active working career to protect against income loss. The cost of disability insurance depends on how much the monthly benefit is, how long the insured is willing to wait before receiving benefits, and how long the benefits last.

These same considerations apply to long-term-care insurance. The cost is dependent on the amount of monthly benefit (with an escalation or inflation provision being advisable), the waiting period before benefits begin (e.g., up to 6 months), and the duration of benefits (with 5 years covering more than 95 percent of the cases). Some policies specify a maximum dollar coverage, and when this amount is spent, the coverage ends.

Older policies required at least a 3-day hospital stay to trigger benefits, which is harder to achieve in this day and age and impossible to achieve if Alzheimer's is the triggering event. Modern policies speak in terms of inability to perform one or more activities of daily living (ADLs) such as eating, toileting, bathing, dressing, and transferring from bed to a chair. The impairment of two or more ADLs generally triggers coverage either in a nursing home or in an assisted-living facility or at home with home health aids provided to help overcome the deficiencies.

With the rise of managed care, more and more long-term-care insurers are providing case management, as well as dollar benefits, to reduce costs.

One innovation in this area is to combine disability insurance, which speaks of inability to carry on one's own occupation from the standpoint of a medical assessment, and long-term insurance based on loss of ADLs. Such a policy recognizes that disability is a more likely occurrence than death for people until they reach their late thirties. Moreover, disability does not stop at age 65 but becomes an increasing hazard until age 85. As a group, senior citizens are the fastest-growing segment of our population; there is almost a 50-50 chance that a person will reach the age of 85. Thus, a person has a far greater risk of becoming disabled than of having a fire destroy his or her home (1 chance out of 1000) or having an auto accident (1 chance out of 100), yet we insure against the latter two possibilities out of ordinary prudence.

I've heard that long-term-care insurance is not such a good deal. How do I know if my agent is telling me the right things?

Long-term-care insurance is a relatively new product. The policies have improved greatly in just the last few years. Some of the stories you may have heard about unscrupulous agents and poor-quality products may well be true. Because of the tremendous need in this area, however, state governments have begun taking an active role in assisting consumers with information and counseling regarding long-term care.

Every state government has set up some sort of counseling system you can benefit from. Call your state's Department of Insurance to find out how the program works in your state. The state counselors can assist in determining your needs and can generically describe the background of the type of agent you're looking for. Your other professional advisors can also assist you in locating a skilled professional long-term-care agent. Your estate planning attorney is often well positioned to provide you with such a referral.

A very helpful brochure is available from the National Association of Insurance Commissioners. It is called *A Shopper's Guide to Long-Term Care Insurance.* You can get it from your insurance professional or contact the National Association of Insurance Commissioners, 120 West 12th Street, Suite 1100, Kansas City, MO 64105-1925, or, by phone, 816-842-3600.

Would you share the biggest concerns, in your experience, with current long-term-care policies?

The two biggest concerns are field underwriting and policy gatekeepers. *Field underwriting* is a business practice in which the agent takes health information from the proposed insured directly and the company issues a contract with little, or even no, review of the client's actual medical records. When the policyholder applies for benefits under the policy, the company then conducts an in-depth review of the health situation. Quite often, the company is able to claim that the original information provided on the application was incomplete or even misleading. In these situations it is not uncommon for the company to deny a claim.

Policy gatekeepers are provisions included in a policy to make it difficult for the policyholder to ever receive benefits. For example, a gatekeeper provision might specify qualification by level of care. Early long-term-care policies provided that a policyholder must receive skilled care before applying for custodial care benefits under the policy. Skilled care is care aimed at rehabilitating a client. Direct entry into a nursing home, therefore, was almost never covered. Another, more direct example is a provision that requires transfer from a hospital to the nursing home. Again, direct entry to the home would not be covered.

How do I protect against these problems?

The best way to protect yourself is to obtain information from your state's Department of Insurance and, most importantly, to select a qualified agent. Each of the problems mentioned above, field underwriting and the use of policy gatekeeper provisions, is decreasing as consumer education increases. When you research this area, mention these two problems and ask your counselor and agent what other problems they are currently seeing in the marketplace. They will see this as an opportunity to demonstrate their value.

Is there a way to combine the purchase of long-term-care insurance with other planning strategies?

One of the most common and effective strategies being utilized under the current Medicaid set of rules is to prepare an estate plan using a revocable living trust and a special durable power of attorney and then purchase long-term-care insurance for a benefit period long enough to cover the 36-month look-back period. In this way, a person can pay for a period of time from his or her assets and have all the benefits of control, including selection of facility. If the need for assistance turns out to be long-term, the person has positioned his or her trustees and agents to make the necessary transfers *without* having to utilize private funds beyond the cost of the premiums for the long-term-care policy.

This strategy has the drawback that the client will eventually be dependent upon the whims of government, but it seems to be a popular "middle ground" due to the difference in premiums for policies providing 3 or 4 years of benefits as compared to those providing lifetime benefits.

One caution with this type of planning is that the federal government may, at any time, increase the look-back period to longer than 36 months. If this is the case, then there may be a shortfall in coverage. This potential problem should be discussed in detail before using this approach.

I have a nursing home policy for long-term care. How will payments from this affect my eligibility for Medicaid?

Insurance coverage is available to help pay the cost of long-term care. Generally most of the policies allow for payments to be made either to the individual or to the nursing facility. If made to the individual, the benefits are counted as income and could adversely affect eligibility. Therefore, you should have the benefits assigned directly to the facility. If you do this, the long-term-care insurance is treated as a third-party resource and does not adversely affect eligibility.

Social Security

What is Social Security?

Social Security is a federal program started in 1936 to provide disability and retirement security to people when their working careers end. The program has come under stress because people are living longer and because the ratio of workers to retirees has changed. When the program was founded, most people died by age 75, and there were thirteen workers paying into the system for every retired worker. Now, a rapidly increasing number of persons are age 85 and older, and the ratio of workers to retirees is now closer to five to one.

Many retirees have the impression that they have "earned" their Social Security benefits, but this is increasingly untrue. One study estimates that by age 75, retirees have used up all their payroll withholdings, their employers' contributions, and the interest earned on both. Social Security benefits paid after age 75 are coming from someone else.

In addition, Congress has been borrowing against the payroll taxes not needed to pay next month's Social Security benefits by issuing special Treasury bonds. Moreover, when the "baby boomers," born between 1946 and 1965, begin retiring in 2010, the ratio of workers to retirees will likely become worse—in the range of three to two.

Present calculations are that a single person who retires in 2029 will have paid in about $250,000 more than he or she will receive in benefits. Young people are increasingly wondering if Social Security will be there for them when they retire.

As a retirement plan, Social Security is limited. For a worker who retires with a salary of $55,000 per year, Social Security and an average pension will make up about 56 percent of that amount. For higher-income people, the percentage falls, making it imperative that private savings be generated to fund an acceptable level of retirement income.

How does early retirement affect one's ability to receive Social Security benefits?

Perhaps one of the most difficult social and economic issues facing many older workers is the early retirement they are forced to take by companies that are either downsizing or going out of business. Many of these workers believe that early retirement includes the right to begin receiving Social Security retirement benefits. They often do not understand that Social Security retirement benefits are not available until they reach the age of 62. Even if they elect to begin receiving benefits at 62, the amount of the benefits is reduced. In order to receive full benefits from Social Security, one must be 65 years of age.

Individuals and couples planning for retirement should understand that there is pending legislation that proposes to increase the age at which Social Security benefits will be paid. This potential change in the Social Security system may have a substantial financial impact on many retirees and should be considered as part of an overall retirement plan.

7

Retirement Planning

This chapter's questions and answers focus on benefits, control, and taxation of the various types of retirement plans rather than on the technical requirements of creating, maintaining, and administering them. This is not surprising, since they were submitted by attorneys who focus much more on planning than on the mechanics of plan operation. The questions and answers offer insights into the practicalities of plan participation, which are very important in an estate planning practice.

Some of the contributing authors treated individual retirement accounts and qualified plans as separate and distinct topics. Others combined them. Because of the different points of view, we thought it might be helpful to the reader to see both approaches. That is why some of the information on individual retirement accounts and other qualified plans is much the same as the information dealing with individual retirement accounts only.

The complexities of the law in the area of retirement planning made this chapter challenging to edit. The result is a chapter filled with practical information and suggestions about planning for qualified retirement plans and IRAs.

The Importance of Retirement Planning

Why is retirement planning advantageous?

Qualified retirement plans and IRAs are important ways to save for retirement because they are funded with pre-income tax dollars. The earnings are also exempt from federal income tax until withdrawn.

I have spent my life accumulating assets in my retirement plans. What goals should I have in planning for significant or large retirement plan proceeds?

There are two general goals for starting and maintaining an IRA or qualified retirement plan. The first is to accumulate as much wealth as possible for retirement. The second is to use the tax-deferred feature of a retirement plan to accelerate the growth of the account by continuing to invest the amounts that would have been used to pay for taxes.

Once your IRA or qualified retirement plan becomes a substantial asset of your estate, the natural instinct of preservation begins to alter your philosophy with regard to planning strategies. These accounts might serve to support you, your spouse, and dependents upon your death or disability. At age 59½, or when the account approaches a value in excess of $750,000, you should begin to coordinate the effects of income and estate taxes on the account as you begin to make the required withdrawals or as you prepare for lump-sum distributions after your death. You should also plan for controlling the use, investment, and distributions of the account upon your death or disability without jeopardizing its income tax–deferred or estate tax–deferred qualities.

Qualified Retirement Plans

What are qualified retirement plans?

The government, as a matter of policy, has decided to encourage everyone to save for retirement. As a supplement to, or perhaps a replacement for, Social Security benefits, the government has created a system of special tax rules under Section 401 of the Internal Revenue Code to encourage the establishment of so-called qualified retirement plans.

The primary types of qualified retirement plans are *pension plans* and profit-sharing plans. There are three types of pension plans:

1. Defined benefit plans
2. Money purchase plans

3. Target benefit plans

Profit-sharing plans are generally categorized into three groups:

1. Corporate/business-entity profit-sharing plans
2. Section 401(k) plans
3. Stock bonus plans

What is an individual retirement account?

An *individual retirement account (IRA)* is a nonqualified retirement plan. It is nonqualified because it is not described in Section 401 of the Internal Revenue Code. IRAs are generally not subject to the Employee Retirement Income Security Act (ERISA) of 1974 because they are not employee benefit plans. Even though IRA participants do not enjoy the protections offered by ERISA, most retirement assets end up in an individual participant's IRA because of the flexibility of IRAs.

IRAs are widely available from banks, insurance companies, mutual fund management companies, brokerage houses, and other sellers of investment products that can be used to fund such an account. An IRA must be in the form of a written trust or custodial account held for the exclusive benefit of the trust maker.

IRAs can be of three types:

1. Those that are established by an individual with a bank, brokerage firm, or similar company that acts as a trustee of the investments
2. IRAs in the form of annuities or endowment contracts purchased by individuals from insurance companies
3. Plans that are established by employers and employee associations and that qualify as IRAs

Distributions from IRAs and Qualified Plans

PRIOR TO REACHING AGE 59½

Can I incur additional taxes over and above the income taxes

that I will pay upon taking distributions from my IRA or qualified plan?

Yes. There is a 10 percent penalty on distributions taken prior to age 59½.

Are there any exceptions to the 10 percent penalty for taking withdrawals from an IRA or qualified plan prior to age 59½?

Yes, there are three exceptions to the 10 percent penalty on early distributions:

1. Distributions made to a beneficiary or participant's estate on or after the participant's death
2. Distributions related to disability or mental incompetency
3. Distributions made in substantially equal annual payments, similar to an annuity, over the participant's lifetime or life expectancy or the joint lifetimes or life expectancies of the participant and the beneficiary

What are the basic rules for making substantially equal annual payments?

1. The substantially equal periodic payments generally must be received for at least 5 years.
2. The method of distribution cannot be changed before age 59½.

Unless a distribution change was because of the intervening death, disability, or mental incompetency of the participant, he or she must wait at least 5 years to change the distribution method even if he or she turns 59½ before the end of that 5-year period.

How can the substantially equal payment requirement be met?

There are three methods of distribution that meet the substantially equal payment requirement:

1. An annual distribution of the required minimum distribution amount, based on the life expectancy of the participant
2. An annual distribution of the required minimum distribution amount, based on either the life expectancy of the participant

or the joint life expectancies of the participant and a designated beneficiary

3. Dividing the plan balance by an annuity factor derived by using a reasonable mortality table at an interest rate which does not exceed a reasonable interest rate on the date that payments commence

Can you give me an example of how these three methods are actually computed?

Table 7-1 presents the results of the three methods for a person age 50, with a 50-year-old spouse and a $100,000 retirement plan balance averaging a 10 percent yearly investment return that had no new contributions. (The so-called annuity exception allows you to receive substantially equal payments over your life expectancy or over the lives of you and your beneficiary or your joint life expectancy as set forth in Appendix E, Life Expectancy Table I, II, or III of IRS Publication 590.)

DISTRIBUTIONS AT REQUIRED BEGINNING DATE

When is the latest date that I can begin taking distributions from my IRA or qualified plan?

Distributions to a participant must begin by the participant's required beginning date, which is generally April 1 of the year following the calendar year in which the participant becomes 70½ years of age. (Should the participant die before age 70½, the required beginning date is the date of death.) Distributions must be paid over one of the following periods:

1. The lifetime of the participant
2. The lifetimes of the participant and a designated beneficiary
3. A period which may be a term certain, not extending beyond that table of life expectancy set forth in IRS tables for the participant or for a combination of the participant and his or her last designated survivor beneficiary

The minimum number of distributions that are required is equal to the total plan benefit divided by the participant's life expectancy or the joint life expectancy of the participant and a designated beneficiary.

The result of using joint life expectancy is that the distributions from a plan are less each year than if only the participant's life expectancy is used. By distributing less each year, income taxes are deferred as long as possible.

Beneficiaries of IRAs and Qualified Plans

Who may be the designated beneficiary of my IRA or qualified retirement plan?

Under the Internal Revenue Code, only an individual or a *qualified trust* can be a designated beneficiary. For a trust to qualify:

1. The trust must be valid under state law.
2. The trust must be irrevocable on the earlier of the date of death or the required beginning date.
3. The beneficiary of the trust must be identifiable from the trust document.
4. A copy of the trust instrument must be provided to the trustee of the plan or to the custodian.

An estate, a nonqualified trust, or a charity cannot be a designated beneficiary.

You may choose anyone as the beneficiary of your qualified retirement plan. You may choose your spouse, your children, your living trust, a testamentary trust, or an irrevocable trust as your beneficiary. Under qualified retirement plans (but not IRAs), if you are married and choose anyone other than your spouse, your spouse must consent to your choosing a beneficiary other than him or her.

A SPOUSE AS DESIGNATED BENEFICIARY

What happens if I die prior to age 70½ and my spouse is the beneficiary of my IRA or qualified retirement plan?

If your spouse is the beneficiary of your IRA or qualified retire-

TABLE 7-1 IRA Distributions under Substantially Equal Payment Requirement

	Single Life Expectancy Method	Joint Life Expectancy Method	Amortization Withdrawal Method
Account balance beginning year 1	$100,000	$100,000	$100,000
Life expectancy	33.1	39.2	
Annuity factor	—	—	33.1 (constant)
Penalty-free amount to withdraw year 1*	$3,021	$2,551	$10,445
Add investment buildup	$9,698	$9,745	
Account balance beginning year 2	$106,677	$107,194	$99,555
Life expectancy	32.2	38.2	
Annuity factor	—	—	
Penalty-free amount to withdraw year 2*	$3,313	$2,806	$10,445
Add investment buildup	$10,336	$10,439	
Account balance beginning year 3	$113,700	$114,827	$99,065

*$100,000 ÷ life expectancy or annuity factor

ment plan, your spouse will have an additional option that is usually not available to any other beneficiary. Your spouse may be able to request a lump-sum distribution from the plan and roll the benefits into his or her own IRA. This is referred to in the Internal Revenue Code as the *spousal rollover.*

If your spouse does choose the spousal rollover, distributions are not required until April 1 after your spouse reaches age 70½. If your spouse does not elect the spousal rollover, the plan benefits are generally required to be distributed over his or her life expectancy, commencing on December 31 of the year following the year of your death.

What happens if I die after I reach age 70½ and my spouse is the beneficiary of my IRA or qualified retirement plan?

If your spouse is your beneficiary at your required beginning date, your retirement plan benefits are generally distributed over the joint life expectancy of you and your spouse. If you die after the required distributions have commenced and you are recalculating your life expectancy for minimum distribution requirements, the retirement plan benefits are required to be distributed over your surviving spouse's life expectancy.

If you are not recalculating, the distributions would continue the same as they had prior to your death.

Don't I lose control by naming my spouse as my beneficiary?

By allowing your spouse the opportunity to elect the spousal rollover, you may gain maximum tax deferral. However, you lose control over a substantial portion of your estate. Once your spouse elects the spousal rollover, he or she may then choose how the plan proceeds are to be distributed on his or her death. You will not be able to give what you have to whom you want, the way you want, and when you want, and you may not be able to save every last federal estate tax dollar possible because you may have insufficient assets outside the qualified plan or IRA to fully fund your family subtrust. In addition, your trust or will-planning probate estate may have insufficient assets to fully utilize your unified credit; therefore, you may not qualify for the $235,000 federal estate tax savings provided by a fully funded family subtrust.

AN INDIVIDUAL OTHER THAN SPOUSE AS DESIGNATED BENEFICIARY

What happens if I die prior to 70½ and an individual other than my surviving spouse is the beneficiary of my IRA or qualified retirement plan?

If you name an individual other than your surviving spouse as the beneficiary of your IRA or qualified retirement plan, then the plan benefits generally must be distributed to that individual by December 31 following the fifth anniversary of the date of your death.

If your plan allows, however, the beneficiary may receive distributions over his or her life expectancy.

What happens if I die after I reach age 70½ and an individual other than my surviving spouse is the beneficiary of my IRA or qualified retirement plan?

If you die after the required distributions have commenced and you are recalculating your life expectancy for minimum distribution requirements, the retirement plan benefits are required to be paid to your designated beneficiary by December 31 of the year following your death. If you are not recalculating, the distributions would continue the same as they had prior to your death.

AN ESTATE AS DESIGNATED BENEFICIARY

What happens if I name my estate as the beneficiary of my IRA or qualified retirement plan?

You should avoid naming your estate as the beneficiary of your retirement plan benefits. If you name your estate as the beneficiary, you take a nonprobate asset and subject it to the probate process. The proceeds are subject to the claims of creditors, as well as the cost, publicity, and delay associated with the probate process. In addition, your estate will be required to receive all of your retirement benefits no later than December 31 following the fifth anniversary of the date of your death.

Under this planning situation, your advisor and your spouse will have no opportunity to maximize income tax savings by deferring the income tax on your retirement plan benefits past the December 31st following the fifth anniversary of the year of your death.

A LIVING TRUST AS DESIGNATED BENEFICIARY

Can my revocable living trust be a designated beneficiary?

A revocable living trust qualifies as a designated beneficiary until you reach your required beginning date; thereafter, it does not qualify because it is not irrevocable. If your living trust is the named beneficiary of your qualified retirement plan on April 1 of the year following your 70½ birthday (required beginning date), you will be able to use only your own life expectancy when calculating your minimum distributions. Because of this, your required minimum distribution will be more than it would be if you used a joint life expectancy. A higher required minimum distribution will cause you to pay more income tax yearly.

Why should I choose to name my living trust as the beneficiary of my IRA or qualified retirement plans?

You may want to name your living trust as the beneficiary of your IRA or qualified retirement plan so that you will be able to give what you have to whom you want, the way you want. Your living trust allows you to provide instructions for your beneficiaries on how and when to use your retirement plan distributions. A living trust may also protect your retirement plan assets, after they are distributed, from your beneficiaries' creditors or from a spouse in the event of a later divorce.

Also, if you name your living trust as beneficiary, your trustee will have the opportunity to obtain the maximum federal estate tax savings possible by utilizing each spouse's unified credit, which is the key to proper estate tax planning for married couples.

What happens if I die prior to age 70½ and my living trust is the beneficiary of my IRA or qualified retirement plan?

If your living trust is your beneficiary, the living trust will qualify as a designated beneficiary. Why? A living trust usually becomes irrevocable on the death of the person who makes the trust. The living trust qualifies as a designated beneficiary because it is irrevocable on the required beginning date, which is the date of your death if you die before age 70½.

The qualified retirement plan is then required to make minimum distributions of your plan benefits over the life expectancy of the oldest beneficiary of your trust. If you are married, this beneficiary is usually your spouse.

What happens if I die after I reach age 70½ and my living trust is the beneficiary of my IRA or qualified retirement plan?

If your living trust is the beneficiary of your IRA or qualified retirement plan when you reach age 70½, your plan benefits will be distributed no slower than over your life expectancy. When you determine your life expectancy for minimum distribution requirements, you may choose whether or not your life expectancy will be recalculated yearly.

If you choose to recalculate, in the year of your death your life expectancy will go to zero and your entire benefits must be distributed by December 31 of the year following your death. The distribution of your entire benefits in one year requires the immediate income taxation of your entire plan benefits. This is not a favorable outcome in most situations.

If you choose not to recalculate, your plan benefits will continue to be distributed over your life expectancy. This will result in additional deferral of the income tax on these plan benefits. If your living trust is the beneficiary of your plan on the April 1st following your 70½ birthday, you should elect *not* to recalculate your life expectancy!

What can I do to avoid the potential loss of tax savings and deferral if I name my living trust as the beneficiary of my qualified retirement plan?

One way to avoid these problems is to name an individual as the beneficiary of your qualified retirement plan before you reach age 70½. However, this will result in your losing control of the qualified retirement plan distributions after your death. You will not be able to give what you have to whom you want, the way you want. On distribution, your benefits pass outright to the named beneficiary. In addition, if your named beneficiary predeceases you and you have not named a contingent beneficiary of your retirement plan, your benefits will become part of your probate estate.

Another way to avoid the income tax problem is to name an irrevocable trust as the beneficiary of your IRA or qualified retirement plan before you reach age 70½. An irrevocable trust will qualify as a designated beneficiary if it satisfies all of the additional requirements as set forth above. When a trust qualifies as a designated beneficiary, the joint life expectancy is calculated using your life expectancy and the life expectancy of the oldest beneficiary of your irrevocable trust.

Although the trust is irrevocable, the beneficiary designation of the qualified plan is not: you may still amend or change this beneficiary designation at any time. Your irrevocable trust can include the same tax and personal death instructions as your living trust. In the event that your goals and objectives change, you would simply change the beneficiary designation of your qualified retirement plan from your existing irrevocable trust to a new irrevocable trust, which would contain instructions based on your new goals and objectives. The only thing that needs to be irrevocable is the trust, not the beneficiary designation of the plan.

By using an irrevocable trust, you may obtain maximum income tax savings and give what you have to whom you want, the way you want, and when you want.

How can I know in advance whether to name my spouse or my living trust as the beneficiary of my retirement plan benefits?

The bad news here is that you can't. This is because even if you could know the date of your death in advance, you can't know what the tax law will be on that date, let alone what the balance of your retirement plan or the size of your estate will be. The good news is that you don't have to know these things. There is a way to "hedge your bets."

As you are probably aware, you can name both primary and contingent beneficiaries for your retirement plan benefits. By naming both your trust and your spouse as potential beneficiaries of your plan, the final decision can be deferred until all the facts are in.

Through a technique called a *disclaimer* your advisors and family can decide after your death what the best course of action will be. A disclaimer is a legal "no thank you." It is a simple, but powerful, document that allows the recipient of property to refuse acceptance. Under the law, when a disclaimer is exercised, the intended recipient is considered to have never received the property involved. Therefore, with a disclaimer, the primary beneficiary can either accept the property (your retirement plan benefits) or sign a disclaimer and allow the benefits to be paid to the contingent beneficiary.

To make this strategy work, however, care should be taken to include special provisions in your revocable living trust and to have the beneficiary-designation paperwork through your retirement plan administrator completed correctly.

This strategy does not work effectively after you have reached age 70½ because your revocable living trust is then not a qualified trust. After age 70½, you should consider using the irrevocable trust strategy discussed above. Under all circumstances, you and your advisors should meet when you turn 69 so that all alternatives can be explored on the basis of your then-current financial and estate status.

I understand all of my beneficiary alternatives. However, my attorney (or CPA or financial advisor) still insists there are negative tax consequences to naming my revocable trust as the beneficiary of my retirement plan. Are you sure this is a good idea?

If satisfying the definition of estate planning is your goal, then naming your revocable living trust as your beneficiary makes sense. Most of the legal and financial world operates on the assumption that income tax planning is all that counts. In addition, most advisors make decisions for clients about tax issues without involving the client. Nowhere is this more evident than in the process of handling beneficiary-designation planning for retirement plans.

Your other advisors are correct when they say that income taxes will be due when the assets are paid to your trust. They are not, however, disclosing the whole picture to you! Retirement plan assets, as you know, are tax-favored investments. Generally, no tax is due when assets are deposited into the plans, and the tax is deferred on the earnings until they are withdrawn. Withdrawals can occur during your lifetime or after your death. Eventually, however, the deferred income taxes *will* become due.

Most advisors only address income tax issues upon the death of the trust maker/retirement plan participant when they talk with clients on this subject. They do not talk about the impact of the estate tax system on retirement plan assets. They also do not, in general, discuss the implications of the client's decision in this area on his or her personal planning instructions.

The advice most commonly given to a married couple is to name the nonparticipant spouse as the beneficiary of the retirement plan dollars. This spouse can receive the benefits and, if received within 60 days of the date of the participant spouse's death, can add the funds to his or her own IRA account. This is known as a *spousal rollover,* or *spousal continuation, IRA*. If the transfer is made within the time frame allowed, no income tax is due.

This advice, in a vacuum, seems sound; however, what if the surviving spouse is involved in a second marriage? Are these advisors so certain that this is the correct course of action? As you can see, the surviving spouse has total control of the assets because he or she can name the beneficiary of the rollover IRA. Individuals in this situation often do *not* place tax concerns above people concerns. And who should make this decision? We believe strongly that only the participant spouse can make this judgment call.

In addition, what are the estate tax effects if the common approach is utilized? The value of the account is included in the estate of the survivor for estate tax purposes. Eventually the deferred income taxes will become due. In the case of a large retirement plan, deferring withdrawals can trigger an excess accumulation tax of 15 percent on the entire balance of the retirement plan. Finally, if the participant spouse does not have sufficient assets outside of the qualified retirement plan or IRA, the result of a spousal rollover is deferred income tax and dramatically increased federal estate tax at the surviving spouse's death.

When these taxes are added together, a huge percentage of the fund can be confiscated by the IRS. In these circumstances, the assumption that the spousal rollover is the only proper course of action can be financially disastrous.

Retirement Plans and Taxes

FEDERAL ESTATE TAXATION OF RETIREMENT PLANS

Are IRAs and qualified plans included in the participant's gross estate and subject to federal estate tax?

Yes, with very limited exceptions. At one time, certain qualified plans and IRAs paid after the participant's death were entirely exempt from federal estate taxes. However, the law has changed a number of times. Now, the unlimited estate tax exemption for plan proceeds applies only if the participant separated from employment prior to January 1, 1983, and has not changed the beneficiary form since that date. No matter when the participant dies, the proceeds will not be included in the participant's estate.

There is a $100,000 exemption available for plan proceeds for a participant who separated from service before 1985 and who did not change the beneficiary form after January 1, 1985. This exemption also applies to those plan proceeds no matter when the participant dies.

All other plan proceeds are subject to federal estate tax.

Because of the law changes affecting the federal estate taxation of plan proceeds, anyone who was part of a plan prior to 1985 should know when and if he or she separated from service. If either the unlimited or $100,000 exclusion is available, no change in the beneficiary form should be made. A change will cause a loss of those exclusions.

EXCISE TAXES ON EXCESS ACCUMULATIONS

What happens if I accumulate too much in my IRA or qualified retirement plan during my lifetime?

The amount distributed yearly in excess of the greater of $150,000 unindexed or $112,500 in 1986 indexed for the cost-of-living adjustment ($155,000 in 1996) is subject to a 15 percent excess distribution tax.

You may elect to receive your qualified retirement benefits in a lump sum. If you do, the threshold amounts are increased to five times the yearly $150,000 or $155,000 in 1996 and indexed for the cost-of-living adjustment.

What happens if I die with too much accumulated in my IRA or qualified retirement plan?

Your IRA or qualified retirement plan assets may be subject to an additional 15 percent excess accumulation tax on an amount called the *excess accumulation.* How is your excess accumulation calculated? It is the excess of your retirement plan benefit on your date of death over an amount equal to the present value of a hypothetical life annuity as provided for in the Internal Revenue Code.

Table 7-2 shows the hypothetical life annuity threshold amount at different ages, with a $150,000 yearly lifetime threshold amount and a 9 percent federal midterm interest rate. This interest rate is determined monthly by the Internal Revenue Service. The numbers shown in the table will change according to fluctuations in the applicable federal midterm interest rate and the yearly lifetime threshold amount. As the federal midterm rate decreases the hypothetical life annuity increases. Also, as the yearly threshold amount of $150,000 increases, so does the hypothetical life annuity.

As an example, if you die at age 70 with $2 million in your IRA, your excess accumulation amount, based on Table 7-2, is $981,065 ($2 million – $1,018,935). Your estate would pay an excess accumulation tax of $147,160 (15 percent × $981,065), in addition to the estate taxes due.

TABLE 7-2 Present Value of a Hypothetical Life Annuity

Age	Amount	Age	Amount
50	$1,413,570	66	$1,116,945
51	1,399,485	67	1,093,365
52	1,384,815	68	1,069,095
53	1,369,530	69	1,044,270
54	1,353,675	70	1,018,935
55	1,337,220	71	993,240
56	1,320,165	72	967,185
57	1,302,435	73	940,725
58	1,284,060	74	913,770
59	1,265,055	75	886,230
60	1,245,465	76	858,045
61	1,225,335	77	829,290
62	1,204,725	78	800,070
63	1,183,635	79	770,640
64	1,162,035	80	741,210
65	1,139,820		

What can I do to avoid either the excess distribution during my lifetime or the excess accumulation tax in the event of my death?

Beginning at age 59½, you should consider commencing distributions so that you receive a distribution equal to or less than the yearly threshold amount (currently $155,000). You will have to pay federal and state income tax on this amount. However, the sooner you start receiving distributions, the better your chance of decreasing the excess distribution when you are required to commence distributions on April 1 following your 70½ birthday or decreasing the excess accumulation on your death.

If you have over $1 million in your qualified retirement plan, each year after you are 59½, you should have your attorneys or accountants or financial advisors make a calculation to determine your potential of being in an excess-distribution or excess-accumulation position. If your plan benefits are in a company-qualified benefit plan, not your own IRA, you must consult with the plan administrator to determine if you may request distributions from your qualified retirement plan prior to your retirement or required beginning date.

What should I do with the retirement plan benefits once I receive them?

If you are taking distributions from your retirement plan prior to age 70½ to avoid excess distributions or accumulations, in all likelihood you will owe federal estate taxes in the event of your death. This means that you will be in the 37 to 55 percent marginal estate tax bracket.

If you reinvest your retirement plan benefits inside of your taxable estate, each dollar that you accumulate after the distribution will be subject to the 37 to 55 percent estate tax. If you do not plan to spend every last dime of your retirement plan distributions, consider using part or all of the plan distribution to purchase a life insurance policy owned by an irrevocable life insurance trust that you create.

The life insurance policy will grow income tax–free, similar to your retirement plan. However, the proceeds of the insurance policy will not be subject to income tax on your death. Also, because the irrevocable trust owns the policy, the proceeds of the insurance policy will be estate tax–free on your death. By taking early distributions from your retirement plan, you can convert the qualified retirement plan asset that is subject to income, estate, excess-distribution, and excess-accumulation taxes to an asset that is income and estate tax–free.

IRAs and qualified retirement plans are excellent ways to accumulate wealth. However, once the wealth is accumulated, you must put in place a plan of distribution which will preserve the wealth that you have taken a lifetime to accumulate.

INCOME IN RESPECT OF A DECEDENT

What is income in respect of a decedent?

Income in respect of a decedent (IRD) is a term that the Internal Revenue Code uses to refer to the income from an asset which is

TABLE 7-3 Effect of Taxes on Qualified Plan Benefits*

Gross qualified plan benefit		$1,000,000
less: Estate tax (assume 55 percent marginal tax rate)		550,000
Net qualified plan benefit after estate tax		$ 450,000
less: Income tax:		
Gross taxable income	$1,000,000	
less: Deduction for federal estate taxes paid	550,000	
Net IRD	$ 450,000	
Income tax rate (assume 40%)	× .40	
Income tax on IRD		180,000
Net plan benefits to beneficiaries		$ 270,000

**Assumptions:* $5 million gross estate, including a $1 million qualified retirement plan benefit; age on date of death: 65.

included in your gross estate and which you did not pay income taxes on during your lifetime. Typical IRD items include nonqualified deferred compensation plans, qualified retirement plan benefits, IRAs, and royalties.

Having IRD items in your estate may be very costly to your beneficiaries. Why? In the event of your death, not only are federal estate taxes due, but your beneficiaries are required to pay income taxes on your IRD items. The calculation in Table 7-3 is an example of what may happen to your $1 million qualified retirement plan. As the table shows, as a result of having an IRD item in your estate at your death, you can lose approximately 73 percent of your qualified retirement plan benefits to estate and income taxes.

What can I do to avoid the IRD on my retirement plan benefits?

To avoid the income tax on your retirement plan benefits at your death, you may want to consider naming a charitable remainder trust as the beneficiary of your retirement plan. If your spouse is the

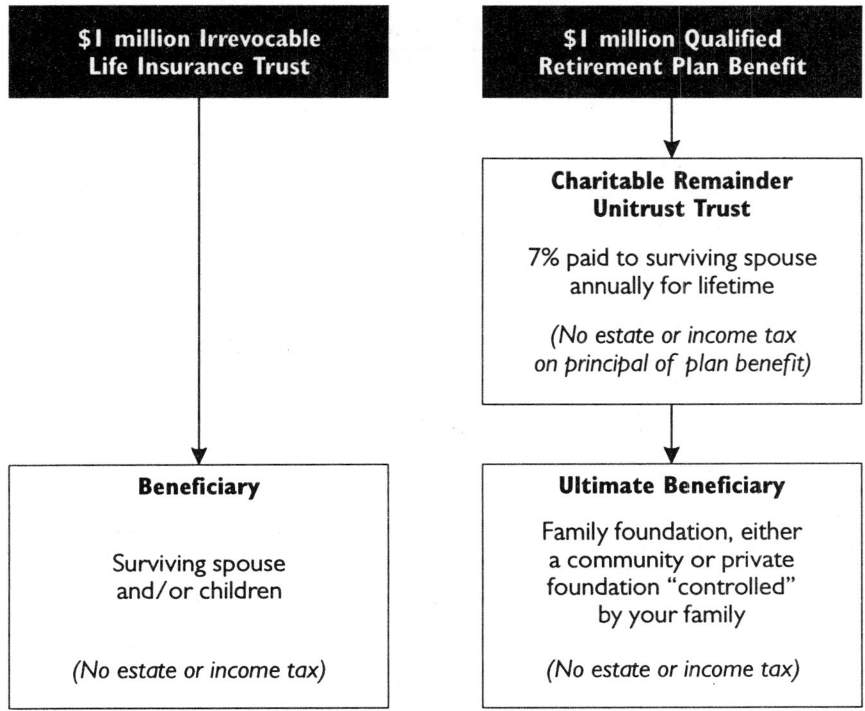

Figure 7-1 Combined strategy to control estate, income, and excess-accumulation taxes.

income beneficiary of your charitable remainder trust, your retirement plan will not be subject to IRD or estate taxes.

Why? On your death, the IRA or qualified retirement plan benefits will be paid to the charitable remainder trust. The trust is considered a tax-exempt charitable organization for income tax purposes. Also, on your death, there will be no estate tax because of the marital and charitable deductions.

This planning strategy, however, does not avoid the excess-accumulation tax on retirement plans. You should combine the above strategy of naming the charitable remainder trust as the beneficiary of your retirement plan benefits with the strategy of purchasing a life insurance policy owned by an irrevocable life insurance trust. By combining these two strategies, you will be able to pass on 100 percent of your IRA or qualified retirement plan benefits to your spouse and control the amount (potentially 73 percent, as shown in Table 7-3) of taxes that would have been distributed to the Internal Revenue Service. The diagram of this strategy is shown in Figure 7-1.

Establishing an IRA

Who is eligible to establish an IRA and to make contributions?

Anyone who is paid earned income may establish an IRA. *Earned income* includes wages, compensation for services, salaries, commissions, or professional fees. It does not include investment income, such as interest, certain partnership distributions, dividends, or capital gains from investments, and it does not include amounts received as a pension or annuity.

A spouse who qualifies for an IRA may be able to set up and contribute to an IRA for the other spouse who has no earned income.

Are contributions to an IRA tax-deductible?

Yes, under certain circumstances.

What is the annual deduction limit for contributions to an IRA?

The annual IRA deduction limit for an individual is the lesser of $2000 or 100 percent of the individual's annual compensation. This annual $2000 limit applies whether the contributions to the account are made by the individual or by his or her employer.

If I am covered by a qualified retirement plan sponsored by my employer, under what circumstances are my contributions to an IRA deductible?

If one spouse is covered under an employer's retirement plan, both spouses may be able to make tax-deductible contributions to IRAs, subject to certain restrictions that apply to the spouse who already is an active participant in an employer's qualified retirement plan.

The IRA deduction limits for individuals who are active partici-

TABLE 7-4 IRA Deduction Limits for Participants in Qualified Plans

	Earnings		
Deduction	Individual	Married Couple Filing Joint Return	Married, Filing Separately
Full	$25,000 or less	$40,000 or less	Full deduction not available
Reduced	$25,000–$35,000	$40,000–$50,000	$0–$10,000
No deduction	$35,000 or more	$50,000 or more	$10,000 or more

pants in a qualified plan are shown in Table 7-4. These contribution thresholds may be raised by congressional action in our current political climate, so be sure to ask your attorney, accountant, or tax advisor to inform you of any changes.

If I cannot make a deductible contribution to an IRA, can I make a nondeductible contribution?

Individuals who are not entitled to a deduction are still permitted to make contributions to an IRA of up to $2000 ($2250 for a regular and a spousal IRA combined) or 100 percent of compensation, whichever is less. While these contributions are not tax-deductible, as long as the contributions are within the allowed contributory limits, the earnings in the account will be tax-deferred until withdrawn.

What types of assets can be used for contributions to an IRA?

All contributions to an IRA must be made in cash or negotiable instruments. IRA deductions are not allowed for contributions of property other than cash. Noncash contributions will not disqualify an IRA but will be considered excess contributions subject to a 6 percent annual excise tax.

When do contributions have to be made?

Contributions to an IRA for a particular year must be made no later than the date the contributor's tax return is due for such year, typically April 15. Extensions of the filing of an income tax return do not extend the contribution date.

At what age can one start making contributions?

Deductions are available for any contributions made by an IRA participant who is between the age of birth and 70½ years of age at the end of the taxable year for which the contribution is made.

SEP-IRAs

What is a SEP-IRA?

SEP-IRAs are *simplified employee pension* arrangements that allow self-employed persons to make IRA contributions for themselves and their employees. SEP rules permit employer contributions for each employee (including a contribution for the self-employed business owner) of up to 15 percent of an employee's compensation or $30,000, whichever is less.

SEP plans may also include an election by the employee to have part of his or her pay contributed to the SEP-IRA.

Employers who participate in SEPs are subject to time limits, employee inclusion or exclusion rules, and contribution limits.

IRAs and Prohibited Transactions

What specific acts are generally considered prohibited transactions between the IRA owner and the account?

1. Borrowing money from the IRA
2. Selling property, real or personal, to the IRA
3. Having the IRA invest in collectibles like artworks, antiques, metals, gems, coins, stamps, and certain other tangible personal property
4. Using the IRA as collateral or security for a loan
5. Using IRA funds to purchase property for personal use

6. Paying the IRA owner for management of the IRA or paying third parties excessively for such services

What are the general categories of prohibited transactions?

1. Making excess contributions
2. Making early withdrawals or premature distributions
3. Allowing excess amounts to accumulate or failing to make or complete timely required withdrawals
4. Receiving excess contributions

What types of additional penalties, beyond regular taxes, accrue for using IRA funds in prohibited transactions?

Excise taxes and penalties ranging from 5 to 100 percent of the prohibited transaction amount or distribution may be levied against the owner or the owner's beneficiary if the owner or owner's beneficiary engages in a prohibited transaction.

Disadvantages of IRAs

What are some of the disadvantages of IRAs?

As discussed below, IRAs may sometimes be subject to creditors' claims. Two main additional disadvantages are that no loan can be made from an IRA to the owner, under Section 408(e)(2) of the Internal Revenue Code, and that, upon withdrawal of the funds, there is no special tax averaging available to the owner.

Differences between IRAs and Qualified Retirement Plans

Are IRAs and qualified retirement plans subject to the claims of creditors?

Qualified plans are exempt from the claims of creditors under the 1992 Supreme Court case of *Patterson v. Shumate.* In this case, the Court held that ERISA, the law governing qualified retirement plans, overrides bankruptcy law in terms of the availability of qualified plan assets to creditors. Prior to this case, the lower courts differed as to this issue.

One of the biggest problems with IRAs is that they are not covered by ERISA's favorable creditor protection rules, so they are subject to the claims of creditors unless there is an exclusion granted under state law. Many states now grant exemptions for IRAs to make them creditor-proof, but you must ask your attorney what the law is in your state.

What are the important differences between an IRA and a qualified retirement plan that might affect my estate and tax planning?

There are two very important differences one must keep in mind when planning for an IRA as opposed to a qualified retirement plan. First, to remove your spouse as beneficiary of your qualified retirement plan, you must obtain written and notarized permission from your spouse to do so. This spousal permission is not required with an IRA.

Second, a qualified retirement plan is written and created by an employer to fit the situation and circumstances of that employer. Consequently, each qualified retirement plan is different and, for the most part, unalterable. This means that you and your advisors must be extremely cautious when planning and drafting documents that may affect the administration or qualification of the qualified retirement plan. An employer may not be willing to change the plan to fit your needs. IRAs are extremely flexible and for the most part can be changed or amended to fit your particular estate planning needs.

Rollovers

What is a "rollover," and how is it accomplished?

As long as amounts distributed from a qualified retirement plan are rolled over into an IRA within 60 days of receipt by the recipient, they will retain their tax-deferred status. There is a 20 percent withholding, however, on distributions that are not made directly from a qualified plan to an IRA or from one IRA to another.

Why do most assets in qualified plans end up in IRAs?

The reason that most retirement plan assets end up in IRAs is that most of these assets are accumulated in qualified retirement plans during the working years. When an employee retires, he or she usually rolls over his or her qualified plan assets into an IRA. Section 401(c) permits rollovers from qualified plans to IRAs and allows the assets to retain their tax-free status until taken out of the IRA by the owner or beneficiary. Moreover, any distribution to an employee or an employee's surviving spouse, which is includable in the income of the employee or employee's spouse, may be rolled over into an IRA and retain the tax-deferred status.

There are three exceptions to this tax-free rollover:

1. Cases where a minimum required distribution is necessary
2. Distributions made over a term certain of 10 years or more
3. Distributions made over life or life expectancy under Section 402(c)(4)(9)

Why is there a tendency for most employees, upon retirement or termination, to roll over their qualified plan assets into an IRA?

While it is sometimes possible for an employee to leave funds in a qualified plan and not roll them over into an IRA, there is an increasing tendency among qualified plans to not permit the employee to leave the money in the plan after retirement or after termination of employment. The reason for this is that it costs the employer money to administer nonemployees' or retired employees' money that is left in the qualified plan.

If an employee does not want to roll over his or her funds to an IRA, the only options remaining are to take the total balance out in a lump sum or a set number of installment payments or to accept an annuity under the terms required by the Internal Revenue Code. Many participants do not like the annuity option because they want to have access to the principal and do not want to rely on a fixed annuity for the rest of their lives. Thus they opt for a self-directed IRA.

An IRA is attractive because it offers the same types of payout possibilities as does a qualified plan (the annuity, lump-sum payments, or installment payments). Thus, the IRA gives greater flexibility to the departing employee. Since the investments in an IRA are not limited to the options provided in the original employer's plan, an IRA may offer some attractive diversification or investment alternatives. The IRA owner is permitted a wide latitude in choosing his or her investments. The only exceptions are collectibles and insurance policies.

The bottom line is that the former employee/participant has greater control over the assets when they are in an IRA rather than a qualified plan.

8

Business Planning

This a practical chapter that differentiates between the benefits and detriments of the many different forms of business organization. It takes a fresh look at many of the "givens" of business organization and provides questions and up-to-date answers that may surprise the reader.

Questions and answers in this chapter emphasize the *limited liability company* as a form of business organization that is very new and exciting to many people. Not surprisingly, little emphasis is given to the regular, or C, corporation as a viable business alternative as compared to limited partnerships, subchapter S corporations, and limited liability companies.

Business continuity and the manner in which business owners can protect and perpetuate their business holdings through stock redemption, entity purchase, cross-purchase, and wait-and-see agreements are discussed at length. Each is compared to the other and in light of what you might wish to accomplish in planning to maintain the value of your business after you are no longer able to serve it. The questions and answers in this chapter center upon the "best ways" you can structure your business agreements to protect your loved ones and business associates upon your retirement from the business, disability, or death.

There are a surprising number of questions and answers on the precise procedures and methodologies that should be used to receive accurate appraisals of business interests for purposes of enacting gift and business continuity programs. There are also a number of helpful tips on the dos and do nots of properly selling your business.

Sole Proprietorships

What is the advantage of operating my business as a sole proprietorship?

A sole proprietorship requires the least amount of red tape in its formation. Because a sole proprietorship is owned by an individual proprietor, there are no formal filing requirements (there are some very limited exceptions in a few states).

What are the disadvantages of a sole proprietorship?

A sole proprietorship is not generally conducive to tax planning, liability planning, or business succession planning.

Unlike a corporation, a limited partnership, or a limited liability company, a sole proprietorship offers no liability protection. A sole proprietor's exposure to outside creditors and business losses is *not limited* to the sole proprietor's investment in the business. A sole proprietor is personally responsible for business losses and claims of business creditors to the full extent of his or her net worth.

A sole proprietorship cannot survive the death of its owner. A sole proprietor may leave his or her business *assets* by will or trust to relatives or employees, but there is no assurance that the business will survive the proprietor's death.

What type of income tax return do I have to file for my sole proprietorship?

A person doing business as a sole proprietor reports income and expenses on Schedule C of his or her federal income tax Form 1040.

Does a sole proprietor have to pay self-employment tax?

If there is net income from the sole proprietorship in excess of $400, the proprietor is responsible for self-employment tax. The purpose of the self-employment tax is to provide Social Security benefits for the sole proprietor. An individual is allowed a deduction equal to 50 percent of the self-employment tax assessed in arriving at his or her adjusted gross income.

Am I required to apply for an employer identification number if I operate my business as a sole proprietorship?

Your sole proprietorship is not required to apply for a federal employer identification number unless the business is going to pay wages to employees who are subject to federal withholding taxes. If the business has employees, it is required to apply for an employer identification number on a federal income tax Form SS-4.

General Partnerships

What is a general partnership?

A *general partnership* is a business entity in which two or more persons or entities agree to capitalize a business venture for profit.

In a general partnership, the liability of the general partners is joint and several: they have unlimited personal liability for the debts and obligations of the partnership, and each partner is authorized by law to bind the partnership in business transactions. This is true even if an individual partner does not have the actual authority to do so.

A general partnership is a flow-through entity. Profit or loss of the partnership will typically flow through to the partners according to their respective interests in the partnership on a percentage basis.

Can one person operate a business as a partnership?

There must be at least two persons involved in the formation of a partnership. If there is only one person, then the business is a sole proprietorship.

Under the Uniform Partnership Act, *person* is defined as a natural person, partnership, corporation, limited liability company, or association. Partnerships of various business entities are a common occurrence in American enterprise.

In the absence of an agreement which states to the contrary, all of the partners have equal rights in the management of the partnership.

Does my general partnership agreement have to be in writing?

If two or more individuals—by spoken or written words—consent to form a partnership, a partnership exists. A partnership contract can be created orally or in writing. Some states add statutory refinements to basic partnership rules.

For example, in New York, a partnership can be created by oral agreement, but if the partnership's terms are not capable of performance within a year, the partnership must be in writing. Also, if the agreement of the partners calls for the contribution of real property or a lease on real property to the partnership business, then it must be in writing.

Should a partnership agreement be in writing?

If you do not have a written partnership agreement, your state's laws have created one for you. If you know what your agreement is but do not know the provisions of your state partnership law, it is advisable that you reduce your particular agreement to writing.

What basic provisions should a properly written partnership agreement contain?

A partnership agreement should spell out the specifics of the relationship between the partners, including partner compensation, management responsibility, required contributions, and how profits and losses are to be shared.

Am I liable for the debts and actions of my partners?

If their debts are partnership debts and their acts are partnership acts, you are 100 percent liable for them, just as you are 100 percent liable for your own.

Limited Partnerships

What is a limited partnership?

A *limited partnership* is a partnership that has both general and limited partners.

General partners control all of the business operations of the partnership and have full responsibility for its debts, liabilities, and obligations. They have unlimited liability with respect to partnership creditors.

Limited partners do not have control of the business operations of the partnership and have very limited or no voting rights. They are not responsible for the debts, liabilities, and obligations of the partnership. Their losses are limited to the amount of their investment in the partnership.

What are the main differences between general and limited partners?

General partners have unlimited joint and several liability; limited partners are liable only up to their capital investment in the partnership.

General partners have total responsibility and control of the partnership business; limited partners have no responsibility or control.

Can I limit my liability as a general partner by creating a corporation to be general partner?

Professionals often suggest that a corporation serve as the general partner of a limited partnership. Because a corporation affords its shareholders limited liability, a corporate general partner further insulates the entrepreneur from the general partner's liability. The corporation, however, must have some assets other than its interest in the partnership.

What are the duties of the limited partners?

Limited partners do not have duties. They contribute capital, and do not participate in the business of the partnership.

How are a limited partnership's earnings taxed?

A limited partnership is a flow-through entity; its profits and losses flow through to the general and limited partners in accordance with their proportionate ownership percentages.

Are limited partnerships good estate planning vehicles?

As we discuss at length in Chapter 3, limited partnerships are an excellent business form to use in transferring assets to family members at discounted values for purposes of federal estate and gift taxes.

This is so for a number of very important reasons. Parents and grandparents can:

- Transfer significant percentages of their ownership interests to other family members and, as general partners, still maintain control of the partnership's affairs
- As general partners, make all management decisions, receive compensation for making those decisions, and do so with as little as 1 percent or less of the partnership's ownership
- Give limited-partner interests to succeeding generations at discounted values often averaging 30 to 50 percent of fair market valuations
- Protect family members from the claims of partnership creditors

Do gifts of limited-partner interests qualify for the annual exclusion, lifetime exemption, marital deduction, and minority discounts?

Gifts of limited-partner interests can qualify for all of these tax benefits.

Is it easy to make limited partnership gifts?

Gifts of limited-partner interests are easy to make because fractional interests can be given. For example, a gift of 1/100 of a real estate section can be easily computed and made by deeding that fraction of the real estate to a family member as a 1 percent limited-partner interest.

If I am interested in creditor protection, why should I consider a partnership over a corporation?

Because the Revised Uniform Limited Partnership Act (RULPA) provides that the assets of a partnership can be seized only through a *charging order,* many people favor it over corporations when they are trying to attain creditor protection.

How does a charging order work?

RULPA provides that a charging order may be obtained by the

judgment creditor of a partner against that partner's distributive share of the partnership. A charging order will attach to whatever distributions the partner receives from the partnership. If he or she does not receive a distribution, it will not attach to anything.

Under federal income tax law the holder of the charging order is deemed to be in constructive receipt of the partnership's income, and the creditor will be taxed on that income proportionate to the interest attached by the debtor partner. If the debtor is deemed to own 40 percent of the partnership, the creditor will be charged with receiving 40 percent of the partnership's income even though that income is not distributed. As a result, the creditor will receive phantom income—income that is not received—upon which taxes will have to be paid for as long as the charging order stays in existence.

Are these limited partnerships the same as the ones I invested in during the 1980s?

No, they are not. The limited partnerships that were so popular in the 1980s were used primarily for purposes of raising capital with the promise of tax write-offs that were often much greater than the amount of the investment behind them. They most often resulted in the loss of their investors' capital and were driven by tax greed rather than basic investment economics.

Who should be the general partner of a limited partnership?

There is no one right answer to this question. The general partner could be an individual, a revocable or irrevocable management trust, a limited liability company, or a corporation. Each of the proposed entities has the advantages or disadvantages associated with that entity's use in business planning in general.

What about using a limited liability company as a general partner?

Many tax planners would agree that state law permitting, a limited liability company provides the best balance of creditor protection and tax planning without undue red tape and complications.

Thus, if permitted by state law, limited liability companies make excellent general partners. They give protection from creditors just as corporations do, but they allow all income to pass through to their members just like a partnership's income flows to its partners.

My attorney and CPA suggested that I create a regular C corporation to be the general partner of my limited partnership. Were they wrong?

Many of the wonderful fringe benefits afforded to shareholder managers of closely held regular corporations have been legislated out of existence. Today's corporation is no longer the *ultimate tax shelter* it was advertised to be in the 1970s. Professional advisors seem to prefer the limited liability company as a more effective general partner for additional liability protection.

What is a management trust? Can it hold my general-partner interest?

A *management trust* is a trust which is created solely to avoid the problems that can occur when a general partner dies or becomes mentally incapacitated. It provides continuance of the partnership upon the death or disability of the general partner without the need for liquidation or court proceedings.

Regular Corporations

How does a regular corporation differ from a sole proprietorship or a partnership?

The owners of the corporation own stock in the corporation and are referred to as *stockholders* or *shareholders*. Since the corporation is a separate legal entity, it is also a separate taxpaying entity.

What is the main disadvantage of a corporation?

Because a regular corporation is a separate taxpaying entity, it is possible that the earnings of the corporation are subject to *double taxation:* the corporation pays taxes on any income it earns, and when the earnings are distributed to individual shareholders, the earnings are taxed again at the shareholders' regular personal income tax rates. The combination of corporate taxation and individual taxation is a major weakness in corporate planning.

What are the main advantages of a corporation?

Corporations have traditionally offered three primary advantages, but over the years the situation has been changing:

- For many years corporations provided fringe benefits to executives that they could not obtain anywhere else. Because of several punishing tax acts over the past 30 years, many of these fringe benefits have been limited or eliminated.
- The ability to shield or protect individual shareholders from various creditors or business losses used to be exclusive to corporations. With the advent and popularity of limited liability companies and limited partnerships, this is no longer the case. Limited liability companies and family limited partnerships can provide the same creditor protection as corporations without the attendant tax disadvantages.
- Many corporations were created purely for their business succession attributes since they can exist perpetually. Once again, however, family limited partnerships and limited liability companies can provide like benefits without the administrative headaches that so often result from doing business as a corporation.

How are corporations created?

Corporations are created by filing a Certificate of Incorporation or Articles of Incorporation with the Secretary of State in the state in which the corporation wishes to be located. The state laws in whichever state the corporation operates determine what statutory powers the corporation has as a business entity.

What is the difference between a corporation and a general partnership?

A corporation is a fictitious entity which, for legal purposes, is considered separate and apart from its shareholders. One person can form a corporation and be its sole shareholder, or a corporation can have hundreds of thousands of shareholders, like IBM does. One reason for forming a corporation is to enable the individual shareholders to avoid personal liability. The corporation is controlled and managed by the board of directors, who are elected by the shareholders.

A partnership, on the other hand, is an association of two or more persons who combine their money, labor, or skill for a lawful business purpose. Partners divide the profits and losses according to certain proportions. Unless otherwise agreed, each partner, regardless of his or her capital contribution and regardless of his or her stake in the profits or losses, has an equal say in the management of the partnership.

Generally, a corporation will give its shareholders limited liability, whereas a general partnership does not afford its partners this same protection. In a general partnership, each partner is jointly and severally liable for the torts of the partnership and jointly liable for the contracts of the partnership. This means that each partner's personal assets are subject to any third-party claims against the partnership. The unlimited liability of partners versus the limited liability of corporate shareholders is a key difference between a general partnership and a regular corporation.

Isn't there a lot of paperwork involved with having a corporation?

While it is true that there is more paperwork and red tape in forming and maintaining a corporation, the promise of limited liability often overrides the administrative inconvenience and professional costs of forming and keeping a corporation current.

Are there any estate planning benefits to incorporating?

Incorporating affords creditor protection through limited liability and ensures the perpetual existence of a corporation, both of which are pluses to an estate plan. Corporate shares of stock are easily given to others, and corporate management structures are complementary to succeeding generations who may own, but not be active in, the corporate business.

S Corporations

What is the difference between an S corporation and a regular corporation?

An S corporation is formed like a regular corporation. The major difference between an S corporation and a regular corporation is that the Internal Revenue Code provides that "a small-business corporation" may elect not to be taxed at the corporate level but, rather, to have the corporation's income and losses pass through to the shareholders and be taxed to them.

S corporation income is passed through to the shareholders proportionate to their ownership of the corporation's shares. Thus, an S corporation is a tax pass-through business entity for federal income tax purposes, much like a sole proprietorship or partnership.

How do I make an S election?

The election to be taxed as an S corporation is made on Form 2553 of the Internal Revenue Service. Form 2553 must be completed and filed with the Internal Revenue Service at any time before the sixteenth day of the third month of the tax year, if filed during the tax year the election is to take effect, or at any time during the preceding tax year. Thus, if the corporation determines to elect subchapter S taxation and has adopted July 1 to June 30 as its taxable year, the election may be made at any time during the preceding fiscal year or by September 15 for the present year.

What are the requirements for an S corporation?

In order to elect to be an S corporation:

- There must be no more than thirty-five shareholders.
- Shareholders must be natural persons, an estate of a natural person, or certain trusts.
- There must be only one class of stock.
- A nonresident alien cannot be a shareholder.
- The S corporation may not own 80 percent or more of the stock of any other active corporation and retain its S status.
- It cannot own a wholly owned subsidiary.

What advantages does an S corporation have over other business entities?

S corporations do not pay double tax because their income and losses flow through directly to their shareholders. They can be owned and created by a single individual, and they have a vast body of federal law behind them which is recognized in every state.

Do I have to decide whether to be an S corporation before I incorporate?

You do not need to tell the Secretary of State whether the corporation is to be a regular C corporation or an S corporation. The election to be taxed as an S corporation is relevant only for income tax purposes.

Corporations are automatically taxed as regular corporations under subchapter C unless the corporation elects to be taxed under subchapter S. A corporation which is originally taxed under subchapter C can later elect to be taxed under subchapter S, and vice versa, by filing the appropriate election with the Internal Revenue Service.

Can my friend's corporation be a shareholder of my S corporation?

A corporation cannot be a shareholder of a subchapter S corporation. Only individuals can hold S corporation stock.

In your particular case, you should consider a limited liability company as a viable organizational alternative. Limited liability company statutes allow corporations to be members (owners) and also allow income and loss to be allocated among the members pro rata to their contributions.

If my living trust owns subchapter S stock after my death, will the S election be disqualified?

A revocable living trust which is owned by an individual who is a citizen or a resident of the United States qualifies to own S corporation stock because it is a "grantor trust."

Another type of trust, called a *qualified subchapter S trust (QSST)* can also hold S corporation stock. The QSST must provide that all of its income will be distributed to a beneficiary, and under a recent private letter ruling, it may provide that a beneficiary can elect to have the trustees retain all or part of its net income.

A QSST may not allow payment of principal to anyone other than an income beneficiary even if the trust first disposes of the S stock. If a QSST is created, notice must be given to the Internal Revenue Service, and the notice must contain the following:

- Name, address, and taxpayer identification number of the current income beneficiary, the trust, and the corporation
- Identification of the election under the Internal Revenue Code

- Specification of the date on which the election is to become effective
- All information necessary to show that the current income beneficiary is entitled to make the election

Limited Liability Companies

What is a limited liability company?

A *limited liability company (LLC)* is a hybrid business entity that possesses certain attributes associated with corporations and certain attributes associated with partnerships.

Instead of partners or shareholders, the LLC has members. Members enjoy limited liability regardless of whether they participate in the day-to-day affairs of the business. This means that LLC members can participate in the management and control of the business without risking their personal liability as a result of the acts of others.

A limited liability company is generally treated as a partnership for purposes of federal and state income taxation. Because partnerships are not subject to the corporate income tax, an LLC offers the limited liability of a corporation without the additional level of income taxation associated with regular corporations.

Most states have only recently adopted limited liability company statutes. Because the LLC is a recent phenomenon as a business entity, the case law concerning limited liability companies is in its infant stages. Therefore, it is sometimes difficult to determine how the Internal Revenue Service will react to LLC situations or what other legal ramifications an LLC will have.

It appears that more and more people will choose a limited liability company as the preferred business entity and that the future looks fairly assured for the LLC as an alternative to the corporation.

What does it take to form an LLC?

Because LLCs are so new and because the laws differ so dramatically from state to state, you will need to check with an attorney in your state to determine the rules and regulations for establishing an LLC.

How many people are needed to form an LLC?

While under some state statutes only one member is needed to create an LLC, it is recommended that you always begin the formation of an LLC with two or more members.

Who can be an LLC member?

Unlike the S corporation, an LLC has no restrictions as to the type or character of its members. This means that any person or entity can be a member of an LLC. An LLC can have corporate wholly owned operating subsidiaries and can create different classes of ownership interests and different priorities within or among different classes of owners.

Unlike the partners in a limited partnership, LLC members can participate in the management and control of the LLC's activities without risking limitation on their personal liability. This allows LLC members to materially participate in the LLC's activities and currently deduct LLC losses and deductions that otherwise might be suspended in a limited partnership.

Are the LLC laws uniform among the states?

The laws regarding LLCs are not uniform among the states. One of the major areas of difference involves whether or not the entity will be classified for federal income tax purposes as a corporation or a partnership. The Internal Revenue Service has looked at the limited liability company statutes of several of the states and has classified the statutes either as "partnership" statutes or as "flexible" statutes. For example, under Colorado's limited liability company statute, an LLC can be taxed only as a partnership. In this regard the statute is deemed to be a "bulletproof" partnership tax statute. On the other hand, the Kansas limited liability company statute is referred to as a flexible statute: the drafter of the LLC can organize the company in such a way that it can be taxed either as a regular C corporation or as a partnership.

The test that the IRS applies to determine whether the LLC will be taxed as a corporation or as a partnership includes an analysis of the following:

- Limited liability
- Continuity of life

- Centralized management
- Free transferability of interests

If an entity lacks two or more of these characteristics, it will be taxed as a partnership.

Obviously, limited liability companies have limited liability as the essence of their existence. The drafter of the entity can then choose from among the other characteristics the two that he or she does not want the entity to have.

It is relatively easy not to have *free transferability of interests* by putting restrictions on the trading of shares. It is also easy to provide in the LLC agreement that any interest in the LLC must first be offered back to the LLC or that the transfer has to be approved by the unanimous vote of all company members.

Continuity of life is another test that is relatively easy to accommodate. Any provision that the company will end upon the death of a member closely resembles a partnership characteristic. It is also possible under some states' statutes to provide that if all of the remaining members vote to continue the entity, it will be continued and does not have to be reconstituted as is required with a partnership. Such a provision does not give the entity the characteristic of a corporation.

Why are LLCs so popular?

They are popular because they have the best attributes of each of the other business entities currently in existence.

Why are LLCs better than regular corporations?

An LLC is free from the double-taxation burden of regular corporations. It avoids unreasonable compensation issues and unreasonable accumulation earnings tax issues. It also avoids many of the corporate formalities.

Why are LLCs better than S corporations?

LLCs are not limited in the number or type of owners. Moreover, an LLC can elect a pro rata step-up of inside basis upon the death of an LLC member. This means that if a member dies and his or her LLC interest receives a step-up in basis, the LLC can elect to allocate the step-up among the LLC's assets. After initial formation, LLCs can receive encumbered property and include their debt or liability in the basis of a member. LLC members can distribute appreciated property to the LLC without recognizing a gain, compared to an 80 percent ownership requirement for subchapter S shareholders.

Why are LLCs better than general or family limited partnerships?

An LLC's members can limit their liability to the extent of their investment even if they participate in the management of the company. General partners always remain liable to creditors or for partnership debts.

Do you think that LLCs will replace general partnerships?

The limited liability company and its counterpart, the limited liability partnership, should replace most existing general partnerships. There is very little advantage to having a partnership in which all of the partners are liable for all the debts of the partnership and all of the acts of each of the other partners.

In addition, the limited liability company has the advantage of being managed like a partnership. Each of the members may have management authority if the state statutes allow such a management style and if it is in fact chosen by the members.

Also, by delegating management to one individual who would be classified as active and materially participating in management, other members may be determined not to be materially participating in management. Under the proposed regulations for limited liability companies, anyone not actively participating in management would not be deemed to have earned income or self-employment income from the LLC. This has a positive tax effect for those members who are seeking to avoid self-employment taxes or to avoid being disqualified for their Social Security retirement benefits.

What asset protection planning is accomplished with a LLC?

An LLC can be structured for tax purposes much like a general partnership but can retain liability protection for the members. As with a corporation, the assets of the limited liability company would be subject to judicial process by any creditor of the company. The assets of the individual members would be protected from liabilities of the LLC, and the assets of the LLC would be protected from the liability of the debts of its members.

An LLC is an excellent candidate for general partner in a family limited partnership in that it has strong control characteristics and no adverse income tax consequences.

Why isn't everyone using an LLC?

The lack of development of case law in this area has caused some practitioners to shy away from recommending the LLC until it becomes better known and is tested in the courts.

If my business associates and I desire to allocate business income and loss among us on a basis that may differ from our cash investment, what type of entity would you recommend we use?

You should consider either a limited partnership, general partnership, or limited liability company. You could consider a C corporation if you know just how you desire to allocate and are willing to create multiple classes of shares.

An S corporation would not be an alternative because all allocations of income and loss are pro rata by law, based upon the shareholder's interest. The IRS allows such entities to distribute items of income and deductions in ways other than on a pro rata basis. However, there are specific rules on how and under what circumstances this can be achieved.

Professional Corporations

What if I am a professional and want to incorporate my practice?

Professional corporations are creations of state statutes that permit certain professionals—such as doctors, dentists, lawyers, architects, and engineers—to run their practices as corporations. Whether or not a professional corporation is a C or S corporation is purely a tax decision.

I have a medical practice. Should I form a professional corporation?

If you practice with one or more other physicians, it is very important for you to form a professional corporation or limited liability company in order to protect your liability. In partnership law, the liability is "joint and several," so if you do not incorporate, each partner is liable for the malpractice of any of the other partners. All of your personal assets will be subject to a malpractice claim against any one or more of your partners, even if you were not involved in the patient's case.

However, if you all form a professional corporation and become its shareholders and employees, or form a partnership of professional corporations, or form a limited liability company, you will protect your liability. In the case of a malpractice claim against one doctor, the physicians who are not involved in the matter will not be liable and their personal assets will be protected from a lawsuit predicated upon the practice mistakes of a colleague.

Is there a way for me to transfer my professional corporation stock into a living trust?

If the trustee who holds the license to practice is sole trustee during his or her lifetime, there is a strong argument that this satisfies any state statute.

In addition, your living trust can provide that if you become disabled, the successor trustees can immediately appoint a *special professional trustee*—who holds the required professional license—to take title to your stock.

Business Continuity Planning

What is business continuity planning?

It is planning that is calculated to keep closely held businesses going upon the deaths or disabilities of their founders and/or leaders.

Closely held businesses face many problems when principals die, become disabled, or resign. These problems can arise when the business is entirely held by family members and also when the business is held among unrelated individuals. The problems are often so severe that only about 30 percent of closely held businesses survive the deaths of their founders.

What planning concerns should I have as a business owner?

The primary planning concerns for all business owners, particularly those who are nonrelated owners of the same business, are:

- Ensuring a market to purchase their stock or other business interest at retirement, death, and substantial disability
- Providing funds for the purchase of the business interests of all of the principals
- Keeping "unwanted partners" such as competitors or nonessential family members from becoming business partners

In addition to dealing with the above concerns, family businesses must make plans to effectively continue the operations of the business, designate business successors, provide surviving spouses and children with sufficient assets, and provide sufficient liquidity for the payment of estate tax obligations so that the business will not have to be liquidated to pay those taxes.

Is there really a need to continue the business?

In most family businesses, the business is built upon the personality, marketing, and operational talents of the principals. The absence of a principal creates a major void. While the grief-stricken family seeks to fill that void, customers will have concerns and may go elsewhere.

Postdeath or disability problems are often complicated by internal family rivalry and disputes as to the ownership, control, and operation of the business.

In many states, unless specific authorization is provided to operate a business, the executor (or agent under a power of attorney) can only wind down the business.

How can I make advance plans for the designation of my business successors?

Ideally, families want children to share equally in the family wealth. However, all children might not have the same interest in participating in the family business or might not be in circumstances that enable them to do so. If one particular child remains in the family business, advance planning is necessary to provide that child with the control and/or ownership needed to successfully operate the business. If one child is active and the others are passive in matters of the family business, the situation is a likely breeding ground for family dissension.

Advance planning should include leaving other or replacement assets, including the benefits of life insurance trusts, to create equality among the children. Additionally, in drafting the estate planning documents, care should be taken to avoid placing a disproportionate estate tax burden upon the children who do not receive the business.

If more than one child will be involved in the family business, the issue of roles and control should be resolved by the family prior to losing the services of the leader parent. Dissension among children could destroy the business and might also adversely affect the family unit. Advance decisions could mitigate or avoid these problems.

Advance planning should also include providing necessary legal authority to continue the business; determining how business decisions will be made and who will make them; instituting early involvement of family members in customer public relations; and providing for funds such as "key person" insurance to provide needed capital during the business hiatus.

How can I provide for the protection of my spouse with the business assets?

The small-business owner frequently invests profits back into the business, and over time this causes the business to become the major asset in the decedent's estate. If the business owner desires to pass his or her business to children, arrangements must be made to provide sufficient replacement resources for the benefit of the surviving spouse. Advance planning for the purchase of life insurance, as well as preparation of installment sale notes, private annuities, and self-canceling notes, is essential.

Are taxes a problem?

Federal estate taxes are a major problem in conjunction with business continuity planning. Often, the family business is a major asset of the estate, and estate taxes are due, in cash, 9 months after the date of death or can be deferred in a few ways. If the business is typical, it will most probably be difficult to value and buyers will not easily be found even at a reasonable asking price. Without business continuity planning, there is every likelihood that the business might have to be sold at a fire-sale price.

Won't I qualify for the installment payment of estate taxes?

Any business that is 35 percent or more of an estate will qualify for the installment payment of estate taxes. This exception applies only to the first $1 million of business value, and the tax must nevertheless be paid over a 14-year-period with interest. However, only interest is paid, at the rate of 4 percent, for the first 4 years. Thereafter, principal is reduced each year, and interest is paid at the current statutory rate.

Are there problems with unrelated owners?

There can also be problems with unrelated owners. When an owner dies, his or her heirs often do not want to own a portion of the business, and the remaining principals do not want the deceased owner's family in the business. Most generally, the remaining principals do not have the liquidity necessary to buy the deceased owner's shares, and the respective sides have widely divergent views as to the value of the interest in question.

Can a fair price be easily established?

Even if cash were available, how will a fair price for the deceased owner's shares be determined? Bitter disputes and hurt feelings can result if the terms of a buyout have not been negotiated in advance. In addition, an S election can be ruined if transfers of stock are not controlled and proper provisions for its repurchase are not in place.

LIFE INSURANCE

How can I provide liquidity to pay for my obligations?

If your spouse is to continue your business, its value will be included in his or her estate. If liquidity is not otherwise provided, the business may have to be sold or heavily leveraged in debt to cover the resulting federal estate tax obligation. Life insurance planning needs to be discussed early in such a situation.

Can I purchase life insurance in an irrevocable trust and then let my family liquidate the family business?

This is a meaningful but often overlooked alternative. If you do not have partners who you wish to have the business upon your death, the combination of life insurance and liquidation could be your best alternative. You can make gifts to an irrevocable life insurance trust that purchases life insurance on your life equal to the value of your closely held business interest. Upon your death, the proceeds will be available for your spouse and children and will pass tax-free to your children upon your spouse's subsequent death.

With this approach, your family members can liquidate your business interest and add the proceeds to the insurance benefits they have already received. The tax on the liquidated value of your business interests will be directly proportionate to their liquidated value and might very well place your estate into significantly lower brackets.

Are premiums paid on business life insurance deductible?

The Internal Revenue Code provides that no deduction is allowed for premiums paid on life insurance.

Are life insurance death proceeds exempt from income tax?

The entire benefit paid to the beneficiary is exempt from the beneficiary's income taxes. However, if an existing policy is sold or otherwise "transferred for value," the proceeds may not be exempt from federal income tax.

Are life insurance proceeds payable to a corporation subject to the alternative minimum tax?

If the corporation is an S corporation, the proceeds received are not subject to the AMT calculation. If it is a regular corporation, however, the proceeds are subject to the AMT calculation.

BUY-SELL AGREEMENTS

I own a business with another person and understand that we

should have an agreement providing that if one of us dies, the other will purchase the interest of the deceased owner. Also, I understand that we should probably have life insurance to pay for the buyout. Both of us want to maximize the amount that we receive from our business, and, most importantly, we want to maximize the amount our children actually receive. Should we purchase more insurance than we need to fund the business purchase agreement?

All of these are basically good ideas. However, you must be aware that the value of your interest in the business will be included in your estate for federal estate tax and other death tax purposes. Thus, the higher the value placed upon the business interest, the more the taxation. If you and the other owner artificially inflate the value of your respective business interests, up to 55 percent of that value could pass directly to the government due to federal estate tax.

Assuming that the other owner of the business is not a family member, one recommendation would be to put the lowest possible value on the business interest, especially if the buyout is to be funded by life insurance.

Assume that your interest in the business is worth between $750,000 and $1 million. If the other owner agrees to buy your interest at your death for $1 million, he or she will have an equal funding need when purchasing life insurance on your life. Your business interest will be included in your gross estate at a value of $1 million. At potential federal estate tax rates of 55 percent, your family members may end up getting as little as $450,000.

If, however, you value your interest at $750,000, the federal estate tax savings will be $138,000. The money saved by funding the buyout with $750,000 of life insurance rather than $1 million of life insurance could be used to purchase a second insurance policy on your life in the amount of $250,000. This second life insurance policy would be for the benefit of your family, and it would be owned by an irrevocable trust referred to as an ILIT or wealth replacement trust. The ILIT will be the beneficiary, and the benefits will not be subject to estate taxation. Thus, your family will receive all $250,000 of the proceeds from the second life insurance policy.

In the end, by valuing your business interest at $750,000 instead of $1 million and by utilizing an ILIT, your family will receive $587,500 ($337,500 from the buyout plus $250,000 from the ILIT) rather than $450,000—an additional benefit of $137,500 without a dime of additional cost.

What are the basic types of buy-sell agreements?

The three basic types of buy-sell agreements are stock redemption agreements (entity purchase agreements in the case of a partnership or LLC), cross-purchase agreements, and hybrid purchase agreements.

A *stock redemption agreement* is made between the individual shareholders and the corporation. The individual shareholders agree that upon the occurrence of a triggering event such as the death of a shareholder, they are obligated to offer their respective stock ownership for sale to the corporation. The corporation is likewise obligated to "redeem," or purchase, the stock. The agreement is usually funded by insurance owned by the corporation on the life of each shareholder.

A partnership can buy back a partner's interest through a similar method often referred to as an *entity purchase agreement.* With this type of agreement, the partnership often purchases life insurance on the lives of the partners and is the beneficiary of that insurance. On a partner's death, the partnership purchases the interest of that partner with the funding provided by the insurance. The result is that the partnership is owned by the remaining partners and the deceased partner's family has cash based upon a predetermined value of the partner's interest. Members of limited liability companies would follow this identical planning pattern.

A *cross-purchase agreement* is made between the individual shareholders, partners, or members rather than between them and their business entity. With a cross-purchase agreement, upon the death, disability, or retirement of a principal, the remaining principals are personally obligated to purchase the business interest on a pro rata basis. In cross-purchase agreements, each shareholder usually owns a life insurance policy on the lives of the other business principals. Cross-purchase agreements step up the basis of the purchasing partners to the cost of their purchase.

A *hybrid purchase agreement* combines both redemption and cross-purchase features. It is referred to as a *wait-and-see* agreement as it enables the remaining shareholders to determine whether the corporation has sufficient funds to make the purchase or whether the purchase should be made by the shareholders. With this agreement, life insurance is generally owned by the shareholders and the selling shareholder is required to first offer the stock to the corporation. If the corporation declines to make the purchase, the shareholders are obligated to make the purchase.

By selecting hybrid agreements, either the business or the business principals can own any life insurance purchased as a funding vehicle.

Which is preferable, a stock redemption (or entity purchase) agreement or a cross-purchase arrangement?

There are several tax and practical factors affecting this decision, but the primary tax issue is for the purchaser to be able to qualify for capital gain taxation rather than ordinary-income treatment on the subsequent sale of his or her business interest. For example:

> In starting a business, Able and Baker each contribute $10,000 for 5000 shares of stock. At the time Able dies, the fair market value of the stock has doubled. If the corporation redeems the stock from Able at his death, Baker will control a $40,000 business but have only a tax basis of $10,000. If a cross-purchase is involved, Baker will purchase the stock at $20,000 and have a $30,000 basis (Baker's $10,000 plus Able's $20,000), which will reduce the gain when the stock is subsequently sold.

Frequently, the controlling practical consideration pertains to funding the buy-sell agreement. Buy-sell agreements are primarily funded with life insurance on the lives of the shareholders or partners. If there are only two shareholders or partners, a cross-purchase agreement can be used, with each owning a life insurance policy on the other. If there are multiple shareholders or partners, it may be simpler for the corporation or other business entity to own the policies. Life insurance owned by a C corporation is subject to the alternative minimum tax, while life insurance owned by individual shareholders is not subject to AMT.

What is the relationship between buy-sell agreements and federal estate taxes?

If the business valuation is properly established, the buy-sell agreement should determine the estate tax value of the business. In buy-sell agreements involving unrelated principals, the appropriate business valuation used in the agreement will generally avoid an after-death valuation dispute with the IRS.

In buy-sell agreements between related parties, the business valuation will almost always be the subject of close IRS scrutiny so that it does not unreasonably reduce the fair market value of the business interest.

In order for the buy-sell agreement to establish the estate tax value of the business, the agreement must be an enforceable, binding agreement established for a valid business purpose. It must be a binding agreement during life as well as at death. In other words, it must restrict a lifetime transfer to the price established by the buy-sell agreement.

The agreement must be for a price that is determinable and reasonable at the time the agreement is made. If the agreement represents full and adequate consideration at the time it is made, then the price will be upheld even if there is a difference between the agreement price and the fair market value at the time of the triggering event. However, agreements among family members will almost always be scrutinized for reasonableness by the IRS.

In order for the taxpayer to set a business value for federal estate tax purposes, the agreement must be comparable to similar arrangements entered into by persons in an arm's-length transaction and not just a device to avoid federal estate taxes. The burden of proof is on the taxpayer to show that each of these tests are satisfied.

TRANSFERS TO FAMILY MEMBERS

We want our oldest daughter to take over our family business; however, we cannot afford to give it to her because we need the income it generates for our retirement, and we are reluctant to sell it to her because of the capital gain taxes we will have to pay. What are our options?

You have a number of planning options which you should consider.

First, an installment sale to your daughter would allow you to transfer the business to her immediately and would provide you with an income stream for the term that you set in the installment note. However, whenever you sell any asset to a family member, you must treat it as an arm's-length transaction; any discounting that you provide your daughter—whether on the price or interest rate on the installment note—may be construed to be a taxable gift by the IRS if the price is too low or the terms are too good.

Under an installment sale, you do not avoid the capital gain tax but are able to defer the tax by paying it over the life of the note.

Second, you may consider a self-canceling installment note. A self-canceling installment note is like the installment note you would receive in an ordinary installment sale. However, a self-canceling installment note has a unique additional provision: the obligation is canceled in the event of your death. Thus, you would receive the income stream that you desire, but your estate will not have to pay estate tax on the unpaid portion of the promissory note at the time of your death.

Third, you could sell the business to your daughter in exchange for a private annuity. A private annuity involves a sale to a family member for a number of fixed payments determined by IRS tables for the remainder of your life. The obligation to make these payments ends on your death. If you live a short time, the payments will end upon your death and your daughter will have acquired the business with very little investment. If, however, you outlive your actuarial life expectancy, your daughter will have paid more than the business was worth.

By using a private annuity, you would sell the business to your daughter and receive a set income every year for the rest of your and your spouse's lives. If the asset does not produce an income to cover these payments, this strategy may not be operable because of the demand on your daughter to produce the money to make the payments.

Fourth, you should consider establishing a family limited partnership and transferring your business into it. Thereafter, you can give limited-partner interests to your daughter over a period of years at discounts ranging from 30 to 50 percent. As general partner, you will be able to retain control over the management of your business until you feel your daughter is ready to take over. You can also provide yourself and your spouse with an income stream for as long as you desire for your duties as general partners.

Fifth, you may also consider creating an irrevocable grantor retained annuity trust (GRAT). You transfer the business to the GRAT and receive a percentage of the value of the business over a period of time and at an interest rate that you select. At the end of the payment period, the business belongs to your daughter. The Internal Revenue Code provides tables that measure the amount of that remainder interest; it constitutes the gift amount upon which you may have to pay gift tax.

The longer the retained term, the smaller the gift will be; conversely, the shorter the time over which the payments will be made, the larger the gift will be for federal gift tax purposes. If you die prior to the expiration of the retained term, the transaction will be treated for federal estate tax purposes as if it never occurred.

EMPLOYEE STOCK OWNERSHIP PLANS

What is an ESOP?

An *employee stock ownership plan (ESOP)* is a retirement plan provided for in the Internal Revenue Code. In an ESOP the company makes contributions to the plan for the benefit of its employees and the contributions to the plan are used to acquire stock in the company, which must be a regular C corporation.

Can you explain to me in simple terms how an ESOP works?

An ESOP is a tax-qualified plan. The employer is allowed to make tax-deductible contributions either of the company stock or of cash to a trust. All of the employee participants then have the benefit of having the assets in the trust, whether stock or cash, allocated to them according to a variety of formulas that are identical for practical purposes to any other deferred-compensation plan. When their employment is terminated or when they retire or die, they or their families will receive amounts of cash or stock in the company as distributions from the ESOP.

From the company's perspective, it can generate income tax deductions by contributing stock rather than cash to the plan and can create a market for its stock which might otherwise not be marketable.

What are the uses of the ESOP in an estate and business planning strategy?

The adoption of an ESOP by a corporation has several potential uses and advantages:

- The first use is to raise capital for the company to purchase existing stock owned by a shareholder, capital assets, or the stock of other companies.
- Second, any stock purchased by the ESOP from a shareholder receives favorable capital gain tax treatment if the shareholder

reinvests the proceeds of the sale in *qualified replacement property (QRP)*—the stock of American operating companies—within 1 year of the sale of the stock of the corporation. In that event, the sale does not have to be recognized as taxable for capital gain purposes in the year of the sale. As long as the selling shareholder retains the QRP, there is no capital gain recognition. However, when any QRP is sold, the capital gain will be recognized. There is a carryover basis from the basis of the original stock to the QRP. An operating company is one that is not a personal service company but has product and inventory for sale constituting more than half of its gross income.

The ESOP area is one in which a great many creative planning opportunities exist.

A unique planning opportunity exists when the shareholder who is selling the stock to an ESOP first transfers the stock to a family limited partnership that he or she creates. The reason for this additional transfer to the FLP is that the value of the partnership interest can be discounted at the death of the shareholder for estate tax purposes and yet may receive a step-up in basis for income tax purposes if the proper election is filed at the death of the partnership owner.

Is there a way for an owner of a private corporation to create a market for his or her stock by using an ESOP?

A corporation can contribute cash to its ESOP on a tax-deductible basis. The cash can then be used to acquire the stock of a majority shareholder.

Most often it is difficult for corporate founders to find somebody in the open market to buy their stock. And even if they find a buyer, they will not generally be willing to sell a controlling interest in the company. Unless they are willing to sell a majority interest in their company, it is highly unlikely that anyone will wish to purchase their stock. Through the use of the ESOP, a majority shareholder can sell less than a majority interest in his or her stock to the ESOP and defer or eliminate capital gain taxes.

ESOP planning provides an ideal way for a majority shareholder to find a "marketplace" for his or her stock. With the proper use of the ESOP, the business owner can even continue to effectively control the company.

Valuations in Business Planning

How important is the valuation of assets in the estate planning process?

The valuation of assets for gift and estate tax purposes is critical. If effective discount planning is implemented with valuation planning, it is possible to achieve a situation where "the sum of the parts does not equal the whole." To achieve this result, it is essential to form a "valuation partnership." This is a team of advisors consisting of the attorney, tax advisor, financial planner, and business valuation appraiser. These professionals must develop and provide the evidence supporting the valuation of the business and any discount that may be appropriate.

The fair-market-value tradition of valuing businesses continues to be effective. The tax concept of "fair market value" requires both the taxpayer and the government to determine the value of a business according to a hypothetical, free-market standard. This means we look at the hypothetical "willing buyer" and "willing seller" to value a business.

For business valuation, the family relationship of the parties in the business is irrelevant. This is to the advantage of families seeking to share wealth on a multigenerational basis. As part of the Revenue Reconciliation Act of 1990, Congress confirmed the viability of "fragmented ownership" discounts by recognizing that the courts generally approve corporate and partnership equity discounts (nonmarketability, minority interests, and other types) often aggregating 30 to 50 percent in relation to underlying business or asset values.

By using a combination of the business valuation discounts available to them, a married couple, using their combined unified credit of $1.2 million, might be able to transfer upward of $2.5 million in assets free of federal gift or estate tax to their children.

In general, what does the business valuation process involve?

The basic IRS pronouncement on valuations is Revenue Ruling 59-60. This ruling requires consideration of:

- The nature of the business and history of the enterprise
- The general economic outlook and the outlook for the particular industry

- The book value of the stock and the financial condition of the business
- The earning capacity of the company
- The dividend-paying capacity of the company
- Whether or not the enterprise has goodwill or other intangible value
- Past sales of the stock
- The market price of comparable stocks

The value of a business is based upon its future earnings. In order to determine future earnings, the first basic step is to adjust prior earnings to reflect economic reality. This involves making adjustments to such items as the business owner's high salary and benefits and one-time expenses; adjusting the inventory accounting system from LIFO to FIFO; and correcting improper accounting methods.

The second step involves attempts to find comparable public and private companies upon which to make comparisons in order to determine the business value. Although a necessary step, finding comparable companies is often difficult and at times impossible.

The third step is to use prior financial statements over a 5-year period to project future earnings. Two popular methods for determining future earnings include the averaging of prior earnings on both a weighted and unweighted basis. And if the business is experiencing financial difficulty, the value of the business could be determined on the basis of its liquidation or net asset value.

The fourth step is to capitalize the business earnings. A capitalization, or yield, rate is selected based upon a safe rate and a risk rate. The safe rate is frequently the interest rate on a long-term or intermediate-term Treasury bond. The risk rate is additional compensation to the investor for investing in a particular business. In other words, the more volatile and unpredictable the business, the higher the rate of return the investor must earn to compensate for the additional risk. Considerations of the risk rate include:

- Evaluation of the economy and specific industry outlook
- Whether the business is diversified in its products and customers
- The ability and depth of management
- The profitability and stability of earnings

- Consideration of the financial ratios of the business and comparing the ratios to those of the industry

For small, closely held businesses, the risk premiums could be approximately 15 to 30 percent in addition to the safe rate.

Once the capitalization rate is determined, it is applied to the appropriate valuation method. The primary valuation methods are adjusted net assets, capitalization of earnings, comparison of the price-earnings ratio of comparable businesses, excess earnings, and discounted earnings dividend. For example, using the capitalization of earnings method with average earnings of $100,000 and a capitalization rate of 25 percent, the value would be $400,000 ($400,000 would be required to yield $100,000 at a capitalization rate of 25 percent).

Although generalized *rules of thumb* might be used in various industries to arrive at a sales price (e.g., earnings times a specified factor), rules of thumb are not accepted as being accurate for formal appraisals.

Once the value of the business has been determined, the valuation is subject to adjustments for either the payment of a premium based upon the ability to control the business ownership (control premium) or discounts for the inability to control the business (minority discount) and the lack of marketability of shares of a closely owned business (marketability discount). The marketability discount could also be affected by a restrictive buy-sell agreement.

Revenue Ruling 59-60 requires the appraiser to consider all alternatives and to select the most appropriate method. Averaging and weighting the results of the various methods is basically not acceptable. A professionally written report meeting IRS and professional standards is necessary to withstand IRS scrutiny. The comprehensiveness and professionalism of the report may well be a factor as to whether the IRS desires to question the valuation.

Why are business valuations important for buy-sell agreements?

Business valuations establish fair market value for gift and estate tax purposes. The Internal Revenue Code provides a substantial penalty for a material understatement of value. If the value claimed is less than its proper value, there is a 20 percent penalty on the underpayment if it exceeds $5000. There is a 40 percent penalty if the value is 25 percent less than its proper value. However, penalties will not apply if there is reasonable cause for underpayment and the taxpayer acted in good faith with respect to the underpayment.

A bona fide business valuation is important prior to commencing any gifting program. A $10,000-per-year gift program cannot be effectively planned unless there is a professional business valuation. Additionally, good estate planning will establish a correct business value for both federal gift and estate tax purposes.

Taxpayers should remember that the burden of proof for establishing a correct business valuation is on them. Arguably, an independent, professionally conducted business valuation would meet the good-faith test to avoid the underpayment penalty. However, the good-faith test will not alleviate the interest which is accruing for underpayments of federal gift tax.

Can you simply explain valuation discounts and how they work?

There are two viable types of discounts: lack of marketability and minority interests. Together, these discounts provide a donor with the opportunity to leverage the transfer of assets during his or her lifetime or upon death.

A *lack-of-marketability discount* is created by restricting the right of an owner to transfer his or her interest in an entity. By making the business interest virtually unmarketable, the holder of the business interest cannot transfer his or her ownership without first complying with the terms and conditions of the agreement. These restrictions, coupled with a restriction of the price to be paid for the business interest if the business or its other owners buy it back, create the lack-of-marketability discount.

A *minority-interest discount* is created by breaking up a block of majority ownership into smaller minority interests. In a death situation, the value of the interest transferred will be based upon the holdings of the decedent at the time of his or her death. A willing buyer will demand a discount from the value of any minority interest because it does not provide the buyer with any means or method to control the entity whose units are being purchased.

Minority-discount planning works as well for federal estate tax planning as it does for gift tax planning. If the business owner holds a controlling interest in a business at death, the value of that interest is not subject to a minority discount. But if the business owner holds only a minority interest in the business, the value of that interest may be eligible for a large minority discount.

While transfers at death are valued upon the interest transferred by the decedent, lifetime transfers are valued based upon the interest received by each individual recipient. Minority discounts are possible even though the gifts in question are to members of a single family. If, however, one individual receives a control block as a lump-sum gift, no minority discount will apply. Gifts of noncontrolling interests will usually be eligible for the minority discount.

While the Internal Revenue Service no longer applies the family attribution doctrine—this doctrine attributes ownership by related family members to the family patriarch or matriarch for purposes of denying an otherwise justified minority discount—issues of "form over substance" and "actual value" may prevent application of a minority discount. If the IRS can show that the underlying transfer was clearly designed to avoid income taxes, a minority discount will be denied.

A tremendous opportunity exists in the use of discounts in estate planning. However, it is critical that the attorney, accountant, financial planner, and appraiser work together to properly structure the business agreements necessary to obtain the appropriate discounts.

What is the Internal Revenue Service's response to the use of discounts?

The IRS has long recognized discounts in valuing property. For example, if three persons own a piece of real estate and one of them wants to sell that real estate and the other two are not willing to purchase it, and the owner of the undivided one-third interest offers to sell that interest to the public, that owner is not likely to receive an amount equal to one-third of the fair market value of the entire parcel if the entire parcel was being sold.

The selling owner controls only one-third of the property and therefore possesses little, if any, control over its use. He or she has little say in the management of the property or the ability to affect its profitability, and this creates the required discounting environment.

What qualifications should an appraiser have to substantiate the discounts claimed?

It is critical to the valuation discount process that the professional drafting the organizational documentation for the business has a thorough working knowledge of valuation discounts and what planning will affect the bottom-line evaluation by subsequent appraisers.

It is even more critical that the appraiser is experienced in business appraisals with an in-depth knowledge in the valuation and discount processes to be able to carefully and meticulously document the factors affecting the bottom line of the valuation.

Appraisers who do not do their homework will not produce appraisals that will support meaningful discounts that will be approved by the Internal Revenue Service. Nevertheless, quality appraisals will result in substantial federal estate and gift tax savings for the clients.

Do I need more than one appraiser?

When it comes to valuation discounts, two types of appraisers are typically required. The first is the *substantive appraiser,* who can properly value the worth of a particular asset as a specialist in that kind of assets. For example, a farm specialist to value farms, a commercial real estate specialist to value commercial real estate, or a fast-food-franchise specialist to value a fast-food franchise. These appraisers must be followed by a *business valuation specialist,* who then values the discounts that will enure to minority-ownership interests in those assets or businesses.

Business Documents

What is a death-benefit-only plan?

A *death-benefit-only,* or *survivorship income, plan* is one in which a corporation agrees to pay to the surviving spouse and children of the decedent employee an amount equal to a percentage or multiple of salary. The corporation receives a benefit in the form of an income tax deduction. This type of plan allows the surviving spouse and children to receive income for a period of time or for life without being an employee of a corporation after the death of the deceased employee.

I am about to buy a business, and I want the seller to sign an agreement that the seller will not compete with me. I also want my

key employees to sign covenants not to compete. I was told that covenants not to compete do not hold up in court. Is that true?

As a general rule, courts do not like covenants not to compete because they restrict a person's ability to earn a livelihood. But courts also recognize that some companies must use covenants not to compete to protect themselves from employees who might take the companies' customers, secret processes, or other items of value. The courts try to achieve both goals: they try to protect the company while not destroying the selling owner or employee's ability to earn a living.

Generally, covenants not to compete are enforceable if they are not too restrictive. In determining whether or not a covenant is too restrictive, the courts usually address three questions:

- How large a geographical area is covered by the covenant?
- How long do the restrictions last?
- In what types of activities is the employee not permitted to engage?

Covenants not to compete are sometimes found to be unenforceable because of lack of consideration. This can occur when employees are asked to sign covenants not to compete. In order to be valid, covenants not to compete must be accompanied by valid consideration to an employee in return for his or her agreeing to sign the covenant. Allowing the employee to remain in your employ is not enough to support a covenant not to compete. It is suggested that you pay your employees a reasonable sum of money in return for their agreeing to sign covenants not to compete.

Sale or Purchase of a Business

What can I do to prepare my business for sale to make it more marketable?

A buyer will usually want to purchase the assets of the business rather than the business entity itself. Purchasing the business entity may result in the purchase of hidden liabilities of the selling entity.

A purchase of the old entity's assets allows the buyer to start anew without the liabilities of the predecessor business.

With this fact in mind, it should be clear that one of the things you can do to improve the marketability of your business is to literally clean up its assets. Whether it be the accounts receivable, rolling stock, equipment, inventory, or goodwill, you can significantly heighten the business value by preparing the assets for sale. For instance, improving the length of time it takes to collect your accounts receivable improves the value of the remaining accounts receivable. Cleaning and improving the outward appearance of your equipment is another easy way to improve the value of the assets.

The financial records of the business will need to be reviewed and brought up to date. The buyer will want to review at least 5 years of business tax returns. The financial statements should be reviewed and prepared according to generally accepted accounting principles.

You would be wise not to overstate or misstate the financial condition of your business, as statements of this sort generally lead to future litigation based upon claims against you for fraud and misrepresentation.

While it is important to prepare accurate financial information, it is also important to prepare information about past financial decisions. For instance, in year-end planning for regular corporations, many accountants will recommend that the profit of the company be spent to prepurchase supplies or equipment. This decision means that the profit will be spent solely to avoid taxation at the corporate level. Additionally, the value of improvements and equipment may only be reflected at the book value and not the true fair market value of the asset. These decisions result in reducing the profit of the corporation so that the financial statements do not accurately reflect the financial situation of the business.

It is important for the seller to prepare emotionally for the sale process. Not only may the seller be selling the family business, which itself can be difficult, but the buyers may be critical of the business or the assets in order to negotiate a lower purchase price. Thick skin and patience are important factors for the seller. Being prepared to walk away from a sale helps keep the price up and contract terms more favorable.

It is important to evaluate the type of business you are selling. A business that is based upon a niche market is easier to sell and worth more money than a business that is relationship-based. A business that has failed to modernize or to retool is not as marketable as a business that is on the cutting edge of technology. The more difficult it is to replicate the business, the more valuable the business.

If the business is a corporation, the minutes and corporate books should be reviewed and updated if they are not already complete. The buyer will likely ask for this information because it can provide insight into the history of the business.

If you are thinking of selling your business, you should plan on consulting with your attorney, accountant, financial planner, and other advisors. They can help structure and prepare you and your business for sale. A little time, energy, and advice should produce a higher price at better terms from a greater number of potential buyers.

In making my decision whether or not to purchase a business, are there any proactive steps that I can take in order to find out the real condition of the business?

The first step you should take in your investigation of the business enterprise is to obtain a copy of the existing lease, if any, from the potential seller. This lease will give you a wealth of information. The lease can have a powerful effect on your business, so it needs to be reviewed carefully by your attorney. In addition, you should review the business certificate of occupancy; it will describe the legal use or uses for the premises.

You should conduct a full judgment and lien search against all proposed sellers and past owners, if any. If the seller is a corporation, this search should be done against the corporation and all individual shareholders. Because any judgments, liens, and other encumbrances can affect your future business, it is imperative that you make this search.

With the aid of your accountant, you should analyze the two most current tax returns, as well as the last 2 years of sales tax returns. Your accountant can help you coordinate with the seller's accountant in order to facilitate the transfer of all the required tax information that will be necessary in a complete investigation.

All of the above can be done after you have entered into a contract of sale. It is imperative that the contract specifically have language conditioning its validity on the favorable outcome of these investigative steps.

Is there a quick and simple way to determine a fair market value for a business?

In order to pay a "fair" price for the business you are planning on purchasing, you should retain the services of a licensed and certified business appraiser. This appraiser should have experience in appraising the type of business that you plan to purchase. He or she will give you a good idea of the business value and should also give you comparable sales against which you can make your assessment.

I am considering the purchase of an existing supermarket. What key points in the purchase contract should I be concerned with?

You should first be aware of exactly what it is you are buying. The business should be described in detail, and you should be sure that all stock-in-trade, fixtures, equipment, contract rights, leases, goodwill, accounts receivable, and so on, are included in the sale. There should always be a schedule attached to the contract of sale that more particularly describes these items.

In addition, you should always be sure that there is language in the contract of sale stating that you are purchasing the business free and clear of any debts, mortgages, security interests, or other liens or encumbrances, except for those, if any, that you are assuming.

Consider including a provision in the purchase contract that guarantees the gross weekly receipts for a reasonable period of time that corroborates the seller's representations. As purchaser, you can be afforded a trial period in the business during which full opportunity will be given to you to keep tally of the business receipts. In the event the total of the actual gross receipts is less than the guaranteed sum, then there could be language in the contract stating that the down payment shall be repaid to you on demand. During this trial period, you should not be deemed to have taken possession of the business.

An important part of the contract is language stating that the seller will provide you with a complete list, which should be made part of the contract, of all the current creditors and the amounts owed to each. Often, this list is sworn and subscribed to by the seller.

The contract might include language stating that the bill of sale will contain a restrictive covenant as to the seller. This restrictive covenant is a contractual promise by the seller and all other persons active in the business, or in any way connected to the business, not to reestablish, reopen, or engage directly or indirectly in any business, trade, or occupation similar to the one that is being currently sold, within a specified geographic area and for a specific time period.

Another important element is the promise by the seller that, at the time of closing, he or she will assign and transfer as part of the sale the existing business lease. In the alternative, the seller can procure the execution and delivery to you of a new lease or an extension of the term of the existing lease covering the premises.

Another element of a good contract of sale is a liquidated damages clause. This clause will cap the extent of liability for either party by providing a specific amount to be paid for any default or breach.

The attorney for the seller will often hold a specified amount of monies in escrow pending receipt of the appropriate sales tax releases. In addition, an amount is often held in escrow for the claims of creditors for a period of time after the closing of the business.

Another consideration that should be addressed in the contract is the seller's representation that there are no violations of record affecting the premises and that the lease is in full force and effect. The seller should also represent that there are no executory contracts affecting the subject premises except for the leasehold.

The warranties and covenants contained in the body of the contract of sale should survive delivery of the bill of sale and continue in full force as though set forth in the contract of sale.

How do you determine the seller's tax basis for the sale of stock or other business interests?

In determining the seller's tax basis, different rules apply depending upon whether the stock is acquired by purchase, by gift, or through inheritance.

Purchase of Stock If the seller purchased stock, the tax basis for a subsequent sale is the cost of the stock plus the expenses of the purchase. For example:

> If John purchased shares at a cost of $8 per share and had expenses of $1 per share, John's tax basis in each share would be $9. If John sold the shares for $14 per share and had sales expenses of $2 for each share, the sale would result in a gain of $3 per share ($12 minus the $9 basis).

Gift The tax basis of a gift depends upon whether the recipient later sells the stock at a loss or gain. The basic concept is what is called a *carryover basis,* which means that the recipient of the gift takes the same basis as the donor.

If stock received by gift is later sold for a gain, the carryover basis is the donor's basis (John's basis of $9) a share. A different rule applies if the recipient sells the stock at less than the donor's basis. If the fair market value of the stock at the time of the gift is less than the donor's basis, the recipient takes the fair market value of the shares at the time of the gift as his or her basis:

> Assume that John has a basis of $9 per share, the fair market value of the stock was $5 on the date of the gift to Donald, and Donald sold the stock for $4 per share. The loss would be $1 per share (the $5 value less the $4 sale).

Inheritance Property interests of a deceased person are valued at the time of the decedent's death. This is frequently referred to as a step-up in basis. Thus, if John's shares were valued at $15 at his death and the shares were given by will or trust to his son, Donald, Donald's basis would be $15 per share for purposes of ascertaining the gain on his subsequent sale of the shares.

How do we redeem stock on a dividend-free basis?

Basically, the tax code requires dividend treatment on a redemption of stock unless certain requirements are satisfied. For a redemption to qualify, one of these tests must be satisfied:

- The redemption cannot be equivalent to a dividend.
- The redemption must be a substantially disproportionate distribution.
- The redemption must terminate a shareholder's entire interest.
- The redemption must be used to pay death taxes.

There is also an exemption permitted to an individual shareholder in a partial liquidation. However, its applicability to business continuity is limited.

The first category is that redemptions are not to be used to circumvent the payment of dividends. An example would be to allow all shareholders to redeem a portion of their stock, for example, 10 percent for capital gain treatment rather than at the ordinary income tax rate.

The second category incorporates the first category but is primarily concerned with a meaningful reduction in control of the corporation. To constitute a meaningful reduction in control, the redeeming shareholder must have less than 50 percent control and an 80 percent reduction in the total voting power and voting stock after the redemption is completed. If the numerical tests are not satisfied, the shareholder is permitted to otherwise demonstrate there is a meaningful reduction in corporate control. This is clearly a last resort and usually results in an uphill battle with the IRS that has very limited chance of success.

The third category is the complete termination of an ownership interest. For example, one of the shareholders desires to retire and is unrelated to the other shareholders. Capital gain treatment is permitted for a complete liquidation of such person's shares.

The fourth category has to do with payment of death taxes. If the value of the corporate stock owned by a deceased shareholder is greater than 35 percent of that shareholder's estate, the corporation can use its assets to pay the federal and state death taxes, funeral expenses, and other death expenses of the deceased shareholder without creating a taxable dividend. Professionals refer to this technique as a Section 303 redemption. A Section 303 redemption is merely the purchase by a corporation of enough of a deceased shareholder's stock to pay these expenses.

How are C corporation redemptions taxed when the shares are owned by related taxpayers?

If the shareholders are related, the tests are calculated on the basis of *attribution*. This means shares owned by certain other family members and legal entities are considered as "constructively" owned by the selling shareholder. Attribution applies to shares owned by a parent, a spouse (unless divorced or legally separated), a child, or a grandchild. It does not apply to shares owned by a brother or a sister. It does include certain shares owned by partnerships, LLCs, S corporations, and various trusts and estates. In very limited circumstances, attribution can be waived with restrictions.

The significance of attribution is that if the shareholder is considered to own additional stock through the means of attribution, the 50 and 80 percent substantially disproportionate distribution tests are difficult, if not impossible, to satisfy. Attribution might also prevent a complete termination which could result in dividend treatment in redeeming a deceased parent's shares.

How are S corporation redemptions taxed when the shares are owned by unrelated taxpayers?

Each year, an S corporation files a tax return which reports the earnings and profits to the IRS. A K-1 form is furnished to shareholders showing their respective shares of the corporation's income or losses. Each shareholder reports the income or the loss on his or her personal tax return and pays the appropriate income tax. Thus, there is no untaxed income inside a subchapter S corporation other than any remaining undistributed income if the S corporation converted from a C corporation.

The rules for redeeming S corporation stock are the same as regular corporation redemptions. However, the effect of the rules are different. The rule is that an S corporation redemption, unless otherwise exempted, would involve ordinary income to the extent of earnings and profits. However, since income taxes have already been paid by the shareholders, there are no earnings and profits trapped in the corporation except those from a prior conversion from a C corporation. If prior C corporation earnings still remain inside the S corporation, the distribution would be a dividend subject to ordinary income tax.

9

After-Death Administration of Wills and Trusts

Of all the statistics that we have heard, the one that is the most telling is that we all have a 100 percent chance of dying. That means that at some point, all of our planning—or lack of it—must be put to the test of actually being used. After-death administration is the process of implementing and supervising a decedent's estate planning.

There are practical as well as administrative and tax considerations when a family member or other loved one dies. Survivors have to face the grief of loss as well as the task of burial or cremation and a myriad of other concerns. When these responsibilities have been taken care of, there are all of the financial aspects of death. There may be very real concerns about how a family can survive because the assets of the family's provider are tied up in probate. There may be issues of what the decedent owned and who his or her creditors are. The list can go on and on.

Little has been written about issues that arise after the death of a loved one. Our contributing authors have provided an excellent overview of many of these points and practical advice as to how they should be approached. This chapter offers a checklist of what all of us need to know about these after-death issues.

Immediate Action Steps upon the Death of a Family Member

What immediate, practical actions should be taken if a family member dies?

- Notify family members and friends of the death.
- Find any information left by the decedent as to funeral arrangements, nature of ceremony, burial or cremation instructions.
- Make funeral arrangements, including placement of an obituary, if appropriate.

When my grandmother died, I called her lawyer and asked for an immediate appointment to take important papers to him so that he could act immediately. The attorney was courteous, but he did not act immediately. He scheduled an appointment for an office conference after the memorial service. Why did the attorney not act immediately?

A skilled estate planning attorney attends first to emotional and spiritual needs of the family and second to financial affairs of the family. If the attorney foresaw no need for an immediate conference, the attorney properly deferred attention to financial affairs.

What are some of the first legal steps that should be taken upon the death of a family member?

Generally, there is no necessity to take immediate action after the death of a family member unless there is some pending legal event that calls for immediate action. After a family member is buried and after a period of grief, the following actions should be taken:

- A family member should locate the decedent's important legal papers, most particularly his or her will or trust.
- The decedent's estate planning attorney should then be contacted as soon as possible. If the decedent did not have an estate planning attorney, the person or institution named as trustee of the decedent's living trust or as personal repre-

sentative of the decedent's will should retain a competent attorney.

- If there are assets that will be passing under a will, the personal representative, or executor, identified under the will should, with the help of legal counsel, proceed to see that the will is probated.
- If the assets of the decedent are already held in the decedent's revocable trust, then any successor trustees should be prepared to list the assets that are in their possession or come into their possession as trustees.
- An inventory of all assets should be made, and assets which need immediate attention should be reviewed. These assets include life insurance policies, stock options, and retirement plans, which, in some instances, may have a death benefit.
- If the decedent was a principal in a business enterprise, care should be taken to determine what obligations and responsibilities the trustees have to continue the operation of that business. A review of any succession planning of operation and control of the business should be undertaken.
- If probate is necessary, the personal representative's attorney may have to petition for the right to take immediate actions, such as selling assets that are perishable or that are time-sensitive and subject to sharp fluctuations in value (e.g., stock options).

If I am named as the personal representative, or executor, in a will, can I immediately start paying bills and collecting assets?

No. Before you have any authority to act, you must file a petition with the probate court to request that you be appointed by the probate court to act as personal representative. This will entail the court's acceptance of the will as valid. The decedent's appointment of a personal representative in a will is a guideline for the court to follow in making that decision. In most states, before you can be appointed, a notice must be given to all of the interested parties (heirs and other family members) and the court must give the interested parties an opportunity to agree with your appointment or contest it, as the case may be.

Ultimately, the probate court will enter an order which gives you or some other person the power to act. It is the probate court's order which empowers you to act, not the decedent's will.

What happens if an individual dies leaving no will?

When a person dies leaving no will, that person dies *intestate.* If the individual is married and his or her spouse is living, all property that was owned as joint tenants with right of survivorship or tenants by the entirety passes to the surviving spouse without any court process. If the decedent owned assets individually, a court proceeding called an *administration* must be started by a family member, friend, or anyone else who knows about the decedent's death.

An administration is similar to a probate proceeding, but there are some additional steps. The court will appoint an *administrator,* who takes on duties similar to those of a personal representative, or an executor, of a will. For the most part, the person or persons who start the administration proceeding request, through a legal document called a *petition,* that they be named as the administrator. In the administration process, unhappy relatives or other interested persons, such as creditors of the decedent, can challenge the petitions of would-be administrators.

Once appointed by the court, the administrator generally must post a bond equal to the value of the gross estate. In addition to other duties, the administrator must prove where the decedent resided and who the decedent's heirs are. These questions must be proved because generally the laws in the state in which the decedent resided determine which of a decedent's heirs receive his or her property.

How does the government know when a person dies?

In most states, the individual handling the funeral or memorial arrangements or the individual who pronounces death is required by law to notify the State Department of Vital Statistics.

The Need for a Lawyer

Do I need legal counsel on a person's death if the estate plan has been set up and funded or beneficiaries have been designated under life insurance, contracts, or retirement plans?

Yes. In every instance, a decedent's family, the personal representative of the decedent's estate, any trustees of the decedent's trust, and an experienced estate planning attorney should review the status of the decedent's estate plan and assets. Usually, when an estate plan was prepared, it was based on the financial, tax, and family situation at that time. In many situations, the estate plan may be fine as executed; but in some situations, there might be opportunities to reduce taxes or optimize other planning on an after-death basis. For instance, if the decedent died at a time when the surviving spouse was gravely ill, it may be wise to reconsider the allocation of assets to the surviving spouse for estate tax purposes.

There are opportunities under the laws to change the estate plan of a person by having potential recipients of the property "disclaim" their interest in the property. In other situations, elections under the estate planning documents may be made which would alter the tax consequences previously envisioned for the estate plan. These potential opportunities should be carefully reviewed with legal counsel and the family members that may be affected by the decisions.

If I hire an attorney to help me administer my spouse's trust upon death, who does that attorney represent?

This question is not asked often enough. In most situations, an attorney is retained to represent the trustee on behalf of the trust. Here, the attorney does not represent the beneficiaries in their individual capacities. The trustee has a fiduciary obligation to the beneficiaries, and the attorney must advise the trustee as to the exercise of these duties. The beneficiaries should retain their own attorneys if they believe this duty has been compromised by the trustee.

When the surviving spouse is a trustee *and* a beneficiary of a deceased spouse's trust, conflicts may arise. This is especially true if the surviving spouse is not the sole beneficiary. Conflicts may arise as to the proper distribution of the trust assets.

It is important that a surviving spouse who is a trustee and a beneficiary resolve the question as to whom the attorney represents before any administration of the trust begins. If there are multiple beneficiaries, the attorney should represent his or her client only in one capacity and all named beneficiaries should be apprised of the representative capacity of the attorney accordingly.

The Probate Process

What is the probate process?

The probate process is more fully discussed in Chapter 1. The *probate process* is, in a nutshell, a court proceeding that establishes the validity of a will and provides legal oversight to ensure accuracy in accounting for a decedent's assets, fairness in the treatment of heirs, and protection for the rights of the decedent's creditors.

Each state provides, by statute and rule of court, for various time limits and procedural steps for full probate of estates. The process begins with the presentation of the will for probate. The probate process can take anywhere from 3 months to 2 years or more, depending on the complexity of the estate and on whether there are any challenges to the validity of the will.

There are filing fees to the designated court as well as attorney fees for the duration of the probate process.

What assets have to go through death probate?

Assets which are titled in the decedent's name alone must go through death probate in order to be retitled into the name of his or her heirs. As an example, if I own some General Motors stock and only my name appears on the certificate, the only way my spouse or my children can gain ownership and control of that stock at my death is through probate. The probate court would actually issue an order assigning the ownership of the probate asset to my heirs. Pursuant to that order, the stock transfer agent would retire the certificate which had my name on it and reissue the certificate in the name of my heirs.

In contrast, assets which are owned by two or more persons as joint owners with right of survivorship do not go through death probate, as long as there is a surviving joint owner. Also, assets which are titled in a revocable living trust are not probated when the trust maker dies because they are titled in the name of the revocable trust, not in the name of the individual.

Are the assets which are in the probate process completely available to the family?

No. One of the major problems with probate is that the assets are for the most part tied up until the process is completed. There are some statutory allowances available for a widow, dependent children, and other family members. These allowances are meager at best and certainly cannot compare to what a family is used to in terms of having complete control over and access to all of a decedent's assets.

Who will handle getting out-of-state property distributed to my heirs?

If you die with property titled in your name and located in another state, an ancillary administration must be opened in the probate court of that state in addition to your residence state.

Certified copies of the will and other filings from your home probate court are sent to a law firm in the other state so that the firm can complete the probate process under its state's procedure. When this out-of-state proceeding is completed, then your heirs can receive their property.

DUTIES OF AN EXECUTOR OR PERSONAL REPRESENTATIVE

What are the differences between an executor, personal representative, and administrator?

All of these terms refer to the person a court appoints to administer an estate. When the law refers to a "person," the term includes bank trust departments and other corporate fiduciaries.

Executor or *executrix* (the legal term for a female executor) is the traditional term for a person named in a will and subsequently approved by the probate court to administer and distribute the property of a person who has died with a will. We inherited this term from England. *Personal representative* is the modern term for "executor." Many states have adopted statutes that replace the term "executor" with the term "personal representative."

An *administrator* or *administratrix* is the person appointed by a court to administer and distribute the property of a person who has died without a will (intestate).

For all but the most technical purposes, these terms can be used interchangeably.

I have been named an executor. What do I have to do with the decedent's assets?

As executor, you have the responsibility to gather all of the decedent's assets and report to the court by preparing and submitting an inventory. You recommend and the court appoints an appraiser to value real estate and anything else that doesn't have readily ascertainable values. The due date of the completed inventory is governed by state law.

You must then take possession of the assets, usually for several months, in order for creditors' claims to be filed and satisfied according to state law. After you have paid the decedent's debts, claims, and taxes from the probate assets, you can distribute the remaining property to the decedent's heirs as provided in the will. You then must prepare a final accounting and submit it to the probate court for approval.

As attorneys, what techniques do you use to determine the decedent's assets?

If a decedent has a previously prepared schedule of assets, this job is much simpler. If there is no schedule of assets, we normally attempt to locate as many of the deceased's financial documents as we possibly can, such as statements from financial institutions (e.g., bank accounts, brokerage accounts, IRA statements). We also attempt to locate deeds and mortgages, stock certificates, and life insurance policies in the decedent's name. Federal and state tax returns can be helpful in ascertaining a decedent's assets. Another technique we use is to contact the decedent's accountant and other attorneys, if possible, as they may have a clearer picture of the decedent's estate.

I have been appointed as personal representative to probate the estate of my great aunt. What are some of the most easily overlooked assets?

Easily overlooked assets include:

- Income tax refunds
- Overpayment of bills
- Prepaid deposits (damage deposits for rental property or utility deposits)
- Collections (coins, stamps, etc.)
- Antiques whose values are not recognized because they are thought to be junk
- Jewelry, precious gems, precious metals
- Corporate share certificates

- Time-share contracts for recreation properties in other states
- Real property in other counties, states, or countries
- Life insurance benefits and disability insurance benefits that are incidental to credit card accounts and savings accounts
- Old life insurance policies for small amounts
- Property entrusted by your great aunt to someone else
- Monies owed to your great aunt under fixed obligations such as mortgages
- Monies owed under obligations which are in dispute
- Monies held by a state agency under an "escheat" statute because your great aunt did not make deposits or withdrawals in bank accounts over a long period of time
- Money lent to loved ones on oral agreements for repayment (You may have to go through many years of your aunt's canceled checks for a long time to learn of the loans and to calculate the unpaid amounts owing at death.)
- Rights to reimbursements under medical insurance policies and long-term-care contracts

I am the personal representative for the estate of my grandfather. My grandfather told me that his estate was about $800,000, mostly in investment securities and bank accounts. My search for assets has disclosed about $400,000 in investment securities and a $400,000 savings account held jointly by my grandfather and the woman who was attending to his living needs. I have asked her to turn over the money in the joint savings account, but she refuses. I want to sue her. Will I win?

Whether you would win the lawsuit depends upon the answers to a number of questions:

- Does the law of your state raise a presumption that a nonspouse named as the surviving owner of a joint account holds that account as trustee for the estate of your grandfather?
- Does the law of your state raise the presumption that the joint account was intended only to permit lifetime withdrawals by the caretaker for the benefit of your grandfather and was not intended to give beneficial ownership to the caretaker upon your grandfather's death?

- Was your grandfather competent when he created the joint account?
- Did the caretaker assert undue influence over your grandfather to get him to create the joint account?
- When your grandfather created the joint account, did the caretaker orally assure him that after his death she would hold and apply the joint account as a trustee for some other person or for some other purpose?
- Would such an oral trust agreement be enforceable under the law of your state?

The attorney representing you as the personal representative of your grandfather's estate will conduct a preliminary investigation and perform preliminary legal research to form an opinion on which you may act. You should not be surprised if your claim against the caretaker is settled for a fraction of the joint account.

Is a personal representative liable to the estate's creditors?

In all states, the personal representative must wait until after the publication of notice to creditors or the expiration of a "nonclaim" period (generally 3 to 9 months, depending on state law) to distribute the estate's assets. If the personal representative does not wait the requisite period of time to distribute the assets of the estate, the decedent's creditors may commence a cause of action against the personal representative for failing to adequately provide for them.

PAYMENT OF LIABILITIES OF THE DECEDENT

What should the personal representative consider before payment of the decedent's debts?

Just as the personal representative has a duty to marshal the estate assets, he or she has the duty to determine all debts or claims against the estate. From the start of administration, the personal representative should keep a separate record of the decedent's debts and the payment of those debts.

The first questions the representative should ask are whether the obligation was created before death and whether the obligation is legally enforceable. If the obligation is not legally enforceable, such as a charitable pledge, the representative should definitely not give such payment equal standing with enforceable claims.

The representative should also determine whether an obligation contains a provision extinguishing the indebtedness upon death. For instance, if the decedent purchased credit life insurance on a mortgage or a major consumer purchase contract, the personal representative should be aware of the insurance contract provisions.

Are there priorities for the payment of a decedent's debts?

Yes. They are provided in your state's probate statute. Generally, first priority is given to administration expenses until paid in full, and the personal representative is protected in paying such expenses ahead of all debts, provided the expenses are reasonable and proper. Funeral expenses as well as those of the decedent's final illness receive second priority. Federal and state taxes receive next priority.

The personal representative should note that bequests cannot be safely paid until the time for presenting claims in accordance with state law has expired.

What procedure must the creditors of an estate follow to protect their rights?

While the procedures that creditors must follow to protect their rights when a debtor dies vary from state to state, typically a creditor of an estate must file a notice of claim within a specified time period, personally or by certified mail with return receipt requested, to the personal representative of the estate at his or her place of residence or to the clerk of the probate court.

If a creditor has not filed a notice of claim in a timely manner, may the personal representative distribute the estate assets?

Generally, yes. If the personal representative distributes estate assets in good faith after the nonclaim period, then he or she is not liable to creditors even if, for some reason, they may successfully receive a subsequent judgment against the estate.

After the beneficiaries have received the funds from an estate, can they be sued by the decedent's creditors?

Yes. The beneficiaries of an estate are liable to the decedent's creditors for up to the sum of money received as a distribution from the estate until the statute of limitations has run out on the creditors' claims.

A friend of the decedent has threatened to file a lawsuit against the estate for services rendered to the decedent. How does this affect the administration of the estate?

The personal representative must resolve every claim against the estate. If the matter cannot be settled or compromised, then a hearing can be set by the court and handled like any other lawsuit.

The person making the claim, in this case the decedent's friend, must prove that the services claimed were actually performed and that a contract was entered into for which payment was clearly to be made. Sometimes a friend may take care of a sick person, without payment, expecting an inheritance after the sick person's death. If the inheritance is not received or it is lower than expected, hard feelings occur. The outcome in any case can differ depending upon the facts.

Postdeath Administration for a Fully Funded Revocable Living Trust

My spouse and I have a fully funded joint revocable living trust. When one of us dies, what has to be done?

When the first trust maker dies, there is very little that the surviving spouse must do if all assets have been transferred to the trust. Probate is eliminated, although in some states you may be required to file the deceased spouse's pour-over will with the probate court as a matter of formality. If the deceased spouse had minor children, then the pour-over will would have to be filed with the probate court in order to determine their guardians. (If the children are from your marriage, this is not a requirement.)

The trustee may have to obtain a separate taxpayer identification number for the trust. The successor death trustees will become the primary trustees of the trust. *Affidavits of successor trustee,* which are legal documents stating that successor trustees have assumed the trusteeship, should be sent to all financial institutions so that these trustees have signatures on file and their authority to act on behalf of the trust is recognized.

If the assets of the deceased spouse are valued at $600,000 or more, then a federal estate tax return must be filed and the assets must be allocated between the marital and family trusts. In states that have an estate or inheritance tax, a return may have to be filed based upon the state's requirements. A final income tax return must also be prepared for the deceased spouse.

Specific bequests and distributions required by the trust should be made and any final bills paid. Within a few months of the death, it is a good idea to review the estate plan to determine if any further planning should be done.

What if my spouse and I have separate revocable living trusts and my spouse dies?

If your spouse's revocable trust was fully funded, the procedures are almost identical to those required for a joint living trust.

In our joint revocable living trust, there are provisions for a marital trust and a family trust. After one of us dies, how exactly are assets put into those trusts?

If provisions have been made in your trust for marital and family subtrusts, they must be established as separate trusts. Typically, the trustee will not have to physically transfer the assets to each trust. Accounting records can be set up which account for each trust. The value of each trust and how assets are allocated to each trust are set forth in your trust document in a *formula clause.* In many cases, the first $600,000 in assets, which is the maximum exemption equivalent amount, is allocated (on paper) to the family trust, with the balance of the assets allocated to the marital trust. This will provide for optimum estate tax planning on the death of the second spouse.

Incidentally, if you both had separate trusts, the process would be almost exactly the same.

If I have a funded living trust but have a $2500 account in my name, will a probate be required?

For small amounts of personal property that have not been funded into a living trust, you might consider a *voluntary administration,* which is allowed by statute in many states. A voluntary administration is not a formal probate; it is an informal probate for modest estates. To qualify, an estate must, as a rule, consist of only personal property valued under a specified statutory amount. If the estate qualifies, the voluntary administrator is not obligated to file a bond nor is he or she required to file an inventory or annual accounting. The voluntary administrator has full power to administer the estate. From the estate assets, funeral expenses and expenses of the last illness must be paid first, followed by debts of the decedent. If any assets remain, the administrator must distribute them to the surviving spouse or, if there is no surviving spouse, in accordance with the laws of intestacy.

If it appears that a voluntary administration will meet the trust maker's intent and will save the fees and delay of a formal probate, it should be considered.

After a maker of a revocable living trust dies, how can a loved one get access to his or her safety deposit box?

Upon the death of a trust maker, his or her living trust now becomes irrevocable. A new trustee(s) steps into the shoes of the trust maker. If the safety deposit box is titled in the name of the trust, the new trustee simply goes to the bank and shows proof of the trust maker's death, typically by showing a certified copy of the death certificate and either an affidavit of successor trustee or a copy of the part of the living trust that discusses successor trustees. After showing identification, the new trustee signs a new agreement allowing access to the box.

If the safety deposit box is not in the name of the trust, it is likely that a probate will have to be initiated in order for the bank to allow anyone to open the safety deposit box.

Of course, it helps greatly if the trust maker has kept his or her records up to date. In a properly drafted living trust plan, a portfolio of documents should include a list of where to find important documents and items such as safety deposit box keys.

DUTIES OF A TRUSTEE

What duty does the death trustee of a revocable living trust have to account to the beneficiaries?

Although the administration of a trust is usually accomplished outside of the review of the probate court, certain rules still apply and these rules may be enforced by trust beneficiaries. Accordingly, the prudent trustee will notify, in writing, all the beneficiaries named in the trust, including any contingent beneficiaries, of the existence of the trust and the death of the trust maker. Unless otherwise prohibited by the trust document, it is wise that all beneficiaries be supplied with a copy of the trust and that they be informed that they have the right to seek and employ legal counsel if that is their wish.

In most jurisdictions, the death trustee will have a duty to report and account to the beneficiaries named in the decedent's trust at least once a year. This requirement may generally be waived by the consent of the named beneficiaries or by express waiver granted in the decedent's trust instrument. However, good practice dictates a full accounting of all trust activity by the trustee to the named beneficiaries at frequent intervals to avoid any misunderstandings among them.

As a trustee, how do I make distributions from the trust and protect myself?

You, as a trustee, hold property for another's benefit and are held to the highest standard of care. This standard of care is called a *fiduciary duty.* You may have personal liability if you are negligent in the handling of trust assets and liabilities.

You must maintain accurate records regarding trust property, including additions of principal and income. Liabilities are even more critical because if an unexpected obligation pops up after you have distributed assets to the beneficiaries, it is difficult to retrieve the funds. You could become personally liable if you distributed funds without properly paying all creditors.

For these reasons it is always a good idea to hold some trust funds back for a year or more in order to allow plenty of time for any adjustments to income and estate tax returns you filed or for any final medical bills. When you are certain that all liabilities are covered, then it is safe to make final distributions to the beneficiaries.

On the death of a single trust maker, does the trust property immediately belong to the beneficiaries?

The trustee must first determine if there is any direction in the trust document from the trust maker or conditions placed upon the trustee which require that the trustee keep the trust in existence. For example, if there are minor or disabled beneficiaries, they probably would not receive their distribution until they reach a certain age or until the disability terminates.

The trust maker may have required that the trustee retain a particular asset in trust or require certain events to occur prior to the distribution or sale of the asset.

Is it true that my death trustee is allowed to distribute trust assets to beneficiaries, usually children, within a few days after my death?

Although your living trust, if fully funded, avoids probate, your death trustee must follow your trust's instructions. Those instructions usually require that your legitimate debts, income taxes, and death taxes be paid and that distributions be made to your beneficiaries. Since your trustee may be personally liable if he or she makes distributions to beneficiaries and then does not have enough money or property left in the trust to pay debts and taxes, your trustee must determine which debts and taxes should be paid from trust assets. This may take some time.

A well-advised trustee will consider partial distributions while the trustee retains assets sufficient to meet the contingencies for unsettled claims and undetermined taxes.

PAYMENT OF A TRUST MAKER'S LIABILITIES

If a decedent placed his or her assets in a living trust, are such assets beyond the reach of his or her creditors?

Upon a trust maker's death, a living trust, in many states, completely cuts off the claims of the maker's unsecured creditors. At least seven states, California, Massachusetts, Michigan, New Jersey, New York, Oregon, and Florida, do not follow this general rule of severing creditors' claims. These states allow creditors of the trust maker to use the maker's assets held in the trust to pay debts.

I am the successor trustee under my mother's revocable living trust. Just how far do I have to go in searching for persons who might have claims against my mother or against her trust?

If you are in a state whose law permits creditors to enforce their claims against such a living trust, the U.S. Supreme Court has made it clear that you must search diligently for creditors. Also, if the trust instrument itself requires that you pay creditors, you must search diligently for creditors.

If you fail to make diligent search and you distribute trust assets to beneficiaries, a successful claim may subject you to liability not only to the creditor but also to the beneficiaries against whom the creditor may seek remedy. Your fiduciary duties as trustee obligate you to exercise care, skill, and diligence in ascertaining the validity and enforceability of claims. If necessary, you are required to deny payment of a claim and to defend the claim in court.

You should find out from your attorney whether the law of your state permits you to publish notice to creditors as a part of the due-diligence process. Publication is one way that you can demonstrate that you have been diligent in searching for unknown creditors.

In a sense, your diligence can keep you from the "hot box" between failing to pay creditors you should pay from trust assets and paying creditors you should not pay from trust assets.

What are some good ways for me, as trustee, to find out who the maker's creditors are?

In your search for creditors, you should examine the maker's canceled checks, previously paid bills, pending unpaid bills, correspondence files, and unopened mail. You should inquire of liability insurers whether there is any known pending claim against the trust maker or against the trust itself.

Beware of creditors who falsely assert that they are entitled to accelerated payment of a debt not due; always insist on examining all written documentation to ascertain if amounts are really due.

If the maker was active in business, it is prudent to inquire whether claims for breaches of warranties or other contracts may reasonably be expected. If the maker was a partner, shareholder, or member in a partnership, corporation, or limited liability company, you should make reasonable inquiry of the other partners, shareholders, or members as to potential claims or debts.

An effective opening step in verification of debts or claims is to send a letter requesting verification of the absence of a claim for previously paid bills or, if there is a claim, the balance due, the amount of each current monthly payment, the absence of default by the maker, and other relevant features of the indebtedness.

What steps should I take if I find a claim against the maker or trust that I do not believe is valid?

Seek legal advice if you plan to reject a claim. Be cautious about rejection if an insurer will be obligated to defend the trust if legal action is brought.

Consider deferring distribution to beneficiaries of an amount that may be held as a contingency fund to cover unresolved claims.

If you are in doubt about whether a significant claim should be paid, consider asking a court for instruction so that you are protected from future personal liability to a creditor or to a beneficiary.

I am the trustee under my deceased father's trust. The trust owns a note secured by a mortgage. The borrower is in default. My lawyer says that the lawsuit to foreclose the mortgage will take 2 years and that the value of the land is only half of the amount of the expected foreclosure judgment. My brothers and sisters, as beneficiaries of the trust, are clamoring for distribution. I believe that I have paid all creditors to whom my father or his trust owed money. There is no death tax. What are my choices?

Here are your choices:

1. Under state law, you, as trustee, can ask for instructions from a court, but the time, expense, and uncertainty in getting instructions may dissuade you from this course of action.
2. You may distribute the note and all of your rights under a pending foreclosure action in fractional shares to the beneficiaries of the trust, allowing all of those beneficiaries to band together to pursue the foreclosure action.
3. You may tell your brothers and sisters to "cool it" while you press the foreclosure action to conclusion, but this may result in your brothers and sisters going to court to ask the judge to instruct you otherwise.
4. You may negotiate with one of more of your brothers or sisters to get an agreement by which the distributive share of one or more of them may include the note and the mortgage at an adjusted, or "discounted," value. These beneficiaries may then take a gamble to try to recover more than the "half" forecast by the estate's attorney.

TERMINATION OF A LIVING TRUST AFTER THE DEATH OF THE MAKER

Does my trust have to continue after I die?

No. Your trust will continue as an "administrative trust" after you die only for a period long enough to ensure that your trustee pays your debts and your taxes and gets the assets ready to make distributions.

Are there reasons to continue a trust for a period of time?

Absolutely. Many trust makers choose to have their trusts continue long after death so that the trustees can carry out their instructions for the benefit of children, grandchildren, and other beneficiaries. It may be that beneficiaries, in the opinion of the trust maker, are not ready to handle assets that otherwise might be given to them outright. A well-drafted living trust enables its maker to lay out loving instructions for each beneficiary.

How can I be sure that my trust won't run on and on when, applying good sense, it should be terminated?

A skillfully drafted living trust may contain permission for your trustee to terminate the trust when the trustee determines that the trust agreement has become uneconomical to administer due to the high cost of administration relative to the value of the trust property. Also, state law may allow the trustee to terminate the trust if continuance of the trust would defeat or substantially impair the accomplishment of the purposes of the trust. The trustee should always seek legal counsel before terminating the trust to avoid violating state law or the terms of the trust agreement.

What happens to the assets in the trust when the trust is terminated early?

If the trustee terminates the trust under the authority stated in the trust instrument, the instrument should spell out who gets the trust assets. Often, early termination gives the assets to the trust maker if the trust maker is living or to the spouse of the trust maker if the spouse is a beneficiary of the trust. If neither of them is living, then other beneficiaries should be listed.

If the trust is terminated early under the authority of a state statute, the state statute usually lists who gets the trust assets. If necessary, a court will clear up the matter, although this should be avoided if possible.

Qualified Disclaimers

What is a disclaimer?

A *disclaimer* is an irrevocable and unqualified refusal to accept an interest in property. The effect of a disclaimer is as if no transfer was made to or from the person making the disclaimer. Most states have statutes that allow disclaimers and set forth how disclaimers are made.

What is a qualified disclaimer?

A disclaimer is "qualified" if it meets the requirements of Section 2518 of the Internal Revenue Code. These requirements are:

- The disclaimer must be in writing.
- The disclaimer must be delivered to the person who is attempting to transfer the interest, to his or her legal representative, or to the holder of the legal title to the property interest.
- The disclaimer must be delivered not later than 9 months after the date of the transfer creating the interest or 9 months after the person making the disclaimer becomes 21.
- The person making the disclaimer must not have accepted the interest or any of its benefits.
- As a result of the disclaimer, the property must pass, without any direction on the part of the person making the disclaimer, either to the spouse of the person making the transfer or to someone other than the person making the disclaimer.

Why would anyone wish to disclaim an interest in property left to him or her by a decedent?

Generally, disclaimers are exercised to redirect property to another person either for tax purposes or as a reallocation of assets for nontax purposes. As an example, if a parent died leaving all his or her property to the parent's two children or their issue and one of the children is terminally ill, it may be to the advantage of that terminally ill child to disclaim the property that he or she would receive from his or her parent. The property, by such a disclaimer, will then pass automatically to the terminally ill child's children without being included in the estate of the terminally ill child. The transfer will be treated as a transfer from the deceased parent directly to the grandchildren. This has the effect of eliminating federal estate tax in the terminally ill child's estate.

The same result may be desirable in the case of a child whose estate is already substantial. That child may prefer to have the property pass directly to his or her children.

As another example, if property was left to two children or to the survivor of the children and one of the children feels that his or her sibling should receive that property, that child could disclaim his or her interest in the property in favor of the sibling.

There are a variety of situations in which a disclaimer of an interest can be particularly useful in planning for family members. Individuals should obtain counsel prior to making decisions to accept or to reject property to determine if disclaimers may be appropriate in specific situations.

My husband just died, and I don't need all of the $500,000 that he left me. I have separate property and separate income, which are more than adequate for my care into my old age. I tried to talk my husband into leaving the $500,000 directly to our children, but he said that his attorney had told him that I could divert the $500,000 by a disclaimer. Can I do that?

Whether a disclaimer is available as a technique to divert the $500,000 to your children depends upon the manner in which you are receiving the $500,000.

First, if the $500,000 is coming to you under a joint and survivor account that you and your husband created, you probably will not be permitted to disclaim the $500,000 and thereby divert it to your children. If your state law permits you to disclaim, it is possible that the diverted amount will have to go through probate.

Second, if the $500,000 comes to you under a trust or a will that also allows property to pass to your children if you do not survive your husband, the disclaimer will divert the benefit to your children.

Third, does your husband's trust or will say that the $500,000 goes to someone other than your children if you should disclaim? Your husband's direction will prevail because you are not permitted to say who receives the disclaimed property. The recipient of the disclaimed property is determined by operation of law or by direction of your husband.

If a disclaimer is not available to you, you can still receive the $500,000 and attempt to give it to your children over a number of years by making gifts within your $10,000 annual exclusion.

It is possible that your estate planning attorney would advise you to use some of your $600,000 exemption equivalent to give the entire $500,000 to your children now. For example, if you have three children and they have an opportunity to use the $500,000 now to purchase an asset that is expected to rise rapidly in value before your death, you might use $470,000 of your unified credit exemption equivalent by filing a gift tax return showing that you have used three $10,000 annual exclusions for your children and $470,000 of your unified credit exemption equivalent. The appreciated, or increased, value of the asset at your death will be excluded from your death taxable estate, but the threshold at which you will pay taxes on your estate at your death will be lowered by $470,000.

It is important to remember that even if a disclaimer is effective in diverting the benefit to your children, it may not be an effective tax strategy because the disclaimed property is not eligible for the marital deduction in your husband's estate. Estate taxes may have to be paid as a result. A disclaimer should be carefully thought out before it is carried out.

I may receive an inheritance from my parents under the terms of their estate plan after they are both deceased. I do not need this money, and I would rather have it pass to my children. Is there a way that I can get the property to my children without incurring gift taxes?

This is a perfect situation for using a qualified disclaimer. If you disclaim your inheritance after your parents are deceased, the assets will pass as if you were deceased at the time of your surviving parent's death. The recipient of those assets in this event will be determined by the terms of your surviving parent's will or trust. If the document provides that in the event of your death, your share will pass to your children in equal shares, then your children will receive the assets which you have disclaimed. You will not be deemed to have made a gift to your children for gift tax purposes.

Please remember, however, that these assets may still be subject to federal estate taxation in your parent's estate. The disclaimer will eliminate disclaimed assets from your estate and allow them to pass to your children free of gift tax; the assets will be included in the estate of the last one of your parents to die.

The disclaimer is an incredibly useful tool for leveraging the amount of gifts which you can make during your lifetime without gift tax liability. There is no limit on the amount you can disclaim, and all assets which you disclaim to your children will escape estate taxes upon your death.

There may, however, be generation-skipping transfer taxes in your surviving parent's estate if the disclaimer results in property passing to beneficiaries who are more than one generation below your surviving parent. Note that your surviving parent has a $1 million exemption for generation-skipping transfers which may eliminate this tax. Generation-skipping transfer taxes should be discussed with your estate planning attorney prior to your making this disclaimer. In fact, because of all the limitations and traps that exist around disclaimers, it is critical that you consult an estate planning attorney immediately after you become aware of your right to any asset which you may want to disclaim.

Can jointly owned property between spouses be disclaimed?

Yes, jointly owned property may be disclaimed. However, state law controls the starting point for the surviving spouse's ability to disclaim his or her *survivorship interest.* The survivorship interest, which is the survivor's right to the property held jointly, may be disclaimed by the surviving spouse if the joint tenancy can be severed or partitioned under state law. Phrased another way, if the surviving spouse had the absolute right to take his or her share of the property during life by partitioning (splitting up) the property without the other spouse's consent, the surviving spouse has 9 months from the date of his or her spouse's death to execute a qualified disclaimer.

Your attorney will look to state law as to whether an interest may be severed by either spouse during life. This is especially true for real property which is owned in tenancy by the entirety. In one case in Maryland, the IRS denied an attempted disclaimer of a real property interest within 9 months after the first joint tenant's death. The IRS determined that under Maryland law, tenancy-by-the-entirety property can be partitioned only with the consent of both parties. Because both parties were required to partition the property, the survivorship interest was created when title to the property was taken, not at the death of the first joint tenant. The disclaimer had to be made within 9 months of the transfer of the property into tenancy by the entirety to be effective, not within 9 months after the date of the death of a joint tenant.

The Spousal Election

What is the spousal election?

In almost all states, a surviving spouse who has not inherited a certain minimum amount provided by state law has a right to take a share of the deceased spouse's estate. This right is known as the *spousal election,* or the surviving spouse's right of election.

States differ regarding not only the amount of this election but also what property the election applies to. In some states, the spousal election is one-third of the deceased spouse's estate. In others, it is one-half or more.

What assets are subject to the spousal election?

This varies from state to state. In many states, these assets include:

- All assets titled in the name of the deceased spouse
- Assets that were given as gifts by the deceased spouse in anticipation of his or her death
- Any property interests transferred by the deceased spouse to or for the benefit of another person within 1 year of his or her death for which the deceased spouse did not receive adequate and full consideration
- Bank accounts in joint names and payable on death
- Money in savings accounts in the name of the decedent in trust for another person
- Any interest in property that is subject to a general power of appointment by the decedent
- Pension benefits and stock bonus or profit-sharing plans

How do I claim my spousal elective rights?

The spousal election statutes are generally very technical and impose strict time limits for claiming the elective share. These statutes vary from state to state and may be amended from time to time. You should consult an attorney with regard to your rights in a particular state immediately after the death of a spouse.

Spousal elective rights are required to be asserted within specific time limits after the death of an individual. The elective rights are considered a personal right of the surviving spouse and in some states cannot be claimed by children or others acting on behalf of the surviving spouse unless specific written authorization is given to make the claim.

I am in a second marriage, and I have a will that excludes my present spouse and transfers all of my assets to my children from my first marriage. Can my present spouse still take part of my probate estate?

Most likely the answer is yes. Most states allow a spousal election for a surviving spouse. If your spouse does not like the terms of your will, he or she can elect to receive that portion of your estate that is allowed by state law.

What if I signed a premarriage agreement waiving my right to an elective share of my spouse's estate?

In most states, a spousal election can be waived in a valid premarriage agreement. If you have concerns, you should have your attorney review your premarriage agreement for its validity and you should ask if your state allows the waiver of the spousal election in a premarriage agreement.

Income Taxes after Death

A DECEDENT'S FINAL INCOME TAX RETURN

Why must an income tax return be filed after the death of an individual?

During that portion of a tax year that a decedent was living, income was received under his or her own Social Security number. That income was reported to the state and federal governments along with appropriate tax withholdings. A final return is required to be filed with the federal, state, and local governments after the death of an individual to pay any remaining taxes or to claim refunds for this tax period.

In the case of a married individual, the final return may be part of a joint return with the surviving spouse.

What items should be reported on a decedent's final income tax return?

Any income actually received on a cash basis as well as any expenses that were actually paid should be reported on a decedent's final 1040 return. The tax period between the beginning of a person's taxable year (almost always January 1) and the date of his or her death is treated as the tax period for which Form 1040 and the state income tax return must be filed.

Can a joint income tax return be filed in the year that a spouse dies?

Yes. A joint return may be filed with the decedent's surviving spouse provided that spouse does not remarry before the close of the tax year. The return must include the surviving spouse's income for the entire tax year. The decedent's personal exemption can be used.

Authorization for the personal representative (or trustee) to file a joint return should be stated in the decedent's will or trust document.

This option should always be explored because a joint return may well reduce total tax liability.

My brother recently died, and I am the executor of his estate. He lived in a nursing home for years and has never filed an income tax return. What should I do?

You should promptly seek the advice of a tax preparer who can examine all of the information that you can make available for the purpose of determining whether, in fact, your brother should have filed income tax returns. If your brother should have filed income tax returns, you should now consider filing returns for prior years and pay necessary tax from estate assets or trust assets as the case may be. As executor of your brother's estate, your failure to file a return can make you individually liable for tax to the extent of the value of the estate assets or the trust assets under your control. You can find yourself in a bind if you ignore your duty to file income tax returns and pay taxes and you distribute assets to your brother's heirs.

INCOME RECEIVED AFTER THE DECEDENT'S DEATH

How is income that is received after the decedent's date of death reported?

Any income received after the decedent's death is reported on the estate's income tax return, the trust's income tax return (if the decedent had a living trust), or the returns of the beneficiaries who received income.

When my mother died, she had some U.S. savings bonds. Who must report this income?

There are some elections that can be made regarding the reporting of certain accrued interest on U.S. savings bonds. The income can be reported on your mother's final income tax return; it can be reported on her estate's tax return; or, under some circumstances, the heirs can report it.

Determining who should report the income is based on a number of factors such as the tax brackets of your mother, the estate, and the beneficiaries. If there is more than one beneficiary, this income may be divided by the number of beneficiaries receiving the income, which may result in insufficient income to place the beneficiary in a higher tax bracket.

In addition, since it is possible to deduct certain expenses on either a federal estate tax return or the decedent's final income tax return, the determination as to who shall pay income taxes on the interest will be affected by which return reflects the expenses.

A prudent trustee or executor will consult with a knowledgeable advisor to determine the existence of a decedent's income. He or she will also consult with the beneficiaries to determine the most beneficial place to report these items.

INCOME RECEIVED IN A LIVING TRUST AFTER THE DEATH OF THE MAKER

Who pays tax on the income generated after the death of a trust maker who had a fully funded revocable living trust?

If a living trust can be terminated quickly after the death of the trust maker and preferably within the same tax year as his or her death, the trustee will pass the income to be reported directly to the beneficiaries who receive the income. If the distributions are made to other trusts, such as a marital or family trust, then the income may have to be reported on that trust's income tax return.

If it appears that the trust cannot be terminated quickly, then the trustee creates an *administrative trust* with its own taxpayer identification number. An administrative trust is much like a probate estate in that it has its own income tax bracket. The administrative trust reports the income.

If the trust is in order and the assets are easy to distribute, why would a trustee create an administrative trust?

The primary reason for creating an administrative trust is to allow the trustee sufficient time to review his or her duties and to make sure that all prudent decisions and elections are made. An administrative trust also allows the trustee and the beneficiaries the time to:

- Decide if disclaimers should be made and then make such disclaimers.
- Make decisions concerning valuation and alternate valuation of assets.
- Determine on what income tax return income should be reported and deductions taken.

Unless there are few income-producing assets and none of the above considerations apply, the better approach is to establish an administrative trust and allow sufficient time to properly evaluate the trust and the correct course of action for complete distribution.

Does the administrative trust pay income tax estimates?

Most trusts must pay quarterly estimates, but under Section

6654(1)(2)(B) of the Internal Revenue Code, an administrative trust whose purpose is to complete the trust in a reasonable time will qualify for a 2-year exemption from quarterly estimates.

AFTER-DEATH INCOME TAX CONSIDERATIONS

What issues should be considered when electing a tax year for a trust or a probate estate?

An executor of an estate may elect a fiscal tax year. The first year can be a full 12-month period or can be a short year followed by a 12-month period. For example, a decedent may die on March 2. The executor may decide that he or she would like to have a tax year that begins on June 1. A short-year income tax return would then be filed for the probate estate income and expenses for the period from March 2 through May 31. Thereafter, the tax year for the probate estate would be from June 1 through May 31.

The successor trustee of a trust has no such option. A calendar year must be used. In the above example, the trust's first tax year would begin on March 2 and end on December 31. Thereafter, the trust's tax year would be a calendar year.

Why did the attorney for my spouse's probate estate specify the close of the tax year for the estate as April 30?

In selecting the ending date for the tax year of an estate, the requirement is that the first tax year end on a date which is at the end of any month and within 12 months of the date of death. For this reason, the first tax year of the estate will usually be less than a full 12 months. Any initial tax year of less than 11 months may be chosen and usually an ending date other than December 31 is selected. An early to midyear ending date for the estate's tax year presents more opportunity for shifting income into a different calendar tax year for the beneficiaries.

The attorney was not simply requiring that an extra tax return be filed. Each estate is required to file a tax return reporting any income that it has received and may also use that tax return to report expenses and losses allocated to the beneficiaries of the estate for deduction purposes. By selecting a tax year with an ending date other than December 31, the estate has some flexibility in timing the distribution of assets. If the estate sells an asset of the decedent at a gain over date-of-death values, the recognition of gain by the beneficiary may be deferred to a later year if the estate's tax year ends in the next calendar year. The gain on that sale may be distributed to the beneficiary and reported for a tax year in which the beneficiary is in a lower income tax bracket. For instance, if the surviving spouse will receive less income in the next calendar year because the decedent's earnings are no longer available, then the surviving spouse may be in a lower tax bracket. If the capital gain on the sale of an asset is carried forward and reported as distributed to the surviving spouse in the later calendar year, a tax savings may result because the surviving spouse is in a lower tax bracket. This income-shifting technique could occur between any two years during the administration of the estate to reduce income taxes.

Is this deferral technique always effective?

One of the problems of deferring income into other tax years is that "bunching" can occur. Bunching means that income is deferred into another year that has high income. This creates taxation at a higher tax bracket because 2 years' worth of income is bunched into 1 year. It is not uncommon in an estate for bunching to occur in the year the estate is closed. That is why great care must be taken when using a fiscal year to defer income; deferral has a habit of biting back!

Are there any tax reasons that I should be paid as personal representative of my father's estate?

Every personal representative performs duties and bears responsibilities which justify the payment of a fee. However, the personal representative is not required to accept a fee. Any fees received are taxable income for local, state, and federal purposes.

If a personal representative is also an heir of the estate, it may be that an estate distribution which is not subject to income tax would produce a greater benefit to the beneficiary/executor.

The income tax on a fee may be avoided only if the fee is waived. To effectively waive the fee, the personal representative should make an early written statement disclaiming the intent to receive the fee. The Internal Revenue Service and some state revenue departments may impose a tax on an imputed fee to the personal representative if the disclaimer is not made early and in a sufficiently definite form.

This tax trap is of more significance in large estates with potentially substantial fees. Attorneys representing estates should place the waiver-of-fees issue near the top of their administration checklist so that it can be discussed and decided upon at the earliest possible time.

Should the personal representative retain income in the estate during the administration or distribute it to the beneficiaries?

Retaining income in a decedent's estate is always a concern because the income tax rates on estates are very compressed and very oppressive. If it appears that the deductible expenses will not zero out the taxable income, it is usually wise to distribute the income to the estate beneficiaries because such a distribution is deductible and avoids payment of income tax at the estate level on the income distributed.

The individual beneficiary who receives the income distribution will pay the income tax on it at typically a much more favorable income tax rate. However, the probate court's permission may be required for such a distribution, and it will be necessary to show that there is sufficient liquidity in the estate to pay any anticipated expenses.

If I receive a distribution of an appreciated asset from a decedent's estate, what is my cost basis for calculating capital gain if I sell the asset?

Your basis is the fair market value of the asset on the decedent's date of death. You receive a step-up in basis from the decedent's basis to the fair market value of the distributed assets.

Federal Estate Taxes

THE FEDERAL ESTATE TAX RETURN

When must a federal estate tax return be filed?

A federal estate tax return (Form 706) must be filed and tax paid, if any, 9 months after the decedent's death. If it is impossible or impracticable for the estate tax return to be filed within 9 months, the IRS may grant a reasonable extension of time for filing. Nevertheless, the tax is still due within 9 months unless an extension to pay the tax is granted and authorized by a specific IRS Code section.

Who must file an estate tax return?

A federal estate tax return is required if a decedent's gross estate is valued at $600,000 or more. If a person made lifetime taxable gifts so that his or her estate is less than $600,000 upon death, these gifts must be added back into the value of the estate. If, after adding them back, the decedent's gross estate is $600,000 or more, a federal estate tax return is required, even if no tax is due.

When assets are included in my estate for estate tax purposes, how are they valued and must they be appraised?

Assets are included in a decedent's gross estate at their fair market values. *Fair market value* is defined, for federal estate tax purposes, as the price at which the property would change hands between a willing buyer and a willing seller, neither being under any compulsion to buy or sell and both having reasonable knowledge of all relevant facts. For example, if you died owning a car, the fair market value of the car would be the retail value of the car: not what a used-car dealer would pay you for the car, but the price at which the used-car dealer would resell the car.

There are special rules, though, for some types of property, such as life insurance policies, interests in trusts, and shares of mutual funds, to name a few.

If you die owning any real estate, that property should be appraised for estate tax purposes. Also, if you die owning an interest in a closely held business, a qualified business appraiser should be hired to determine the fair market value of that business interest. As for your personal property—such as your household furniture, your camping equipment, your kitchen utensils, and so on—it generally does not need to be appraised. However, if you own some very valuable personal property, then the person who administers your estate should balance the cost of an appraisal of your personal assets against the likelihood that the IRS will challenge the value and initiate a potentially expensive legal battle.

Who will be responsible for valuing my assets after my death?

Assets that have readily ascertainable values, such as CDs and bank accounts, do not have to be appraised in order to determine their value. Assets such as real estate or business interests should be appraised because their fair market values are sometimes subjective and thus subject to IRS challenge.

In probate, the probate court will appoint either an appraiser recommended by the personal representative or a person from a list the court maintains. If you have done trust planning, your trustee will hire certified appraisers to value your property as needed.

How are U.S. Series EE and H bonds valued for federal estate tax purposes?

They are valued at their redemption value on the applicable valuation date.

ALTERNATE VALUATION DATE

What happens if the value of my assets plummets soon after I die? It doesn't seem fair to make my estate pay taxes on the value of my assets on the date of my death if my assets are worth much less by the time my estate actually pays the taxes.

The general rule is that assets are valued for estate tax purposes at their fair market values on the date of the decedent's death. But if certain conditions are met, the assets can be valued on the *alternate valuation date* rather than on the date of death. The alternate valuation date is the date that is 6 months after the date of death. Or if the estate sells some assets within that 6-month period, then, for those assets that were sold, the alternate valuation date is the date of the sale.

For example, assume that you die on January 1 owning a car and some General Motors stock. Also assume that the personal representative of your estate sells your General Motors stock on March 1 but does not sell your car. If your estate elects to value your property on the alternate valuation date, your General Motors stock will be valued on March 1 and your car will be valued on July 1. Note that you cannot value some assets on the date of death and other assets on the alternate valuation date. You must value all assets on the date of death, or you must value all assets on the alternate valuation date.

What are the requirements for electing to use the alternate valuation date?

There are three requirements that must be met to be eligible to elect the alternate valuation date:

1. The total value of the decedent's gross estate must decrease by using the alternate valuation date.
2. The amount of the estate taxes must decrease by using the alternate valuation date.
3. The person who files the decedent's estate tax return must make the proper election on the return.

A word of caution: There might be adverse income tax consequences to utilizing the alternate valuation date, and they should also be considered. If the alternate valuation date is chosen, the cost basis of the assets will not be the date-of-death value; it will be the alternate valuation date value. Thus, if assets appreciate in value and are then sold, the income taxes may be greater. This issue should be thoroughly explored by the estate's or trust's tax advisors before deciding which valuation date should be used.

Is there any disadvantage if a death trustee of a revocable living trust distributes assets that have gone down in value prior to the elapse of 6 months after the date of death?

The alternate valuation of assets for calculating federal estate tax is available only in the event that a reduction in tax is ultimately realized. The date of disposition of an asset determines its value for tax purposes. Accordingly, if an asset is depreciating in value or is likely to further depreciate in value during the 6 months after a decedent's death, the prudent trustee will wait until the full elapse of the 6-month period. Any distribution made prior to that time will "arrest" the value as of the date of disposition, while the additional passage of time may have allowed the trustee to have taken advantage of an additional depreciated value.

THE ELECTION FOR QUALIFIED TERMINABLE INTEREST PROPERTY

What does the estate tax QTIP election do?

QTIP stands for "qualified terminable interest property." A QTIP election must be made on the federal estate tax return to ensure that qualified terminable interest property qualifies for the marital deduction.

How does my personal representative or trustee make the election to treat the property I leave for my spouse as QTIP property?

When you die, the person who is responsible for administering your estate (your personal representative or trustee) must file an estate tax return (Form 706) with the IRS. All of the property that is part of your gross estate must be listed. This includes all of the property which is being transferred to your surviving spouse and for which your estate is to receive an estate tax marital deduction.

Your representative makes the election to treat certain property as QTIP property simply by listing that property on Schedule M of Form 706.

In order for the election to be valid, the estate tax return must be filed on time. Also, the election must be made on the first estate tax return to be filed—it cannot be made on an amended return. Furthermore, once the election has been made, it cannot be revoked.

PAYMENT OF FEDERAL ESTATE TAXES

I understand that federal estate taxes are due within 9 months after my death. Is there any way to arrange installment payments of federal estate taxes?

Yes. If a substantial portion of your wealth consists of an interest in a farm or a closely held business, your estate may not have enough liquid funds to pay the estate taxes attributable to that farm or closely held business. Unless your estate can postpone the payment of some of the estate taxes, your estate might be forced to sell the farm or business interest at a distress price in order to pay the estate taxes within 9 months after your death.

The Internal Revenue Code contains an exception to the 9-month rule for estates which consist largely of a farm or business interest. If certain requirements are met, your estate can elect to defer the payment of some of the estate taxes for 5 years. During that 5-year period, your estate will have to pay interest on the deferred taxes. Then, at the end of the fifth year, your estate must begin to pay the estate taxes (while continuing to pay interest on the unpaid amount) in ten or fewer equal annual installments.

Not all of your estate taxes can be paid in installments. Only that portion of your estate taxes which is attributable to your farm or business interest can be paid in installments.

To be eligible for installment payments, the following requirements must be met:

- The decedent must have been a U.S. citizen.
- The value of the farm or business interest must be more than 35 percent of the decedent's adjusted gross estate.
- The person who files the decedent's estate tax return must make an election on the return to pay the taxes in installments.

SPECIAL-USE VALUATION

I heard that if I own a farm or a small business, I might be able to avoid some estate taxes. Is that true?

The Internal Revenue Code contains a *special-use valuation* provision by which the land on which a farm or a small business is operated can be valued for estate tax purposes at an amount well below its fair market value.

Generally, land is valued at its highest-and-best-use value, meaning that if the property would be worth more if you had been using it in a different way, then the property is valued at a higher value as though you had been using it in that different and more valuable way. For instance, assume that you owned a building in the middle of downtown in which you rented apartments. If valued as an apartment building, that building may be worth $500,000, but if you had been renting out office space in that building, rather than apartments, the building would be worth $600,000. The building is valued for estate tax purposes at its highest-and-best-use value—$600,000—even though you were not using it for its highest and best use.

Farmers and owners of small businesses are typically hardest hit by this highest-and-best-use rule. There can be a huge difference between the value of land used for farming and the value of the same land if it were subdivided and developed into a new neighborhood. Also, land often is the primary asset of farmers and small-business owners. So in order to meet the high estate taxes attributable to the land, farmers and small-business owners might have to sell the land, usually at distress prices.

Congress, in recognizing that this result is often inequitable, amended the Internal Revenue Code to permit farmers and small-business owners to value their land at its special-use value rather than at its highest-and-best-use value. The total decrease in value, from the highest-and-best-use value to the special-use value, cannot exceed $750,000.

Numerous detailed requirements must be met to be eligible for special-use valuation. These requirements can be summarized as follows:

- The land must be located in the United States.
- The decedent or a member of the decedent's family must have owned the land for 5 out of the 8 years immediately preceding the decedent's death.
- The decedent or a member of the decedent's family must have used the land as a farm or in another business for 5 out of the 8 years immediately preceding the decedent's death.
- The decedent or a member of the decedent's family must have actively participated in the farming or other business for 5 out of the 8 years immediately preceding the decedent's death.
- Fifty percent or more of the adjusted value of the decedent's estate (valued at its highest-and-best-use value) must consist of the adjusted value of the land and personal property that was used for the farm or business. The *adjusted value* is the value of the land or personal property reduced by any debt that is secured by the land or personal property.
- Twenty-five percent or more of the adjusted value of the decedent's estate must consist of the adjusted value of the land that was used for the farm or business.
- The land must pass from the decedent's estate to members of the decedent's family, and those members of the decedent's family who receive the land must agree to continue to operate the farm or business on the property for at least 10 years after the decedent's death.

FLOWER BONDS

What are flower bonds, and why did my attorney include a reference to flower bonds in my trust?

Flower bonds are specifically designated pre-1971 U.S. Treasury securities which may be useful in reducing federal estate taxes. These

U.S. Treasury bonds bear low interest rates and trade on the open market at a discount from their face value. If such bonds are held by the decedent at the date of death, they may be used for the payment of federal estate taxes at their face value.

These bonds are said to "flower" because they then have an added, untaxed value for the estate. The bonds themselves, of course, are estate assets and are taxable at their market value.

The savings to the estate result because the bonds are redeemable at the higher face value if they are surrendered to pay federal estate taxes even though they were purchased at a discount. Your trustee under a revocable living trust should be authorized to use such bonds on your behalf to make this benefit available to your estate.

USING A SECTION 303 REDEMPTION TO PAY FEDERAL ESTATE TAXES

What is a Section 303 redemption and when is it used?

Internal Revenue Code Section 303 allows a C or S corporation to make a distribution in partial redemption of stock from the decedent's estate. There are generally no income tax consequences to the estate because of the step-up-in-basis rules.

A Section 303 redemption is used to allow the estate to keep control of the family corporation and redeem stock to meet the estate's death taxes and other administrative and funeral costs.

APPENDIX A

How to Find, Work with, and Pay a Qualified Estate Planning Attorney

The inability to find the *right* estate planning attorney is an often-expressed frustration of many people. It is difficult for nonprofessionals to know what degree of legal sophistication an attorney should have to plan their estates. People often take on faith that "any attorney" is competent to plan an estate, and this misplaced confidence most often works to their and their families' detriment. And competent estate planning attorneys often voice their disappointment that potential clients yield to the temptation of shopping for price rather than quality when it comes to legal services.

The truth is that attorneys have varying degrees of skill in any area of the law; they are no different from physicians, athletes, or any other paid professionals. The fee an attorney charges is certainly one of the many relevant factors that should be measured in making the appropriate "hiring decision," but it is not—by any means—the only factor.

An attorney-client relationship should be based on a bond of trust and understanding that is developed by open and honest communication. It should necessitate a mutual commitment that both the client and the attorney will help each other in maintaining this bond of trust and respect.

Our contributing authors were very concerned about the entire aspect of choosing and working with a qualified attorney. They went to great lengths to describe all of the criteria by which an attorney should be assessed. The result is a comprehensive discussion of the competence needed for an attorney to be able to design, draft, and implement a better-than-average estate plan.

We found particularly interesting the use of estate planning software to create one's own estate plan. Technology has changed the lives of Americans and has given us more access to more information than at any time in history. Whether this wealth of new information has helped or hindered the search for knowledge is a topic that will be debated for years, but the exposure to the information has certainly expanded the horizons for all of us.

Technology, and the information that goes with it, does not grant instant understanding or expertise. It merely allows us to become broader generalists who can know just enough to ask the right questions. This chapter addresses the questions of technology very well and demonstrates the folly that a little knowledge can create.

This chapter is must reading for anyone who is concerned with or confused about how to find a competent estate planning attorney and how to work successfully within the attorney-client relationship. It answers some very tough questions about fees and the quality of services that people should expect. We hope that you enjoy the perspectives found in this chapter as much as we did in editing them.

Who should prepare my estate plan: an insurance agent, an accountant, a financial advisor, a stockbroker, or an attorney?

Each of these professionals can be a valuable and integral member of an estate planning team that is led by a qualified estate planning attorney.

It is illegal for a person who is not licensed to practice law to perform legal services, and the preparation of estate planning documents is the practice of law.

There are many businesses and salespeople masquerading as estate planning professionals. They offer to sell estate planning documents such as wills, revocable living trusts, or irrevocable life insurance trusts without involving an attorney in the design or drafting of the estate planning documents on the pretense that it will be "cheaper" for the clients. In truth, they are in the business of deceiving consumers.

Florida, Iowa, Kansas, Minnesota, Maine, Massachusetts, Nebraska, New Mexico, Ohio, Texas, and Wisconsin, to name a few states, have brought legal proceedings against companies allegedly using scare tactics to sell boilerplate living trusts for thousands of dollars more than they are worth.

Invariably, the boilerplate documents create major problems, and when these problems ultimately surface, both the companies and their salespeople will have disappeared.

What is the unauthorized practice of law as it relates to estate planning?

By law, attorneys have exclusive authority to draft legal documents and to render legal advice, just as physicians are licensed to practice medicine.

In relation to estate planning, many courts have ruled that meeting with clients to advise them about estate planning, retitling assets for their plans, and assembling, drafting, and executing estate planning documents are the practice of law. Therefore, if any organizations or individuals that are not licensed to practice law perform these functions, even if they are not working directly with clients, they are engaging in the unauthorized practice of law.

What's wrong with estate planning packages sold by nonattorneys?

Estate planning documents prepared by nonattorneys create major problems for loved ones, including:

- They may not work in your state because they may have been prepared under another state's law.
- They are pure boilerplate and not likely to meet your planning situation.
- They may cause you unnecessary taxes and expenses.
- Even if drawn properly, they most likely will not work unless they have been funded properly as well.
- Their many mistakes and deficiencies will not come to light until after your death.

People should not shy away from living trusts and other estate planning tools just because they are being improperly sold but, rather, should seek out the advice of qualified attorneys with regard to them.

One commentator's wry observation on will and living trust hucksters says it all: "There is no reason to buy anything from anybody who comes to the door unless they are about four feet tall and selling Girl Scout cookies."

Can I have a paralegal or someone other than an attorney prepare my trust?

Paralegals are legal assistants who may or may not have formal training. By law, paralegals are allowed to assist attorneys and laypersons in filling out paperwork, but they are not licensed to practice law.

Many insurance agents, certified financial planners, stockbrokers, and others hold seminars throughout the community extolling the virtues of proper estate planning and the use of living trusts. These people, as long as they are not giving individual advice to the seminar attendees or preparing documents for these people, provide a valuable educational service.

There is no substitute, however, for a fully qualified estate planning attorney, and presentations that do not have attorneys present should be suspect.

I am working with a financial planner in whom I have a great deal of confidence. Why can't she prepare my estate plan?

A competent financial planner can provide you with a wide variety of professional and educational services. Depending upon his or her level of expertise, qualifications, and certification, he or she may perform comprehensive financial planning/analysis; assist in the creation, development, and implementation of short-, medium-, and long-range financial planning goals; act as the registered broker/dealer for purposes of purchasing various investments; recommend various estate planning concepts; and act as a sounding board regarding the performance of various investments.

Despite all of these beneficial services that a financial planner can provide, one service that a financial planner cannot legally provide is the preparation of legal documents.

Undoubtedly, some estate planning attorneys have reviewed living trust documents that were prepared by nonattorney financial planners. In most cases, the documents are found to be completely inadequate; in all cases, the preparation of the legal documents by any nonattorney constitutes the unauthorized practice of law.

Many financial planners are well versed with estate planning matters and work closely with competent attorneys to serve the needs of mutual clients. They participate in the right way with one another to better serve the client, and these financial planners are to be sought after.

Can the staff attorneys in my bank's trust department prepare a revocable living trust document for me if I name the bank as trustee?

It is common and often advantageous to name an institutional or professional trustee in estate planning documents. In most instances, a bank or trust company is named as a trustee. For many trust makers, naming a bank trust department makes a great deal of sense because it has a highly trained staff of trust specialists who have ongoing and daily experience with the administration of trusts.

However, a bank trust department should, at no time, actually create the living trust documents. This activity is unauthorized in the law—even if the documents are prepared by bank attorneys—because legal ethics require that an attorney must be independent and represent only the client. An attorney employed by a trust department represents the bank, not its customers, and as a result, an inherent conflict of interest is created.

A bank trust officer should be utilized as a valuable member of your estate planning team and can be helpful in designing various terms and provisions of the trust in working with your independent counsel.

Can members of my bank's trust department assist me in finding competent counsel?

They are in the trust business and know the most competent professionals in their communities. If asked, they will be pleased to give you a number of names.

Do-It-Yourself Estate Planning

I see various will and trust kits advertised in the media. Can I do my own estate planning?

We represent a great many attorneys who do not specialize in estate planning; they follow the adage, "An attorney who has himself or herself for a client has a fool for a client," and instead hire us. The law is highly technical and complicated, and unless the practitioner possesses a high degree of professional training, a great deal of harm can be done. It would be foolish for uneducated, inexperienced, and unlicensed people to plan their estates and equally foolish for educated, experienced, and licensed people to plan their own estates as well.

A recent *Wall Street Journal* article observed that proper estate planning is like brain surgery: it is not a hobby.

Planning kits are not innocent attempts at saving money; they are potential weapons that can do serious damage to a family. The peace of mind that you seek for yourself and your family in knowing that your planning is properly completed is best achieved by having a competent and experienced attorney assist you in the preparation of your estate planning documents.

I have seen living trust software programs on the shelf of my computer store for less than $100. Why shouldn't I do my own?

Software without the training to use it is no different from the issues we have already discussed. This is particularly true in planning for taxable estates that requires sophisticated knowledge of estate and gift tax statutes. Innocent mistakes or oversights in tax planning can disqualify major exemptions, deductions, and credits.

The use of forms, whether they are preprinted or programmed on software, is no substitute for experience, judgment, and legal training.

Would your answer be different if I told you that I am very intelligent and have some legal training?

Many of our Network members are law professors, and they agree with an overwhelming consensus that even their best law students do not turn out workable estate plans on their first attempts. Unfortunately, your competency will not be challenged until after your disability or death.

Can I get an attorney to review and correct the plan I drafted myself?

Most attorneys will not go to the time and expense of explaining the seemingly endless reasons why an amateurish attempt does not work. They prefer to keep both their sanity and their clients' legal fees within reason by starting a professional plan afresh.

One-Size-Fits-All Estate Planning

Isn't the preparation of a trust agreement really a "fill-in-the-blank" exercise for attorneys?

It is not uncommon to see an advertisement placed by an attorney offering to prepare a trust agreement for a low fixed fee. Much has been written in the past 5 to 10 years about the desirability of the revocable living trust as the best estate planning technique, often based solely on the concept of probate avoidance. This has led some attorneys to attempt to capitalize on this popularity by advertising their low-cost preparation of a trust agreement.

Unfortunately, in many instances, these attorneys do not possess estate planning experience and expertise but are trying to latch on to the popularity of the revocable living trust as a way to generate volume fees with little effort or concern for the client's individual needs. This has led to a dangerous misconception by many people that a "one-size-fits-all" trust agreement is a reasonable solution to effective estate planning.

In reality, nothing could be further from the truth. Proper planning and use of revocable living trust–centered estate planning techniques require detailed analysis of the client's assets and personal financial situation, as well as his or her individual hopes, plans, dreams, and ambitions.

A true estate planning professional will make certain that the trust document is individually tailored and designed to satisfy the intensely personal concerns and goals of each client.

Don't attorneys just use forms?

Compare two attorneys: Attorney A started practicing right out of law school and has taken every matter that came to him; he has no particular estate planning experience but does have a few *very good forms* he copied from books and documents that came his way. Attorney B has specialized or limited her practice to estate planning law throughout her 25-year career; she has attended hundreds of professional symposia, lectured to bar groups, and written articles and books on the subject. She, too, has forms—thousands and thousands of them—upon which she has labored tens of thousands of hours over the years. In which practitioner's forms would you have the greatest confidence?

Knowing which language to place where and in juxtaposition to other language within a document is the art of the competent estate planner. Practitioners who do not have many hundreds or thousands of forms upon which to extract the perfect language to achieve the desired result are like pharmacists who do not have drugs. Physicians are trained to diagnose and prescribe; pharmacists are trained to fill those prescriptions; attorneys are trained to do both; and clients are trained to do neither.

The goal of an experienced and dedicated estate planning attorney is to tailor each document and its provisions specifically to the particular needs of each client.

What Makes an Attorney Qualified to Do Estate Planning?

Can just any attorney prepare a living trust plan?

Any attorney who is licensed to practice law can legally prepare estate planning documents, including revocable living trust–centered plans. However, few attorneys graduate from law school with much knowledge or background in trusts or estate planning. Most graduates would agree that they need practical experience and guidance from a senior attorney prior to tackling any but the most basic of estate plans.

A generalization that holds much truth is that those attorneys who have dedicated themselves to continuing education and practices concentrated on estate planning generally possess the requisite skills to accomplish better-than-journeyman estate planning.

An article in *Elder Law Forum* (January–February 1995) alerted its readers to the problems that can arise from the practice of an unskilled and untrained attorney. In one situation over 300 people in Oregon and northern California were put at risk because of flawed documents created by the ineptitude of a now-disbarred attorney.

Are there established standards of practice for qualified estate planning attorneys?

Unfortunately, there are no national standards of practice for estate planning attorneys such as those required for patent attorneys, who must take and pass a written examination given by the U.S. Patent and Trademark Office in order to hold themselves out to the public as patent attorneys. A few law schools, such as the

University of Miami and the University of Denver, offer master of law in estate planning degrees, and other law schools offer master of law in taxation degrees. However, they are currently the exception rather than the rule among the nation's law schools.

A few states certify practitioners as specialists in estate planning, but they are by far in the minority. There is some movement in the American Bar Association to establish a national certification program for qualified estate planning attorneys. However, this proposal has yet to be adopted.

Some attorneys take courses sponsored by the American Law Institute, American Bar Association, and state and local bar associations that are offered through continuing education programs. Fortunately or unfortunately, depending upon your perspective, these courses are usually attended by a small cadre of specialists.

There are two major national organizations which recognize attorneys with expertise in the estate planning field. These are the American College of Trusts and Estates Counsel and the National Network of Estate Planning Attorneys. Members of these two organizations are committed to excellence in estate planning, and membership in them is a recognition of these attorneys' serious commitment to their clients and their individual professionalism.

What should I look for in an attorney who is reasonably qualified to plan my estate?

Following are some of the characteristics that a qualified estate planning attorney will possess:

1. An attitude that puts the client's well-being ahead of everything else
2. A good reputation for the highest levels of honesty, integrity, and ethics
3. Discipline and diligence in staying legally current through constant study, research, reading, and interaction with other specialized members of the profession
4. Organizational methods and technological systems which will allow him or her to provide superior legal services and documents in a timely manner
5. The ability to freely acknowledge when a matter is beyond his or her experience or expertise

6. Relationships that will enable him or her to enlist the aid of specialized colleagues or advisors in situations that call for that expertise
7. A number of clients who are pleased with his or her legal services

What are some specific standard practices that qualified estate planning attorneys use?

- Qualified estate planning attorneys are willing to discuss fees openly and reach an agreement before beginning work.
- They offer and adhere to a reasonable turnaround time for the preparation of the clients' estate plans. (Unless your situation is unusually complex, the drafting of your plan should be accomplished within 2 to 6 weeks.)
- They create efficiency for their clients by using state-of-the-art automation.
- They discuss the pros and cons of the various estate planning tools, yet let the clients make the decision as to what strategies or solutions are best for them.
- They focus on the clients' goals, desires, fears, and expectations rather than their own.

What is one of the most important skills required of an estate planning attorney?

The ability to *listen and question* effectively, which is how an attorney:

- Determines your objectives, desires, dreams, concerns, and fears
- Learns about your family situation, assets, and special needs

An attorney who listens carefully can make an accurate diagnosis of your estate planning needs by fully understanding your situation, goals, and objectives. An attorney who listens poorly and misdiagnoses your situation can do great harm to you and your family.

How do I find an attorney who specializes in estate planning?

Ascertaining the type of professional organizations to which your attorney belongs is usually a good indication of whether he or she concentrates on estate planning. Keep in mind that few organizations require that their members demonstrate a minimum level of professional expertise. Thus membership in a professional organization does not always equate with professional competence.

A number of souces provide meaningful referrals to competent counsel. Recommendations from the following institutions, groups, or individuals are usually very helpful:

- Attorneys you know but who do not emphasize estate planning in their own practices.
- Accountants, financial planners, insurance professionals, and stockbrokers.
- Bank trust departments and private trust companies.
- Your local Estate Planning Council. This group is usually comprised of attorneys, accountants, bank trust officers, life insurance agents, and financial planners who meet regularly to share estate planning ideas. A copy of its roster should give you a number of good leads.
- American College of Trusts and Estates Counsel and the National Network of Estate Planning Attorneys. These national organizations are committed to excellence in estate planning, and membership in them is a recognition of that commitment. A copy of their state membership roster should be of assistance to you.
- The *Martindale-Hubbell Law Digest.* This directory can be found in any legal library and in many public libraries. It describes attorneys by geographic location, with credentials and ratings by their colleagues. As you peruse the listings, ask yourself: What does his or her listing tell me? How has he or she been rated by colleagues? What credentials are special or missing?

The professionals listed above will either work closely with estate planning attorneys or have the opportunity—firsthand—to see their work product and professional demeanor.

Should I look for specific types of experience?

Your attorney must have broad estate planning experience (in addition to will and probate experience). He or she must have reasonable experience in drafting all types of fully funded revocable living trusts and irrevocable trusts including:

- Life insurance trusts
- 2503(c) minor's trusts
- Qualified personal residence trusts
- Charitable remainder and charitable lead trusts
- Grantor retained annuity trusts
- Testamentary private foundations

In addition, you should look for a practitioner who has experience in creating family limited partnerships and limited liability companies, as well as in business continuity planning if you have a family business.

Besides *experience*, what else should I look for in an estate planning attorney?

The best technician in the world will not necessarily make the best practitioner. You must feel personally comfortable with the attorney you select. Ask yourself these questions:

- Does he or she communicate well with me, and do I communicate well with him or her?
- While in his or her presence, do I feel secure and trusting, or do I feel nervous and ill at ease?
- Will my family like or dislike his or her personality?
- Are his or her fees commensurate with the value that he or she will provide to me and my family?

Should I call the local bar association for a recommendation?

In our collective experience, bar associations cannot make qualitative judgments. They will simply give you the next few names on their referral list, a list that ensures nothing other than the attorney's interest in receiving referrals.

I am somewhat intimidated by this search process. Isn't there an easier way?

Share your need with:

- Friends and acquaintances
- The person you deal most with at your bank, and ask for an introduction to someone in the bank's trust department if it has one
- Your accountant and life insurance advisors

What do I do once I have a few names?

Telephone their offices and state your business (you will almost always get their secretaries or assistants). Ask for an appointment, inquire as to how long you should spend together, and whether or not there will be a charge for the first meeting. Do not make your choice until you have completed your investigations.

If I can talk with prospective attorneys on the telephone, what questions should I ask?

Tell the attorneys you want an estate plan which includes a living trust as its foundation. If they attempt to talk you out of a living trust–centered estate plan, suggest only a will, or tell you that your estate is not large enough to need a living trust–centered estate plan, you should be on your guard or find someone else.

Ask the attorneys how long they have been preparing estate plans and how many they have done. Ask them what kind of clientele they have, and the average size of estate they plan (if the estates are much larger or smaller than yours, you probably should look elsewhere).

Ask the attorneys about their background and education. Do they belong to estate planning–oriented organizations? Do they have any specialized degrees or training?

If an attorney is a member of a large firm, ask who in the firm will supervise and be responsible for preparing the documents. You want to make sure the attorney you retain does as much of your work as possible.

Ask how long it will take to complete the process. If an attorney is not willing to commit to a reasonable schedule for completing your plan, you might try another attorney.

If a call is positive from your perspective, ask if you may make an appointment and inquire about the charge for that first meeting.

Should I check with the advertisements in the newspaper or the Yellow Pages?

Advertising in newspapers, the Yellow Pages, or other media is less an indication of legal expertise than of a willingness to buy advertising. Beware of advertisements promising extraordinary tax savings or freedom from creditors at the stroke of a pen. If it sounds too good to be true, it probably is too good to be true.

I have noticed advertisements in the newspaper for estate planning seminars. Should I go to one of these seminars before making an appointment with an attorney?

It would be a good idea to attend one or more of these seminars. The more information you can acquire on the estate planning process, the better position you will be in to talk knowingly to the attorney you ultimately select about your planning. If you do attend one or more educational seminars, be sure to notice whether or not the seminar turns into a sales pitch for a particular product or service.

A seminar should be, first and foremost, dedicated to providing information and education. The host of the seminar should never attempt to give specific legal advice to you or anyone else in the audience. If you are invited to participate with the host or one of his or her associates one-on-one after the seminar, be sure that it is on a no-cost, no-obligation basis. You should always know what you are buying before committing to anything.

What criteria should I utilize in deciding which attorney to hire to complete my estate plan?

One of the most important criteria is the "creation of a relationship" between you and your estate planning attorney. If an attorney fails to show genuine interest in you, your family, and your affairs or is discourteous to you in any way, it is unlikely that he or she will have the necessary ability and personality to create a plan with which you will be comfortable.

Any attorney you select should be well aware of your goals, wishes, and aspirations as they pertain to your family background, assets, and estate planning objectives. This personal knowledge will be a direct by-product of a positive working relationship and can only result from the attorney's asking you the right kinds of questions in a kind tone and polite manner.

Make sure that you do not permit any attorney to think that he or she has been retained by you until you receive a well-defined indication of how your estate plan will be designed, specifics regarding the number and type of documents, and the fees for the design of your plan and the preparation of your documents.

In summary, the attorney you select should be someone with whom you feel comfortable, who has the level of expertise for which you are looking, and who will charge a fee that you feel is fair for the value you receive and which you feel good about paying.

Are there any other attorney-related criteria that I need to consider?

Estate planning is not a transaction, such as the sale or purchase of residential real estate. It should be the beginning of a long-term relationship between you and the attorney. You should ask the attorney if he or she believes that having a relationship with you is fundamental to helping you plan (the National Network of Estate Planning Attorneys believes in a relationship-oriented practice rather than a transaction-oriented practice).

Some of the other factors that you should consider are:

- Does the attorney have permanency such as an established office and presence in the community?
- Does the attorney have a well-trained support staff?
- Is the attorney capable of providing ongoing services?
- Does the attorney regularly attend estate planning meetings and seminars to maintain his or her skills on the cutting edge in order to keep your affairs on that edge?
- Does the attorney concentrate on or emphasize estate planning in his or her practice?
- Has the attorney spoken professionally on estate planning topics to colleagues?
- Has the attorney written professional articles or books regarding estate planning?
- Is the attorney an active member of a professional group, bar association, estate planning committee, Estate Planning Council, or a nationally recognized professional group such as the American College of Trusts and Estates Counsel or the National Network of Estate Planning Attorneys?

What should I do after each meeting?

Evaluate your meeting. Was the attorney prompt, courteous, organized, and knowledgeable? Did the attorney speak in plain and understandable language and fully answer your questions? Did he or she seem genuinely interested in you and your family?

Trust your instincts. If you feel good, then you should proceed, but do not forget to determine the cost up front. If something just does not feel right, you should probably keep looking because it is likely that you will find a practitioner not only who will meet all of your qualifications and criteria but whose company you enjoy as well.

As an attorney, what would you look for in another attorney?

We would ask ourselves whether the attorney seems to be:

- The kind of person we enjoy talking with for hours, and in whom we feel comfortable sharing our most intimate thoughts and secrets that relate to the planning at hand
- A respectful and a good listener who strives to understand our concerns and needs
- Enjoying what he or she does
- Focused in his or her estate and tax planning practice
- Evidencing a strong commitment to serve us as his or her clients
- Able to provide us with quality work in a timely manner
- Attending a significant number of continuing legal education programs
- Comfortable in explaining his or her fees and costs
- Reflecting the same persona as described by the referral

Is my present attorney the right one to do my estate planning?

Reread the past few pages, and put your attorney through the same scrutiny. If there is a good possibility that he or she will qualify, set a meeting and ask all of the questions we provided you earlier in this chapter.

Please remember that estate planning is a highly technical and legal specialty; it requires that your attorney be up to date with all state-of-the-art strategies to ensure that you and your family can avoid taxes and administrative and professional fees to the greatest extent possible.

In general, we believe that you are most likely to achieve these goals when you work with an attorney who has considerable experience in the area of estate planning, with an emphasis in the area of living trust–centered estate plans with all related documents.

I know and trust two attorneys: the first has a will-planning probate practice and the other does a lot of living trust–centered planning. The will-probate attorney tells me that wills are cheaper and are not difficult to probate. What do you recommend that I do?

A good relationship with your attorney begins with confidence and trust. Obtain as much practical information about estate planning as possible so that the decision you make will be based upon your common sense and your personal knowledge of the planning experiences of others. Skim and read good books on the subject. We would recommend *Loving Trust* (Viking-Penguin, 1994), *The Living Trust Revolution* (Viking-Penguin, 1992), and *Protect Your Estate* (McGraw-Hill, 1993), all written by attorneys and authors Robert A. Esperti and Renno L. Peterson. They will directly address the major issues you need to address—head-on—and will help you to make a wise decision.

I am 61, near retirement, and want to proceed in preparing a comprehensive estate plan. Should my attorney be someone near my age?

The age of the attorney who will be completing your estate plan is, for the most part, irrelevant. What is important is the attorney's expertise.

There are many older attorneys who have taken the time to stay current and flexible within an ever-growing and changing body of law. They have remained knowledgeable regarding the multitude of estate planning vehicles that are available to assist their clients in the estate planning arena and have the advantage of years of experience that their juniors have yet to experience.

However, there are also a number of older, well-established attorneys who have become comfortable practicing in a probate-dominated arena and who promote (from lack of education or otherwise) the usage of simple wills or other estate planning documents that will result in your estate going through the probate process. Often, these same attorneys do not use, or are not aware of, various other estate planning vehicles that have as their primary purpose the reduction and/or elimination of estate taxes at the federal level or the elimination of probate.

Many clients nearing retirement age have a strong preference for working with an attorney who is 10 to 20 years younger than they are, not so much from an assumption that the younger attorney will possess any more expertise than the older attorney but, rather, because the clients see various advantages in having the younger attorney available after their deaths to counsel their children and grandchildren.

Fees and Costs of Estate Planning

How do I find an attorney who will charge me a fair and reasonable fee?

Abraham Lincoln is attributed with saying, "An attorney's time and advice are his stock in trade." In our experience, his statement still holds true, even in this era of advanced information systems and computers.

Many people believe that if an attorney charges $150 to $300 per hour, he or she must make about $250,000 to $300,000 per year. But a law practice has overhead, including staff salaries and expenses, that must be paid first, just as in any business. An attorney not only must complete a minimum of 7 years of schooling past high school but must continue that education for the remainder of his or her professional life. Because of this continuing educational commitment, not all of an attorney's time can be spent producing results for his or her clients. In our experience, an established and experienced attorney who can convert two-thirds of his or her time to billable hours is working very hard and responsibly.

Attorneys who do more than provide clients with standard forms or fill-in-the-blank planning should be appropriately compensated. Most attorneys are dedicated professionals who are trained by experience to listen carefully to the facts, separate the wheat from the chaff, and provide solutions and results that give value to the client's pocketbook and lead to peace of mind.

While a fee may sometimes seem large, its size in relation to the value of the service and to the methodology employed in achieving a particular result is generally relatively small.

To evaluate your attorney's fee quotes, you might consider:

- The value to you of the services which were provided

- The time the attorney spent on the project
- The skill that went into the result as compared to the skill levels of other attorneys you did not select
- The dollar relief in saved costs, expenses, and taxes provided to you and your family
- The speed with which the result may be obtained, and your confidence in the professional, his or her process, and the likely results

What are the various types of fee arrangements used by attorneys?

Attorneys use various types of billing methods which include:

- *The hourly rate:* The attorney and the attorney's colleagues, associates, paralegals, and assistants all charge for their time at standard hourly rates allocated to the values of their respective time as chosen by the attorney or the partners of the firm. Progress billings are usually sent out monthly. Time records are typically kept in increments of one-tenth of an hour (i.e., 6-minute segments), one-sixth (10-minute segments), or one-quarter (15-minute intervals) of an hour, depending upon the standard practice of the particular attorney.
- *Value-added billing:* In addition to standard hourly billing, the client is billed for any significant or unusual value that is added by the attorney's efforts. This type of billing is generally used when an attorney comes up with a particularly innovative solution that has great economic value to the client.
- *Contingency fees:* The amount of the attorney's fee is contingent upon successful results being achieved for the client in the particular matter. The amount of the fee is expressed as a fraction or percentage of the amount of the client's recovery or the savings generated by the attorney's efforts.
- *Flat or fixed fees:* The attorney and client agree in advance on the amount that will be charged for the particular matter regardless of the time spent or the results achieved.
- *Combination fees:* Typically an hourly rate or contingency fee is charged, but there is a guaranteed maximum.
- *Retainer:* The attorney charges a fixed amount for undertaking representation. Depending on the circumstances, the amount

of the retainer can be either nonrefundable or applied against another billing method agreed upon by the attorney and the client.

Because of the nature of estate planning legal work, contingency fees are not generally appropriate. Estate planning services are usually performed by experienced estate planning attorneys on either a straight hourly rate basis, an hourly rate with a guaranteed maximum, a value-added billing arrangement, or a flat or fixed fee. A retainer may or may not be required depending upon the attorney's or firm's policies.

What factors will the attorney take into account in establishing his or her fee for my estate plan?

Fees are often determined by using some or all of the following factors:

- *Cost of doing business:* The amount of overhead and other expenses involved in running the practice are usually considered. (In our experience, there are few attorneys who can keep their true overhead below 50 percent of their gross fees.)
- *Credentials:* The attorney's level of expertise, reputation, and achievements usually affect billing.
- *Time requirements:* Emergencies and unusually quick timelines almost always generate value-added billings.
- *Responsibility and liability:* The degree of responsibility and liability that must be assumed by the attorney plays a huge role in determining the fee. Because malpractice insurance rates are raging upward, this is a sensitive issue with most attorneys.
- *Value of the estate:* The complexity, nature, and value of the assets that comprise the estate are generally always taken into consideration.
- *Results and benefits:* The economic value resulting from the avoidance of probate and ancillary administration and the dollar value of saving estate, gift, income, capital gain, and excise taxes are always taken into consideration in determining the appropriate billing.
- *Complexity:* The involvement of extraordinary legal, financial, or business issues is important to the billing decision.

- *Novelty:* The novelty of the issues presented and the question, "Are the issues routine or uniquely difficult?" play a large part in the billing decision.
- *Service:* The speed and the overall level of service provided throughout the relationship are important to many attorneys. If the attorney determines that a particular client demands *right-now service,* the billing will usually be higher.
- *Time:* How much time did the attorney spend on the matter that could not be spent on other equally or more profitable matters?

How do you determine your fee?

We refer to the above criteria and attempt to arrive at a charge or fee that is reasonable to all parties including us and which we feel good about from the perspectives of fairness, morality, and good ongoing relationships with our clients.

What is your candid opinion of the pros and cons of the various billing methods ?

The Hourly Rate

- If fees were based on time alone, the most inefficient attorneys would be paid the highest fees.
- The world's greatest performers don't get paid unless they perform.
- A wonderful incentive to never finish anything.
- To be used as a last resort by attorneys and clients alike.

Contingency Fee

- Attorneys who generate substantial tax and expense savings for their clients like contingent fees, which are usually calculated on the present dollar value of all savings generated for their clients.
- Contingent fees are popular with wealthy entrepreneurial clients but not suitable for most estate planning clients.

Flat Fees

- Flat fees encourage attorneys to work quickly and protect their clients from future "surprise" billings.
- They work well for specialist practitioners who can estimate accurately what resources, expertise, and time a project will most likely take. They work poorly for nonspecialist attorneys who have little or no idea what they are going to encounter in working on an unfamiliar project.
- In our experience, most clients prefer this billing method over all others.

Value-Added Billing

- A very popular billing method with some attorneys.
- A very unpopular billing method with most, but not all, clients who want to know up front what their costs are going to approximate.

Combination Fees

- Very suitable for living trust–centered planning where the attorney may quote a flat fee for work he or she can estimate closely, such as the preparation and implementation of documents, and couple that work and fee quote with an hourly rate for work that cannot be estimated such as funding the trust.
- In our experience, a highly popular method of billing with both attorneys and their clients.

When should I discuss fees with my attorney?

You can discuss fees at any time, but it is preferable that you do so as early as possible in your relationship and prior to giving your attorney the go-ahead to do any work.

We would urge you to use caution in comparing the relative value between attorneys solely on the basis of the amount of their fees or their fee structures. As professional insiders, we believe you would be far better off to compare the value that each will likely provide you and to compare the value of their respective services—less the amount of their fees—one to the other on an apples-to-apples basis.

Is it necessary for me to have a written fee agreement with the attorney doing my estate planning?

So as to avoid the potential for misunderstanding, it is generally a good idea for you and the attorney to have a written fee agreement establishing the parameters of the attorney's services and the amount and nature of the billing. Some states, such as California, require fee agreements. Whether required by law or not, fee agreements are beneficial to both you and the attorney. They should establish a clear description of the exact services the attorney will provide and the terms of the payment.

A number of experienced attorneys with sophisticated clientele eschew fee agreements on the basis that they are unprofessional and can create an aura of distrust in the attorney-client relationship. If you are uncomfortable dealing with such an attorney on a *handshake,* request that your agreement be put into writing to protect both parties. In our experience, the attorney will gladly comply and will not be offended.

Should I have to pay an attorney for an initial consultation?

Some attorneys charge for initial consultations, and some attorneys do not charge for them. It is entirely dependent upon each attorney's billing policies.

What else do I need to know about fee arrangements?

Some attorneys require a refundable or nonrefundable retainer. If the attorney uses the client's retainer to offset subsequent hourly or flat fees for work and returns the unused portion to the client, the retainer is refundable. If the attorney does not return the unused portion of the retainer, it is considered nonrefundable.

What other items of expense might I have in working with an estate planning attorney?

Costs not usually included in the fee you pay to the attorney for his or her professional services generally include expenses such as:

- Fees to county clerks or registrars of deeds for filing deeds
- Appraisals of real estate, personal property, or other assets for purposes of making gifts or for establishing values in closely

held corporations, family limited partnerships, and limited liability companies

- Out-of-state counsel fees to assist in preparation and filing of deeds for out-of-state property
- Agency expenses effecting the transfer of vehicles to a trust
- Mortgage companies' administrative fees to place the identity of the trust of record in the mortgage department when mortgaged property is transferred to a trust
- Out-of-pocket costs for photocopying, facsimile transmissions, long-distance telephone calls, online research, and other such direct expenses

Are there any annual or additional costs of keeping the trust plan updated?

A revocable living trust–centered plan does not require annual minutes or memoranda of meetings held by directors or members, as might be the custom with corporations, partnerships, and limited liability companies.

The routine conduct of transactions with your trust will not require you to change or amend the trust documents. Putting assets in the trust and taking assets from the trust generally do not require you to change or amend the trust documents. One of the characteristics of a well-prepared estate plan is that amendments can be made without major redrafting of the entire trust document and at relatively reasonable cost.

However, significant changes in your family makeup, significant events in the lives of the individual members of your family, changes in the way you want assets distributed at death, or substantial changes in your overall tax plan are events that will likely generate higher fees to amend or restate your trust.

Your doctor will tell you that it is wise for you to have periodic medical examinations or checkups; likewise, it is considered good practice for you to consult and review your overall estate plan on some predetermined regular interval with your estate planning advisors and attorney. At a minimum, we would suggest that you consider having a general review meeting with your attorney and your other advisors every 3 to 5 years.

What should I expect to pay to have a comprehensive estate plan designed and drafted by a qualified estate planning attorney?

The legal fees for estate planning vary a great deal nationwide, much the same way that the prices of real estate vary. They will also vary depending upon the expertise and experience of the practitioner that you choose to retain and the complexity of your planning needs and desires.

Because of these dramatic variances, any general numbers we might quote would not have any significance to your particular situation.

Can you make some general observations about estate planning fees?

When it comes to legal fees, we believe that you almost always get what you pay for. In our collective experience, you would be well advised, especially over the long run, to spend more money with a highly qualified attorney than to spend less money for someone less capable or experienced.

The fee for a comprehensive plan will be based upon its complexity and will vary with every case and every family. Typically, the larger the estate size, the more planning is needed to effectively protect it from confiscatory taxes. More planning requires more attorney time, more expertise, and a greater variety of planning tools.

Very simple estate plans might generate fees in the hundreds or low thousands of dollars; complicated multimillion-dollar plans will generate fees in the tens of thousands; and very large estates could generate fees in the hundreds of thousands of dollars.

A plan that makes use of a combination of revocable living trusts, irrevocable life insurance trusts, family limited partnerships, charitable trusts, offshore asset protection trusts, grantor retained annuity trusts, and so on, may require a legal fee of $100,000 or more and will likely save millions of dollars of taxes and expenses.

Regardless of the size and complexity of the estate, the amount spent for legal fees should pale by comparison to the tax and cost savings generated for the family.

Can you make any further general observations on fees?

To determine how much you ought to pay an attorney for estate planning services, you need to determine in your own mind what you perceive to be the value of estate planning for you and your family. We believe that people are only willing to pay legal fees commensurate with the value they place on the work product.

If person A believes the planning is critical to his happiness and his family's well-being, he will gladly pay far more than person B, who sees little, if any, value in the exercise. This is true even if person B receives a far greater objective result than person A.

Why does it cost so little to get a will done?

Most attorneys have been reluctant to charge adequate fees for wills because they generally put very little effort into drafting them. Their work, and corresponding fees, begins upon your disability or death, when the probate process begins.

This "don't pay me now, but pay me later" situation is changing. Many practitioners, and the profession as a whole, are moving toward living trust–centered estate planning that avoids probate. Because living trust–centered planning requires a great deal more effort on the part of the attorney, the fees are higher initially but much lower later on.

A detailed comparison between will-planning probate and living trust–centered estate planning can be found in Chapter 2 of *The Living Trust Revolution,* by Esperti and Peterson (Viking-Penguin, 1992). In general, their research found that living trust–centered estate planning saved 75 percent of total fees.

What would you be willing to pay your attorney if he or she was able to demonstrate to your satisfaction that a properly conceived and written living trust–centered estate plan could save you and your family $235,000 in federal estate taxes and $40,000 in probate fees compared to your current estate plan? What would you be willing to pay if the tax and expense savings were double, triple, or ten times these amounts?

Is it appropriate for me to negotiate an attorney's fee?

It depends upon the attorney, but in our experience, the majority of skilled and experienced attorneys not only do not negotiate their fees but will be offended by the experience.

Is there anything I can do to reduce my legal fees?

In order to render competent legal advice, it is critical that your estate planning attorney have a detailed inventory of all of your financial assets and holdings and copies of all of your relevant legal documents. Most qualified estate planning attorneys will request that you provide them with this personal, financial, and legal information prior to your first strategy meeting. If you are thorough in your preparation, you will save the attorney significant time and effort, which should reflect itself in your bill or fee quote.

You can also facilitate the estate planning process by familiarizing yourself with basic estate planning concepts prior to meeting with your attorney. The ideas and concepts contained in this book should adequately prepare you to be an active participant in the estate planning process, resulting in faster and more enjoyable communication with your attorney and potential cost savings to you.

Additionally, the participation of your accountant, financial planner, stockbroker, and insurance professional in your planning process will greatly assist your attorney and should also result in reduced billing.

Can I expect to receive a fee quote over the telephone?

Professional attorneys do not quote their fees over the telephone, nor do they give advice to people they do not know. They wish to practice law the old-fashioned way, in that they wish to:

- Meet with the client to determine if representation would be appropriate.
- Ascertain the client's legal needs by taking the time to carefully diagnose the client's overall situation.
- Familiarize and make the client comfortable with the laws and strategies that are relevant to his or her situation and the legal documentation that will be necessary.
- Prepare the needed documents on a tailored-to-fit basis, and have them signed after thoroughly explaining them to the client.
- Prepare all ancillary documents, and initiate funding procedures for whatever trusts or other planning entities have been created.

Physicians do not practice medicine by phone, nor do professionally responsible attorneys.

We hear of so many varied and different prices being charged for living trusts. What causes this difference in fees?

A complete estate plan for you and your family does not come in boxes or in cans but, rather, from a process that involves your attorney listening to your hopes, dreams, and aspirations for you and your family, followed by him or her making recommendations and giving you options to accomplish your goals.

A living trust is only one piece of a complete estate plan, which would also include a pour-over will, health care powers of attorney, durable funding powers of attorney, a property agreement, memorial and funeral instructions, a living will or directive to physician, and provisions for division of personal property.

Depending upon the size of the estate, a complete plan might also include generation-skipping tax provisions, charitable remainder trusts, charitable lead trusts, irrevocable life insurance trusts, family limited partnerships, limited liability companies, S corporations, and offshore trusts, all of which will need to be customized to fit your and your family's particular needs.

Some attorneys are more talented than others—like fine art painters, their canvases command higher prices than those of their less skilled colleagues.

Attorneys are free to run their businesses as they see fit as long as they observe the ethics of the profession. Some choose to cut corners, and spend as little time with the client or his or her documentation as possible, and they reflect this preference in a billing system that emphasizes reduced or even cheap legal fees. However, most attorneys take great pride in their work, and work diligently to make sure it is the best effort they can produce in meeting their clients' needs. Their prices will most generally always be significantly higher than those of their cost-cutting brethren.

Is the cost of my estate plan deductible on my federal income tax?

Pure estate planning fees are not a deductible expense. However, a substantial part of the estate planning attorney's work involves tax planning and lifetime asset management planning that protects and conserves income-producing property. These additional components of the fee may be deductible depending upon your individual tax situation.

The percentage of the estate planning fee that will be deductible will vary from attorney to attorney and from client to client depending on the nature of the work performed. It is therefore very important that you discuss this issue with your estate planning attorney at your initial meeting.

The Team Approach to Estate Planning

What is the team approach to estate planning?

A *team approach* to estate planning is an approach highly recommended by the National Network of Estate Planning Attorneys. Network attorneys believe that it is most generally impossible to achieve the highest levels of professional competence and service without the utilization and assistance of the client's other professional advisors. Accountants, insurance professionals, financial planners, stockbrokers, and investment counselors are invaluable resources to you and your attorney as you mutually work toward meeting your overall goals and objectives.

These other professionals have specific knowledge of their professions and the work they have done for you; they can add much to the discussion from their experiences in serving you and your family over the years. Their participation in the planning process can be invaluable to your attorney.

The use of the professional team approach is especially important and recommended during the funding stage of living trust–centered estate planning. Other professionals can help you and your attorney ensure that the necessary assets that you own are properly and legally placed within the various trusts and entities that have been created.

How can my other advisors be meaningfully involved in my estate plan?

In addition to expertise in the law, estate planning depends upon the expertise of professionals in the fields of accounting, charitable giving, financial planning, insurance underwriting, and securities investment. Financial planners and securities brokers focus on maximizing your resources through investment. Insurance underwriters help to protect assets against disability and death and coordinate the insurance contracts with the trust documents. Accountants focus on the immediate and projected income tax ramifications of the decisions overseen by the other professionals and put them to work in their annual computer pro formas.

It is sometimes useful to think of the professionals involved in estate planning in terms of their place on a continuum with "maximizing assets" on one end and "protecting assets" on the other. As experts in their respective subspecialties of estate planning, each is trained to look for and resolve issues beyond the purview of the others. Most professionals in the estate planning field enjoy and recognize the necessity of working with each other.

How can I find additional advisors for my estate planning team?

If your attorney is an estate planning specialist, he or she will know a number of local qualified professionals who should be part of your team. It will be very easy for your attorney to introduce these professionals to you.

How to Begin the Estate Planning Process

How do we get started? What will my spouse and I need for the first meeting with our estate planning attorney?

Once you have found an estate planning attorney who is right for you, you should ask the attorney what you need to do to get the estate planning process under way. Most estate planning attorneys will have some sort of information sheet which you can fill out in order to outline in detail the specifics of your finances for the initial consultation.

This information sheet will ask you to provide a list of all of the assets you own, including real estate, bank and investment accounts, life insurance, motor vehicles, business interests, and so on, and the way you hold title to each of the assets—individually, jointly, tenancy in common, tenancy by the entirety, or as community property—on your financial statement. You should have a reasonably accurate idea of the fair market value of each of your assets and the amounts of the indebtedness against them.

If you are married, both of you should attend the first meeting with your attorney and be prepared to discuss, at least in general terms, how your property and assets should be administered if one or both of you should become disabled; how your property and assets should be administered and distributed after one of you dies; and how your property and assets should be administered and distributed after you both have died.

During your meeting, your attorney will be able to help you

define your very specific goals and objectives to an extent that you might not have been able to do in advance of your first meeting.

What else do I need to bring to the first planning session?

It would be very helpful to your attorney if you would bring the following items with you (the attorney's assistant will be glad to make copies of them for his or her files):

1. Any prior wills, trusts, or other estate planning documents
2. Deeds to real estate
3. Life insurance policies showing owner, insured, and beneficiaries
4. Statements from savings accounts, certificates of deposit, checking accounts, and other bank accounts
5. Certificates of title for motor vehicles
6. Stock certificates and any other bonds or negotiable instruments, or brokerage account statement
7. Copies of stock certificates for private corporate ownership, copies of shareholder or other corporate agreements, and partnership and limited partnership agreements
8. Notes receivable and trust deeds or mortgages or other documents representing security for the notes
9. IRA trust agreements and other retirement plan documents
10. Information regarding names, birth dates, and other facts you deem pertinent concerning you and your family

How long does the planning process take?

There are essentially three blocks of time that will be required of you during the estate planning process:

- The first block constitutes that time in which detailed information is accumulated and shared with the estate planning attorney in setting forth your hopes, dreams, aspirations, and planning expectations.
- The second block of time will be when you meet with the attorney to help design the specifics of your plan and to ulti-

mately review and sign the estate planning documentation that he or she prepared on your behalf.

- The third block of time is involved in transferring the ownership of your assets into your various trust and planning vehicles.

The amount of time involvement for the first and last blocks is largely dependent on the number of assets you own and the degree of organization that exists prior to the planning process.

Generally speaking, for most but not all clients, the initial meeting with the attorney is accomplished in 1 to 4 hours; the review and signing of the estate planning documents is usually accomplished in 1 to 4 hours; and the process of transferring the assets ("funding") is a function of how well-organized you are and how rapidly you wish to go about funding assets into your trust.

Regardless of the time requirement you will have to commit to the planning process, it is generally a wonderful experience that should provide you with much satisfaction and comfort and an overall sense of well-being.

How much of my confidential information must I disclose to my attorney?

Communications between an attorney and his or her client are privileged and the attorney has a duty to keep all client information confidential. In order to do a complete job of estate planning, the attorney must not be given partial information or incomplete truths. If you keep important matters to yourself, your estate plan will potentially suffer as a result.

How can I determine if I am getting a high-quality living trust plan?

There are several factors that distinguish the comprehensive, high-quality living trust plan from a run-of-the-mill or inadequate plan. A quality living trust–centered estate plan is:

1. *Prepared by a licensed attorney who emphasizes estate planning in his or her practice.* Usually, attorneys who devote substantially all of their practice to estate planning attend extensive continuing legal

education courses devoted to estate planning and are best-suited to draft plans that most accurately capture their clients' needs.

2. *Prepared in a "user-friendly" manner.* Many attorneys feel it is necessary to draft trusts in legalese to make their clients feel that they are getting their money's worth. Actually, the main goal of the estate planning attorney is to draft documents so that the client's objectives are met and the client can understand what his or her documents say and do not say. The mark of a caring attorney is his or her zeal to incorporate mechanisms into the living trust plan which explain and provide easy-to-read instructions for the family and the trust maker's fiduciaries—trustees and personal representatives—as to how the plan works upon the death or incapacity of its maker(s).
3. *Funded with the appropriate assets after the documents are made operational.* All too often we see plans for which the attorneys did not take the appropriate steps to ensure that the clients' assets were transferred into the trusts. Vehicles without fuel do not work very well, nor do trusts without assets.
4. *Prepared by an attorney who has a desire to maintain a continuing relationship with the family.* After the preparation of a trust plan, it is essential that the clients have access to the attorney and his or her staff for interpreting matters concerning the plan.

What documents should I expect to have in my estate plan?

At a minimum, a proper estate planning portfolio using living trust–centered documentation will often contain:

1. A section for personal and family information
2. A list indicating the location of original documents
3. A listing of the names, addresses, and telephone numbers of professional advisors and representatives
4. A thorough and easy-to-understand revocable living trust agreement for you or, if you are married, for you and your spouse, or a joint trust for both (appropriate only in certain circumstances and in particular states)
5. Pour-over will(s)
6. Special powers of attorney which designate agents to fund your revocable living trust with any assets that you may acquire after you are disabled and are unable to fund the trust yourself

7. A memorandum of distribution to dispose of items of your personal effects (what form this takes will depend upon the state in which you reside)
8. A durable special power of attorney for health care which grants your designated agent the power to make medical decisions on your behalf
9. A living will which directs your physician to discontinue life-support systems and invasive medical procedures
10. Memorial instructions which contain your burial or cremation wishes and information on the type of memorial service that you would like to have
11. An anatomical gift form which allows you to make a gift of all or part of your body for medical or dental education and research, therapy, or transplant
12. A list of all insurance and annuity contracts which you own so your intended beneficiaries will not overlook these assets
13. A property agreement which severs and terminates your joint tenancy interest to allow such interest to be properly transferred into your respective revocable living trusts
14. An affidavit of trust which contains pertinent facts about your trust which can be used to prove the trust's existence while preserving the privacy of the detailed provisions of your trust
15. A section for you to insert documentation of those assets which have been transferred into your revocable living trust
16. A detailed letter from your attorney setting forth complete instructions for transferring assets into your trust (*The Living Trust Workbook,* by Esperti and Peterson, Viking-Penguin, 1994, is a complete guide on the subject.)

APPENDIX B

Contributing Authors

DeWayne E. Allen, J.D.
Allen & Associates
1718 S Cheyenne
Tulsa, OK 74119
(918)587-7773 Fax: (918)592-1999

David C. Anderson, J.D.
David C. Anderson, P.C.
404 Camino del Rio South, Suite 605
San Diego, CA 92108
(619)220-8688 Fax: (619)220-8788

David B. Atkins, J.D.
David B. Atkins & Associates
566 W Adams, Suite 501
Chicago, IL 60661
(312)648-0107 Fax: (312)648-0563

David F. Bacon, J.D.
Roth Bacon Young
50 Court Street
Upper Sandusky, OH 43351
(419)294-2232 Fax: (419)294-2488

Jerry D. Balentine, J.D.
Balentine & Balentine, P.C.
6303 N Portland, Suite 305
Oklahoma City, OK 73112
(405)946-4500 Fax: (405)946-4757

Michael R. Bascom, J.D.
Whiteside, Coyle, Bascom & Bergman, P.C.
1000 Cambridge Square, Suite C
Alpharetta, GA 30201
(770)475-1126 Fax: (770)475-4551

Thomas F. Bean, J.D.
Thomas F. Bean Co., L.P.A.
34950 Chardon Road, Suite 210
Willoughby Hills, OH 44094
(216)953-1151 Fax: (216)953-1962

Gary J. Boecker, J.D.
Boecker & Co., L.P.A.
395 Springside Drive, Suite 100
Fairlawn, OH 44333
(330)665-5000 Fax: (330)665-4365

Robert E. Bourne, J.D.
Robert E. Bourne, P.C.
412 Ashman
Midland, MI 48640
(517)835-6511 Fax: (517)835-6521

C. David Clauss, J.D.
P.O. Box 1172
Jackson, WY 83001
(307)733-1191 Fax: (307)733-4718

Nathaniel E. Clement, J.D.
100 Europa Drive, Suite 403
Chapel Hill, NC 27514
(919)929-9298 Fax: (919)968-9413

William A. Conway, J.D.
Law Offices of William A. Conway
1445 Emerson Avenue
McLean, VA 22101
(703)448-7575 Fax: (703)448-0059

Austin J. Doyle, J.D.
Plans & Trusts, P.C.
3201 New Mexico Avenue, Suite 350
Washington, DC 20016
(202)785-8900 Fax: (202)244-5660

Brian A. Eagle, J.D.
Eagle & Fein
8500 Keystone Crossing, Suite 555
Indianapolis, IN 46240
(317)726-1714 Fax: (317)475-1270

Sidney Eagle, J.D.
Eagle & Fein
342 Madison Avenue, Suite 1712
New York, NY 10173
(212)986-3211 Fax: (212)986-3219

William L. Eaton, J.D., LL.M.
Woodman & Eaton, P.C.
801 Main Street
Concord, MA 01742
(508)369-0960 Fax: (508)371-1343

Marie Mirro Edmonds, J.D.
Marie Mirro Edmonds Co., L.P.A.
807 E Washington Street, Suite 100
Medina, OH 44256
(216)725-5297 Fax: (216)722-5932

Richard Egner, Jr., J.D.
657 NE Hood Street
Gresham, OR 97030
(503)665-4186 Fax: (503)665-2038

Edward J. Enichen, J.D.
Guyer & Enichen, P.C.
202 W State Street
Rockford, IL 61101
(815)965-8775 Fax: (815)965-8784

Robert A. Esperti, Cochairman
National Network Incorporated
Post Office Box 3224
125 S King Street
Jackson, WY 83001
(307)733-6952 Fax: (307)739-9191

Isauro Fernandez, J.D.
Isauro Fernandez, P.C.
342 Madison Avenue, Suite 1712
New York, NY 10173
(212)986-3211 Fax: (212)986-3219

Richard L. Ferris, J.D., LL.M.
Ferris & Associates
460 McLaws Circle, Suite 105
Williamsburg, VA 23185
(804)220-8114 Fax: (804)220-8029

Marvin J. Frank, J.D., CPA
Frank & Kraft, A Professional Corporation
135 N Pennsylvania Street, Suite 1100
Indianapolis, IN 46204
(317)684-1100 Fax: (317)684-6111

Jon B. Gandelot, J.D.
Jon B. Gandelot, P.C.
19251 Mack Avenue, Suite 580
Grosse Pointe Woods, MI 48236
(313)885-9100 Fax: (313)885-9152

Guy B. Garner, III, J.D.
Guy B. Garner, III, P.C.
1101 W Randol Mill Road
Arlington, TX 76012
(817)261-5222 Fax: (817)277-6424

Robert A. Goldman, J.D., CPA
Goldman & Associates
600 California Street, Suite 1350
San Francisco, CA 94108
(415)956-4245 Fax: (415)956-7637

Carol H. Gonnella, J.D.
125 S King Street, Suite 200
Jackson, WY 83001
(307)733-5890 Fax: (307)739-9191

Scott J. Hamilton, J.D.
Law Offices of Scott J. Hamilton
351 Pleasant Street
Northampton, MA 01060
(413)586-1173 Fax: (413)586-1306

Lewis B. Hampton, J.D.
Hampton & Bolliger
1815 SW Marlow Avenue, Suite 206
Portland, OR 97225
(503)291-1515 Fax: (503)291-7197

Darrel E. Johnson, J.D.
White & Johnson, L.L.P.
P.O. Drawer O
701 Vilymaca
Elkhart, KS 67950
(316)697-2163 Fax: (316)697-2165

Peter R. Johnson, J.D., LL.M.
Woodman & Eaton, P.C.
801 Main Street
Concord, MA 01742
(508)369-0960 Fax: (508)371-1343

Steven D. Kaestner, J.D., CPA
Brett & Kaestner
2601 NW Expressway, Suite 405W
Oklahoma City, OK 73112
(405)842-3555 Fax: (405)842-3492

Stuart B. Kalb, J.D., LL.M.
Speiser, Krause & Madole, P.C.
5430 LBJ Freeway, Suite 1575
Dallas, TX 75240
(214)404-1401 Fax: (214)404-9797

Kenneth T. Kelley, J.D.
Kenneth T. Kelley Law Associates
2307 Silas Deane Highway
Rocky Hill, CT 06067
(860)257-1679 Fax: (860)257-1795

Yung Mo Kim, J.D., Ph.D.
6470 Main Street, Suite 6
Williamsville, NY 14221
(716)631-2300 Fax: (716)631-2316

Paul A. Kraft, J.D.
Frank & Kraft, A Professional Corporation
135 N Pennsylvania Street, Suite 1100
Indianapolis, IN 46204
(317)684-1100 Fax: (317)684-6111

Jay H. Krall, J.D.
Law Offices of Jay H. Krall
96 State Street
Augusta, ME 04330
(207)626-3330 Fax: (207)622-9115

Howard M. Lang, J.D.
Law Offices of Howard M. Lang
755 S Milwaukee Avenue, Suite 245
Libertyville, IL 60048
(708)367-4460 Fax: (708)367-0090

Tim J. Larson, J.D.
Larson & Schainost, L.L.C.
P.O. Box 367
602 S State
Iola, KS 66749
(800)388-8529 Fax: (316)365-2278

Richard Alan Lehrman, J.D.
777 Arthur Godfrey Road, Fourth Floor
Miami Beach, FL 33140
(305)534-1323 Fax: (305)531-0314

Ellen Check Levy, J.D.
Law Office of Ellen Check Levy
1220 Valley Forge Road, Suite 68-A
Valley Forge, PA 19482
(610)983-3670 Fax: (610)983-3671

Con P. Lynch, J.D.
336 Leslie Street SE
Salem, OR 97301
(503)378-1048 Fax: (503)371-2959

Carol Elyse Magett, J.D.
Magett & Associates
381 Park Avenue South
New York, NY 10016
(212)684-1911 Fax: (212)213-1092

Grant R. Markuson, J.D., LL.M.
Grant R. Markuson & Associates, Ltd.
408 N Ardmore Avenue
Villa Park, IL 60181
(708)832-9200 Fax: (708)832-9202

William J. Maxam, J.D.
William J. Maxam, P.C.
404 Camino del Rio South, Suite 605
San Diego, CA 92108
(619)220-8666 Fax: (619)220-8788

Edward D. McGuire, Jr., J.D.
Law Offices of Edward D. McGuire, Jr.
4306 Evergreen Lane, Suite 103
Annandale, VA 22003
(703)941-3620 Fax: (703)941-4524

Susan Wolff McMakin, J.D., LL.M.
8002 Discovery Drive, Suite 101
Richmond, VA 23229
(804)285-3807 Fax: (804)285-8209

John J. McQueen, J.D., CPA
John McQueen and Associates
4815 S Harvard, Suite 505
Tulsa, OK 74135
(918)742-5920 Fax: (918)742-2142

Ellen Gay Moser, J.D.
E.G. Moser & Associates, P.C.
1112 S Washington Street, Suite 117
Naperville, IL 60540
(630)355-6064 Fax: (630)355-7808

Lucas R. Nardini, J.D.
Nardini & Sheehan, P.C.
31 W Miner Street
West Chester, PA 19382
(610)431-6700 Fax: (610)431-9502

Peter J. Parenti, J.D., LL.M.
Law Offices of Peter J. Parenti, P.C.
8122 Datapoint, Suite 800
San Antonio, TX 78229
(210)614-7766 Fax: (210)692-9066

Renno L. Peterson, Cochairman
National Network Incorporated
2 N Tamiami Trail, Suite 606
Sarasota, FL 34236
(941)365-4819 Fax: (941)366-5347

Chester M. Przybylo, J.D.
Przybylo, Kubiatowski & Associates
5339 N Milwaukee Avenue
Chicago, IL 60630
(773)631-2525 Fax: (773)631-7101

Gerald J. Rachelson, J.D., LL.M., M.L.T., CPA
5040 Roswell Road, Suite 250
Atlanta, GA 30342
(404)851-9399 Fax: (404)256-1422

David H. Radcliff, J.D.
David H. Radcliff, P.C.
2216 Walnut Street
Harrisburg, PA 17103
(717)236-9318 Fax: (717)236-9354

Richard L. Randall, J.D.
Randall Law Offices, P.C.
10333 N Meridian, Suite 265
Indianapolis, IN 46290
(317)574-9911 Fax: (317)574-9922

F. David Resch, J.D.
Resch & Root, Attorneys at Law
2715 Tuller Parkway, Suite 102
Dublin, OH 43017
(614)889-0990 Fax: (614)889-5250

Robert E. Ridgway, Jr., J.D.
P.O. Box 710
93 Chandler Center
Hartwell, GA 30643
(706)376-3991 Fax: (706)376-1155

Mark S. Roberts, J.D.
Mark S. Roberts & Associates, APLC
1440 N Harbor Boulevard, Suite 800
Fullerton, CA 92635
(714)449-3353 Fax: (714)680-0906

John L. Rolfe, J.D., LL.M.
Rolfe & Rosenbaum, P.C.
222 Lancaster Avenue, Suite 349
Devon, PA 19333
(610)989-9911 Fax: (610)989-9915

William K. Root, J.D.
Resch & Root
2715 Tuller Parkway, Suite 102
Dublin, OH 43017
(614)889-0990 Fax: (614)889-5250

Jeffrey P. Roth, J.D.
Roth Bacon Young
50 Court Street
Upper Sandusky, OH 43351
(419)294-2232 Fax: (419)294-2488

Merek S. Rubin, J.D., LL.M.
Rubin, Hay & Gould, P.C.
205 Newbury Street
Framingham, MA 01701
(508)875-5222 Fax: (508)879-6803

Robert J. Saalfeld, J.D.
Saalfeld, Griggs, Gorsuch, Alexander & Emerick, P.C.
P.O. Box 470
250 Church Street SE, Suite 300
Salem, OR 97308
(503)399-1070 Fax: (503)371-2927

Gary A. Sargent, J.D.
Backman, Clark & Marsh
68 S Main Street, Suite 800
Salt Lake City, UT 84101
(801)531-8300 Fax: (801)363-2420

Jeanie L. Schainost, J.D.
Larson & Schainost, L.L.C.
P.O. Box 367
602 S State
Iola, KS 66749
(800)388-8529 Fax: (316)365-2278

Duke Schneider, J.D.
Weinstein, Schneider & Kannebecker
50 Sheffield Lane
West Chester, PA 19380
(610)918-0700; (215)654-7664 Fax: (215)654-1498

John J. Schneider, J.D.
Weinstein, Schneider & Kannebecker
501 Broad Street
Milford, PA 18337
(717)296-6471 Fax: (717)296-2653

Arnold L. Slavet, J.D.
60 State Street, Suite 700
Boston, MA 02109
(617)894-1022 Fax: (617)647-1436

David A. Straus, J.D., LL.M., CPA
Law Offices of David A. Straus
900 Rancho Lane
Las Vegas, NV 89106
(702)474-4500 Fax: (702)474-4510

Andrew A. Strauss, J.D.
One W Pack Square
Asheville, NC 28801
(704)258-0150 Fax: (704)258-1305

Jeffrey B. Strouse, J.D.
Jeffrey B. Strouse, P.A.
200 Pierce Street
Tampa, FL 33602
(813)226-0074 Fax: (813)224-9153

Daniel P. Stuenzi, J.D.
Law Firm of Daniel Stuenzi, P.C.
7105 Virginia Road, Suite 20
Crystal Lake, IL 60014
(815)477-5515 Fax: (815)356-7724

Thomas C. Sturgill, J.D.
Elam, Miller & McKee, P.S.C.
2401 Regency Road, Suite 201
Lexington, KY 40503
(606)277-4849 Fax: (606)278-2207

Dennis B. Sullivan, J.D., LL.M., CPA
Dennis Sullivan & Associates
888 Worcester Street
Wellesley, MA 02181
(617)237-2815 Fax: (617)237-3141

Samuel T. Swansen, J.D.
640 Sentry Parkway, Suite 104
Blue Bell, PA 19422
(610)834-9810 Fax: (610)834-9932

Daniel P. Trump, J.D., LL.M.
Trump, Alioto, Trump & Prescott
2280 Union Street
San Francisco, CA 94123
(415)563-7200 Fax: (415)346-0679

I. Michael Tucker, J.D.
Law Office of I. Michael Tucker
29 E Pine Street
Orlando, FL 32801
(407)649-7103 Fax: (407)649-1491

T.A. "Rusty" Ward, Jr., J.D.
2243 W 42nd Street
Casper, WY 82604
(307)472-4544 Fax: (307)472-4544

John J. Whitney, J.D.
Spieth, Bell, McCurdy & Newell Co., L.P.A.
925 Euclid Avenue, Suite 2000
Cleveland, OH 44115
(216)696-4700 Fax: (216)696-6569

Scott A. Williams, J.D.
400 W Bagley Road
Berea, OH 44017
(216)891-8850 Fax: (216)891-9633

Addison E. Winter, J.D.
The Winter Law Firm
205 S Broadway
Riverton, WY 82501
(307)856-1929 Fax: (307)856-4456

William T. Winter, J.D.
The Winter Law Firm
205 S Broadway
Riverton, WY 82501
(307)856-1929 Fax: (307)856-4456

Byron E. Woodman, Jr., J.D., LL.M.
Woodman & Eaton, P.C.
801 Main Street
Concord, MA 01742
(508)369-0960 Fax: (508)371-1343

Mark W. Worthington, J.D.
94 Highland Street
Worcester, MA 01609
(508)757-1140 Fax: (508)795-1636

Guy R. Youman, J.D.
The Law Offices of Rupp & Youman
P.O. Box 745
4302C W Crystal Lake Road
McHenry, IL 60050
(815)385-7444 Fax: (815)385-7480

John G.W. Zacker, J.D.
9 Sixth Street
Locust Valley, NY 11560
(516)674-2261 Fax: (516)674-8319

Glossary

ancillary administration The probate and administration of a decedent's estate performed in a jurisdiction other than the one in which the decedent lived at the time of death. Occurs if decedent owned property in more than one state at death.

annual gift tax exclusion A federal gift tax exclusion of $10,000 for a gift of a present interest to each recipient annually without limit as to the number of recipients. For married couples who consent to split gifts, the exclusion is $20,000 each year.

annuity A fixed amount of money which is paid to the person establishing the annuity, called the annuitant, for life or for a fixed period of time.

basis Generally the cost of property. Basis can be increased by such items as capital improvements or decreased by items such as depreciation. Basis is used to compute taxable gain on the sale or exchange of property.

beneficiary One who receives property pursuant to a will, a trust, an insurance policy, an individual retirement account, or other third-party beneficiary contract.

bypass trust *See* **family trust.**

capital gain (loss) The difference between the amount received in a sale or exchange of an asset and its basis.

charitable lead trust A trust in which a charity has the right to receive distributions of an income or annuity interest from the time the trust is created until it terminates.

charitable remainder trust A trust in which the beneficiary has the current right to receive income from the trust with the remainder interest going to a charitable entity.

CLAT (*charitable lead annuity trust*) A trust in which a fixed dollar amount or a percentage of the initial value of the trust assets is paid to charitable entities for a term of years, after which the trust principal is transferred to designated beneficiaries of the grantor. The charitable interest "leads" the beneficiaries' interests in a CLAT or CLUT.

CLUT (*charitable lead unitrust*) A trust in which a fixed annual percentage of the value of the trust assets, revalued annually, is paid to charitable entities for a term of years, after which the trust principal is transferred to designated beneficiaries of the grantor.

community property Property ownership in which property acquired during marriage is deemed to be owned equally by both spouses. Community property states are Wisconsin, New Mexico, Louisiana, Nevada, Arizona, California, Idaho, Washington, and Texas.

CRAT (*charitable remainder annuity trust*) A trust in which a fixed dollar amount or a percentage of the initial value of the trust assets is paid to the grantor and/or other designated beneficiaries (usually the grantor's spouse) for a term of years or for the life of the grantor, after which the trust principal is transferred to designated charitable entities chosen by the grantor. The charitable entities receive the remainder interest in a CRAT or CRUT.

credit shelter trust *See* **family trust.**

Crummey power The noncumulative right of a beneficiary to withdraw property transferred to a trust in order to convert a future-interest gift to a present-interest gift such that the gift will qualify for the $10,000 annual gift tax exclusion.

CRUT (*charitable remainder unitrust*) A trust in which a fixed annual percentage of the value of the trust assets, revalued annually, is paid to the grantor and/or other designated beneficiaries (usually the grantor's spouse) for a term of years or for the life of the grantor, after which the trust principal is transferred to designated charitable entities chosen by the grantor.

defective trust A trust that is drafted in such a way that the trust maker is treated as the owner of the trust for income tax purposes, but not to such an extent that it is included in the estate of the trust maker upon death.

disclaimer The refusal by a beneficiary or other recipient to accept a gift or bequest.

durable power of attorney for health care A power of attorney that enables the power holder to make health care decisions for the principal in the event of the principal's inability to make health care decisions for himself or herself, usually because of incapacity.

estate tax An excise tax levied by the state or the federal government on the privilege of transferring wealth at death. The estate has the obligation to pay estate tax.

family limited partnership A limited partnership established under state law and used by family members to facilitate the transfer of assets to other family members, often at a discount (i.e., the value of the partnership interests are discounted from the value of the assets held by the partnership and represented by those partnership interests).

family trust A trust created at the trust maker's death to take advantage of the trust maker's $600,000 exemption equivalent amount. It will often provide for income and discretionary distributions of principal to the surviving spouse but be drafted in such a way that when the surviving spouse dies, none of the trust assets are included in the surviving spouse's estate. Sometimes called a *credit shelter, bypass,* or *B trust.*

grantor A person who creates a trust; also known as a *trust maker, settlor, trustor,* or *donor.*

GRAT (*grantor retained annuity trust*) A trust in which the grantor retains the right to receive a fixed amount paid at least annually for a term of years.

GRIT (*grantor retained income trust*) A trust in which the grantor retains a right to income for a term of years. Most GRITs are no longer effective except for a "house GRIT," more commonly called a *qualified personal residence trust.*

GRUT (*grantor retained unitrust*) A trust in which the grantor retains, for a term of years, a right to a fixed percentage of the trust, as valued annually.

GSTT (*generation-skipping transfer tax*) A flat federal transfer tax assessed on property transferred from one generation to another generation which is more than one generation removed from the donor of the transferred property (e.g., the transfer of property from a grandparent's trust to a grandchild with a skip over the generation in between).

GSTT exemption An exemption amount of $1 million for the benefit of each transferor with respect to federal generation-skipping transfer tax.

ILIT (*irrevocable life insurance trust*) A trust which holds life insurance as a principal asset, the death proceeds of which are neither estate-taxed in the estate of the insured nor income-taxed to the beneficiaries of the trust; sometimes also referred to as a *wealth replacement trust.*

inheritance tax A tax levied by certain state governments on the privilege of receiving or inheriting transferred wealth at death. The recipient has the obligation to pay inheritance tax.

inter vivos trust A living trust.

living trust A trust created during the trust maker's lifetime. A living trust can be either revocable or irrevocable.

living will Not actually a will, but a set of instructions or an expression of wishes and desires regarding the use or nonuse of medical treatments or procedures that would artificially prolong life.

LLC (*limited liability company*) A hybrid entity possessing the liability limitation characteristics of an ordinary corporation and the tax characteristics of a partnership.

marital deduction A gift tax deduction or an estate tax deduction which is allowed with respect to transfers made from one spouse to another either during life or after death.

Medicaid A federal medical assistance program created under Title XIX of the Social Security Act of 1965 and operated in combination with each state. It is not a federal entitlement program, as is Medicare. One must be financially needy to qualify for Medicaid.

minority discount A discount allowed in the valuation of a minority interest (less than 50 percent) in a limited partnership or a corporation which is closely held.

NIMCRUT (*net income makeup charitable remainder unitrust*) A trust which provides the flexibility of accumulating distributable funds (the "makeup account") to a later date or dates while continuing to increase trust assets in a tax-deferred environment. Often used as a pension plan alternative.

power of appointment A power granted to a person allowing him or her to designate who is to receive the property controlled by the power.

private foundation A tax-exempt charitable entity established by a member or members of a family for the purpose of carrying out charitable purposes.

probate A court proceeding to determine competency or custodial rights (*living probate*), or to determine the validity of a will and the oversight of the procedure by which the assets of a decedent are administered under the provisions of a will.

QPRT (*qualified personal residence trust*) A trust owning a personal residence of the trust maker in which the remainder interest value of the property, after being held for the benefit of the trust maker for a period of years, is given to a beneficiary or beneficiaries.

QTIP (*qualified terminable interest property*) Property in which the surviving spouse has an income interest for life.

revocable trust A trust that can be changed or revoked by the trust maker.

spendthrift trust A trust which contains provisions limiting the ability of a beneficiary to access the trust assets.

testamentary trust A trust that is created through the operation of a will after death.

trustee A person or institution that has the fiduciary responsibility for carrying out the instructions set out in a trust.

unified credit A credit (under existing law) of $192,800 which is allowed against the federal gift tax imposed on gifts made during life or against the federal estate tax on estate transfers made after the death of the trust maker. This equates to a pretax amount of $600,000, which is often referred to as the unified credit.

will A legal document containing the instructions for the disposition of one's assets after death.

Index